Jesus Christ

God's Revelation to the World

Jesus Christ

God's Revelation to the World

Michael Pennock

ave maria press notre dame, indiana

The Subcommittee on the Catechism, United States Conference of Catholic Bishops, has found this catechetical text, © 2010, to be in conformity with the *Catechism of the Catholic Church*.

Nihil Obstat: The Reverend Michael Heintz
                    Censor Liborum

Imprimatur: Most Reverend John M. D'Arcy
                    Bishop of Fort Wayne-South Bend

Given at: Fort Wayne, Indiana, on 6 August 2009

The *Nihil Obstat* and *Imprimatur* are official declarations that a book or pamphlet is free of doctrinal or moral error. No implication is contained therein that those who have granted the Nihil Obstat or Imprimatur agree with its contents, opinions, or statements expressed.

Founded in 1865, Ave Maria Press is a ministry of the Indiana Province of Holy Cross.

Engaging Minds, Hearts, and Hands for Faith® is a trademark of Ave Maria Press, Inc.

www.avemariapress.com

ISBN-10 1-59471-184-4   ISBN-13 978-1-59471-184-8

Project Editor: Michael Amodei

Cover and text design by Andy Wagoner

Photography credits listed on page 312

Printed and bound in the United States of America

To the many thousands of students
the Lord sent into my classroom.
May he continue to bless them
and do great things through them.

—Michael Pennock

Engaging Minds, Hearts, and Hands for Faith

"An education that is complete is one in which the hands and heart are engaged as much as the mind. We want to let our students try their learning in the world and so make prayers of their education."

—Fr. Basil Moreau
Founder of the Congregation of Holy Cross

In this text, you will find:

 knowledge about how Jesus Christ is the unique Word of Sacred Scripture and how God's mission of Salvation is revealed in both the Old Testament and New Testament.

 ways to quench the human desire to know and love God, especially through praying with Sacred Scripture.

 Scripture-inspired projects and activities to further Christ's social mission to the world and especially to the poor.

Contents

1

SEARCHING FOR GOD

*As the deer longs for streams of water,
so my soul longs for you, O God.
My being thirsts for God, the living God.
When can I go and see the face of God?
My tears have been my food day and night,
as they ask daily, "Where is your God?"*

—Psalm 42:2-3

True Happiness

Without God, true happiness is fleeting
if achievable at all.

God: The Source of
True Happiness

Our hearts are restless until they find rest
and satisfaction in God our Creator.

Knowing God through
Natural Revelation

Through our God-given intelligence, we have
the capacity to come to know there is a good
and loving God.

Knowing God through
Divine Revelation

It is only through God's willingness to reveal himself that
human beings get a fuller idea of who he is.

Faith: Our Response
to Divine Revelation

Faith is the virtue that allows us to respond "yes"
to God's invitation to believe in and follow him.

True Happiness

John D. Rockefeller, founder of the Standard Oil Company, was one of the world's richest men. He confessed that his great wealth brought him no happiness. He said that he would trade it all to go back to the time when he worked in an office for three dollars a week.

His contemporary was the fabulously wealthy industrialist Andrew Carnegie, famous for endowing public libraries throughout the country. Carnegie observed that millionaires seldom smile. He also said, "I would as soon leave my son a curse as the almighty dollar."

Otto von Bismarck was instrumental in unifying the many states of Germany in the nineteenth century. Known as the Iron Chancellor, he was one of the most powerful and feared men of his day. However, toward the end of his life, he said, "I have seldom been a happy man. If I reckon up the rare moments of real happiness in my life, I do not believe they would make more than twenty-four hours in all."

What these men discovered is that money and power cannot buy true happiness. Neither can possessions, popularity, physical beauty, athletic skill, or intellectual achievement.

A verse from the Psalms gives us a hint as to the source of true happiness: "Happy the people so blessed; happy the people whose God is the LORD" (Ps 144:15). An important point in that verse is that only God can make us truly happy since God created us and made us with longing souls that only he can satisfy.

What Is Happiness?

Read the following definitions of happiness. Which one resonates most closely with your own belief about happiness?

"If you love what you are doing, you will be happy."

"Happiness if JOY:
Put Jesus first, then Others, finally Yourself."

"Money can buy happiness."

"The source of true happiness is a loving family."

"Happiness is a choice."

"If you want happiness for an hour—take a nap.
If you want happiness for a day—go fishing.
If you want happiness for a month—get married.
If you want happiness for a year—inherit a fortune.
If you want happiness for a lifetime—help someone else."
(Chinese proverb)

"Happiness is secured through virtue; it is a good attained by man's own will." (St. Thomas Aquinas)

For Reflection

- Write your own definition of happiness. Then describe a time when you were happiest. What ingredients went into your being happy?

- "Holiness and happiness go together." What does this statement mean to you?

God: The Source of True Happiness

We all want to be happy. In other words, we want to be joyful, content, and satisfied. We also associate happy people with a cheerful disposition. Yet why do so many people you meet seem to be sour and outright miserable? Why do so many people you read about or see on television seem unsatisfied, restless, looking for something else? Could it be that they are pursuing happiness down the wrong path?

What about you? Are *you* basically a happy person? Or do you need some cheering up?

One thing is true: We were made to be happy. Yet we will only achieve true happiness if we understand, accept, and live God's plan for us. This makes sense since God made us. As the loving Creator, God has a plan for all of his creatures, and especially for human beings, who are made in his image and likeness.

And what is this plan? Simply put, out of God's sheer goodness, God created us to share in his own blessed life. God is totally blessed in himself. He does not need us. Yet because he is so good and so generous, God wants to share his love. This is why he created humans—beings who can recognize and respond to his love. Only when people come to understand this truth will they achieve true happiness. The *Catechism of the Catholic Church* puts it this way:

> True happiness is not found in riches or well-being, in human fame or power, or in any human achievement—however beneficial it may be—such as science, technology, and art, or indeed in any creature, but in God alone, the source of every good and of all love. (*CCC*, 1723)

The Restless Human Heart

> The desire for God is written in the human heart, because man is created by God and for God. (*CCC*, 27)

Modern psychology claims you won't be happy until certain basic needs are met. Among these are the needs to be loved and understood, to be recognized and appreciated, and to be able to achieve a goal using the talents you have.

But even if you are lucky enough to have all of these needs met at one time or another, they won't ever be *perfectly* fulfilled. For example, no one can understand you perfectly. (You probably don't even understand yourself perfectly.) Yet you want to be understood.

The truth is that nothing in this life—no matter how good—can make us fully content or perfectly happy. Why is this? Simply, it is because God gave us an unquenchable hunger for happiness that only he himself can fulfill. We all have deep yearnings for completeness, for satisfaction, for happiness that is implanted in us by God himself and is only satisfied by God.

The bottom line is that God wants you to be happy. But you won't be perfectly happy until you rest in him. This explains why even when you get what you want—say the recognition of a classmate, the victory in a soccer tournament, new clothes—the feeling of contentment does not last. No good thing—pleasure, fame, or possessions—can make you perfectly, fully happy. Only God can.

You have a restless heart because God made you this way—to help you find him. St. Augustine (354–430), in his famous *Confessions,* put it this way: "Our heart is restless until it rests in you." We are like carrier pigeons that God created with homing devices deep within us to guide us to our true home—the source of true happiness, union with our God.

Questioning Minds

We not only have restless hearts, we also have active, questioning minds. Have you ever looked up at the sky on a star-filled night and questioned what is way out and beyond what you see? Have you wondered why you live in the time and place that you do? When close friends or relatives died, did you question the meaning of life and wonder why they had to die and where they are now? Do you ever think about where your life is going? Do you wonder what will happen to you after you die?

People have been asking these kinds of questions from the very beginning. Just like your heart

religion

The relationship between God and humans that results in a body of beliefs and a set of practices: creed, cult, and code. Religion expresses itself in worship and service to God and by extension to all people and all creation.

irreligion

A vice contrary to the virtue of religion that directs us away from what we owe to God in justice.

secularism

An indifference to religion and a belief that religion should be excluded from civic affairs and public education.

monotheistic

Religions that believe there is only one God. Christianity, Judaism, and Islam are three great monotheistic world religions.

polytheistic

Religions that believe in the existence of many gods and goddesses.

atheist

A person who denies the existence of God.

yearns for love and happiness, you are searching for truth about human existence. Like every thinking person ever made, you want to know what is the meaning of life.

Your questions help you search for the One who can help you discover the meaning of human existence . . . and why *you* are here. It is no accident that you ask these kinds of questions, simply because God made you with an inquiring mind to help you find him. God made you, and all humans, in his image and likeness. Being made in God's image endows us with the abilities to choose and to think. These powers enable us to love God, to satisfy our restless hearts, and to know God, to satisfy our quest for truth.

World Religions

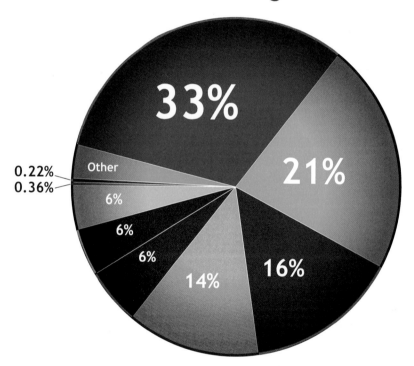

- ■ **Christianity** (including Catholic, Protestant, Eastern Orthodox, Pentecostal, Anglican, Monophysite, AICs, Latter-day Saints, Evangelical, SDAs, Jehovah's Witnesses, Quakers, AOG, etc.)
- ■ **Islam** (Shiite, Sunni, etc.)
- ■ **Nonreligious** (including agnostic, atheist, secular humanist, people answering "none" or "no religious preference." Half of the group is "theistic, but not religious")
- ■ **Hinduism**
- ■ **Primal-Indigenous** (including African traditional/diasporic)
- ■ **Chinese Traditional**
- ■ **Buddhism**
- ■ **Sikhism**
- ■ **Judaism**
- ■ **Other**

Note: Total adds up to more than 100% due to rounding and because upper bound estimates were used for each group.

We Are Religious by Nature

Because God made humans with restless hearts and questioning minds that seek love, understanding, truth, and happiness, human beings are naturally religious. Scholars believe that the word **religion** is related to the Latin word meaning "reconnecting to the divine" or "binding to God."

Throughout history, humans have discovered that they are not whole or complete persons unless they are connected, bound to, or related to God. Humans have always searched for God and they have always given expression to their quest through their beliefs and behavior. Countless religions through the ages have produced prayers, sacrifices, rituals, meditations, and so forth to express belief in a divine being who created them and the universe.

No one can determine how many religions have actually existed throughout human history. You have probably read about religions in the ancient world, for example, that of the Egyptians, Greeks, or Romans. In your study of world history, you may have also learned about some of the beliefs of the Aztecs in Mexico or of Native American tribes like the Navajos or Lakota. Even with the prevalence today of **irreligion** and **secularism**, the vast majority of people still belong to an organized religion (see the chart on the previous page).

The two largest religions (Christianity and Islam), as well as Judaism, are **monotheistic**, that is, they believe in one (*mono*) God (*theos*). Popular Hinduism is **polytheistic**, holding that there are many (*poly*) goddesses and gods. Buddhism does not believe in a personal god, but it does hold that there is a sole ultimate reality in the universe.

A person who does not believe in God is known as an **atheist**. One modern branch of atheism is secular humanism, which claims that people don't need God to live in the world and reach satisfaction. Secular humanists make the person the center of the universe. **Agnosticism** (from the Greek word for "don't know") is similar to atheism. Agnostics claim that since people can't know for certain if God exists or not, they "decide not to decide" on the question of God.

agnosticism
The belief that God's existence cannot be known.

Divine Revelation
The way God communicates knowledge of himself to humankind, a self-communication realized by his actions and words over time, most fully by his sending us his divine Son, Jesus Christ.

 ## Basic Beliefs of World Religions

Write a short synopsis of one of the world's religions (other than Christianity and Judaism). Include in the report answers to the following:

- What do they believe about the divine?
- What do they believe about the meaning of human existence?
- What do they believe about the afterlife?

Agnostics live for all practical purposes as though God does not exist.

Atheists and agnostics are relatively few in number. In contrast, most people believe in God. The existence of so many religions through human history makes a powerful statement that it is eminently reasonable to believe in God. Humans throughout history seem to know deep in their hearts that there is a Power or Spirit in the universe that makes life meaningful, that we were put here for a purpose beyond day-to-day survival.

More significantly, most people are religious because God calls us first. He speaks to us through our human reason—telling us to look at his creation—the vast universe and the beautiful persons in it. Through prayer, he tirelessly calls us to a union with himself. The human mind can look at the Creator's awesome universe and contemplate the Divine Artist who made it. God also speaks to us through the human heart since it is he who fashioned the human beings who will not be satisfied until they come into union with their Maker. Our human faculties make us capable of coming to a knowledge of the existence of a personal God. This is often termed *natural revelation*. But God speaks to us in yet another way. To keep us from confusion in discovering him, God speaks directly to us through **Divine Revelation**. In the next sections, we explore in more depth these particular ways of coming to know God.

For Review

1. How is true happiness found?
2. Why is God the source of true happiness?
3. According to St. Augustine, how did God make us?
4. Define *religion*.
5. What is the difference between monotheism and polytheism?
6. What belief do Christianity, Judaism, and Islam have in common?
7. What is the difference between atheism and agnosticism?

For Reflection

- What does happiness mean for you?
- How do you plan to find true happiness in your life?

Knowing God through Natural Revelation

Johannes Kepler (1571–1630) was a famous German astronomer who discovered that the Earth and planets travel about the sun in elliptical orbits. One of his closest friends insisted that God did not exist because he believed that the universe began and operated by its own means.

To try to convince his friend that God exists, Kepler made a model of the sun with the planets circling around it. When the friend saw the ingenious model, he commented, "How beautiful! Who made it?"

Tongue-in-cheek, Kepler answered, "No one made it; it made itself."

His friend replied, "That's crazy. Tell me who made it."

The famous astronomer then answered: "Friend, you say that this toy could not make itself. But listen to yourself. This model is but a very weak imitation of this vast universe, which, I think you said, made itself."

At this point, Kepler made his point. *Something* does not come out of *nothing*. Logically, there must be a Creator behind everything that exists.

Contemplating Creation (CCC, 31-32)

In the first verse of the Bible, we learn that God is the Creator of the universe. It stands to reason that by looking at the natural universe, we can discover the handiwork of the Creator. The Book of Psalms describes it this way: "The heavens declare the glory of God; the sky proclaims its builder's craft" (Ps 19:2). The Letter to the Romans emphasizes Church teaching that humans can discover the existence of God by studying his creation:

> Ever since the creation of the world, his invisible attributes of eternal power and divinity have been able to be understood and perceived in what he has made. (Rom 1:20)

Simply put, because we are created in God's image, we are endowed with intelligence. We should use our human reason by opening our eyes to look at the beautiful world in which we live. And then we should ask, where did all these beautiful things come from if not from the beautiful one who made them? St. Augustine made the same point:

> Question the beauty of the earth, question the beauty of the sea, question the beauty of the air distending and diffusing itself, question the beauty of the sky . . . question all these realities. All respond: "See, we are beautiful." Their beauty is a profession. These beauties are subject to change. Who made them if not the Beautiful One who is not subject to change?[3]

The First Vatican Council (1869–1870) stated authoritatively that human intelligence can discover God: "The Church teaches that the one true God, our Creator and Lord, can be known with certainty from his works, by the natural light of human reason" (*CCC*, 47). Earlier St. Thomas Aquinas (1223–1274) set out five proofs for God's existence. These are not proofs in the sense that science would define them. Rather, they are "converging and convincing arguments" that allow us to be certain that there is a Creator.

1. *Unmoved Mover.* The world is in motion (for example, neutrons, electrons, protons, atoms, etc.). For the world to move, there must have been a "First Mover" who started everything. That "unmoved mover" is God.

2. *First Cause.* Nothing causes itself. As in Kepler's example above, a model needs someone to make it. Everything that exists resulted from something or someone that came before it. Trace it all the way back to the beginning. Logically, there has to be a first cause or uncaused cause that is eternal and started the universe off. Today, many who accept the "big bang" theory of the universe's origins conclude that the original matter and spark of energy must have been created by a divine being. No other explanation makes sense.

3. *Everything Comes from Something* (known as the "cosmological argument"). "Nothing" cannot create "something." For anything to exist, there must be a necessary, eternal being (God) who always existed and brought other beings into existence.

4. *Supreme Model.* We all recognize in the world degrees of perfection in qualities like goodness, truth, justice, beauty, and so forth. For example, think of the words "good, better, best" or "most beautiful." We can only speak of these different qualities by comparing them to a supreme model or reference point. This

supreme model of goodness, truth, and beauty is the perfect being we call God.

5. *Grand Designer.* The world contains beauty, symmetry, order, and power that must have been put in it by a grand designer. You can see this when you look at a leaf under a microscope, marvel at a spider spinning its web, or look at the beauty of a newborn child. Prominent scientists marvel at the statistical impossibility of human life forming in the universe out of chance alone. For example, the ratio of the weight of the proton to the electron is balanced perfectly; if it were different, there would be no life here on earth. Someone must have put the laws into nature that make human life in a well-ordered universe possible. That someone is God!

If you were to combine all these arguments into one, you might simply ask, "How did I come into existence?" No scientist has yet been able to explain how living beings evolved from matter. No mathematical formula can prove that human life appeared by chance. Take a deeper look at human history. For example, think only about the technological explosion of the past century. Does there not seem to be a superior intelligence leading and guiding us? It is logical to conclude that the mystery of how and why we are here is because God is at the heart of the universe.

Contemplating the Human Person (CCC, 33)

Of course, when we think about God's creation, we must also think about the human person. We have already considered how the human heart longs for happiness, love, and understanding. Nothing in this world can satisfy this thirst. Is this yearning and tug of the heartstrings, which is felt by every human being, merely accidental? Might not a better explanation be that our Creator made us this way so we can find him? Additionally, don't you sense that life has meaning? You sense this because it is true: our lives

 ## Caring for God's Creation

Knowing God as Creator naturally leads us to take care of his creation, the environment. Consider these facts:

- For every ton of paper that is recycled, the following is saved: 7,000 gallons of water; 380 gallons of oil; and enough electricity to power an average house for six months.

- You can run a television for six hours on the amount of electricity that is saved by recycling one aluminum can.

- By recycling just one glass bottle, you save enough electricity to power a 100-watt bulb for four hours.

- For every ink cartridge that is recycled, 2.5 lbs. of petroleum products are kept out of our rivers and oceans.

On your own or with classmates, devise a recycling project to help protect the environment. For example, collect empty ink cartridges and turn them in at an office supplies store or some other recycling center. Calculate how much you have contributed to preserving some of the resources of God's good earth.

have meaning. Your study, hard work, self-discipline, and desire to develop your talents all mean something because they help you become the person God created you to be. Here are other elements of our humanity that lead us to God.

Beauty and truth. God gives us a taste of Heaven here on earth. Think of a beautiful piece of music or song lyrics that seem to take you out of yourself. Or the pleasant, peaceful feeling you get when looking at a gorgeous sunset or a sleeping baby, so innocent and calm. Imagine the great satisfaction you get when you grasp the truth of a mathematical formula. The experiences of joy in the presence of beauty and intellectual completeness in the face of truth are but hints of what God's beauty and truth are like. The God who made, understands, and loves us gives us a glimpse of what is in store for us when we finally are united with him in eternity—the source of all beauty and truth.

Moral goodness, personal conscience, and justice. Deep inside each of us, we sense the call of **conscience** that tells us to do good (for example, treat others with respect) and avoid evil (for example, don't steal). As we look within, we sense a God of goodness and justice who teaches us how to act as beings created in his image and likeness. This is why we are disgusted and angry when we hear of cheaters who defraud poor people, terrorists who kill innocent people, or sexual predators who commit unspeakable crimes against children. We sense that some behaviors are simply wrong because they go against how God made us. Our sense of justice tells us that those who have violated the moral order should be held accountable for their actions, if not in this life, then in the next.

Love and intelligence. Free will, which enables us to love, and intelligence, which enables us to think, are spiritual realities that cannot be explained by a material universe. Love and intelligence can only come from love and intelligence itself, that Supreme Being who possesses these qualities because he is those qualities.

As mentioned before, the vast majority of people throughout history have looked at the physical world and reflected on the spiritual nature of humans and come to the correct conclusion that there is a God. But not everyone has found God.

Some people refuse to believe in God because they see suffering in the world. Others look at the sins of believers and are shocked that anyone who claims to believe in a loving God could act this way. So they choose not to believe. Other people are simply lazy or indifferent. Still others are afraid that if they did believe in God, they will have to change their behavior.

Though honest, thinking humans can discover God's existence, human reason and human perception are limited. **Original Sin** has weakened our minds and hearts so that we fail to perceive and follow the truth.

This is why man stands in need of being enlightened by God's Revelation, not only about those things that

conscience
A practical judgment of reason that helps a person decide the goodness or sinfulness of an action or attitude. It is the subjective norm of morality we must form properly and then follow.

Original Sin
The sin of disobedience committed by Adam and Eve that resulted in their loss of original holiness and justice and their becoming subject to sin and death. Original Sin also describes the fallen state of human nature into which all generations of people are born. Christ Jesus came to save us from Original Sin (and all sin).

exceed his understanding, but also "about those religious and moral truths which of themselves are not beyond the grasp of human reason, so that even in the present condition of the human race, they can be known by all men with ease, with firm certainty and with no admixture of error" (*CCC*, 38).

Part of the Good News of the Catholic faith is precisely this: God did not leave us alone to discover him. He actually spoke to us, entered human history, and gave himself to us in his Son, Jesus Christ. The topic of Divine Revelation will be examined in more detail in the next section.

For Review

1. What does it mean to be made in God's image and likeness?

2. Discuss any three ways to demonstrate the existence of God.

3. Why do some people not believe in God's existence?

For Reflection

- Which "proof" for God's existence is the most convincing? Why?

- "In God we live and have our being. We are like fish in the water or a bird in the air. We are always in the presence of God. He is the Lord who watches over us, like a good mother who takes care of our needs." What does this statement mean to you? Give an example of a time when God has taken care of you.

Knowing God through Divine Revelation

By looking at creation and reflecting on the human person, we can discover that God exists. We can even say some things about what God must be like when we reflect on his creation, especially human

♥ Finding God in Nature

Nature is essential to our lives. Without air, sunlight, water, and the food that nature provides, we could not live. God gave us nature to live and to enjoy life. Nature also helps us to discover God since he is its Creator.

Take a walk in a favorite place outdoors, preferably away from other people: in the woods, a field, climbing a hill, a garden. On your walk, place

yourself in God's presence. Imagine yourself swimming in an ocean of his love. Take note of all that you see, smell, hear, taste, and touch. Enjoy God's goodness in nature: his beauty, power, creativity, majesty, love.

Take some photos of objects or scenes that strike you: for example, a flower, an interesting rock formation, grass blowing in the wind, or a majestic tree.

After your walk, develop a collage with your photos. Use the collage to help you pray. For example, you might praise God for his goodness. Or thank him for giving you the ability to see his splendor in creation. Share your collage and prayer with your classmates.

beings. Consider this analogy to think about how this is so: Say you just finished playing a complicated video game, and you started to think about the person who dreamed it up. You judge that the game designer must have been both brilliant and imaginative—brilliant because she knew intricate computer code to make the game work, and imaginative because the graphics, design, and exciting level of play are "awesome."

Now think about the designer of the universe: God. When you think about how vast the universe is, you must come to the conclusion that the one who made it must be all-powerful (**omnipotent**), almighty, and all-knowing. Then, when you see qualities like intelligence in creatures like humans, you rightly judge that the Creator must have a supreme intellect. Similarly, when you are struck by the beauty of a sunrise, you can say its Creator must embody all that is beautiful.

When we talk about God, though, we must recognize that human language is really imperfect in describing the perfect one. God transcends or goes beyond all creatures. God is a mystery so beyond human understanding as to be incomprehensible to the human mind. Human language always falls short of describing what God really is.

Just as human language cannot fully describe God, human reason alone cannot really know what God is like. Consider all the religions that exist. Believers in these religions know there is some kind of God out

there, but they cannot clearly know just who God is. Some will worship the sun or the moon or the stars or the mountains or the wind because they believe these bodies have power and must be the source of all that is. Others will worship several gods because they see different qualities of the divine in the universe and conclude that there must be a god behind each power. Still others think of God as distant and uncaring, something like a "divine watchmaker," one who creates the universe and gets it ticking but does not get involved with it after the initial creation.

What we can conclude from all this is that humans can know there is a God—and they can name some qualities about God—but left to themselves, they cannot get a true picture of who God really is. God is truly a mystery; his ways are way beyond our ways; his thoughts are not our thoughts (see Is 55:8). However, there is more to it than that. God does not leave us to our own limited knowledge. He has spoken to us through Divine Revelation.

What Is Divine Revelation?

God is infinitely loving and good. Because of this he entered human history. God revealed himself to us.

omnipotent
An attribute of God that he is everywhere, unlimited, and all-powerful.

Salvation History
The story of God's saving action in human history.

covenant
A binding and solemn agreement between human beings or between God and people, holding each to a particular course of action.

Sacred Tradition
The living transmission of the Church's gospel message found in the Church's teaching, life, and worship. It is faithfully preserved, handed down, and interpreted by the Church's Magisterium.

Sacred Scripture
The written record of Divine Revelation found in the books of the Old Testament and the New Testament.

Revelation means "unveiling, uncovering." God, whose existence we can discover, stepped into human history to tell us *who* he really is. He did this through the events of **Salvation History**, through the Law given to the Chosen People and the words of the prophets, and most perfectly through his only divine Son, Jesus Christ. Creation is the foundation of God's saving plan and the beginning of Salvation History that reaches its goal in the new creation in Christ.

Divine Revelation is God's free gift of self-communication by which he makes known the mystery of his divine plan. "Through an utterly free decision, God has revealed himself and given himself to man" (*CCC*, 50). Remarkably, God's divine plan is "to communicate his own divine life to the men he freely created, in order to adopt them as his sons in his only-begotten Son" (*CCC*, 52).

We learn about the plan of revelation in the Bible. This plan involves both deeds and words that are intimately related, shedding light on each other. The Scriptures teach that God invites humans to live in **covenant** with him. God's covenant is a wholehearted commitment of unconditional love between God and humans. God will always be faithful to us; we are called to be faithful to God.

The greatest sign of God's love was the sending of his Son, Jesus Christ, to be our Savior from sin and death. Jesus Christ is the Word of God, God's fullest, complete, and final revelation. He is the perfect sign of God's

covenant with humans. The Letter to the Hebrews puts it this way:

> In times past, God spoke in partial and various ways to our ancestors through the prophets; in these last days, he spoke to us through a son, whom he made heir of all things and through whom he created the universe, who is the refulgence of his glory, the very imprint of his being, and who sustains all things by his mighty word. (1:1–3)

The Church was ordained by the Lord from the beginning of time to spread the Good News of God's Salvation in Jesus Christ. The Church is guided by the Holy Spirit, who was sent by Jesus and his Father to guide the Church in truth (Jn 16:13). The Church is both the means and goal of God's plan. Church Fathers of the first century said that "the world was created for the sake of the Church" (see *CCC*, 760). The truths about Jesus and Salvation History are found in the **Sacred Tradition** and **Sacred Scripture**, both of which are faithfully taught, interpreted, and preserved by the successors of the Apostles known as the **Magisterium**.

More complete definitions and explanations of these elements follow.

Salvation History

God revealed himself gradually to humans, preparing them in stages for the fullest Revelation that was to come—the sending of Jesus Christ. This gradual Revelation is told in Salvation History, which is the account of God's saving activity for mankind. Both the Old and New Testaments record how God revealed himself in human history, working in both events and people to bring us into union with him. The story's happy ending is Salvation won through Jesus Christ.

God's creation of the world begins Salvation History. We learn in the Book of Genesis that God created a world that is "very good." God intended from the very beginning to invite humans to live in intimate union with him, blessing them with grace and justice. However, the Original Sin of Adam and Eve broke their intimate friendship with God. But God did not abandon humankind.

God remained faithful to the creatures he made, inviting them to live in friendship with him, promising them Salvation and redemption. Despite human sin, God always desired to give eternal life to the members of the human race. God refused to abandon humans who had turned their backs on him out of pride.

Out of his never-ending love, the Lord established a series of covenants with humankind. A covenant is a solemn agreement, an open-ended contract of love in which God commits himself totally to human beings. Time and again, the Old Testament records how God always keeps his promises to his people. He continually offered Salvation, redemption, and eternal life. The story of Salvation from the Old Testament to the time of Jesus includes covenants and dramatic heroes, especially the prophets. Highlights of this period include:

- *Covenant with Noah.* Human sin destroyed the unity God intended for humanity. The Flood was divine punishment for prideful ambition. After the Flood, God entered into an everlasting covenant with Noah, his descendants, and "every living creature," promising never again to destroy the earth with a flood. The purpose of the covenant was to unify all God's children into one family through our Lord Jesus Christ.

- *Covenant with Abraham.* To work for the unity of a scattered humanity, God made a covenant with Abraham. He called him out of his land, gave him a new

name, and promised him many descendants. The patriarch Abraham became the father of faith for the Jewish people. He also became a spiritual father for all believers because of our shared ancestry with God's Chosen People. God promised Abraham that he would be his God and the God of his descendants for all time. **Circumcision** for Jewish males was a sign of the covenant with Abraham as a way to set his

Magisterium
The official teaching authority of the Church. The Lord bestowed the right and power to teach in his name on Peter and the Apostles and their successors. The Magisterium is the bishops in communion with the successor of Peter, the bishop of Rome (pope).

circumcision
The surgical removal of the male foreskin; it was the physical sign of the covenant between God and Abraham.

descendants apart as God's People. God was faithful to his covenant when he blessed the aged Abraham with a son, Isaac. Isaac's son, Jacob, renamed Israel, fathered twelve sons who became the ancestors of the tribes of Israel. These descendants, the Chosen People, were "called to prepare for that day when God would gather all his children into the unity of the Church" (*CCC*, 60; see Rom 11:17–18, 24). This was the family of Jesus.

- *Covenant with Moses, the Sinai Covenant.* After the era of the patriarchs like Abraham, Isaac, and Jacob, God formed Israel as his People. He did so by freeing the Israelites from slavery in Egypt at the time of the great event known as the Exodus. On Mt. Sinai in the desert, God revealed his name as **YHWH** ("I Am Who Am"), showing that he is the source of all that is. The word YHWH is written without vowels because there were no vowels in the Hebrew alphabet. Also, because of the sacredness of God's name, the Jews did not say YHWH aloud. Rather, they substituted Adonai, or "My Lord." God also gave the Chosen People his Law through Moses. The purpose of the Law was to help people recognize God and serve him as the one, true, living God, a just judge. The Law would help form the Israelites

as God's special people, a priestly people, and help them look to the day of the coming of the promised Savior.

- *Kings and Prophets*. God promised the Israelites their own land in Canaan. They settled the land and eventually were governed by judges and kings. The greatest Israelite king, David, made Jerusalem his capital city; his son Solomon built the Temple in this city, where the Jewish priests offered sacrifices and worshiped God.

After Solomon's rule, the Chosen People split into a northern kingdom and a southern kingdom. Because of the sinfulness of the people, including the worship of false gods, difficult times fell on the Israelites. During this period, God sent **prophets** to help form in his people the hope of Salvation. The prophets warned against abuses like greed and failure to follow God's Law, but they also encouraged God's people when the Assyrians conquered the northern kingdom in 722 BC and the Babylonians conquered the Southern Kingdom in 586 BC. They never failed to mention that God would always be faithful to his promises. They continued to unveil God's plan for humanity by promising a new and everlasting covenant. The New Covenant they described is to be written on human hearts. The prophets—men like Elijah, Ezekiel, Isaiah, and Jeremiah—"proclaim a

THE GREAT FLOOD AND GOD'S COVENANT WITH NOAH

Read Genesis 6:5–9:29, the story of the Great Flood and God's covenant with Noah. Write your answers to the following questions:

1. Why did God want to destroy the earth?
2. What were the names of Noah's sons?
3. How old was Noah when the flood began?
4. How long did the flood last?
5. What sign convinced Noah that the waters were receding?
6. Write out the words of the covenant found in Genesis 9:11.
7. What did Noah's youngest son do that merited a curse from his father?

radical redemption of the People of God, purification from all their infidelities, a Salvation which will include all nations" (*CCC*, 64).

- *Wisdom Literature.* God inspired a body of writings of proverbs, riddles, stories, warnings, questions, and similar types of writings to serve as a guide to daily, successful living. The Book of Psalms, a collection of prayers to God, is an essential part of Wisdom Literature. In beautiful poetic verses, the Psalms praise God for his creation and for the great things he did for the Chosen People. They also express every human emotion in heartfelt prayers of thanksgiving, grief, fear, confidence, and repentance. In the Psalms, we learn about the Creator God, the source of all life, who holds each human being precious. The Psalms share the hope that God will finally triumph, restore Israel among the nations, and right all wrongs. Notably, some Psalms tell of the coming of a future Messiah.

- *Jesus Christ, the New Covenant.* The climax of Salvation History is the entrance of Jesus Christ into the world. His birth took place several centuries after the Jews returned from exile, during the rule of the Romans. Jesus Christ is God's total Word, his fullest Revelation. He is the only Son of the Father; he is God himself. John the Baptist, a relative of Jesus, was sent as a final prophet to prepare the way for the Lord's public ministry. Teaching a message of repentance,

John baptized Jesus and recognized that he was the Messiah. The Son of God lived among us. He taught us in words and deeds about God. His Passion, Death, Resurrection, and Ascension (glorification) accomplished our Salvation. Jesus Christ is God's final Word. Why? As Jesus said to Philip, "Whoever has seen me has seen the Father" (Jn 14:9).

Handing Down Divine Revelation

Most people are interested in their family's story. When did your great-grandparents come to this country? Where did they come from? What made them leave their native lands? What were their jobs and accomplishments once they got here? A curious mind asks questions like these and many more. You can learn about your family's story by talking to older relatives, viewing old photos and letters, researching family trees, and reading family diaries.

How do we learn about the story of Salvation History, events that took place so long ago yet are so very important to how we live our lives today? God revealed himself fully through his Son, Jesus Christ. Jesus turned over this revelation to the Apostles after he ascended into Heaven. It is a single **Deposit of Faith** contained in Sacred Scripture and Sacred Tradition. Inspired by the Holy Spirit, the Apostles handed down this deposit, or "heritage of faith," to the Church. They did this through their oral preaching and their writings, both done under

prophet
The word *prophet* is from the Greek, meaning "one who speaks before others." God entrusted the Hebrew prophets with delivering the divine message to rulers and the people. Most of them were unpopular in their own day. Their style was poetic and memorable. Most of their prophecies were written only at a later time.

Deposit of Faith
"The heritage of faith contained in Sacred Scripture and Tradition, handed down in the Church from the time of the Apostles, from which the Magisterium draws all that it proposes for belief as being divinely revealed" (*CCC*, Glossary).

the inspiration of the Holy Spirit. Therefore, all future generations can hear about God's love for us in Jesus Christ until the Lord comes again at the end of time. We find this single deposit in two places: Sacred Tradition and Sacred Scripture.

Sacred Tradition

The word *tradition* means "handing down." Sacred Tradition is the living transmission or "handing down" from one generation to the next of the Church's gospel message.

The Apostles obeyed Jesus' command to preach the Gospel to all nations. Strengthened by the Holy Spirit, they preached the message throughout the Roman Empire. They proclaimed their beliefs in a heroic way. All of the Apostles but St. John died as martyrs for preaching the Gospel. They called people to repent of their sins and to believe in, accept, and live the Lord's teaching. They also baptized their converts and blessed and broke bread with them, which was nourishment from Christ himself in the Sacrament of the Eucharist. The Apostles served other people, especially the poor.

The Apostles wisely chose men to succeed them after they were gone. These men were the bishops, headed by the Bishop of Rome. St. Peter was the

first Bishop of Rome; his successors are the Popes. Their job through the ages is to "faithfully preserve, expound, and spread . . . by their preaching" (*Dogmatic Constitution on Divine Revelation*, No. 9, *CCC*, 81) the gift of faith given to the entire Church.

Today, we find the living Sacred Tradition—both the handing down and what was handed down—in the teaching, life, and worship of the Church:

Through Tradition, "the Church, in her doctrine, life, and worship perpetuates and transmits to every generation all that she herself is, all that she believes." (*Dogmatic Constitution on Divine Revelation*, No. 8, *CCC*, 78)

Sacred Scripture

God is like a fountain. Two streams flow from his fountain: Sacred Tradition and Sacred Scripture. Sacred Scripture is the written form of what the Apostles and early Christians handed down:

Sacred Scripture is the speech of God as it is put down in writing under the breath of the Holy Spirit. (*Dogmatic Constitution on Divine Revelation*, No. 9; *CCC*, 81)

Chapter 2 presents a full overview of Sacred Scripture—how it came to be, how we are to read it, and so forth. As a way of introduction, think of Sacred Scripture, or the Bible, as a library of divinely inspired writings. The word *bible* means "books." The Bible is one book, and this book is Christ. By inspiring the writers of Sacred Scripture, God used the human authors and their unique talents to put into writing exactly what he wanted written, and nothing more. We can be confident that when we read Sacred Scripture we are reading the Word of God:

> The books of Scripture firmly, faithfully, and without error teach that truth which God, for the sake of our Salvation, wished to see confided to Sacred Scriptures. (*Dogmatic Constitution on Divine Revelation*, No. 11, *CCC*, 107)

Sacred Scripture records the events of Salvation History and the covenants God made with humanity. It is divided into two parts: The Old Testament and the New Testament. Both the words *covenant* and *testament* come from the same Greek word and are often used interchangeably.

Thus, the forty-six Old Testament books report the workings of God in the history of the Chosen People, his fidelity to his covenants, and his promise to send a Savior. Because of this Christ is clearly present in the books of the Old Testament. The twenty-seven books of the New Testament tell the story of God's saving action through his Son Jesus Christ, the covenant sealed in His death and Resurrection. It also recounts the story of the early Christian communities and their beliefs in their Lord Jesus. The New Testament, especially the four Gospels, is the most important part of the Bible. The Gospels are the primary documents of the life and teachings of our Savior, Jesus Christ, God's Son.

When Jesus entrusted the Deposit of Faith—both Scripture and Tradition—to the Apostles, he gave them the authority to interpret God's Word authentically. This authority keeps the Church free from error. It also guarantees that the true Gospel of Jesus Christ is preached from generation to generation.

Christ passed on this teaching authority to the successors of the Apostles—the Bishop of Rome (the Pope) and the bishops in communion with him. This teaching authority, which resides in the Pope and the bishops, is known as the Magisterium of the Church. Under the guidance of the Holy Spirit, the Magisterium serves the Word of God by teaching

EXPLAINING THE FAITH

Why do Catholics believe in and do things that are not in the Bible?

The Bible is not the only means God used to hand down the truths of Revelation. Revelation is handed on or transmitted by the Church through the ages in two ways: Sacred Scripture and Sacred Tradition. Some Catholic beliefs, for example, Mary's Assumption into Heaven, come from Tradition. Although beliefs like the Assumption cannot be explicitly found in the Bible, the teachings from Tradition never contradict Scripture since both of them come from Jesus Christ through the Apostles.

Apostolic Tradition refers to those things that Jesus taught to the Apostles and other early disciples that were at first passed down by word of mouth. St. Paul makes reference to these in one of his letters: "Therefore, brothers, stand firm and hold fast to the traditions that you were taught, either by an oral statement or by a letter of ours" (2 Thes 2:15). The New Testament itself comes from the Apostolic Tradition because the Apostles preached what they learned from Jesus before they committed anything to writing. It is interesting to note that the very last verse of the Gospel of John tells us that not everything was written down: "There are also many other things that Jesus did, but if these were to be described individually, I do not think the whole world would contain the books that would be written" (Jn 21:25).

Tradition is the living transmission of the Church's Gospel. The Pope and the bishops, the successors of the Apostles, conserve and hand down the single Deposit of Faith which is made up of two components: the inspired Sacred Scripture and Sacred Tradition. The beliefs that come from Tradition are part of God's Revelation to us.

ST. PETER

Impetuous. Brave. Headstrong. Compassionate. Heroic. Born leader. These are some of the adjectives that describe Simon bar Jonah. His brother Andrew introduced him to Jesus. Both were humble fisherman working out of the village of Capernaum on the Sea of Galilee. Peter was also a married man. (We know this because Mark 1:29–30 reports that Jesus cured his mother-in-law of a fever.) Jesus nicknamed Peter "Rock" to indicate that Peter would be the rock-like foundation on which he would build his Church.

Peter was perceptive enough to recognize who Jesus was when he proclaimed him to be the Messiah, the Son of God. But he argued with Jesus when the Lord told him he must go to Jerusalem to die. Christ had to rebuke Peter, comparing him to the devil, for trying to turn Jesus away from his mission. Peter later realized that he would rather die than betray Jesus. Yet, after the Lord was arrested, Peter three times denied knowing him.

Peter did repent for his sinful error and wept bitter tears of sorrow. The Lord forgave him. After his Resurrection, the risen Lord gave Peter authority over the other Apostles and his Church. The Book of Acts recounts the bold preaching of Peter to the nations and some of his missionary activity. Tradition has it that he died a martyr in Rome in AD 64 under the Emperor Nero. He requested that he be crucified upside down since he was not worthy to die as his master did.

Do one or more of the following:

1. Read the following passages about Peter: Matthew 4:18–22; 8:5; 14:22–33; 16:15–28; Mark 14:27–31, 66–72; Luke 9:28–36; John 21:1–19. Note in your journal some significant facts about Peter.
2. Name some key points of one or more of St. Peter's early sermons in the Acts of the Apostles: Acts 2:14–36; 3:11–26; 10:34–43.
3. Check out the following website and report on something you learn: Capernaum: http://www.bibleplaces.com/capernaum.htm
4. Take a virtual tour of St. Peter's Basilica in Rome at http://www.virtualsweden.se/projects/peters/. Report on something that you learn.

THE KEYS represent the authority given to St. Peter as head of the Church. "And so I say to you, you are Peter, and upon this rock I will build my church, and the gates of the netherworld shall not prevail against it. I will give you the keys to the kingdom of Heaven. Whatever you bind on earth shall be bound in Heaven; and whatever you loose on earth shall be loosed in Heaven" (Mt 16:18–19).

This power to forgive sins in Christ's name is celebrated in the Sacrament of Penance in which Christ proclaims his mercy and love to sinners. In art, St. Peter is often depicted as having the keys to the "pearly gates" of Heaven.

THE LATIN CROSS turned upside down symbolizes the manner of St. Peter's execution.

EXPLAINING THE FAITH

Isn't the Bible just another piece of literature?

While the Bible contains many literary forms and types of literature—poetry, history, stories, letters, Gospels—it is not just another piece of literature. The Bible is the inspired Word of God.

Because the Bible is God's own Word, we cannot read or understand Scripture in the same way as other literature. We need to read and interpret it with the help of the Holy Spirit. The Spirit guides us to proper interpretation through the Magisterium, whose Christ-given role is to guide the Church in the truth of Jesus Christ.

only what has been handed down. It listens to what it has received, preserves it through the centuries, and explains it so Christians can live as Christ wants us to live.

With the help of the Holy Spirit, the Magisterium teaches with Christ's authority. This is especially true when the Pope and bishops define a **dogma**, that is, a central truth of Revelation that Catholics must believe.

Jesus said this to his Apostles: "Whoever listens to you listens to me. Whoever rejects you rejects me. And whoever rejects me rejects the one who sent me" (Lk 10:16). This is why Catholics should humbly listen to and obey the teachings of the Holy Father and bishops.

For Review

1. Define *Divine Revelation*.
2. Why do humans need Divine Revelation?
3. What are the terms of God's covenant with humankind?

4. Briefly summarize Salvation History from creation to the birth of Jesus.
5. What are the two elements of the single Deposit of Faith?
6. What special role does St. Peter have in Salvation History?
7. Define *Magisterium*.

For Reflection

- Reread the St. Augustine quotation on page 3. What do his words mean to you?
- How do you view your own place in Salvation History?

Faith: Our Response to Divine Revelation

When a friend congratulates you for a good test grade, you naturally say, "Thank you." It is natural and right to

dogma
A central truth of Revelation that Catholics are obliged to believe.

faith

A gift from God; one of the three theological virtues. Faith refers to personal knowledge of God; assent of the mind to truths God has revealed, made with the help of his grace and on the authority and trustworthiness of his revealing them; the truths themselves (the content of faith); and the lived witness of a Christian life (living faith).

virtues

"Firm attitudes, stable dispositions, habitual perfections of intellect and will that govern our actions, order our passions, and guide our conduct according to reason and faith" (CCC, 1804).

theological virtues

Three foundational virtues that are infused by God into the souls of the faithful: faith (belief in and personal knowledge of God), hope (trust in God's Salvation and his bestowal of the graces needed to attain it), and charity (love of God and love of neighbor as one loves oneself).

respond to good things that happen to us.

So it is with the Good News of our Salvation in Jesus Christ. We are privileged to hear it and have been invited to live it with a community of believers. Our response to God's invitation, which comes to us through the Church, is **faith**.

Faith is a **virtue**, one of the three **theological virtues**; hope and charity are the other two. These virtues are known as theological because they relate us to God (*theos* is the Greek word for God). The Holy Spirit bestows these gifts on us to help us live in relationship to God, the Blessed Trinity. In fact, the Blessed Trinity is the origin, motive, and object of all the theological virtues.

What does this gift of faith, which has been given to us by the Holy Spirit, enable us to do? Simply, it enables us to respond "yes" to Divine Revelation, God's free gift of self-communication. It enables us to believe in God and all that he has revealed to us. Faith also helps us to accept Church teaching. Faith enables us to commit ourselves totally to God, both our intellects and our wills. The gift of faith:

- makes it possible for us to accept Jesus Christ as our Lord. It helps us imitate him and put his teachings into practice.

- enables us to partake of the life of the Holy Spirit who enlightens us as to who Jesus is—the Second Person of the Blessed Trinity.

- requires free acceptance. God does not force his love on us. He invites us to respond to him freely with our minds and hearts. Our own free will cooperates with the grace of God's invitation.

- opens up the gates of Heaven to us. Faith is necessary for our Salvation. When we use the gift of faith and live Christlike lives, we are on the path to eternal life—a life of union with God.

Divine Revelation is God's gift to us. By responding to this gift through faith in Jesus Christ, we position ourselves for happiness both in this life and forever in eternity.

For Review

1. What is a virtue?
2. What does the gift of faith enable us to do?

For Reflection

Describe a person of faith you know. How does that person manifest the gift of faith?

Main Ideas

- Human beings are made to be happy (pp. 2–3).

- Only God can satisfy our desire for happiness (pp. 2–4).

- "The desire for God is written in the human heart" (p. 3).

- People are naturally religious; religion helps people to connect to God (pp. 5–6).

- In spite of the prevalence of irreligion and secularism, most people still belong to an organized religion (pp. 4–5).

- The one true God can be known with certainty from human reason (pp. 6–10).

- St. Thomas Aquinas developed five precepts that prove the existence of God (pp. 7–8).

- However, human reason alone cannot really know what God is like (p. 11).

- God revealed himself through the events of Salvation History, beginning from Creation through covenants he formed with the Chosen People (pp. 12–15).

- Jesus Christ is God's fullest, complete, and final Revelation. He is the only Son of the Father; he is God himself (p. 15).

- Divine Revelation is received through a single Deposit of Faith that is found in two places: Sacred Tradition and Sacred Scripture (pp. 15–19).

- The Church's Magisterium conserves and hands out the single Deposit of Faith (pp. 15–16).

- Faith, one of the three theological virtues, is our response to Divine Revelation (pp. 19–20).

Terms, People, Places

Complete each sentence by choosing the correct answer from the list of terms below. You will not use all of the terms.

agnosticism	atheist
circumcision	conscience
covenant	Deposit of Faith
Divine Revelation	dogma
faith	irreligion
Magisterium	monotheistic
omnipotent	Original Sin
St. Peter	polytheistic
prophets	religion
Sacred Scripture	Sacred Tradition
Salvation History	secularism
theological virtues	St. Thomas Aquinas
virtue	

1. Because humans are created with a longing for God, they naturally seek out _____ to allow themselves to reconnect to the divine.

2. By claiming people can't know for certain if God exists or not, _____ is similar to atheism because its adherents live as though God does not exist.

3. Looking at the vastness of the universe and realizing it is the product of the Creator God, we become more aware that God is _____, that is, almighty and all-knowing.

4. The single _____, turned over by Jesus to the Apostles, is contained in both Sacred Scripture and Sacred Tradition.

5. _____ was a sign of God's covenant with Abraham and his descendants.

6. The Holy Spirit's gift of _____ enables us to believe in God and all that he has revealed to us.

Primary Source Quotations

Discovering the Lord

For all men were by nature foolish who were in ignorance of God, and who from the good things seen did not succeed in knowing him who is, and from studying the works did not discern the artisan;

But either fire, or wind, or the swift air, or the circuit of the stars, or the mighty water, or the luminaries of Heaven, the governors of the world, they considered gods. Now if out of joy in their beauty they thought them gods, let them know how far more excellent is the Lord than these; for the original source of beauty fashioned them.

—Wisdom 13:1–3

Finding the Lord in Creation

When we see the beauty of creation and recognize the goodness present there, it is impossible not to believe in God and to experience his saving and reassuring presence. If we came to see all the good that exists in the world—and moreover, experience the good that comes from God himself—we would never cease to approach him, praise him, and thank him. He continually fills us with joy and good things. His joy is our strength.

—Pope Benedict XVI

God is not what you imagine or what you think you understand. If you understand, you have failed.

—St. Augustine

God is closer to us than water is to a fish.

—St. Catherine of Siena

Research the context of one of these quotations. Write a short report that includes information on the source of the quotation and what else the author wrote on God and how people come to know him.

Ongoing Assignments

As you cover the material in this chapter, choose and complete at least three of these assignments:

1. Psalm 104 praises God for his creation. Create a PowerPoint presentation to illustrate this Psalm. Choose appropriate background music to accompany the text and pictures.

2. In your journal, create a list of the Twelve Apostles (see Matthew 10:1–4, Mark 3:13–19, or Luke 6:12–16). Then, consult one of the following websites to read a biography of one of the Apostles. Write a one-page report. Download an image from the Internet for an illustration of the Apostle or one of his symbols.

   - American Catholic.org–Saints: www.americancatholic.org/Features/Saints/byname.asp
   - Catholic Information Network: www.cin.org/saints.html
   - Catholic Online Saints: www.catholic.org/saints/stindex.php
   - Patron Saints: www.catholicforum.com/saints/indexsnt.htm
   - Theology Library: www.shc.edu/theolibrary/saints2.htm

3. Identify four of the happiest people you know, including at least two adults. Record interviews (either audio or video) asking them to define what it means to be happy. Then ask them for their secrets to a happy life.

4. At a Church function, interview at least five people on why they believe God exists. Prepare a report on your findings.

5. Write a letter from God to you telling you why you should be happy and how to find happiness. Make sure your letter includes a description of your strengths and talents.

6. Check out LifeTeen.com. Read some entries under "Teen Talk." Report on some faith statements you read there.

7. Check out Disciplesnow.com. Under "It's Catholic," find and report on an article about God or faith.

8. Check out "Interview with Jesus": www.interviewwithgod.com. Look at some of the presentations, for example, "Interview with God." Transcribe some favorite Scripture passages into your journal.

9. Create a dialogue skit in which a believer answers the arguments of a nonbeliever about the existence of God.

10. Find the *Dogmatic Constitution on Divine Revelation* (*Dei Verbum*) on the Vatican website: www.vatican.va. Read Chapter 4 of that document (paragraphs 14–16). Write a one-paragraph summary of the purpose of the Old Testament.

11. Interview several members of the older generation of your family. For tips on how to do oral history, check out Cyndi's List: www.cyndislist.com/oral.htm. See if you can find answers to these questions:

    - Where did your family come from?

    - When did they settle in this country?

    - Are there any famous relatives?

    - Are there any family legends? Are they true or false?

    As part of this activity, perform a service in gratitude for your relative: do some housekeeping or yard work, run an errand, or help to bind some family photos.

Prayer

Make it a habit to recite this hymn of praise to begin each day:

> Come, let us sing joyfully to the LORD;
> > cry out to the rock of our Salvation.
> Let us greet him with a song of praise,
> > joyfully sing out our psalms.
> For the LORD is the great God,
> > the great king over all gods,

> Whose hand holds the depths of the earth;
> > who owns the tops of the mountains.
> The sea and dry land belong to God,
> > who made them, formed them by hand.
> Enter, let us bow down in worship;
> > let us kneel before the LORD who made us.
> For this is our God,
> > whose people we are, God's well-tended flock.
>
> > —Psalm 95:1–7

- *Reflection:* What *for you* is God's greatest creation for which you want to thank him?

- *Resolution:* Take time this week to thank one person who brings you happiness.

2

INTRODUCTION TO SACRED SCRIPTURE

Do you not know or have you not heard?
The LORD is the eternal God,
creator of the ends of the earth.
He does not faint nor grow weary,
and his knowledge is beyond scrutiny.
He gives strength to the fainting;
for the weak he makes vigor abound.
Though young men faint and grow weary,
and youths stagger and fall,
They that hope in the LORD will renew their strength,
they will soar as with eagles' wings;
They will run and not grow weary,
walk and not grow faint.

—Isaiah 40:28-31

The Game of Life

God is the source of our strength as we face the challenges of daily living.

The Bible Is the Inspired Word of God

God is the author of the Bible. The Holy Spirit inspired the human authors of the sacred books.

How to Read the Bible

The Scriptures must be read in light of the same Spirit by whom they were written and in communion with the whole Church.

How to Understand the Bible

There are three spiritual senses of Scripture—allegorical, moral, and anagogical—that help us look to the deeper meaning of God's Word.

Biblical Translations

The Bible was originally composed in Hebrew, Aramaic, and Greek. St. Jerome translated it into Latin, from which many English editions have been drawn.

Modern Approaches for Studying Sacred Scripture

Historical, source, form, and redaction criticism help us to read Sacred Scripture prayerfully and interpret it critically.

The Game of Life

Baron de Coubertin, a key founder of the modern Olympic games, borrowed the words for the Olympic motto from Fr. Henri Martin Dideon, the headmaster of Arcueil College in Paris: *Citius, Altius, Fortius*, Latin for "Swifter, Higher, Stronger." Fr. Dideon used the motto to describe the athletic achievements of the students at his school. Coubertin thought these same words would be appropriate to describe the world's greatest athletes. The Olympic creed also reads:

> The most important thing in the Olympic Games is not to win but to take part, just as the most important thing in life is not the triumph but the struggle. The essential thing is not to have conquered but to have fought well.

The Olympic motto and creed are inspirational because they challenge us to be the best people, not just athletes, we can possibly be. Compare these words to the passage from the Book of Isaiah that opens this chapter. The source of our strength is the good God who will never let us down. He will always carry us through the tough times. The goals are similar: We participate in the journey of life, hoping to be all that God intends for us, the best people we can be.

● How to Locate and Read Bible References

A typical Bible reference looks like this: Jn 1:1–18. Follow these steps to locate and read the passage:

1. "Jn" is an abbreviated title of the book, in this case the Gospel of John. (Common abbreviations for the books of the Bible can be found in your own Bible or on page 266.)

2. The first number listed is the *chapter* number; the *verse* number follows the colon (:). In this example, we should look at chapter 1 of the Gospel of John, verses 1–18.

3. The hyphen (–) indicates several chapters or verses. Study these two examples:

    *   Gn 1–2 (Genesis, chapters 1 through 2, inclusive)
    *   Ex 32:1–5 (Exodus, chapter 32, verses 1 through 5, inclusive)

4. A semicolon (;) separates two distinct references; a comma (,) separates two verses in the same chapter. Study these two examples:

    *   Lk 6:12–16; 7:18–23 (Luke, chapter 6, verses 12 through 16 *and* Luke, chapter 7, verses 18 through 23)
    *   Is 9:1, 3, 8 (Isaiah, chapter 9, verses 1, 3, and 8)

5. Sometimes you'll see something like this: Prv 6:6*f*. The "*f.*" means the following verse; "*ff.*" means an indeterminate number of subsequent verses. Thus, Prv 6:6*f.* means Proverbs, chapter 6, verses 6 and 7, while Prv 6:6*ff.* means Proverbs, chapter 6, verse 6 and several verses that follow.

Write in your journal the full citations for the following biblical passages. Follow the format of the examples given above.

*   Ps 8:1–5, 9
*   Pss 8; 50; 145

- Jl 1:1–2:5*ff.*; 2:28–3:17
- Is 40:12–41:4; 65:17*f.*
- 1 Cor 10:1–13; 12:1–13:13

For Reflection

- What one area of your life best fits the Olympic creed? Explain.
- Reread Isaiah 40:28-31. When was a time when the Lord carried you to greater heights?

The Bible Is the Inspired Word of God

The Bible is the written record of God's Revelation. God comes to us through this collection of writings. "Through all the words of Sacred Scripture, God speaks only one single Word, his one Utterance in whom he expresses himself completely" (*CCC*, 102). The Bible is a great source of strength to help us live "Swifter, Higher, and Stronger."

Because Sacred Scripture is the Word of God, the Church teaches that:

- God is the author of the Bible,
- the Holy Spirit inspired the writers of the sacred books, and
- the Sacred Scriptures teach the truth.

Furthermore, if the Bible is to mean something for our daily lives, we need the Holy Spirit to enlighten our minds to understand and apply his holy word to our lives.

After Jesus rose from the dead, he appeared to the disciples in Jerusalem. The Gospel of Luke reports that "he opened their minds to understand the scriptures" (Lk 24:45). The Bible is not a religion textbook that we study from as if we were learning world history, geography, or languages. It is a living book. For it to remain so, we must call on Christ, through the Holy Spirit, to open our own minds to its Good News.

What Is Inspiration?

We use the words "inspired" and "inspirational" in common speech. For example, you might have read a story about how a teenager overcame cancer. Her faith, courage, and the support of her family and friends *inspired* her through her battle. Or say a classmate gave a particularly good talk in his bid to run for class officer. You told him his talk was "inspirational," that is, it aroused confidence in you that he would be a great class representative.

When we say that God inspired the sacred writers of the Bible, we are using the term a bit more technically. Used in this sense, it means that God is the author of the Bible; he used the human authors as his instrument to convey Divine Revelation to us. Just as you use a ballpoint pen or a pencil to take class notes, so God used the human authors as instruments to commit to writing those truths that are necessary for our Salvation, and to do so without error.

Take this analogy another step: When you take notes in class, you are the author of the notes that end up in your notebook. The pen or the pencil is the instrument you use to get the notes down on paper. Each instrument has its own characteristics (for example, black ink for your pen or erasable lead for your pencil), but the notes that result from either the pen or the pencil will be the same. You are the author of them, even though the writing will look different depending on the instrument you used.

God used the human authors of the books of the Bible as his instruments to reveal the truths of our Salvation. Under the influence of the Holy Spirit, the human authors drew on their own background, education, skill and talent as writers, vocabulary, and so forth to write what God intended for people to know. God respected the freedom of the human writers, but in every case, the Holy Spirit guided the author in the truth. The end product is the inerrant Word of God:

The inspired books teach the truth. "Since therefore all that the inspired authors or sacred writers affirm should be regarded as affirmed by the Holy Spirit, we must acknowledge that the books of Scripture firmly, faithfully, and without error teach that truth which God, for the sake of our Salvation, wished to see confided to the Sacred Scriptures" (*Dogmatic Constitution on Divine Revelation*, No. 11; *CCC*, 107).

For Review

1. How is the Bible the inspired Word of God?

2. How is the Bible inspired?

3. Why should we accept the Bible as inerrant?

For Reflection

• Write your own definition of *inspirational*.

• What is the most inspirational book you've ever read? Why?

• What kind of music inspires you? Explain.

• Who is the most inspirational person you know? What qualities does this person possess? How would you like to be like this person?

How to Read the Bible

The purpose of interpreting the Bible is to discover what God wanted the biblical authors to reveal for the benefit of our Salvation. Because God speaks to us in a human way, when we read the Bible we must pay attention to what the human authors wished to say and to what God wanted to reveal through their words.

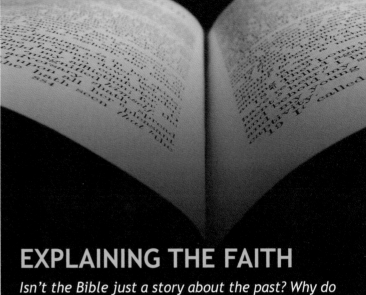

EXPLAINING THE FAITH

Isn't the Bible just a story about the past? Why do people today think it applies to them?

It is true that Sacred Scripture contains stories, history, poetry, and many teachings about events in the past, but these events are part of Salvation History. The message it contains is timeless, just as Jesus Christ and the Salvation he won for us are timeless.

The Bible is the living Word of God. Although the content is rooted in specific historical events, the message of Sacred Scripture will never grow old. God continues to speak to us through his holy Word. The Church recognizes this in her liturgies, which always contain readings from Sacred Scripture. It is also important to focus our personal prayer on Scripture.

To discover the human authors' intentions requires diligence. It requires learning how the history of their time and culture influenced them. It also means studying their language and how they used it to express themselves. A major factor in getting at the authors' intention is to identify the literary form or genre of their writing. (See below for various types of literary forms.)

In addition, since Sacred Scripture is inspired, it "must be read and interpreted in the light of the same Spirit by whom it was written" (*Dogmatic Constitution on Divine Revelation*, 12 §3; *CCC*, 111). The Second Vatican Council taught three ways for interpreting Scripture in accordance with the Holy Spirit who inspired it.

First, note the content and unity of the whole Scripture. Even though the various books may be different, Jesus Christ is the Word of God, the center and heart of Sacred Scripture. The Old Testament prefigures him and illuminates the New Testament. The entire Bible must be read in light of the Death and Resurrection of Jesus. Similarly, because the Old Testament retains its own value as Divine Revelation, the New Testament must be read and understood in light of the Old Testament. As St. Augustine put it, "The New Testament lies hidden in the Old, and the Old Testament is unveiled in the New" (quoted in *CCC*, 129).

Second, "read the Scripture within 'the living Tradition of the whole Church'" (*CCC*, 113). Recall that Sacred Scripture is one of two parts of a *single* Deposit of Faith. The other part is Sacred Tradition. God gave Sacred Scripture to the whole Church. Therefore, to interpret the Bible properly, we should read it within the living Tradition of the Church. Christ left the authority to interpret Sacred Scripture with the Magisterium, which is the Pope and the bishops united with him. Just as the Holy Spirit enlightened Church leaders to recognize which ancient books were inspired, so he guides the Magisterium to help us understand the meaning of God's Word and how to apply it to our daily lives. Without the help of the Magisterium our personal interpretations of Scripture may be wrong.

Third, pay attention to the "analogy of faith." The analogy of faith is the unity "of the truths of the faith among themselves and within the whole plan of Revelation" (*CCC*, 114). Simply put, this means that truths revealed in Sacred Scripture cannot contradict each other. God's revealed truths make sense, one with the other. Therefore, in explaining what the Bible means, it should be done in such a way that it is in harmony with all of God's Revelation, including the teaching of the Magisterium.

AN ANALOGY OF FAITH

What is meant by "analogy of faith"? Consider the following example: Psalm 34:16 says, "The Lord has eyes for the just and ears for their cry."

But John 4:24 says, "God is Spirit, and those who worship him must worship in Spirit and truth."

At first glance, these passages seem to contradict themselves. How can a spirit have eyes and ears? But the analogy of faith holds that Revelation in the Sacred Scripture is not contradictory. The difference is understood by recognizing how the passage from the Book of Psalms uses a *figure of speech*. The intent was to emphasize how God watches over his people and listens to their prayers for help. It does not mean to communicate that God is a physical being like humans, endowed with eyes and ears.

The context of the passage in John's Gospel concerns Jesus' dialogue with the woman he met at a well in Samaria. She believed that God could only be properly worshiped in a particular place, either in the Jerusalem Temple for the Jews, or in the Temple erected on Mount Gerizim for the Samaritans. But Jesus tells her that the physical place of worship is not important since God is a spirit. He can be worshiped anywhere with the help of the Holy Spirit and in truth.

literal sense (of the biblical text)

"The literal sense is the meaning conveyed by the words of Scripture and discovered by exegesis, following the rules of sound interpretation" (*CCC*, 116).

literary genre

A type of writing that has a particular form, style, or content.

exegesis

The process used by scholars to discover the meaning of the biblical text.

Literary Forms

Part of the task of interpreting Scripture is to identify the kinds of writing or various literary forms so we can understand and interpret God's Word correctly. Imagine reading this headline in your local paper: "Padres Slaughter Tribe!" If this appeared on the front page of the newspaper, you could possibly conclude that some missionary priests went crazy and decided to eliminate some native people. But if you read the same headline on the sports page, you would probably conclude that the San Diego baseball team defeated the Cleveland Indians, and by a wide margin!

The context of the headline is crucial in this example. Additionally, editorial writing differs from news reporting. What appears in a horoscope differs from news analysis. Sending an e-mail to your girlfriend is not the same as writing a letter to your grandmother. Instant messaging a friend about an upcoming party differs from filling out your first job application.

Context is also vitally important in scriptural interpretation. Determining context in the Bible first involves identifying the **literary genre** being used by the author. A literary genre or form is a type of writing that has a particular style or content. The seventy-three books of the Bible contain many literary genres.

Catholics typically rely on the work of biblical scholars working under the Magisterium to understand the meaning of difficult biblical texts. **Exegesis** is the process used by

scholars to discover the meaning of the biblical text. Some of the work they do in their studies will be described in the section "Modern Approaches for Studying Sacred Scripture" (pages 39–41). Identifying the literary genre helps anyone who reads the Bible to determine the literal meaning or **literal sense** of the biblical text. "The *literal sense* is the meaning conveyed by the words of Scripture and discovered by exegesis, following the rules of sound interpretation" (*CCC*, 116).

There are several types of literary genres in the Bible. In some cases, entire books of the Bible consist of one literary form. For example, the First Book of Samuel is a *historical book*, Amos is *prophecy*, the Psalms are *poetry*, and most of the books attributed to St. Paul are *letters*. Even within these larger works, we find smaller literary forms like *genealogies*, *miracle stories*, *prayers*, and *parables*. Examples of these and other literary genres from the Old Testament and New Testament are listed below:

- *Allegory*: an extended comparison where many elements of a story stand for deeper realities like abstract ideas, moral qualities, or spiritual realities (see Proverbs 9:1–6).

- *Biography*: a written account of a person's life (see Jeremiah 26).

- *Creed*: a formal statement of religious belief (see Deuteronomy 26:5–10).

- *Etiology*: a story that gives the cause of something (see Genesis 32:22–32).

- *Fable*: a brief story with a moral; often uses animals that act and speak like human beings (see Judges 9:7–15).

- *History*: a chronological narrative or record of events, as in the life or development of a people, country, or institution (see 1 Kings 1–2).

- *Law*: a rule of conduct or standard of behavior established by proper authority, society, or custom (see Ex 20:1–17).

- *Prophecy*: an inspired utterance made by a prophet, which expresses God's will (see Amos 1–2).

- *Genealogy*: a record of one's ancestors (see Matthew 1:1–17).

- *Hyperbole*: a deliberately exaggerated saying to highlight the topic under discussion (see Matthew 18:8).

- *Miracle Story*: for example, a nature miracle is a report of a powerful sign performed by Jesus to show his mastery over the elements (see Luke 8:22–25).

- *Riddle*: a question or statement that teases the mind; it requires thought and application (see Matthew 11:11).

EXPLAINING THE FAITH

Who are fundamentalists? How do they read the Bible? What is the difference between a "literal" reading and a "literalist" reading of the Bible?

Christians known as "fundamentalists" believe in the sole primacy of Scripture. They also allow for private interpretation of biblical texts and a literalist interpretation of Scripture. This view is not correct. Christian faith is not a "religion of the book." Rather it is a religion of the living Word of God. Catholics look to both Scripture *and* Tradition as having their common source in the Revelation of Jesus Christ. Further, only the Church's Magisterium can give an authentic interpretation of Scripture.

Fundamentalists read the Bible in a literalist sense. This means they ignore various literary forms and the cultural and historical factors of the period in which the biblical authors wrote.

There is a major difference between the "literal" sense of Scripture and a "literalist" approach. The literal interpretation takes into account what the author intended to convey. For example, "It's raining cats and dogs" means, in a literal sense, "It's raining hard." In contrast, a literalist interpretation takes the exact meaning of the words without considering any other factors. "It's raining cats and dogs" means cats and dogs are falling from the sky.

Note how a literal reading of the two creation accounts in Genesis (1:1-2:2 and 2:4-22) can explain apparent contradictions. A literalist interpreter would be at a loss to explain how God created humans last in the first creation account but first in the second account. Fundamentalists would conclude that God created the earth in seven twenty-four hour days, the equivalent of one of our weeks. This literalist, fundamentalist way of reading the Bible does not consider changes in language over the centuries, nor does it account for the cultural differences between our age and that of biblical times.

The Church holds that the Bible faithfully teaches the truth that God wishes to convey to us. The primary purpose of the Bible is to present the religious truths that God wishes to reveal through the events of Salvation History. In sum, under the guidance of the Magisterium, biblical scholars and individuals work to find the literal sense of the biblical words—what the author intended. Literalism fails to do this.

- *Parable*: a vivid story told to convey religious truth, usually with a surprise ending (see Matthew 13:33).

- *Pronouncement Story*: a passage whose purpose is to set up an important saying (see Mark 3:1–5).

For Review

1. Read each of the following passages. Identify its likely literary genre: 1 Samuel 17:1-54; Leviticus 23:1-14; Acts 19:1-12; 1 Corinthians 15:1-8; Luke 12:49.

2. What is meant by the "analogy of faith"?

3. What is the *literal sense* of the biblical text?

4. Define and give an example of five literary forms found in Sacred Scripture.

5. What is the difference between a "literal" and a "literalist" reading of the Bible?

For Reflection

Share an example from your experience (other than the Bible) where reading in context was crucial to your understanding of the material.

How to Understand the Bible

The starting point for understanding Sacred Scripture is what the author intended by the words he wrote, the literal sense. But the Bible also has a *spiritual sense* that depends on the literal sense. The literal sense concerns the meaning of the words of Scripture; the spiritual sense refers not in the words themselves but by the "realities and events" that can be signified by them. It is the spiritual sense that looks to the deeper meaning of various scriptural passages as part of God's overall plan of Salvation. There are three spiritual senses of Scripture:

1. *The allegorical sense.* An allegory is a metaphor or "sustained comparison." In an allegorical work of literature, for example, the story line conveys more than one level of meaning at the same time. Taken in total, an allegorical reading of Scripture looks at the entire Bible, especially the Old Testament, in light of its fulfillment in Christ. Therefore, when we study the crossing of the Red Sea by the Israelites, we see it prefiguring Christ's victory over sin. We can also understand the waters of the Red Sea as a symbol for Christian Baptism, a sign of our freedom from sin in Jesus Christ. Or, the Paschal Lamb sacrificed for the feast of Passover is a clear foreshadowing of the Lamb of God—Jesus Christ—who gave up his life to win our Salvation.

2. *The moral sense.* God's Word is intended to lead us to live a good life, to act justly on behalf of God and other people. Thus, the words of the prophets telling the Chosen People to obey God's Commandments also apply to us. When reporting the punishments that resulted from the sins of the Chosen People, St. Paul wrote, "These things happened to them as an example, and they have been written down as a warning to us" (1 Cor 10:11).

3. *The anagogical sense.* Still another way to view God's Word is to look at earthly events and other realities in the context of leading us to Heaven. Our final goal is to get to Heaven, and the Bible shows us the way. (The word *anagogical* comes from the Greek word for "leading"). For example, we can see the Church as a symbol of the heavenly Jerusalem. The Church, which is the Body of Christ, leads us to our eternal destiny.

In summary, there are four senses of Scripture:

EXPLAINING THE FAITH

Are historical and scientific truths and Biblical truth at odds?

We must always remember that the Bible is not a science book or a history book. Its purpose is not to explain scientific facts from modern biology, chemistry, or astronomy, or historical facts that have to do with exact dates for events like the creation of the world. The Bible is a written record of Divine Revelation. God inspired its authors to reveal religious truths. As noted, the Bible contains many literary forms, including poetry, parables, prayers, and, of course, historical narratives. One of the main responsibilities of the Magisterium is to help identify the truths of the faith revealed in Sacred Scripture and explain how they relate to scientific and historical research. These truths reveal who we are in relation to God and the world he created. They tell us that we are material-spiritual beings made in God's image and likeness. And they reveal our destiny—eternal life of union with a loving, Triune God.

The Catholic Church welcomes the research of historians and scientists because "truth does not contradict truth." For example, consider the work of historians who have examined the events depicted in Sacred Scripture to see if there is any record of them elsewhere. Nothing is more important than the existence of Jesus himself. Was there really such a person? Or was he just the invention of the early Christians? Historians, including non-believers, have looked into this question. And, drawing on records from Roman and Jewish historians, and judging the New Testament to be historically reliable, they have proven the following:

- Jesus of Nazareth did indeed exist.
- The Romans under the prefect Pontius Pilate crucified him.
- He established a Church that persists to this very day.

Believers have nothing to fear from open-minded historical research. This is why popes have opened up the Vatican archives to researchers. Pope John Paul II even appointed a commission of historians, scientists, and theologians to reexamine the famous case against Galileo Galilei (1564-1642). The result of the open search for truth was the commission report that said that the judges who condemned Galileo were in error.

Similarly, the Church appreciates the efforts of scientists who help explain the workings of the universe. Their research reveals the marvelous genius of our Creator God, who brought everything into existence.

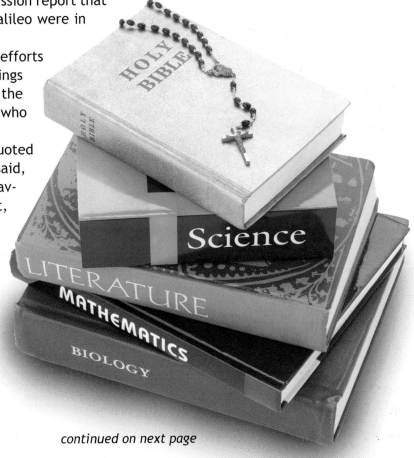

Cardinal Baronius (1538-1607), quoted often by Galileo, put it well when he said, "The Bible teaches us how to go to Heaven, not how the heavens go." Simply put, scientific research and Christian faith do not exclude each other. Consider the theory of evolution and the origins of human life. Nothing in this theory denies or is opposed to the existence of a loving, Divine Creator as depicted in Genesis, who brought everything into existence out of nothingness. Good science does not, and cannot, say that humans resulted from chance in a random universe. Good science cannot exclude the existence of God, who is the first cause of creation.

continued on next page

1. The literal sense teaches history, for example, what the words say in a historical context.

2. The allegorical sense teaches what you should believe, that is, what the words mean in the larger context of Salvation History.

3. The moral sense teaches what you should do regarding how to live your life.

4. The anagogical sense teaches where you are going, building up the virtue of hope while leading us to Heaven.

For Review

1. What are the three spiritual senses of Scripture? Give an example of each.

2. For the passages given below, briefly summarize the *literal sense* of the passage by answering the questions that follow:

   • Compare Genesis 1:1-2 and Matthew 3:16. What is the connection?

   • Read 1 Corinthians 10: 1-14. List three behaviors Christians should avoid by learning from the bad example of the Chosen People in the desert.

   • Read Matthew 7:1-5. Interpret both literally and in an anagogical sense.

3. Why does the Church not fear scientific or historical studies?

EXPLAINING THE FAITH *continued*

Again, there is no conflict between the religious truths that Scripture reveals and the truths that science or history discover and report. The *Catechism of the Catholic Church* (159) says it well:

> Though faith is above reason, there can never be any real discrepancy between faith and reason. Since the same God who reveals mysteries and infuses faith has bestowed the light of reason on the human mind, God cannot deny himself, nor can truth ever contradict truth (*Dei Filius* 4; DS 3017).
>
> Consequently, methodical research in all branches of knowledge, provided it is carried out in a truly scientific manner and does not override moral laws, can never conflict with the faith, because the things of the world and the things of faith derive from the same God. The humble and persevering investigator of the secrets of nature is being led, as it were, by the hand of God in spite of himself, for it is God, the conserver of all things, who made them what they are (*GS* 36 §1).

Share God's Word: Make a Bookmark for Christ

Matthew's Gospel ends with Jesus commanding his disciples to share the Gospel with all people (Mt 28:18-20). Here is an activity to help you to take up that charge:

1. Locate your favorite Scripture passage, one you wish to share with others. For ideas for good verses, search the Internet under the topic "famous Bible quotes."

2. Then create your own bookmarks. Insert appropriate clip art and the verse(s) you selected.

3. Print on card-stock paper, perhaps of different colors. Cut out the bookmarks.

4. Distribute to parishioners after the weekend Mass or to grade school students at the local parish school, or pass them out with classmates at a public place like the local mall.

For Reflection

- Name an allegory with a moral message outside of the Bible that has had an influence on your life. Tell why this is so.

- In the past, what approach have you taken to reading the Bible?

Biblical Translations

Most of the Old Testament was composed in Hebrew. The Hebrew language has origins as an ancient Canaanite language adopted by the Israelites when they entered the Promised Land. Hebrew was the living language of the Israelites until the end of the Babylonian Exile. Aramaic, the common language spoken in Babylon and the whole Middle East, then became the spoken language of the Jewish people. Small sections of the Old Testament were written in Aramaic. Jesus spoke Aramaic. By the first century AD, Hebrew disappeared as the ordinary spoken language, but it remained the sacred and literary language. Seven Old Testament books were also written in Greek.

The entire New Testament was written in Greek. *Koine,* or "common," Greek had become the spoken language in the Roman Empire of the first century AD. Later, the common spoken language of the Roman Empire changed from Greek to Latin. In

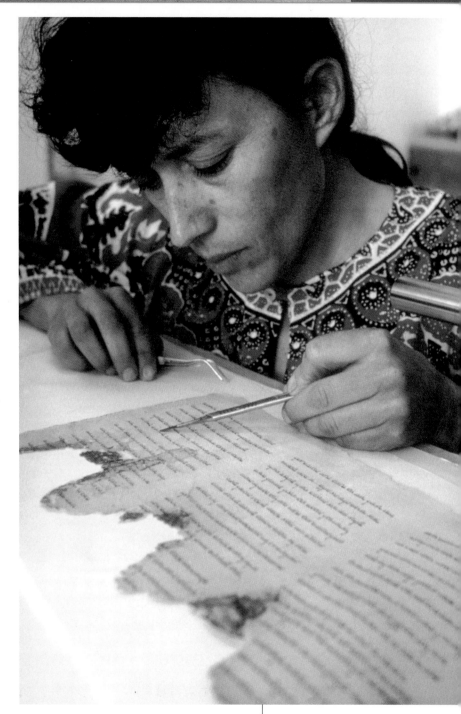

390, St. Jerome completed the Latin translation of the Old and New Testaments. This translation, known as the **Vulgate**, became the Church's official translation of the Bible from the original languages.

Today, only scholars and other linguists are able to read and understand the Bible in its original languages.

Vulgate
St. Jerome's fifth-century Latin translation of the Bible into the common language of the people of his day.

Dead Sea Scrolls

Discovered in 1947 in caves near the Dead Sea, these manuscripts belonged to the Jewish Essene sect, which lived in a monastery at Qumran. The scrolls contain Essene religious documents, commentaries on certain Hebrew Scriptures, and ancient Old Testament manuscripts. They have proved very valuable to scholars in studying the Old Testament and for learning about some Jewish practices at the time of Jesus.

Church Father

A traditional title given to theologians of the first eight centuries whose teachings made a lasting mark on the Church.

Your Bible is an English translation. If you include translations of individual books of the Bible, there have been almost five hundred new translations or revisions of older English versions of the Bible. None of the translators worked from the original biblical books because none of these exist. What translators use are meticulous copies of copies of the Bible. Some important biblical manuscripts have been discovered in the past two hundred years. For example, the **Dead Sea Scrolls** (discovered in Israel in the late 1940s) produced some Old Testament books that predate the birth of Christ. This was an important discovery because until the Dead Sea Scrolls were unearthed there were few Old Testament manuscripts preserved that were composed from earlier than 950 AD. In contrast, there are manuscript copies of virtually the entire New Testament books that date before 300 AD.

Some of the more important English translations of the Bible under both Protestant sponsorship and Catholic sponsorship are listed below.

Protestant Translations of the Bible

For centuries Protestants have been using the popular King James Version (1611). Other Protestant translations include the following, all of which are available in editions approved for Catholic reading:

- *New Revised Standard Version* (1989). Using a good sense of English and sound modern scholarship, this is the most important modern revision of the King James Bible.

- *Revised English Bible* (1992). The British equivalent of the New Revised Standard Version.

- *New International Version* (1973–1978). A conservative translation by scholars from thirty-four different denominations. Many excellent study versions of this Bible are available.

Catholic Translations of the Bible

Until the twentieth century, Catholics relied heavily on the *Douay-Rheims Version* (1582–1609) and its revision done by Bishop Challoner (1749–1763). The *Douay-Rheims* Bible was a translation of the Latin Vulgate. In 1943, Pope Pius XII encouraged the translation of the Bible from the original languages. Two very popular and important English translations by Catholic scholars include:

- *New American Bible* (1952–1970; 1987). The Church uses this translation for the readings at liturgies in the United States. It is solid, faithful to the original text, readable, and scholarly. It is the translation cited in this text.

- *New Jerusalem Bible* (1985). The *New Jerusalem Bible* borrowed heavily from the French Bible, *La Sainte Bible*, which in turn is an important and scholarly translation from the original languages. It contains many helpful introductions and notes to guide the reader.

DEFENDER OF THE FAITH:
ST. JEROME (342–420)

St. Jerome, the translator of the Bible from its original languages into Latin, is also an important **Church Father**.

Jerome was born in northeast Italy. He went to Rome as a young man to study Latin and Greek literature and had an early devotion to some non-Christian scholars. This education in the classics inspired him to lifelong study. At the age of eighteen, Jerome was baptized. After further travels and study, he entered a strict monastic community near his home at Aquileia. There he mastered the difficult language of Hebrew. Later, in Antioch, Jerome had a vision that criticized him for his devotion to secular learning, for being "a follower of Cicero and not of Christ."

Ordained a priest in Antioch, Jerome then traveled in 380 to Constantinople and studied under the Church Father Gregory of Nazianzus. He eventually made it back to Rome to serve as Pope Damasus' secretary. Jerome had an explosive temper, often using his sharp pen to write fierce letters to his opponents. However, the Pope saw beneath

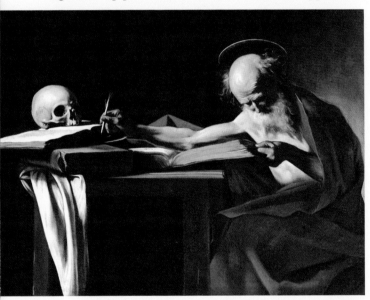

Jerome's sometimes-prickly personality. He discovered in him a man of unique holiness, learning, and integrity. As a result, the Pope commissioned him to translate the Bible into Latin, a task that eventually took Jerome to Bethlehem. There he founded a monastery for men and several convents for the women who studied Scripture under him.

Laboring relentlessly in a cave, Jerome, with the help of his disciples, completed his translation and commentary of the Bible into Latin, a task that took twenty-three years. Known as the Latin Vulgate translation (382–405), it became the authorized Bible used in the Catholic Church from that time on.

In his later years, Jerome also wrote against various heresies. He corresponded regularly with St. Augustine. As an old man worn down with a number of infirmities, he died peacefully. He is recognized as one of the Church's greatest minds and defenders of the faith. St. Augustine said of him, "What Jerome is ignorant of, no man has ever known."

Read more about the life of St. Jerome. See, for example, www.americancatholic.org/Messenger/Sep1997/feature2.asp. Report on something you learned about Jerome's life or write a commentary on one of this writings.

Faithful Disciple

יְהוֹשֻׁעַ

יְהוֹשׁוּעַ

יֵשׁוּעַ

Figure 1: Three ways of writing Jesus' name in biblical Hebrew

Ιησους Χριστος

Figure 2: "Jesus Christ" in Greek

For Review

1. In what languages was the Bible written?

2. Name two important English translations of the Bible.

3. Identify St. Jerome.

For Reflection

Note how the following versions of the Bible translate Psalm 23. Then explain which translation you prefer and why.

- *New American Bible*: www.usccb.org/ nab/bible

- *New Revised Standard Version*: www .devotions.net/bible/00bible.htm

- *Douay-Rheims*: www.intratext.com/X/ ENG0011.htm

- *King James Version*: www.bartleby .com/108

EXPLAINING THE FAITH

How important is the Bible for Catholics?

Sacred Scripture is an integral part of the Catholic Church. The Bible has a central role to play in Catholic prayer life. For example, Scripture readings are integral to every Mass and all the other sacraments. Scripture is also at the heart of the Liturgy of the Hours, or Divine Office, which is the public prayer of the Church that praises God and sanctifies the day. The Psalms are featured in a special way in the Liturgy of the Hours, which consists of Morning and Evening Prayer, Daytime Prayer, and Night Prayer. As official representatives of the Church, priests pray the Divine Office each day, but all Catholics are encouraged to pray the Liturgy of the Hours as a way to join in the daily prayer of the Church.

Especially since the Second Vatican Council (1962–1965), the Church encourages us to use the Bible in personal prayer. Today, many parishes foster Scripture study and prayer groups as a way to grow in holiness. St. Jerome knew the importance of the Bible when he said, "Ignorance of Scripture is ignorance of Christ." The Church has taken this saying much to heart, teaching in the *Catechism of the Catholic Church*:

> The Church "forcefully and specifically exhorts all the Christian faithful . . . to learn 'the surpassing knowledge of Jesus Christ,' by frequent reading of the divine Scriptures." (*CCC*, 133)

Modern Approaches for Studying Sacred Scripture

Sacred Scripture contains God's Revelation. When we read it prayerfully, we can grow closer to God and to each other. But how should you read it? Are you to take everything you read as the absolute, literal truth? How are you to understand what you read?

As we have seen, not everyone agrees on answers to these questions. Fundamentalists, for example, take a literalist approach, believing in the exact meaning of the words without taking into consideration other factors. Others treat the Bible as good albeit fictional literature that is meant to inspire us to live good lives.

In contrast to these positions, the Catholic Church teaches us to read Sacred Scripture prayerfully and to interpret it critically. The Bible is the inspired Word of God. It requires careful reading so that we can understand the literary forms, symbolism, and cultural realities that influenced it. The Magisterium, with the help of biblical scholars, authentically interprets the Word of God. The scholars use techniques of biblical criticism to study the Bible. Don't think of the term *criticism* in a negative way. Rather, it means looking carefully at the biblical texts in their historical and literary contexts. Historical, source, form, and redaction criticism involve scholarly detective work. Their purpose is simply to help us interpret what God wanted to communicate through the original Bible writers.

Historical Criticism

Historical criticism tries to determine the historical context of the biblical text. Historical criticism uses dating techniques, archaeology, and historical research to accomplish this task.

Consider an example of how archaeology assists historical criticism. Archaeology is the branch of science that studies prehistoric or historic people and their cultures. It does so by looking at artifacts, monuments, inscriptions, and the like. Biblical archaeology was popularized with the now-classic film *Raiders of the Lost Ark*. In that movie, the hero, Indiana Jones, unearths the Ark of the Covenant. The events in the film are fictional, but they raise questions like these: Was there an Ark of the Covenant? And if so, what did it look like? And

Liturgy of the Hours
The prayer of the Church; it is also known as the Divine Office. The Liturgy of the Hours utilizes the Scriptures, particularly the Psalms, for specific times of the day from early morning to later evening.

where is it today? Historical criticism helps to answer these types of questions.

For example, historical research reveals that the Ark of the Covenant was a wooden chest, built by the Chosen People after Moses received the Ten Commandments. Exodus 25:10–22 describes its design. Exodus 37:1–9 describes its construction. Its biblical measurements were in cubits (a cubit was the average length of a forearm). It would have measured approximately four feet by two-and-a-half feet. The original tablets of the Ten Commandments—and nothing else—were placed in the Ark. The Ark traveled with the Israelites in the desert. King David brought it to Jerusalem around 1000 BC. Around 930 BC, it was in the Holy of Holies in the Temple built by King Solomon. The High Priest visited it once a year, on the sacred feast of Yom Kippur.

The last time the Ark is mentioned in the Old Testament is when the Babylonians demolished the Jerusalem Temple in 586 BC. When the Temple was rebuilt around seventy years later, there was no mention of the Ark. The scholarly consensus is that the Babylonians destroyed the Ark, melting it down for its gold. There are other theories as to what happened to it, but all these theories are speculative.

Source Criticism

Source criticism is like literary detective work that helps discover where the biblical authors got their material. For example, scholars believe that the history in the Book of Kings came from court records that royal scribes wrote down. Source criticism has also noted that the author of Luke's Gospel used three main sources when he wrote his Gospel. These sources were the Gospel of Mark, a collection of writings also used for Matthew's Gospel, and a list of materials that only Luke had.

Form Criticism

Form criticism involves studying small units of biblical text to attempt to determine how each book took shape in the period of oral tradition before the actual writing of the biblical books. Second, form criticism identifies the literary genre or form. Form criticism is important for proper interpretation because each type of literature has its own way of presenting the truth.

Consider the parable of the Good Samaritan (see Luke 10:25–37). Form critics tell us that this was a story that Jesus told. Because the literary form is parable, we know that Jesus was not speaking of an actual, *historical* person. Rather, Jesus used a story to make the point to be compassionate and loving to all people, including enemies. Jesus' lesson was so important that the early Christian preachers repeated his parable in the early years of the Christian Tradition. Eventually, Luke drew from this Tradition and included it in his version of the Good News.

Redaction Criticism

Think of a redactor as an editor. *Redaction criticism* zeros in on how the various editors put together their sources and arranged them the way they did. Redaction criticism tries to determine what theological insight a given biblical author had that influenced him in his organization of the material.

For example, consider the genealogy of Jesus. When the Evangelist Luke recorded Jesus' family tree, he traced it to Adam. Adam is the common ancestor of *all* people. This helps us to know that Luke's Gospel was written for Gentile Christians. Gentiles were non-Jews. Luke wanted to emphasize that Jesus is the Savior for all people.

The author of Matthew's Gospel, on the other hand, shows how Jesus descended from Abraham, the father of Judaism. Writing for a predominantly Jewish-Christian community, Matthew wanted to show that Jesus Christ fulfilled the prophecies made to the Chosen People, starting with the father of the faith, Abraham.

There are other types of biblical criticism, like sociological studies, but the four discussed here are among the most important. Chapter 3 takes a closer look at how the Bible came into existence. We will also study the official list of sacred books (the canon of the Bible) and discuss some of the tools you can use to read God's Word with more appreciation.

🌐 For Review

1. List three types of biblical criticism. Explain what each tries to do.

2. Identify the Ark of the Covenant. What is most likely to have happened to it?

3. What is the point of the parable of the Good Samaritan?

🌐 For Reflection

What is one book, story, person, or event of the Bible that you would like to investigate to find out more details about it? Which form of biblical criticism would help you most in your search?

Main Ideas

- Sacred Scripture is the written record of God's Revelation (pp. 27–28).

- The Holy Spirit guided human authors to write the truths of Salvation (pp. 27–28).

- The Bible is inerrant (pp. 27–28).

- Sacred Scripture must be read and interpreted in light of the Holy Spirit (pp. 28–29).

- There are three ways for interpreting the Sacred Scripture in accordance with the Holy Spirit. They involve (1) noting the content and unity of the whole Scripture; (2) reading the Scripture within the context of the living Tradition of the Church; (3) paying attention to the analogy of faith (pp. 28–29).

- Identifying the literary genres of Scripture helps in interpreting God's Word (p. 30).

- There are several literary genres in the Bible, including history, prophecy, letters, and many others (pp. 30–32).

- There are three spiritual senses of Scripture that help us to understand its meaning: the allegorical sense, the moral sense, and the anagogical sense (pp. 32–34).

- There are several translations of the Bible, only some of which are approved for Catholics (pp. 35–36).

- St. Jerome translated the Bible from its original languages to Latin (the Vulgate) (p. 37).

- The Church teaches Catholics to read the Scripture prayerfully and to interpret it critically under the wisdom of the Magisterium (p. 39).

- Historical criticism, source criticism, form criticism, and redaction criticism are four ways to interpret the original biblical source (pp. 39–41).

Terms, People, Places

Write your answers to the following questions.

1. Name and define one literary genre from the Old Testament and one from the New Testament. Give an example of each that is not named in this chapter.

2. How are source criticism, form criticism, and redaction criticism examples of Scripture exegesis?

3. How does St. Jerome meet the definition of *Church Father*?

4. What is the English translation of *Lectio Divina*?

5. What is meant by a literal sense of the biblical text? What is the difference between a *literal* reading of Scripture and a *literalist* reading of Scripture?

6. How did the discovery of the *Dead Sea Scrolls* aid biblical scholarship?

7. What is another term for the *Liturgy of the Hours*?

8. Where did St. Jerome undertake the task of translating the Latin Vulgate?

Primary Source Quotations

God Can Utter Nothing That Is Untrue

It is a lamentable fact that there are many . . . whose chief purpose in all this is too often to find mistakes in the sacred writings and so to shake and weaken their authority. Some of these writers display not only extreme hostility, but the greatest unfairness; in their eyes a profane book or ancient document is accepted without hesitation, whilst the Scripture, if they only find in it a suspicion of error, is set down with the slightest possible discussion as quite untrustworthy. It is true, no doubt, that copyists have made mistakes in the text of the Bible; this question, when it arises, should be carefully considered on its merits, and the fact not too easily admitted, but only in those passages where the proof is clear. It may also happen that the sense of a passage remains ambiguous, and in this case good hermeneutical methods will greatly assist in clearing up the obscurity. But it is absolutely wrong and forbidden, either to narrow inspiration to certain parts only of Holy Scripture, or to admit that the sacred writer has erred. For the system of those who, in order to rid themselves of these difficulties, do not hesitate to concede that divine inspiration regards the things of faith and morals, and nothing beyond, because (as they wrongly think) in a question of the truth or falsehood of a passage, we should consider not so much what God has said as the reason and purpose which He had in mind in saying it—this system cannot be tolerated. For all the books which the Church receives as sacred and canonical, are written wholly and entirely, with all their parts, at the dictation of the Holy Ghost; and so far is it from being possible that any error can co-exist with inspiration, that inspiration not only is essentially incompatible with error, but excludes and rejects it as absolutely and necessarily as it is impossible that God Himself, the supreme Truth, can utter that which is not true.

—Pope Leo XIII
(*Providentissimus Deus*)

St. Jerome's Belief in the Inerrancy of Scripture

Jerome further shows that the immunity of Scripture from error or deception is necessarily bound up with its Divine inspiration and supreme authority. He says he had learnt this in the most celebrated schools, whether of East or West, and that it was taught him as the doctrine of the Fathers, and generally received. Thus when, at the instance of Pope Damasus, he had begun correcting the Latin text of the New Testament, and certain "manikins" had vehemently attacked him for "making corrections in the Gospels in face of the authority of the Fathers and of general opinion," Jerome briefly replied that he was not so utterly stupid nor so grossly uneducated as to imagine that the Lord's words needed any correction or were not divinely inspired. Similarly, when explaining Ezechiel's first vision as portraying the *Four Gospels*, he remarks: That the entire body and the back were full of eyes will be plain to anybody who realizes that there is nought in the Gospels which does not shine and illumine the world by its splendor, so that even things that seem trifling and unimportant shine with the majesty of the Holy Spirit.

—Pope Benedict XV
(*Spiritus Paraclitus*)

St. Jerome wrote that "Ignorance of Scripture means ignorance of Christ." How does this statement apply to the entire Bible—Old Testament and New Testament?

Ongoing Assignments

As you cover the material in this chapter, choose and complete at least three of these assignments.

1. Report on the history of the Bible's translation into English. Use this website for reference: www.biblesociety.ca/about_bible/english_bible/index.html.

2. Report on the Dead Sea Scrolls. Here are some websites to start your research:
   - Library of Congress: www.ibiblio.org/expo/deadsea.scrolls.exhibit/intro.html
   - West Semitic Research Project: www.usc.edu/dept/LAS/wsrp/educational_site/dead_sea_scrolls
   - Old Testament Gateway: www.otgateway.com/deadseascrolls.htm

3. Report on seven names for God found in the Old Testament. Present your findings

Chapter 2 Quick View

on poster board, duplicating the Hebrew lettering and English translation. Check this website for more information:

- The Names of God: www.Ldolphin.org/Names.html.

4. Prepare a PowerPoint presentation on two or more archaeological sites in Israel. The following links can get you started on your research:

- The Foundation for Biblical Archaeology: www.tfba.org/finds.php
- Archaeology and the Bible: www.christiananswers.net/archaeology
- The Jewish History Research Center: htttp://jewishhistory.huji.ac.il/links/Archaeology.htm
- Old Testament Gateway: www.otgateway.com/archaeology.htm

5. Locate some of your favorite Scripture passages. Create a parchment-like, elegant, illustrated manuscript of your biblical passage. Do it this way:

- Use heavy-bond paper.
- Transcribe the verse in ink in your best handwriting or use an appropriate computer font.
- Find an appropriate illustration that visually captures the spirit of your passage.

6. Report on the Galileo Affair. See www.catholiceducation.org/articles/history/world/wh0005.html.

7. Copy the Lord's Prayer in a language other than English, perhaps one you are studying. Use Matthew's version of the Lord's Prayer (Mt 6:9–13). You can find various foreign language Bibles at this website:

- Internet Christian Library: www.iclnet.org/pub/resources/christian-books.html#bibles

8. Individually or with a partner construct a model of the Ark of the Covenant.

9. Read both of these articles. Report on at least three new insights you gained from your reading:

- Elizabeth McNamer, "The Bible from Square One": www.americancatholic.org/Newsletters/SFS/an0194.asp
- Sandra Schneiders, I.H.M., "Interpreting the Bible: The Right and the Responsibility": www.americancatholic.org/Newsletters/SFS/an0997.asp

 Prayer

Yet another time-honored way to pray the Sacred Scriptures, and to meet the living God, is the devotional reading of the Bible. For centuries Catholics have practiced a method of prayer derived from the Benedictine tradition known as *Lectio Divina*, that is, "sacred reading." The purpose of the sacred reading of God's Word is not necessarily to cover a lot of territory or to use study aids or take notes. Its purpose is simply to *meet* God through his written word and allow the Holy Spirit to lead us into an even deeper union with him. Therefore, it is best to take a short passage, read it slowly and attentively, and let your imagination, emotions, memory, desires, and thoughts engage the written text.

Pray with the Bible using *Lectio Divina*. Select your Scripture readings from the Mass readings for the day (see www.usccb.org/nab/index.shtml). Then follow these steps:

1. *Reading (lectio).* Select a short Bible passage. Read it slowly. Pay attention to each word. If a word or phrase catches your attention, read it to yourself several times.
2. *Thinking (meditatio).* Savor the passage. Read it again. Reflect on it. This time feel any emotions that may surface. Picture the images that arise from your imagination.

Pay attention to any thoughts or memories the passage might call forth from you.

3. *Pray (oratio).* Reflect on what the Lord might be saying to you in this passage. Talk to him as you would to a friend. Ask him to show you how to respond to his Word. How can you connect this passage to your daily life? How does it relate to the people you encounter every day? Might there be a special message in this Scripture selection just for *you*? Pay attention to any insights the Holy Spirit might send you.

4. *Contemplation (contemplatio).* Sit in the presence of the Lord. Imagine him looking on you with great love in his heart. Rest quietly in his presence. There is no need to think here, just enjoy your time with him as two friends would who quietly sit on a park bench gazing together at a sunset.

5. *Resolution.* Take an insight that you gained from your "sacred reading" and resolve to apply it to your life. Perhaps it is simply a matter of saying a simple prayer of thanks. Perhaps it is to be more patient with someone in your life. Let the word the Holy Spirit spoke to you come alive in your life.

- *Reflection:* Which passage spoke most deeply to your heart? Why?

- *Resolution:* Try the form of praying for at least ten minutes for the next two weeks.

Chapter 2 Quick View

3

SURVEYING THE BOOKS OF THE BIBLE

But you, remain faithful to what you have learned and believed, because you know from whom you learned it, and that from infancy you have known (the) sacred scriptures, which are capable of giving you wisdom for Salvation through faith in Christ Jesus.

—2 Timothy 3:14-15

Best Seller

The Bible is the most-read book of all time.

Formation of the Old Testament

The forty-six inspired books of the Old Testament were drawn from the oral tradition of the Chosen People and written over a period of approximately nine hundred years.

Survey of the Old Testament Books

Every book of the Old Testament—organized in four main categories and written in several styles—all prepared for the coming of the Savior, Jesus Christ.

The Writing of the New Testament

The Gospels form the heart of the Sacred Scripture. They were formulated in three stages: the life of Jesus, the oral tradition, and the written Gospels.

Survey of the New Testament

The twenty-seven books of the New Testament—composed in different styles and written in *Koine* Greek—were written from the second half of the first century to the early second century AD.

canon
The official list of inspired books of the Bible. Catholics list forty-six Old Testament books and twenty-seven New Testament books in their canon.

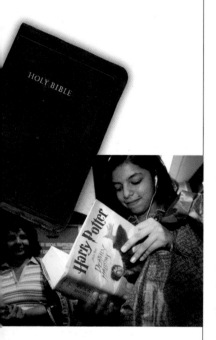

patriarchs
The "fathers of the faith," male rulers, elders, or leaders. The patriarchs of the faith of Israel are Abraham, Isaac, and Jacob.

Best Seller

As God's Word, it is only natural that the Bible would be the most read of all books in history. The Bible was first printed in 1454. Through the beginning of this century the Bible has been translated into more than two thousand languages. The Bible is always at the top of any best-seller's list. For example, in a recent year it sold twenty-five million copies in America alone, twice as many as the final Harry Potter book.

Researchers discovered that forty-seven percent of Americans read the Bible every week. In addition, ninety-one percent of American households have one Bible, while the average is four Bibles per household. To say the least, the Bible is a popular book.

The Bible has had a great impact on our language and culture. Consider these common phrases that all come from the Bible:

- "A house divided" (Mt 12:25, Lk 11:17)
- "Apple of his eye" (Dt 32:10)
- "Can a leopard change his spots?" (Jer 13:23)
- "Don't cast your pearls before swine" (Mt 7:6)
- "One does not live by bread alone" (Dt 8:3, Mt 4:4)
- "It is more blessed to give than to receive" (Acts 20:35)
- "Am I my brother's keeper?" (Gn 4:9)
- "Out of the mouths of babes" (Ps 8:2)
- "The love of money is the root of all evils" (1 Tm 6:10)
- "Where there is no vision, the people perish" (Prv 29:18)

The Bible is filled with knowledge, wisdom, and truth. The more we read from Sacred Scripture, the more we discover God's plan for our happiness. This chapter explores the Bible in more depth, taking up the formation of the individual books of the Bible and the development of its **canon**.

More Familiar Sayings from the Bible

Here are six more familiar sayings that have origins in the Bible. Choose at least two of the passages. Read the accompanying notes on the passage from a biblical commentary (usually on the same page in the Bible) and write an explanation of their meaning.

1. "Handwriting on the wall" (Dn 5:5)
2. "Labor of love" (1 Thes 1:3)
3. "The truth will set you free" (Jn 8:32)
4. "Many are called, few are chosen" (Mt 22:14)
5. "By the skin of my teeth" (Jb 19:20)
6. "Eat, drink, and be merry" (Eccl 8:15)

For Reflection

Research and share the history of a Bible that is part of your family life.

Formation of the Old Testament

The Old Testament is the first part of the Bible; it is the inspired record of Salvation History prior to the coming of Jesus Christ. In the Catholic Bible, there are forty-six books in the Old Testament. The Old Testament centers on the covenant God entered into with the Jewish People. The Old Covenant is distinguished from the New Covenant initiated by Jesus Christ. The Old Testament is made up of the Pentateuch, or Torah, and the Historical, Wisdom, and Prophetic books. Most of the books of the Old Testament are also part of the Jewish Bible, called the Hebrew Scriptures. The Hebrew Scriptures are traditionally divided into three categories:

- *Torah*, meaning "Law," the first five books of the Bible, or the Pentateuch,

- *Nebiim*, meaning "Prophets," and

- *Ketubim*, meaning "Writings."

The first letters of these categories make acronym *TaNaK*, which is a popular designation for the Hebrew Scriptures.

How the Old Testament was finally written and collected is a complex story that spans centuries. Before the actual physical writing took place, there was a period of *oral traditions*. These traditions came from the experiences the people had with God and with each other. Take, for example, the Genesis stories that tell of God's interactions with **patriarchs** like Abraham, Isaac, Jacob, and Joseph. These "fathers in the faith" were real people who encountered a God who cared for them. Before any of their

experiences were committed to writing, they were related by word of mouth. For centuries, ancient peoples of many tribes and cultures recounted laws, told stories, sang songs, and celebrated sacred events through oral tradition to preserve the history of their people. So it was with the Chosen People as well.

In our modern world where data is preserved digitally and on tape, not to mention print, you might think that oral storytelling is not very reliable. However, nonliterate peoples depend greatly on their memories. After all, the human brain can absorb and memorize huge amounts of information. Many of the biblical traditions were in story form because stories are more easily remembered. For example, Genesis 1–11 is a story form.

Eventually, though, God's Chosen People began to preserve their stories in writing. Many historians think this started to take place during the reign of King Solomon, perhaps around 950 BC. Solomon's monarchy would have been rich enough to employ scribes who did the actual writing. The first things the scribes wrote were oral traditions about Israel's

King Solomon welcoming the Queen of Sheba.

Septuagint

An important ancient Greek translation of the Old Testament. The word "Septuagint" comes from the Latin word for "seventy," referring to the legendary seventy (or seventy-two) scholars who translated the work in seventy-two days.

apocryphal books

Apocryphal is a Greek word that means "hidden." For Catholics, it refers to pious literature related to the Bible but not included in the canon of the Bible. Two examples from Old Testament times are 1 Esdras and the Book of Jubilees. However, Protestants and Jews also use this term to refer to several Old Testament books that Catholics consider inspired—Sirach, Wisdom, Baruch, 1 and 2 Maccabees, Tobit, and Judith. These books were not part of the Jewish canon of the Hebrew Scriptures at the end of the first century, although they were found in the early Christian Greek translations of the Old Testament. Catholics refer to this same list of books as "deuterocanonical."

history up to the conquest of Canaan and the stories about the creation of the world.

Writings about the early kings (e.g., Saul and David) followed. At times, the scribes would incorporate ancient fragments like Lamech's Taunt (Gn 4:23–24) and Miriam's Song (Ex 15:21). They also quoted from books that are not part of the Old Testament like the "Book of the Kings of Israel" (e.g., 1 Kgs 14:19; 15:31). Next came the writings of the prophets and sages. The sages were wise men who taught about the ways of God for a people struggling to live as a community. Some of the prophets and sages wrote their own books. However, their disciples and secretaries were often the ones to collect and record their prophecies, sayings, and teachings.

The last of the Old Testament books dates to around 100 BC. During the centuries of writing, many unnamed editors were involved. Their job was to collect, combine, add, and improve the texts before them. Most of the editing took place after the Babylonians destroyed Jerusalem in 586. Their work resulted in many of the Old Testament books being *compilations*, that is, the work of several writers and editors. It kept the material timely for the people living in the current generation.

When you think about how the Old Testament was formed over the course of about nine hundred years, it is easy to see how many of the Old Testament books are a patchwork of earlier works. This is why some books have many, and sometimes confusing, repetitions. It also explains how some books like the Psalms and Proverbs are really anthologies containing the writings of many people over a long time.

The Old Testament Canon

The word *canon* comes from the Hebrew word *kaneh,* which was a tall reed used to measure something, somewhat like our yardstick. Eventually, the word took on the meaning of "standard, measure, rule." The canon of Sacred Scripture, therefore, is the standard list of books recognized as genuine and inspired Holy Scripture.

Why do we refer to *Catholic* and *Protestant* Bibles? The reason is that while Catholics and Protestants agree on the official list of twenty-seven books contained in the New Testament, there is disagreement on the canon of the Old Testament. Protestants accept only thirty-nine books of the Old Testament as inspired, while Catholics accept forty-six. The discrepancy results from which ancient versions of the Hebrew Scriptures are used to form the canons.

This issue began about the third century BC when there was an increasing need to translate the Hebrew Scriptures. Prior to that time, many Jews had been deported to Babylon during the invasion of 586 BC. Most of their descendants did not return to Palestine when the exile ended. Still other Jews had fled Palestine in the wake of persecutions by cruel Seleucid rulers. These dispersed Jews had settled in important cities like Alexandria, Rome, Athens, and Corinth. They spoke Greek, the popular language of the time, and needed the sacred Hebrew Scriptures translated into Greek. The translation that resulted in the **Septuagint** took place in Alexandria, Egypt, beginning sometime in the third century BC during the Ptolemaic reign. The name Septuagint in Latin means "seventy," which refers to a traditional story that seventy scholars were brought from the Holy Land in Palestine to Alexandria to accomplish the task.

By the time of Jesus and the first Christians, the Septuagint was the most common and popular translation

of the Hebrew Scriptures. As Greek was the common language of the Roman Empire during this period, it was also natural for both Jews and Christians to use this version. For example, St. Paul would certainly have used it in his various missionary journeys when speaking to potential converts. Early Church authorities, important Church Fathers, and eventually the Council of Trent (1547) accepted the Septuagint and all the books it contained as the standard for the Old Testament portion of the Bible.

Meanwhile, in AD 90, Jewish scholars who had survived the Roman destruction of the Temple in AD 70 assembled at Jamnia, a city in northern Palestine. They noted that some material in the Septuagint translation—including whole books—was added to older versions of the Hebrew Scriptures. The Jewish rabbis in Jamnia decided to consolidate their sacred books. At that time, they accepted into their official list of books only thirty-nine books, all written in Hebrew. They dropped seven books that appeared in the Septuagint. These seven books were all written in Greek sometime in the two hundred years before Christ. They are 1 and 2 Maccabees, Judith, Tobit, Baruch, Sirach, and the Wisdom of Solomon. In contrast, the Catholic Bible includes these seven books from the Greek translation. The Magisterium, which has the Christ-given authority to determine which biblical books are inspired, accepted them as canonical.

At the time of the Protestant Reformation, the Reformers adopted a different Old Testament canon. They accepted the official list of Hebrew Scriptures accepted by rabbis in AD 90. However, many Protestant Bibles today print the disputed books in a separate section at the back of the Bible. They refer to these books (as well as some passages in Daniel and Esther) as **apocryphal books**, that is, "hidden" or "withdrawn from common use." Catholics refer to these books as **deuterocanonical**, meaning "a second canon," to indicate that they are not accepted in the official Jewish canon.

deuterocanonical
The Greek term for "second canon." It refers to those books in the Old Testament that were not found in the Hebrew scriptures. These books are Sirach, Wisdom, Baruch, 1 and 2 Maccabees, Tobit, Judith, and certain additions to Esther and Daniel.

The chart below lists the four major categories of Old Testament writings found in a Catholic Bible. It also gives the abbreviation (in **boldface**) of each Old Testament book and a short explanatory note about each category. Deuterocanonical works are in italics. The section to the right of each category further summarizes the contents of each of the Old Testament books.

PENTATEUCH [5]

Genesis (**Gn**)
Exodus (**Ex**)
Leviticus (**Lv**)
Numbers (**Nm**)
Deuteronomy (**Dt**)

The Pentateuch refers to "five books." These sacred books, also known as the Torah, contain the Jewish Law and important instruction on belief and practice. They include many memorable stories of our faith: Creation, Adam and Eve, Noah, Abraham, and the patriarchs. They recount the stories of Jewish slavery in Egypt, YHWH's covenant with the Chosen People, the Exodus, and Moses. They provide the Old Law, including the Ten Commandments.

HISTORICAL BOOKS [16]

Joshua (**Jos**)
Judges (**Jgs**)
1 & 2 Samuel (**1 Sm**; **2 Sm**)
1 & 2 Kings (**1 Kgs**; **2 Kgs**)

1 & 2 Chronicles (**1 Chr**; **2 Chr**)
Ezra (**Ezr**)
Nehemiah (**Neh**)

Ruth (**Ru**)
Esther (**Est**)
Judith (**Jdt**)
Tobit (**Tb**)
1 & 2 Maccabees (**1 Mc**; **2 Mc**)

The Historical Books narrate how the Chosen People lived out the covenant in the Promised Land. The first six books have the same style as the book of Deuteronomy and describe how the Holy Land was conquered and settled. They also describe the Chosen People's desire to be ruled by a king. Saul, the first king, and David are described along with the declining monarchy up to the time of the Babylonian Captivity in 586 BC.

The next four books are written from the vantage point of a priestly writer. They tell the story of the Babylonian Captivity and the return under Ezra and Nehemiah.

The period after the Exile also produced some short moralistic tales to uplift and inspire the Jews. First and Second Maccabees record the successful revolt of the Jews against the Greek rulers in Syria.

WISDOM BOOKS [7] Job (**Jb**) Psalms (**Ps[s]**) Proverbs (**Prv**) Ecclesiastes (**Eccl**) Song of Songs (**Song[Sg]**) *Sirach* (also called *Ecclesiasticus*) (**Sir**) *Wisdom* (**Wis**)	These works contain some of the most beautiful and practical religious literature in the world. Job wrestles with the ever-current problem of suffering and good versus evil. The Psalms contain many exquisite hymns and prayers for both public and private use. The Song of Songs is an allegorical love song that treats God's love for his people.
PROPHETIC BOOKS [18] Isaiah (**Is**) Jeremiah (**Jer**) Lamentations (**Lam**) *Baruch* (**Bar**) Ezekiel (**Ez**) Daniel (**Dn**) Hosea (**Hos**) Joel (**Jl**) Amos (**Am**) Obadiah (**Ob**) Jonah (**Jon**) Micah (**Mi**) Nahum (**Na**) Habakkuk (**Hb**) Zephaniah (**Zep**) Haggai (**Hg**) Zechariah (**Zec**) Malachi (**Mal**)	The prophets were powerful figures who spoke for YHWH, often warning the people to remain faithful to the covenant or face dire consequences. Their words remain forceful reminders of a just and faithful God who loves justice and requires believers to live faithfully and compassionately.

◯ For Review

1. What is the meaning of TaNaK?

2. When were the first Old Testament books committed to writing?

3. Why do the Catholic and Protestant canons of the Old Testament differ?

4. Identify the term *deuterocanonical*. What are the deuterocanonical books of the Bible?

5. What are the four major divisions of the Old Testament?

6. Here are some abbreviations of some Old Testament books. Identify the full name of each book: Lv, 2 Chr, Jos, Jb, Sir, Is, Mi, Mal.

7. What is another name for the Pentateuch?

8. When did the Babylonian Captivity take place?

For Reflection

In your experience, what do your friends of different Christian denominations believe about the Bible?

Survey of the Old Testament Books

The Old Testament prepares for the coming of the Savior, Jesus Christ. Recall that *testament* means, "covenant," a solemn contract of love between God and his Chosen People. Every book of the Bible underscores God's love, which comes to its fullness in our Lord. The following sections survey the contents of the forty-six books of the Old Testament.

Pentateuch

Penta in Greek means "five" (e.g., a pentagon is a five-sided shape). The first five books of the Bible comprise the Pentateuch: Genesis, Exodus, Leviticus, Numbers, and Deuteronomy. These important books lay the foundation for Christ's coming.

Traditionally, Moses was thought to have written the books of the Pentateuch. There is no doubt that he was an influential figure behind these books. However, some scholars believe there were four different oral traditions that went into the writing of these foundational books: Yahwist, Elohist, Priestly, and Deuteronomic. (These oral traditions are explained in more detail in Chapter 4.)

Genesis

The word *genesis* means "beginning." The first eleven chapters of Genesis contain stories of prehistory, that is, a time before there was writing. Passed down by word of mouth, they tell stories of God's creation of the world, the sin of Adam and Eve, Cain and Abel, Noah and the Flood, and the Tower of Babel.

The last chapters of Genesis relate the story of the Patriarchs, that is, the fathers of the Chosen People. They tell of God's calling Abram (later named Abraham) and the covenant God made with him. They relate the stories surrounding the first four generations of Patriarchs: Abraham, Isaac, Esau and Jacob (later named Israel), and Jacob's twelve sons. The tribes of Israel descended from these sons. Genesis closes with the story of Joseph, his father, and his brothers and their families living in Egypt, where they escaped famine.

Exodus

This central book of the Old Testament tells how Jacob's descendants, now named Israelites after him, were enslaved by the Egyptian pharaoh and freed by God in the great event known as the Exodus ("departure"). The Book of Exodus recounts the Israelites' wandering in the desert for forty years. Its highlight is God's meeting with Moses on Mount Sinai, where God entered into a covenant with the Chosen People. He gave them the Law, including the Ten Commandments, to help them live the terms of the covenant. The Law formed Israel's identity as God's Chosen People. It guided them socially, politically, and religiously.

Leviticus

The third book of the Pentateuch examines the particulars of the Law. It deals with the theme of holiness in all aspects of life. One of the oldest layers of priestly law is contained in Leviticus 17–26, sometimes called the "Holiness Code."

Numbers

This book gets its name from two censuses of the Chosen People detailed in chapter 1 and chapter 26. The Book of Numbers picks up the story of the Jews in the desert and takes them to the border of the Promised Land. It stresses the need for Israel to be totally dedicated and committed to God if it is to succeed as a nation.

Deuteronomy

The name of this book means "Second Law." In the form of sermons delivered by Moses, it repeats much of the material of the three previous books.

Deuteronomy appeals to obedience and loyalty to God. It also warns of dire consequences if the Chosen People do not follow the Law and live up to the terms of the covenant. At the end of the book, the Israelites are on the threshold of Canaan, the Promised Land. Moses appoints Joshua as his successor and delivers his farewell address. Moses dies before entering the Promised Land.

The Historical Books

The Historical Books deal with the events of Salvation History, namely, how God remained faithful to the covenant and how the Israelites struggled to live its terms. The Historical Books, bracketed in chronology by the Book of Joshua and the Second Book of Maccabees, cover almost nine hundred years of history, from about 1020 BC to 142 BC.

Joshua

Joshua, a military leader, led the Israelites into the Promised Land, conquered it, and divided the land among the various tribes. The Book of Joshua contains a pattern of judgment on Israel that was first introduced in Deuteronomy, that is, (1) apostasy (abandoning God), (2) oppression by Gentiles, (3) repentance by Israel, and (4) deliverance to freedom.

Judges

The judges of the Old Testament were military leaders who directed campaigns of various Israelite tribes versus their neighbors. The basic framework of the

A Reading from the Pentateuch: Abraham, Father of Faith

Abraham is a pivotal Old Testament figure. His original name was Abram: his wife's name was Sarai. They lived in Haran, a land in the northern part of Mesopotamia (now Iraq) when God called him to leave their home. God changed their names to Abraham and Sarah when he made a covenant with them. He promised that from them would come many nations and that they would have numerous descendants.

Abraham is a symbol of faith, of one who trusted God totally. This was especially evident when God asked him to sacrifice his only son, Isaac. Abraham trusted God, who held back Abraham's hand from slaying his son. A great nation did indeed come from Abraham and Sarah. Abraham is "the father of a host of nations" (Gn 17:5) that began with the Israelites and which would later include the Gentiles who grafted onto them once they came to believe. Hence, both Christians and Jews consider Abraham the first patriarch of faith. Muslims also profess to hold the faith of Abraham.

Read about Abraham in Genesis 12:1-25:11. Reflect on each of the following assignments. Write your responses in your journal.

- When were you asked to trust someone? How was your faith put to the test? What did you think at the time? What did you do? How did things turn out?

- Imagine that you are Abraham. Describe what thoughts and feelings you might have when God asks you to sacrifice your only son.

- Pretend you are Isaac. Writing in first person, describe that fateful day from your point of view.

Book of Judges is as follows: Israel sins by worshiping false gods; the Lord punishes Israel by allowing an enemy to conquer it; the Israelites cry to God for help; God sends a judge—like Samson, Deborah, or Samuel—to deliver Israel from the enemy.

Ruth

The Book of Ruth is a short story centering on the life of two women: Naomi and Ruth. It shows how God can work things for the best even in the midst of suffering. Ruth was a foreign heroine who showed great fidelity to her Jewish mother-in-law, Naomi. God rewarded her kindness by giving her a son, Obed, who was King David's grandfather. Ruth is named in Jesus' genealogy in Matthew 1:5. She is a Gentile ancestor of Jesus.

First and Second Books of Samuel

Originally one book, the First and Second Books of Samuel tell of the transition from the period of the judges to the coming of the monarchy. The prophet Samuel is a key figure. He is also the last of the judges. The First Book of Samuel recounts how the people wanted a strong leader—a king—to rule them. Samuel told them that YHWH is their only king and that they should live the covenant under his reign, but the people persisted in their request, and God allowed Samuel to anoint Saul as king while warning them that they would regret their request. At first, Saul was a good leader, but then he faltered through disobedience to God. Samuel then anointed David. The Chosen People would look on David through the centuries as the ideal ruler. The Second Book of Samuel reports of David's rule and some of his adventures and misadventures, including his affair with a married woman, Bathsheba.

First and Second Books of Kings

These books tell the story of David's death and the reign of his son Solomon. King Solomon is known for his wisdom. He was the mastermind of the construction of the Temple in Jerusalem, but his building projects taxed the people to the limit, both finan-cially and in the form of forced labor. When he died, the kingdom split into two: the northern kingdom of Israel and the southern kingdom of Judah. The history of these events—from the founding of the kingdom of Israel by Jeroboam I until the Assyrian conquest in 722 BC—is recounted in 1 Kings 12–2 Kings 17. The remaining chapters of the Second Book of Kings tell of the kingdom of Judah from Hezekiah until the Babylonian conquest in 586 BC.

First and Second Books of Chronicles

These books retell the stories of the First and Second Books of Samuel and Kings, but from a priestly perspective. In some cases, these books quote exactly from the Books of 1 and 2 Samuel and 1 and 2 Kings; in others, they condense the material. The First and Second Books of Chronicles emphasize David as founder of worship in Jerusalem and Solomon as the builder of the Temple.

Ezra and Nehemiah

The Books of Ezra and Nehemiah were once a single book. The authors of Ezra and Nehemiah were likely the same authors of the First and Second Books of Chronicles. These books tell the story of the Chosen People after they returned from exile in Babylon. They report details of the rebuilding of the Temple in Jerusalem (in 515 BC) and the reorganization of Jewish life. From this time on, the Israelites were known as the Jews because the only tribal identity that survived the Exile was that of the tribe of Judah.

Tobit, Judith, and Esther

The Books of Tobit, Judith, and Esther were written as three short novels. Tobit recounts how God works in people's lives in order to further his plans. It shows how God rewards people who remain faithful. Judith tells how God cared for Israel, working through the hand of the brave heroine Judith. Esther reveals how God worked through the actions of humans to preserve the Chosen People when they were threatened with destruction in a hostile world.

First and Second Maccabees

The First and Second Books of Maccabees trace the history of the Jews up to the second century BC. These books relate how the rulers who followed Alexander the Great tried to stamp out Jewish identity by imposing a Hellenistic (Greek) culture. The cruelest of these rulers was Antiochus Epiphanes, who desecrated the Jewish Temple. This sacrilege led Judas Maccabee (a name meaning "hammer") and his brothers to lead a rebellion against the evil ruler. Their efforts led to religious and political freedom for the Jews, though fleeting. The Maccabees ruled Judah, free from foreign powers, from 135 BC until the Roman general Pompey conquered Palestine in 67 BC. Today, the Jewish Feast of Hanukkah (Festival of Light) celebrates the rededication of the Temple (in December of 164 BC) after the Maccabees' victory.

The Wisdom Books

Wisdom literature is an application of how God works in our everyday lives. God created an ordered universe. For us to live wisely, it is important to perceive the order God placed in his creation and live accordingly. Wisdom literature offers instruction on the right way to live. Details of the individual Wisdom Books of the Bible follow.

A READING FROM THE HISTORICAL BOOKS: LESSONS OF RUTH

The Book of Ruth is positioned appropriately in the Old Testament between Judges and the First and Second Books of Samuel because it is set during the era of the Judges. It tells the heartwarming story of Ruth, a Moabite woman who became the great-grandmother of King David. An important lesson we can take from this book is that God's love extends not only to the Chosen People, but to everyone, even foreigners.

The story involves Naomi, who—with her husband and two sons—had gone to Moab to escape a famine. The men of the family died, leaving Naomi with two daughters-in-law: Ruth and Orpah. When the famine ended, Naomi instructed the women to stay with their own people. Orpah did just that, but Ruth insisted on remaining with her mother-in-law. Ruth declared, "Do not ask me to abandon or forsake you! For wherever you go I will go, wherever you lodge I will lodge, your people shall be my people, and your God my God" (Ru 1:16). Ruth's faithfulness was rewarded when she was noticed by a rich landowner, Boaz, for gathering leftover grain for her mother-in-law. He was moved by her story and married her. Together they had a son, Obed. Obed was the father of Jesse, who in turn was the father of King David.

The story of Ruth also teaches God's loving concern for those who suffer in the midst of tragedy. It shows that good comes from devotion to one's family. It reveals how God's plan of Salvation takes place in unexpected ways. Finally, Ruth herself serves as a symbol of God's faithfulness and loving care for the Chosen People.

- Read the entire Book of Ruth. In your journal, list three qualities that describe Ruth's character. Record the verses that support your descriptions.

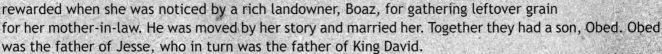

- Write of a time when a friend was loyal to you. What did you feel at the time? Contact this friend and express your appreciation in some way for the friendship.

Job

This famous story tells the trials of an innocent man and raises the question of why bad things happen to good people. The Book of Job teaches the important lesson that God's ways are not our ways.

Psalms

The Psalms are a collection of five books of poetry or song lyrics, something like a hymnal without the musical notes. Their composition spans five hundred years of Jewish history. Many of the 150 Psalms were sung in Temple worship. They praise and thank God. They petition him for help or are lamentations, crying out to God in the midst of suffering. The Psalms also offer valuable religious lessons or truths.

Proverbs

The Book of Proverbs lists short sayings, often poetically, of rules or lessons for moral living. They educate the reader on how to live a good life.

Ecclesiastes

The title of the book is the Greek translation of the Hebrew word *Qoheleth*, meaning "someone who calls an assembly." The title likely does not refer to a historical person. Rather, Qoheleth gives quotes,

A READING FROM THE WISDOM BOOKS: EXPLORING PROVERBS

One of the most well known sayings from the Book of Proverbs is this: "The fear of the LORD is the beginning of knowledge" (Prv 1:7). "Fear" here does not mean that we *dread* God. Rather, it means that we *respect* God and that we love and *appreciate* him. It also means that we do not want to do anything to displease God for he is all-good and worthy of our love. For us to know God, then, means that we must have an attitude of humility, of knowing that he is the Creator and we are the creatures. This kind of attitude leads to true wisdom. And wisdom is a virtue that enables us to live upright lives in God's presence.

King Solomon was known for his wisdom. The First Book of Kings reports that he wrote three thousand proverbs (1 Kgs 5:12). Solomon is credited as the author of Parts 2 and 5 of the Book of Proverbs. Other authors contributed to this work, which was finally edited in the early part of the fifth century BC.

Proverbs is a poetic book. It makes comparisons in pithy two-line sayings. It uses the technique of parallelism, in which the second line restates, contrasts, or advances the thought of the first line. An example of parallelism that contrasts is:

> A wise son makes his father glad,
> but a foolish son is a grief to his mother. (Prv 10:1)

Parallelism makes it easier to remember the wise saying, whose purpose is to encourage us to live virtuous lives and to avoid sin that leads us astray.

- Read Proverbs 25:1–29:27, the second collection of proverbs ascribed to Solomon.
- Note in your journal five of your favorite proverbs from your reading.
- Rewrite these proverbs in a form that would appeal to a contemporary person your own age. Find a picture to illustrate one of your proverbs. Reproduce your proverb and picture on poster board for display.

proverbs, and questions to teach important lessons on how to live. A key passage is that "all things are vanity" (Ecc 1:2), that is, nothing is permanent. The important lesson to learn is that only God is eternal, so we should put our faith and hope in him.

Song of Songs

Not solely representative of wisdom literature, Song of Songs is a poem that celebrates the ideal of romantic love between a woman and man. It is a beautiful reflection on God's great gift to human beings. The Church also reads this book as an allegory of God's love for Israel and Jesus' love for his Bride, the Church.

Wisdom

The Book of Wisdom, written about a hundred years before the coming of Jesus Christ, encourages Jews living in Egypt to remain faithful to their heritage. The complete title of the book is "Wisdom of Solomon," though the author was actually a Jew living in Alexandria, Egypt. The Book of Wisdom clearly states the belief in an afterlife where those who lived a good life will be rewarded.

Sirach (Ecclesiasticus)

Sirach is the only book of the Old Testament whose author is identified: Jesus, Ben (son of) Sira. Likely a sage, he recounts many wise sayings and maxims, ones like "Let not your hand be open to receive and clenched when it is time to give" (Sir 4:31). The Book of Sirach has also been called *Liber Ecclesiasticus*, meaning "Church Book," because it was used extensively by the early Church in preparing catechumens.

Prophetic Books

A prophet speaks for God. Prophets of the Old Testament received a direct call from God and their prophecies are God's Word, messages to the Chosen People and to all people. The idea of a biblical prophet was not primarily one who could foretell the future. Rather, the biblical prophet was a messenger of God, one God called in difficult times to challenge or comfort the people. The prophetic books in the Bible contain the heart of the prophets' preaching, recorded by them directly or by someone associated with them.

Major themes in the messages of the prophets include these:

- *Worship the one, true God.* The Chosen People were often tempted to fall back into **idolatry**. The prophets warned them that only YHWH was deserving of their worship since he rescued them from Egypt. He is the ruler of the universe and is above all.

- *Accept God's love and mercy.* The Chosen People despaired of God's love after the northern and southern kingdoms were destroyed. The prophets preached that sin was reprehensible, but assured the people of God's never-ending love and mercy.

- *Be just, especially to the poor.* The prophets continually railed against greed and injustice. They warned that the nation would be punished if the rulers and people did not turn from their sins. The call to repentance and justice are major prophetic themes. This message often brought the prophets in conflict with the rulers who treated them harshly.

- *Know that God will ultimately triumph.* Despite the setbacks the people experienced, God will ultimately prevail. The prophecies sometimes speak of a restored Jerusalem. At other times, they speak about rewards and punishments after death. Still other prophecies point to a future time when an ideal ruler would come on the scene: a Messiah who would save the people.

For us to understand the prophetic message, we need to know the historical background to the times and places in which the prophets worked. For example, consider the Book of Isaiah, the longest and perhaps most important prophetic book. To understand this book properly it is important to know:

idolatry
Giving worship to something or someone other than the true God.

major prophets
Four of the latter prophets—Isaiah, Jeremiah, Ezekiel, and Daniel—whose books in the Old Testament are quite lengthy.

minor prophets
The twelve prophets of the Old Testament whose recorded sayings are much briefer than those of the major prophets: Hosea, Joel, Amos, Obadiah, Jonah, Micah, Nahum, Habakkuk, Zephaniah, Haggai, Zechariah, and Malachi.

- Isaiah 1–39, or First Isaiah, corresponds to the original Prophet Isaiah, whose career began under King Uzziah in the southern kingdom. He warned against dangerous alliances with foreign powers and railed against social injustice.

- Isaiah 40–55 is the work of an unnamed prophet—Second Isaiah—who wrote when the Jews were captive in Babylonia. He comforted his people with the message of the famous "Servant Songs" in Isaiah 42, 49, 50, and 53.

- Finally, Isaiah 56–66 is the work of Third Isaiah, yet another unnamed prophet. He wrote after the Jews returned from exile. He too warned his people to be just toward one another, and even to the Gentiles. He spoke of a time when people would finally obey God's plan, a time when God would create "new heavens and a new earth" (Is 65:17).

Classifying the Prophets

The prophets of the Old Testament can be classified as **major prophets** and **minor prophets**. Isaiah is one of the major prophets.

Jeremiah, Ezekiel, and Daniel are other major prophets because the books named for them are lengthy. Jeremiah preached during the reigns of the last kings of the southern kingdom. He wrote that God would make a new covenant in the future, one written on the hearts of the people (Jer 31:33–34). Ezekiel used many symbolic images to spread his message of God's presence and power

and the need to take personal responsibility for one's actions. Daniel used apocalyptic writing to encourage his persecuted people that God would be faithful and rescue them. An **apocalypse** is a highly symbolic form of literature used to give hope to a persecuted people that God's goodness will triumph over evil.

The minor prophets are Hosea, Joel, Amos, Obadiah, Jonah, Micah, Nahum, Habakkuk, Zephaniah, Haggai, Zechariah, and Malachi. They are called minor prophets because their Scripture sayings are briefer than the major prophets.

Other ways for classifying the prophets are as *non-writing prophets*, who appear in the historical books (e.g., Samuel, Nathan, Elijah, Elisha), *pre-exilic prophets* (e.g., Hosea and Amos in the northern kingdom and Jeremiah, Isaiah, Obadiah, Micah, Nahum, Habakkuk, and Zephaniah in the southern kingdom), *prophets of the exile* (e.g., Ezekiel, "Second Isaiah," author of Lamentations), and *post-exilic prophets* (e.g., Haggai, Zechariah, Malachi, "Third Isaiah," Joel, Baruch).

◉ For Review

1. Who is traditionally named as the author of the Pentateuch?

2. Identify what took place at the Exodus.

3. When did the Israelites become known as the Jews?

4. Identify the meaning of the Feast of Hanukkah.

5. Which Old Testament book identifies its author?

6. What are four major themes in the preaching of the Old Testament prophets?

⬤ For Reflection

- Who are prophets in the world today?

- Who is someone you trust to provide direction in your life? Why did you choose this person?

The Writing of the New Testament

The Gospels are the heart of the Bible because they contain Jesus' principal teachings and information about him. There were three stages involved in the formation of the Gospels: (1) the time of Jesus' own life; (2) the years after he returned to Heaven when the Apostles and early disciples of Jesus orally preached the Good News; (3) the actual writing of the Gospels. The three stages are distinguished in the following sections.

apocalypse
A Greek word for "revelation." It also refers to a type of highly symbolic literature that contains apparitions about the future and the Final Judgment. This form of literature was used to give hope to a persecuted people that God's goodness will triumph over evil.

remnant
The exiles and former exiles who remained faithful to YHWH during the time of captivity and who were expected to restore Jerusalem.

A READING FROM THE PROPHETS: MICAH'S MESSAGE OF JUDGMENT

The Prophet Micah was from a small country village and was a contemporary of the Prophet Isaiah, during the reigns of Kings Jotham, Ahaz, and Hezekiah (between the years of approximately 740 and 687 BC). His poetic images are drawn from rural life, and his viewpoint was that of a peasant outraged by the injustices landowners committed against the poor.

The first three chapters of the Book of Micah condemn the leaders of both the northern kingdom of Israel and southern kingdom of Judah. He railed against their sins, that is, for hating good and loving evil (3:2). Micah prophesied the destruction of the Temple, using an image from farming (3:12) to show that the Temple would become plowed like a field and Jerusalem would be destroyed.

But Micah also offered hope, saying that a ruler would come from Bethlehem to lead Israel to peace and justice. This ruler would gather God's remnant, a righteous group that would survive God's chastisement of the nation. This remnant would lead nations to true worship of God. The Gospel of Matthew reports that the birth of Christ fulfilled this prophecy.

The Book of Micah ends on a positive note. Micah reminds the people of God's unending mercy.

- Read Micah. Answer these questions in your journal: What are some of the social evils that the prophet criticizes (see Mi 2)? What roles will the future ruler and remnant have (see Mi 5)?

- Print Micah 6:8. Commit yourself to doing this act in the coming week.

Modern Nazareth and basilica of annunciation

kerygma

The core or essential message of the Gospel that Jesus Christ is Lord. One example is found in Acts 2:14—36.

Evangelist

One who proclaims in word and deed the Good News of Jesus Christ. "The Four Evangelists" refers to the authors of the four Gospels: Matthew, Mark, Luke, and John.

Stage 1: The Historical Jesus: 6 BC—AD 30/33

Scholars date Jesus' birth at around 6 BC, based on Gospel evidence that Jesus was born before 4 BC, the year Herod the Great died. He lived a typical life of a Jewish boy growing up in Nazareth, a town in Galilee. There he likely learned the carpenter trade from his foster father, Joseph. He came onto the public scene probably in AD 28. During his public life, he traveled the countryside and into the small towns where he taught, healed, and proclaimed the coming of God's Kingdom. He went to Jerusalem for the great feasts. With the cooperation of some religious leaders who saw Jesus as a threat, the Roman prefect, Pontius Pilate, crucified him there, probably in the year AD 30.

Three days after his crucifixion, Jesus rose from the dead on the first day of the week. His disciples were at first frightened and confused by his Resurrection, but they were convinced that Jesus was alive and glorified as God's Son and present to them by the power of the Holy Spirit. Their hearts burned with love, joy, and excitement.

Stage 2: Oral Tradition: AD 30-50

The disciples begin to live in light of the Resurrection of Jesus. With the grace of the Holy Spirit, they believed that Jesus was the Messiah, the Promised One, the Son of God, and the Lord. The Apostles remembered Jesus' command to "Go out to the whole world; proclaim the gospel to all creation" (Mk 16:16). They first announced in Palestine the marvelous things God had accomplished in Jesus. Remaining pious Jews, the early Christians believed that Jesus was the very fulfillment of God's Old Testament promises. He was literally the New Testament, that is, the New Covenant between God and humanity. However, when their message met with resistance from their Jewish brothers and sisters, Christians began to preach to Gentiles throughout the Roman Empire.

Their preaching took three key forms:

1. *The **kerygma**, or preaching to unbelievers.* The Acts of the Apostles records several sermons that St. Peter and St. Paul preached about Jesus. To help them in this preaching, they and the other followers of Christ would have kept in mind a basic outline of Jesus' life, Death, Resurrection, and Ascension. They would also have used many passages from the Hebrew Scriptures to show how the prophecies made about the Messiah were fulfilled in Jesus. During this period, the disciples began to assemble collections of material about Christ—for example, miracle stories, parables, and the Passion narrative. Later, the four **Evangelists**

would draw on these sources to help compose their Gospels.

2. *The didache, or teaching.* This teaching was really further catechetical instruction for those who accepted Jesus. *Catechesis* literally means to "sound down," that is, to repeat the message and explain it in more depth. Early converts needed further knowledge about how to live a more Christ-filled life. Lists of sayings of Jesus (for example, the Sermon on the Mount) were probably assembled to help in this instruction.

3. *The liturgy, or worship of the Christians.* The celebration of the Eucharist helped shape many of the Jesus stories that the Christian community preserved. The way people pray reflects their beliefs. Certain key events, teachings, and prayers of Jesus were recalled in the early Eucharistic celebrations. Some examples include Jesus' words at the Last Supper, the Lord's Prayer, and recalling of Jesus' Passion. In some cases, different local communities slightly varied the wording of what was prayed at liturgy. However, they faithfully recounted the spirit of what Jesus did and said.

The early Church shaped the Gospel that Jesus lived and proclaimed, which was shared orally after his Death and Resurrection. The Church's primary interest was to interpret the *meaning* of the main events, deeds,

and sayings of Jesus. They wanted to enliven the faith of the believers. As a result, they did not set out to report a full-blown biography of Jesus. However, what they remembered, saved, and proclaimed was the heart of Jesus' message—related to the Old Testament and adapted to the audiences who heard it.

Note that although the four canonical Gospels were composed AD 65–100, preaching about Jesus based on oral traditions carried on well into the second century.

Stage 3: The New Testament Writings (AD 50-ca.120)

Since many have undertaken to compile a narrative of the events that have been fulfilled among us just as those who were eyewitnesses from the beginning and ministers of the word have handed them down to us, I too have decided, after investigating everything accurately anew, to write it down in an orderly sequence for you, most excellent Theophilus, so that you may realize the certainty of the teachings you have received.

—Luke 1:1–4

The final stage in the process was actually recording the written record of the Gospel and various directions for Christian living. The first written books of the New Testament were the letters of St. Paul. Note again that the four Gospels and other writings like

didache
A Greek word that means "teaching." In Christian times this term refers to the earliest known writing in Christianity aside from the New Testament.

catechesis
Process of systematic education in the faith for young people and adults with the view of making them disciples of Jesus Christ.

liturgy
The liturgy is the official public worship of the Church. The liturgy is first Christ's work of Redemption, and his continuing work of Redemption as he pours out his blessings through the sacraments. The Holy Spirit enlightens our faith and encourages us to respond. In this way, the liturgy is the participation of the People of God in the work of the Trinity. The sacraments and the Divine Office constitute the Church's liturgy. Mass is the most important liturgical celebration.

Acts and the Book of Revelation were recorded from the latter half of the first century to the early second century. The quote from Luke above gives a good account of how the Gospel was recorded. The Evangelist Luke examined the sources, including those from eyewitnesses, and then organized the material into a written account.

All four Gospel accounts tell of the Good News God accomplished for us in his Son, Jesus Christ, but each Gospel has its own way of telling the story. For example, Mark stresses Jesus' deeds. He also highlights Jesus as a *Suffering Messiah*, one who freely

gave his life for us. Matthew emphasizes Jesus as a *Teacher* who perfectly fulfilled the Jewish prophecies made about him. Luke presents Jesus as a *Savior* for all people, a merciful and compassionate Lord who has a special place for the poor and neglected. John's Gospel, written approximately 10 to 30 years later than the others, near the beginning of the second century, portrays a majestic, divine Jesus, the *Word of God* who proclaims the truth that brings life.

Why did the early Church wait years after the events of Jesus' life, Death, and Resurrection before writing anything down? Recall that in those days the ordinary way of teaching and learning was through oral transmission. For his part, Jesus taught in easy-to-remember, vivid stories, short sayings, striking images, poetic language, and similar devices. For their part, ancient peoples had remarkable memories, especially compared to people today, who rely more on the printed word and visual images. But

eventually the oral preaching about Jesus and his teaching had to be committed to writing for three main reasons:

1. *The end of the world was not coming as quickly as the early Christians at first thought it would.* Many of the earliest Christians expected that Jesus would come back "to judge the living and the dead" sometime in their lifetimes. As a result, why bother to write anything down? There were more urgent things to do, like preaching the Gospel and preparing for the Lord's return. However, they were mistaken about the hour of the Second Coming of Christ. Eyewitnesses began to die or, even worse, be put to death. It became increasingly necessary to preserve in a more accurate manner the apostolic testimony concerning Jesus.

2. *Distortions to the Gospel were occurring.* As the New Testament letters reveal, after the Apostles preached in a certain community, often someone would follow along and distort the original and authentic message. In the Second Letter to the Corinthians, St. Paul wrote he was "afraid that, as the serpent deceived Eve by his cunning, your thoughts may be corrupted from a sincere [and pure] commitment to Christ" (2 Cor 11:3). To combat heretical teachings and make them standardized, early Christians needed an objective written record of their beliefs—hence, the New Testament.

3. *More instruction was needed.* A written record of the Apostles' preaching could serve as a handy teaching device for Christians and converts who needed more instruction. Second, writings could also serve as helpful guides for liturgy. The Church included the Epistles and Gospels in the Eucharistic liturgy. Finally, the Church could send writings—for example, St. Paul's letters—to new and growing local churches. These written records would provide handy sources for further instruction

and, thus, help new converts maintain proper belief.

For Review

1. Why are the Gospels at the heart of the Bible?
2. Discuss the three stages that went into the writing of the New Testament.
3. Describe the three forms of oral tradition in New Testament times.
4. What years were the Gospels composed?
5. Why were the Gospels eventually written?

For Reflection

- Why is the story of Jesus Christ Good News to you?
- Describe an occasion you have shared the Good News with another.

Survey of the New Testament (*CCC*, 120; 130; 139)

The history of the New Testament canon is complex. The Sacred Tradition of the Church, administered by the Apostles and their successors, determined which books were to be included in the canon and which were not under the inspiration of the Holy Spirit. By AD 200, the four Gospels, Pauline Epistles, Acts, and some of the other Epistles were generally accepted as inspired. By AD 367, Church Father St. Athanasius was a prominent figure in fixing the New Testament canon at the present twenty-seven books. The Council of Trent (1545–1563) taught as a matter of Church doctrine that this canon was the inspired Word of God.

Types of Writing in the New Testament

All twenty-seven books of the New Testament were written in *Koine* (common) Greek, the spoken language of the ordinary people, stretching across the Roman Empire. The language the New Testament was recorded in also was influenced by the Greek Septuagint translation of the Old Testament. Biblical scholars question the exact dates of the various New Testament books. A listing of the various types of writing in the New Testament and their approximate dates of composition follows.

Gospels (4)

"The Gospels are the heart of all the Scriptures 'because they are our principal source for the life and teaching of the Incarnate Word, our Savior'" (*CCC*, 125). The Gospels are narratives about Jesus' public ministry of teaching and healing, and his Passion, Death, Resurrection, and Ascension. The four Gospels are:

1. Mark (60–75; most likely 68–73)
2. Matthew (80–90; +/– a decade)
3. Luke (85; +/– 5 years)
4. John (80–110; probably in the 90s)

Acts of the Apostles (1)

The Acts of the Apostles (85; +/– 5 years) is really the second part of the Gospel of Luke. Note how the first verse of Acts is in common with Luke: "In the first book, Theophilus, I dealt with all that Jesus did and taught until the day he was taken up, after giving instructions to the apostles whom he had chosen" (Acts 1:1). Acts tells of the early history of the Church, reporting the spread of the Gospel from the period immediately after Jesus' Resurrection to the imprisonment of St. Paul in the late 50s.

The preaching of St. Peter plays an important role in Acts. One of the central debates concerned the inclusion of Gentiles in the Church. The issue was addressed and resolved at the Council of

Jerusalem. Other main features of Acts are the three missionary journeys of St. Paul.

Pauline Letters (13)

Letters written by Paul or circulated in his name by his disciples are also called Epistles. The letters are addressed to local churches or individuals and are arranged in the Bible in order from longest to shortest. As listed below, a "P" designates that Paul probably wrote the letter; "D" means it was probably written by a disciple of Paul. The earlier of the two dates listed is more exact if Paul did the writing.

St. Paul founded the church in Thessalonica (now northern Greece). The First Letter to the Thessalonians (P—50/51) is the oldest New Testament writing. It reminds Paul's converts how they should live until Christ comes again. Similar themes are presented in the Second Letter to the Thessalonians (D—51 or 90s), warning those who had been lazy or staid to persevere in working for God's Kingdom.

In the Letter to the Galatians (P—54/55), Paul defends his role as a true Apostle of Jesus Christ. He also says that the Gospel should be preached to Gentiles because Christ's love extends to all. He stresses the necessity for faith in the Lord Jesus Christ.

Paul writes the Letter to the Philippians (P—56) from prison to Christians in northern Greece (Macedonia). A deeply personal and joyful letter, Paul tells his readers to rejoice in Christ the Savior, the one who teaches us the meaning of true humility.

In the First Letter to the Corinthians (P—56/57) and the Second Letter to the Corinthians (P—57), Paul addresses problems his converts were having after he left Corinth. In the First Letter to the Corinthians he also gives important instructions on the Eucharist and Jesus' Resurrection (see 1 Corinthians 11:23–24). Also included is the beautiful passage on the meaning of love (see 1 Corinthians 13:1–13). In the Second Letter to the Corinthians, readers are encouraged to forgive each other and to be generous in a collection for the church in Jerusalem. St. Paul also defends his work as an Apostle.

A READING FROM A NEW TESTAMENT LETTER: PAUL'S APPEAL FOR MERCY

St. Paul wrote the very short Letter to Philemon while in prison, sometime between AD 61 and 63. Paul sent the runaway slave Onesimus back to his master, Philemon, asking Philemon to accept Onesimus as a brother in Christ. Read this letter and answer these questions:

- Who else does Paul address in this letter?
- Why did Paul want to keep Onesimus with him?
- What argument does Paul make to appeal to Philemon on behalf of Onesimus?
- Who is in prison with Paul?

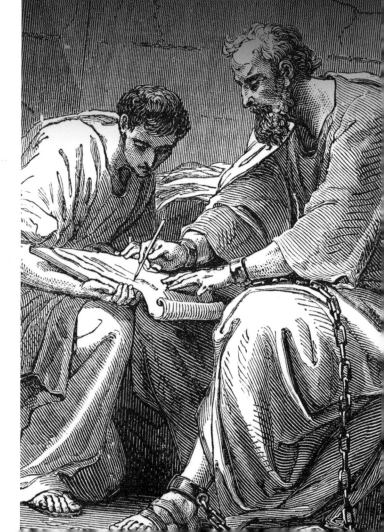

The Letter to the Romans (P—57/58) is Paul's longest letter and contains his most advanced theological reflection on Jesus. The letter stresses the necessity of faith in Jesus Christ, who justifies and saves all believers. It also offers instructions on Christian living.

Three other letters are often categorized as "Prison Letters." Paul wrote the very short Letter to Philemon (P—55) to encourage Philemon to forgive his runaway slave, Onesimus. The Letter to the Colossians (D—61–63 or 80s) instructs the Colossians to reject false teachings and to accept only Jesus Christ as the true Lord of creation and the source of new life. The Letter to the Ephesians (D—61–63 or 90s) develops the theme of the Church as the Body of Christ and the Bride of Christ. It also emphasizes the unity of Gentiles and Jews in Christ, teaching how Christians should live in God's Spirit as his children.

The Letter to Titus (D—65 or 95–100), the First Letter to Timothy (D—65 or 95–100), and the Second Letter to Timothy (D—64–67 or 95–100) are called "Pastoral Letters" because they are correspondences between those who shepherd or pastor Christians. These letters are also unique because they are written to individuals, not entire communities. They give advice on issues of Church leadership (e.g., the qualifications of bishops), Church organization, and instructions for Christian worship and living. They also warn against certain false teachings and the need to be faithful to the true doctrine passed on by the Apostles.

The Letter to the Hebrews (1)

Though identified as the Letter to the Hebrews (60s if by Paul, or most probably in the 80s), it is more likely a sermon or homily and probably not written by St. Paul. It emphasizes Christ's superiority over all creation and that he is greater than all the angels and all the prophets, including Moses. Christ is the High Priest. His perfect sacrifice of Death on the cross took away sin, fulfilling all the promises made in the Old Testament.

Catholic Epistles (7)

The Catholic Epistles are letters intended "for all." (Catholic means "universal.") These letters are catholic or universal because they contain general advice that is helpful to all the churches, both in the East and West. Also, these letters help us understand better how the Church was founded and formed in the first century.

The Letter of James (62 or 80s or 90s) advises its readers to treat people justly, to take care of the poor, and to control one's speech. Faith in Jesus should lead to good works.

The First Letter of Peter (60–63 or 70–90) focuses on how Christians should imitate Jesus when they suffer by not returning evil for evil. Good example will lead others to Christ.

The Letter of Jude (90s) warns Christians to remain firm in their faith against false teachers. It speaks of the punishment that will come on false teachers.

The Second Letter of Peter (c. 130) borrows heavily from Jude. It encourages readers to remain strong and faithful to true teaching.

The Letters of John were written approximately at the turn of the first century. The First Letter of John says to love as proof of our faith in Jesus Christ. God is love; therefore, God's children must love one another. The Second Letter of John speaks of love for others and our need to obey God, who is truth. The Third Letter of John was written to a Church leader with instructions to continue to support missionary efforts to spread the Gospel.

Revelation (Apocalypse of John) (1)

In this highly symbolic work, the seer John relates (probably 92–96) visions he had of God, the Risen Christ, and the future. The purpose of the book was to encourage Christians who were undergoing persecution for their faith in Jesus Christ. God will triumph and watch over them. Using apocalyptic language, the author reassured his reader that Christ will reward the faithful with a heavenly home at the end of time.

🌐 For Review

1. Check your copy of the New Testament. Transcribe into your journal the name of each book of the New Testament with its abbreviation.

2. Write the four Gospels in the chronological order of their composition.

3. Which New Testament letters are attributed to St. Paul or one of his disciples? Which are not?

🌐 For Reflection

What is your favorite Gospel? Why?

Main Ideas

- The Bible is filled with knowledge, wisdom, and truth, often applied in familiar sayings (p. 48).

- The Old Testament is the first part of the Christian Bible that recounts details of Salvation History through the story of the Jews, God's Chosen People, prior to the coming of Jesus (p. 49).

- A majority of the Hebrew Scriptures make up the Old Testament (pp. 50–53).

- From a base of oral traditions, eventually the Chosen People began to record their stories about the time of King Solomon's reign (pp. 49–50).

- The Old Testament was formed over the course of nine hundred years (pp. 49–50).

- Catholics accept forty-six books of the Old Testament; most Protestant Bibles include only thirty-nine books. The differences have to do with which books of the Jewish Bible have been accepted (pp. 50–53).

- There are four major divisions of the Old Testament: Pentateuch, Historical Books, Wisdom Books, and Prophetic Books (pp. 52–60).

- The Gospels are at the heart of the New Testament; they were recorded in three stages (p. 61).

- There are twenty-seven books in the New Testament (p. 65).

- The books of the New Testament were written in different styles and composed from the latter half of the first century to the early second century (pp. 65–68).

Terms, People, Places

Match the following terms with the definitions below.

apocalypse

apocryphal books

canon

catechesis

Evangelist

kerygma

patriarchs

Septuagint

deuterocanonical

idolatry

major prophets

minor prophets

remnant

didache

liturgy

1. The core or essential message of the Gospel
2. Also referred to as deuterocanonical
3. The official public worship of the Church
4. For example, Isaiah, Jeremiah, and Ezekiel
5. Matthew, Mark, Luke, and John
6. Twelve prophets who have books of the Old Testament named for them
7. "teaching"
8. From a word that means "seventy"
9. Refers to books in the Old Testament not found in the Hebrew Scripture
10. Education in the faith
11. Exiles and former exiles who remained faithful to YHWH during the time of their captivity
12. Abraham, Isaac, and Jacob
13. A Greek word for "revelation"
14. Worship of something other than the true God
15. The official list of inspired books in the Bible

Primary Source Quotations

Live the Word of God

I wish that the Scriptures might be translated into all languages, so that not only the Scots and the Irish, but also the Turk and the Saracens might read and understand them. I long that the farm-labourer might sing them as he follows the plough, the weaver hum them to the tune of his shuttle, the traveller beguile the weariness of his journey with their stories.

—Desiderius Erasmus

A man who is well grounded in the testimonies of the Scriptures is the bulwark of the Church.

—St. Jerome

Just as at the sea those who are carried away from the direction of the harbor bring themselves back on course by a clear sign on seeing a tall beacon light or some mountain peak coming into view, so Scripture may guide those adrift on the sea of life back into the harbor of the divine will.

—St. Gregory of Nyssa

Humbly welcome the word that has been planted in you and is able to save your souls. Be doers of the word and not hearers only, deluding yourselves. For if anyone is a hearer of the word and not a doer, he is like a man who looks at his own face in a mirror. He sees himself, then goes off and promptly forgets what he looked like.

— James 1:21–24

These passages tell us not only to read the Word of God, but to live it as well. The purpose of Sacred Scripture is to meet the living God and then to take him into the world. In your journal, write two paragraphs describing how you live your faith, how it makes a difference in your life and in the lives of others.

Ongoing Assignments

As you cover the material in this chapter, choose and complete at least three of these assignments.

1. A *biblical atlas* provides maps to help you navigate around the ancient biblical world. Your Bible might also contain some good maps. You can also find maps online. Print, photocopy, or create your own map of the ancient biblical world at the time of Abraham. Search under the title "Biblical Maps." Here are two helpful links:
   * http://ancienthistory.about.com/od/biblicalmaps/qt/BiblicalMaps.htm
   * www.bible.ca/maps

2. Create a slide show or PowerPoint presentation of key biblical towns. Check sites like these:
   * Pictures of Palestine: www.trekearth.com/gallery/Middle_East/Palestine
   * Bible Places: www.bibleplaces.com

3. Create a timeline of important events of Old Testament history. Consult reference books or the Internet for information.

4. *Biblical dictionaries* (for example, *Harper-Collins Bible Dictionary*, John L. McKenzie's *Dictionary of the Bible*, or *Eerdmans Dictionary of the Bible*) have short articles on themes, names, places, and other topics found in the Bible. Locate a good biblical dictionary. Use this to research a topic of interest or write a short report on one of the following topics:
   * main events in the life of Abraham
   * the Dead Sea
   * some of the meanings of the words *prophet* and *prophecy*
   * the origination and meaning of the word *Jew*
   * some facts about the Exodus

5. A *biblical commentary* analyzes, evaluates, and explains biblical texts. Some can be quite scholarly, for example, the *Anchor Bible* series. Others are designed for the beginning Bible student. Two time-tested Catholic biblical commentaries are the *Collegeville Bible Commentary* and the *New Jerome Biblical Commentary*. The *Catholic Study Bible*, second edition, also has extensive commentaries. Read about

Noah's flood in Genesis 7–8. Locate one of these biblical commentaries and report on what it has to say about the Flood.

6. A *biblical concordance* lists the occurrences of a word that appears in the Bible. With the advent of computers, it is relatively easy to do word searches online. Do one of the following:

- Go to this website: http://bible.crosswalk.com. Find and list ten references to the name *Moses* in the *New Revised Standard Bible*.

- Go to this website: www.biblegateway.com. Find five references to the word *hope* in the Book of Job. Use the *New International Version*.

- Locate the *New American Bible* online at www.usccb.org/nab/bible. Locate 1 John 2. Do a search for the word *love*. Write out two passages that contain that word.

7. Read and report on a brief history of Israel before the coming of Christ at http://netministries.org/BBasics/BBHOI.htm.

8. Outline the Twelve Tribes of Israel as given at the website of Fr. Felix Just, S.J.: http://catholic-resources.org/Bible/History-Abraham.htm.

Prayer

The Book of Numbers contains Moses' instructions to Aaron and the priests on how to bless the Chosen People. A blessing conveys prosperity and well-being on another. To receive God's blessing greatly honors us. It reveals the great dignity we have as God's children. Meditate on the words of this familiar blessing:

> The LORD bless you and keep you!
> The LORD let his face shine upon you,
> and be gracious to you!
> The LORD look upon you kindly and give
> you peace!

—Numbers 6:24–26

- *Reflection*: How has God revealed himself to you? Who has best shown you what God is like?

- *Resolution*: You can be a living blessing to others. Think of several people who need your smile, good cheer, and loving help. Do something special for these people during the coming weeks.

4

THE PENTATEUCH, CREATION, COVENANT, AND THE EXODUS

Hear, O Israel! The LORD is our God, the LORD alone! Therefore, you shall love the LORD, your God, with all your heart, and with all your soul, and with all your strength. Take to heart these words which I enjoin on you today.

—Deuteronomy 6:4-6

Obedience

Cooperating with and obeying God facilitates contentment.

The Writing of the Pentateuch

While Moses is cited as the traditional author of the Pentateuch, there are four major sources of its material, known as the Yahwist (J), Elohist (E), Deuteronomist (D), and Priestly (P) sources.

The Creation Stories

There are two creation stories in the Book of Genesis that each reveal important truths about God, creation, and human beings.

Sin Enters the World

Sin entered the world when the first humans, Adam and Eve, consented to the temptation of evil that came from an outside source.

Covenant with Abraham

God made a covenant with Abraham and his descendants, promising that he would always bless them and remain with them.

The Exodus and the Giving of the Law

God's deliverance of the Chosen People from Egypt was followed closely by the sealing of the event in the giving of the Sinai Covenant.

Obedience

Roger Staubach was the legendary quarterback of the Dallas Cowboys during the 1970s. A graduate of Purcell High School (now Purcell Marian) near Cincinnati, Roger also attended the United States Naval Academy, where he won the Heisman Trophy in his junior year. After completing his military requirement and serving in Vietnam, he joined the Dallas Cowboys. He led his team to six NFC championship games, winning four of them. He also was the quarterback for the Cowboys' victories in Super Bowls VI and XII.

An interesting part of his story is that his coach, the famed Tom Landry, called all of the team's offensive plays from the sidelines. This was unusual for that era, when the quarterback himself was given a game plan but also the freedom to call the plays in the huddle. Roger said that having the coach dictate the plays was a trial for him. It was only in emergencies that the quarterback could adjust the play. Roger knew that his coach was a genius at football strategy, but his personal pride told him that he ought to be able to guide his teammates.

Roger admitted the challenge before him when he later reflected on the situation: "I faced up to the issue of obedience. Once I learned to obey, there was harmony, fulfillment, and victory."

Obedience equates with following the commands, wishes, or instructions of someone else. Roger learned that the result of obeying proper authority led to harmony, fulfillment, and victory. Disobedience, on the other hand, can lead to disharmony, emptiness, and defeat. This lesson parallels what so often happened to God's people in the Old Testament. The Lord asked for their obedience. When the people listened to God, they thrived. When they disobeyed him, they suffered.

This chapter explores selected passages from the Pentateuch where a constant theme emerges throughout: Despite the rebelliousness and disobedience of humans, God remained faithful to the covenants he made.

⬤ Living the Ten Commandments

The Ten Commandments summarize the Law. They tell us how to respond in love to God and our neighbor. Read the commandments from Exodus 20:1–17 (listed below). Reflect on the applications for each of the commandments. Then, write your own personal applications for the commandments, explaining how you are applying them to your life.

1. **I, the LORD, am your God . . . You shall not have strange gods before me.**

   - I put God before all else.
   - I am loyal to the Lord more than to my success, prestige, popularity, possessions, etc.

2. **You shall not take the name of the LORD, your God, in vain.**

   - I respect God's name and everything else that is holy.

3. **Remember to keep holy the LORD's day.**

   - I make sure I go to Mass on Sunday.
   - I renew my spirit through rest, healthy activities, and prayer on the Lord's Day.

4. **Honor your father and your mother.**

   - I honor and obey the wishes of my parents.
   - I respect other family members.
   - I listen to others who have proper authority over me.

5. **You shall not kill.**

   - I respect all life as a gift from God.

   - I don't do anything that would harm others or me.

   - I show care for those who most need love.

6. **You shall not commit adultery.**

   - I respect my own sexuality.

   - I do not tell off-color jokes, watch sexually explicit movies, or visit Internet sites that degrade sexuality.

7. **You shall not steal.**

   - I am honest in all my dealings.

   - I do not cheat on my schoolwork.

8. **You shall not bear false witness against your neighbor.**

   - I refrain from gossip, taking care to protect the reputation of others.

9. **You shall not covet your neighbor's house.**

   - I am not envious of others' good fortune.

   - I am not a jealous person.

10. **You shall not covet your neighbor's wife.**

    - I guard against lustful thoughts.

⬥ For Reflection

Roger Staubach said, "Spectacular achievements come from unspectacular preparation." Write of a time when this was true in your own life.

The Writing of the Pentateuch

Moses has traditionally been named as the author of the Pentateuch. Jesus even referred to the Pentateuch as "the Book of Moses" (Mk 12:26). However, modern scholarship understands that the Pentateuch only reached its final form after centuries of retelling, adapting, and reinterpreting the many stories of God's dealings with the Chosen People. Without a doubt, Moses is the central figure in the Pentateuch, so naturally the Israelites would look to him as the source of the laws and traditions recorded there, but he could not have written everything in these books. For example, Deuteronomy 34:5–12 reports the death of Moses.

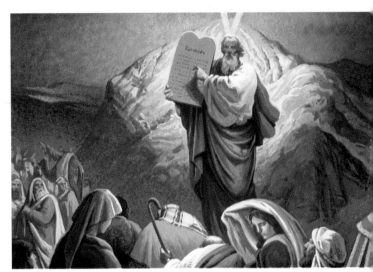

Sources of the Pentateuch

The Pentateuch resulted from the weaving together of several sources that went through various steps of editing.

These steps included incorporating the life and personality of Moses along with the oral transmission of various laws, speeches, stories, narratives, reflections, genealogies, poetry, and liturgical celebrations. Some of these were written down.

How was this done? Authors and editors, inspired by God, collected the sources into a continuous narrative. Often no attempt was made to reconcile all the differences between the narratives. Hence, there are places in the Bible where two versions of the same story exist (e.g., the creation stories of Genesis 1:1–30 and 2:4b–3:21). There are four major sources that make up the Pentateuch. They are known as the Yahwist (J), Elohist (E), Deuteronomist (D), and

anthropomorphic

A literary device in which human emotional qualities (e.g., sadness, anger) and physical traits (e.g., eyes) are attributed to God.

Elohim

A common Semitic word for God used in the Bible. Elohim appears in Hebrew names like Mich-a-EL, Dan-i-EL, and Ari-EL.

Enuma Elish

The Babylonian creation myth.

Priestly (P) sources. More explanation of each source follows:

1. *Yahwist (J):* This source usually uses the name *YHWH* (in German, *Jahweh*) for God. It employs a vivid, earthy style of writing with an **anthropomorphic** view of God. The Yahwist source refers to Mount Sinai as the place for the study of the Law and gives the basic framework for the Pentateuch: human origins, patriarchs, slavery in Egypt, the Exodus, wandering in the desert, the Mount Sinai covenant, and entry into the Promised Land.

2. *Elohist (E):* This source uses the term **Elohim** for God, a name that likely originated from Ephraim in the northern kingdom around 850 BC. Writings that use Elohim for God place emphasis on prophecies, especially those of Elijah and Elisha. The Elohist source retells stories from the northern kingdom's point of view with emphasis on the monarchy. Abraham is a central figure. Around 750 BC, an editor combined J and E into one narrative. He did not bother to drop repetitions or contradictions.

3. *Deuteronomist (D):* The term "Deuteronomist" comes from the Greek meaning "second law." This source places great emphasis on morality and the Law and was likely composed by a priest in the northern kingdom at the shrine of Shechem around 650 BC. Israel's history as a cycle of reward for fidelity to the covenant and punishment by YHWH for sin is also a major theme of this writing. The "D" sources especially highlight speeches of Moses. "Listen, Israel" is a constant refrain.

4. *Priestly (P):* This source is known by its singular census lists and genealogies; numbers and dates; proper ways to worship; and clean and unclean animals. It refers to God as Elohim. As the latest of the four traditions put in writing, it contributed a coherent framework to the Pentateuch.

⬤ **For Review**

1. To whom is the writing of the Pentateuch attributed?

2. Briefly discuss each of the four sources in the writing of the Pentateuch: J, E, D, and P.

⬤ **For Reflection**

What is something God has inspired you to do?

The Creation Stories

The Old Testament creation stories reveal great truths about the world's and humanity's origins. While there are some similarities between the creation stories of the Bible and creations stories of other civilizations (most notably the Babylonian *Enuma Elish*), the Genesis stories reveal that there is one God, in contrast with the many gods of other religions. They tell us that humans were created out of God's goodness, not as a byproduct of some conflict between warring gods.

The two creation accounts in the Old Testament have some differences in organization and themes, but both are preserved as they reveal import truths about God, creation, and human beings.

The first creation story—Genesis 1:1–2:4a—comes from the Priestly tradition. Its style is forceful, stately, and grand. Creation is an awesome, dramatic act by a glorious and majestic God.

The second creation account—Genesis 2:4b–25—comes from the Yahwist tradition. It is much lighter in tone and down-to-earth. It paints a picture of an anthropomorphic God and is the older of the two accounts.

The First Creation Story

The first creation story draws on the Israelite tradition of the seven-day week, in which the seventh day, the Sabbath, was a day of rest and prayer. Creation took place in six days, with each day representing a higher level of creation. God created humans, the pinnacle of his design, on the sixth day. The story describes all that God made as very good.

The Priestly account does not attempt to give a scientific explanation of the universe. Rather, under God's inspiration, the author drew on popular images known by the people of the time to convey *religious* truths that God wanted to reveal. For example:

1. *There is only one God.* Myths of that day taught that there were many gods. Rather, the biblical first creation story emphatically insists there is only *one* God and that this one God created everything that exists.

2. *God planned creation.* Creation did not result from chaotic forces or warring gods. God created the world in an orderly manner to share his life and goodness with us.

3. *Everything that God made is good.* Like many ancient peoples, the Babylonians believed that much of material reality was evil and at war

 ## Deciphering the Creation Stories

Read the creation stories from the Book of Genesis. Create a two-column chart—labeled P and J—that records answers to the following questions:

1. What name does the author of each account give the Creator?

2. From what does God make the world? (P: Gn 1:2) (J: Gn 2:5-7)

3. Describe the creation of humans. (P: Gn 1:27) (J: Gn 2:7, 21-22)

4. What are humans instructed to do? (P: Gn 1:26-30) (J: 2:15-20)

5. The Hebrew word *ruah* means "spirit, wind, breath." How is it used in each story? (P: Gn 1:2) (J: Gn 2:7)

6. What is the relationship between *man* and *woman* in each story? (P: Gn 1:27) (J: Gn 2:18-25)

with the spiritual elements in the universe. The Genesis account rejects this pessimistic view of creation. Genesis gives a positive view of reality. God is pleased with everything, especially human beings, who are made in his own image and likeness. Moreover, God entrusted humans with the responsible development of the rest of creation.

4. *The Sabbath is a special day of rest and worship.* The priestly author tells how God rested on the seventh day. God, of course, does not need to rest. The point of the story is for God's creatures to take time for rest and renewal. More importantly, we need to take the time to worship, in prayer and thanksgiving, a kind and loving God who is the source of our existence.

These four truths powerfully state the revealed truths about the one, powerful, good, and loving God who freely shares his life with his creatures.

The Second Creation Story

The Yahwist author of the second creation story portrays God as a potter who molds Adam's body like a delicate sculpture. Into this form YHWH breathes his spirit, the breath of life. This creation account shows the intimacy between God and the first human

being, a loving relationship of shared life. This image of human and divine closeness radically contrasts with the view of most ancient peoples, who feared God as a distant and powerful being.

The J source describes a compassionate God. YHWH cares for Adam by planting a garden and sending animals for companionship. God puts Adam in charge of other creatures by allowing him to name the animals. (In the ancient world, the power to name signaled control over what was named.) Animals, however, are not enough to fulfill the human need for companionship.

Thus, the story tells of the creation of Eve from Adam's rib. This is an important image of the dignity of women and their equality with men. The second creation account also provides the reason why men and women leave their parents to form their own families. YHWH wants the couple "to become one," to enter into a close relationship that mirrors God's own relationship with them. Man and woman are equal and complementary, intended to be true companions in a stable union open to life and to love.

The story also tells us that Adam and Eve felt no shame, even though naked. Their natural condition of intimacy with God and each other was one of total openness. Only after they sinned did humans feel ashamed and want to hide.

Why Include Two Creation Stories in the Bible

After reflecting on the meaning of both stories, it is clear why God inspired the final editors to include both stories in the final edition of the Pentateuch. God, the awe-inspiring Creator who made everything out of nothing, created humans in his image and likeness, endowing them with great dignity. In this first story, God is great and mysterious and powerful, and he has created human beings who reflect his glory. In the second creation story, we learn that the Creator God, who is goodness and love himself, is also intimately involved in the life of his creatures, especially the man and woman who are the jewels of his creation. He communicates with them and loves them as his own children.

The two creation stories also reveal much about Jesus. These beautiful stories foreshadow the fullness of Divine Revelation: Jesus Christ. As the Gospel of John reports,

> In the beginning was the Word, and the Word was with God, and the Word was God. . . . All things came to be through him. . . . And the Word became flesh and made his dwelling among us. (1:1, 3, 14)

These words echo Genesis—"In the beginning"—and connect the Old Testament to the New Testament. The powerful opening verses of John's Gospel teach about the **Incarnation**, the union of divine and human natures in the one person of the Word, Jesus Christ. The perfect, almighty Son of God became man to live among us, to teach us directly about the ways of God, to show us how God intended humans to live, and to reveal the depth of God's love for us by his own Death and Resurrection.

Incarnation
The dogma that God's eternal Son assumed a human nature and became man in order to save us from our sins. (The term literally means "taking on human flesh.") Jesus Christ, the Second Person of the Trinity, is both true God and true man.

Good Stewards

> God created man in his image; in the divine image he created him; male and female he created them. God blessed them, saying: "Be fertile and multiply; fill the earth and subdue it. Have dominion over the fish of the sea, the birds of the air, and all the living things that move on the earth." (Gn 1:27-28)

These verses from Genesis reveal that God intended human beings to be stewards of creation. A steward is a person who manages another's property or affairs. Made in God's image and likeness, humans have the abilities to think, to choose responsibly, and to use their imaginations to manage the sacred trust God gave to us. God calls each of us to be good stewards. Choose and enact at least one of the following plans for good stewardship. Report on your findings.

- Read a Psalm about God's love for his creation, for example, Psalms 8, 19, 29, 33, 65, or 104. Design a poster or prayer card with several verses from the Psalm you choose.
- Save water by turning off the faucet while you brush your teeth.
- Donate something you own, but do not use, to a charitable organization like the St. Vincent de Paul Society.
- Pick up litter you see today at school or in your neighborhood.
- Think about things you use that you can recycle. Map out a plan of action for how to do so.
- Talk to your family about ways to conserve energy. Map out a plan (e.g., purchase fluorescent light bulbs, turn off lights when not in use, figure out ways to conserve water, save the daily newspaper for recycling, etc.).

Jesus Christ's saving actions, and his and the Father's gift of the Holy Spirit, bring new life to humanity—eternal life. This is the great news of the New Testament.

🌐 For Review

1. Discuss four religious truths revealed in the two creation stories of Genesis.

2. Describe how the two creation accounts in Genesis point in a veiled way to the coming of Jesus Christ.

3. What biblical verse teaches humans to be good stewards of God's creation?

🌐 For Reflection

Rate yourself as a steward of God's creation. How important to you is it to preserve the resources of the earth? How are you effectively helping to do that?

Sin Enters the World (*CCC*, 396-421)

Genesis 3–11 relates how humans declared independence from God through disobedience, the abuse of freedom, and lack of trust in him. These chapters tell us how sin entered the human race and report its tragic consequences. But, in the midst of all the tragedy, the lesson is taught that God does not abandon humans. The next sections trace the entrance of evil into the world—the Original Sin—and God's response. Genesis 3:15 records the *Protoevangelium*, or "first gospel," the announcement of a Messiah and a Redeemer.

The Fall

The second creation story reveals two important truths: First, God created human beings in his image and in his friendship. We were created to be happy and to live forever. Second, as these things are not true for people on earth, the second creation story explains why not. Adam and Eve, tempted by the devil, preferred themselves over God, ignoring the fact that they were only creatures and not God. Their choice had tragic consequences for them and for all their descendants. Original Sin results in the deprivation of grace in fallen human nature.

The story of the Fall includes a serpent and a "tree of the knowledge of good and evil." A serpent has become a symbol of evil. Later, the Jews would associate the serpent with the devil. A message of the confrontation with the serpent is that sin does not originate from *within* humans. Sin comes from human beings freely consenting to an outside temptation.

Genesis 2:16–17 introduces the tree of the knowledge of good and evil and YHWH's command not to eat its fruit on pain of death. The serpent distorts the

EXPLAINING THE FAITH

How did sin spread in the world?

The Book of Genesis answers clearly how sin spread in the world following the sin of Adam and Eve. Within the explanation, Genesis also points out how God never abandons human beings. For example:

- *Cain and Abel (Genesis 4).* In this story of the sons of Adam and Eve, it is revealed that sin can lead to the serious crime of murder and, even worse, fratricide (the killing of one's brother). God condemns Cain to a nomadic life, but the "mark of Cain" (Gn 4:15) protects him against death. Although serious crime deserves punishment, God will not abandon us. God loves the sinner. The Lord God, though a just Judge, is faithful and loving.

- *Noah and the Flood (Genesis 6:5-9:29).* In the Great Flood, recounted by both Yahwist and Priestly authors, we learn how God punishes wicked and depraved humanity. But God does not destroy the human race. Rather, he instructs Noah and his children to repopulate the earth. God then enters into the first biblical covenant with Noah and all his posterity. Never again would the world be destroyed by a flood. The sign of this covenant is the rainbow, a symbol of God's presence. It serves to remind us of God's love for us despite our sins that require correction and punishment.

- *The Tower of Babel (Genesis 11:1-9).* This story highlights humanity's pride in trying to erect a multistoried temple-tower called a *ziggurat* to reach the heavens. Humanity sinned by trying to get to Heaven on its own efforts and by disobeying God's command to disperse and populate the earth. Humanity's ambition and desire "to make a name for itself" was a foolish act of pride. Rebellion and "going it alone" apart from God results in punishment and separation.

The story contains a play on the Hebrew word *balal*, "confusion," to explain the origin of the world's different languages. *Babel* (the Hebrew word for Babylon) is the place where human pride caused the Lord to confuse the speech of the world. (Babylon would later conquer the southern kingdom and take the Israelites into captivity.) The punishment for defying God is the great difficulty in human communication and cooperation caused by speaking different languages.

truth, promising Adam and Eve that if they eat the forbidden fruit, they will be like God. The forbidden fruit symbolizes knowledge only God should have—the knowledge of good and evil. In the words of the *Catechism of the Catholic Church*:

> The "tree of the knowledge of good and evil" symbolically evokes the insurmountable limits that man, being a creature, must freely recognize and respect with trust. Man is dependent on his Creator, and subject to the laws of creation and to the moral norms that govern the use of freedom. (396)

Through their own willful choice, both disobeying and defying God, Adam and Eve tried to make themselves gods. Their act did indeed give them "new" knowledge, but the unfortunate knowledge of shame and guilt. Their self-centered choice alienated them from each other; they sensed their nakedness and were ashamed.

Their disobedience also alienated them from God. They lost the grace of their original holiness and justice and became afraid of God. They tried to hide. When questioned by God about their disobedience, Adam blamed Eve, and Eve blamed the snake. The truth is that their free, defiant choice led them to disobey God. They no longer had harmony between themselves. "The union of man and woman becomes subject to tensions, their relations henceforth marked by lust and domination" (*CCC*, 400).

Sin also broke their harmony with the natural world. With sin came sweat-producing work, painful childbirth, and, sadly, death. The worst consequence of sin, though, is the destruction of close intimacy with God, symbolized by banishment from the Garden of Eden.

The Protoevangelium

God did not abandon our first parents or their descendants. Rather, he promised,

> I will put enmity between
> you and the woman,
> and between your offspring
> and hers;
> He will strike at your head,
> while you strike at his heel.
> (Gn 3:15)

concupiscence
An inclination to commit sin that arises from our human desires or appetites. It is one of the temporal consequences of Original Sin, even after receiving the Sacrament of Baptism.

prehistory
A period of time that refers to events or objects that date before the written record existed.

Examining Sin in My Life

Complete at least one of the following activities:

- A rainbow symbolizes God's presence. Write a short essay describing three "rainbows" in your life that speak of God's care for you.

- Write a poem that laments the effects of sin in your life.

- Make a poster or collage contrasting sinful behaviors with positive ways that sin is overcome. For example, contrast an article about a person who has been arrested for drug use with another article about a person who has turned his or her life around after abusing drugs.

This passage shows how much God still loves his disobedient children. God condemned the evil one and promised that one day the serpent (devil) will be destroyed by the offspring of the woman. The Church understands this passage to be an announcement of the "New Adam," Jesus Christ, the Son of God. Unlike the first Adam, whose disobedience led to death, Christ obeyed, sacrificing his life on a cross. His obedience led to the forgiveness of sin, the defeat of Satan, and eternal life for God's children. Mary, Christ's Mother, is the New Eve. She gave her Son to the world. Her offspring—Jesus Christ—attained the final victory over the power of the evil one. In his Resurrection, he conquers one of the worst effect of sin—death.

Because the human race descends from our first parents, all people are implicated in the sin of Adam and Eve. "By yielding to the tempter, Adam and Eve committed a *personal sin*, but this affected *the human nature* that they would then transmit in a *fallen state*" (*CCC,* 404). Our human nature is wounded by Original Sin. All humans are deprived of the original holiness and justice that God intended for us in the beginning. The consequences of Original Sin include a weakened human nature that is subject to ignorance, suffering, and death; and an inclination to commit sin, known as **concupiscence**.

The *Protoevangelium* gives great hope to the world. God created human beings out of love. The human race is affected by sin, but we can be set free by Christ Jesus, whose Passion, Death, and Resurrection have broken the power of the evil one.

For Review

1. What is the meaning of the "tree of the knowledge of good and evil" in the Adam and Eve story?

2. Name three effects of the sin of Adam and Eve.

3. Identify the *Protoevangelium.*

4. What covenant does God make with Noah? What is its symbol?

5. What is the meaning of the Tower of Babel story?

For Reflection

Write or share about a time you have been shown mercy by another and a time you have been merciful to another.

Covenant with Abraham

The Tower of Babel passages conclude what is called the **prehistory** portion of Genesis. The remaining chapters of Genesis tell the story of the patriarch Abraham and his famous descendants. God called Abram to leave his home and travel to a new land where God would lead him. There, God said:

> I will make of you a great nation,
>   and I will bless you;

I will make your name great,
   so that you will be a
   blessing.
I will bless those who bless you
   and curse those who curse
   you.
All the communities of the earth
   shall find blessing in you.
(Gn 12:2–3)

Abram believed and obeyed God's summons. The Book of Genesis details Abram's travels, along with the birth of his children, their exploits in Egypt during a time of famine, and their survival so that God's promise to them could be fulfilled.

Most importantly, Genesis 15 describes the covenant God entered into with Abram. To seal the covenant, Abram sacrificed two animals as an ancient ritual required. The parties to the covenant were to walk through the two halves, implying that if either were to violate the covenants they would be killed like the animals. But Abram fell into a deep sleep. In his dream, God promised him land and many descendants. He also told Abram of the enslavement of his people but that God would rescue them and remain in continuous friendship with his descendants.

In the dream, Abram saw a smoking pot fire and flaming torch—symbolizing God's presence—pass between the animals. God had made a covenant with him. Interestingly, the biblical text does not say that Abram walked through the split animals. The covenant relied on God's fidelity alone. Nothing Abram's people did could destroy it.

God repeated his pledge in Genesis 17, where he changed Abram's name to *Abraham* to signify that he would be the "father of a multitude."

Twelve Tribes of Israel
The name for the descendants of the twelve sons of Jacob (Israel). See Exodus 1:2—5, Numbers 1:20—43, or 1 Chronicles 1: 1—2.

THREE NAMES FOR THE CHOSEN PEOPLE

Throughout the Old Testament, God's people are alternatively known by three primary names: Israelites, Hebrews, and Jews. An explanation of the origins of each name follows:

- When God changed Jacob's name to Israel (see Genesis 32:28-29), his descendants were known as the *Israelites* or sons of Israel (see, for example, Exodus 1:1,7).
- The Chosen People were also called the *Hebrews*, perhaps after the patriarch Eber, the ancestor of several Semitic peoples who lived in Canaan, a territory that included modern-day Israel and Jordan, the Sinai desert, Lebanon, and the costal areas of Syria. The name might also be derived from "one who crossed over," that is, a wanderer or nomad. The name is used most frequently in relationships with foreigners.
- After the Chosen People entered the Promised Land and the kings came from the tribe of Judah,

For his part, Abraham and his descendants must believe in the Lord's word and be circumcised as a sign of the covenant.

Against all odds, Abraham's wife, Sarah, who was previously barren, conceived a child, Isaac. God was true to his word.

God's covenant with Abraham was tested in Genesis 21–23 when God asked Abraham to sacrifice his only son with Sarah, Isaac. Abraham trusted and obeyed God without protest, bargaining, or hesitation. He knew that all he was and all he had was pure gift from God. He was not about to question what God required of him.

Happily, at the last minute, the Lord's messenger stopped the sacrifice. We can see in this disturbing story many important lessons. Perhaps there is a veiled condemnation of child sacrifice, which had been practiced by some of the Israelites' neighbors. Here Abraham is a model of faith, one who put aside his doubts to follow his Lord God. Also, in Isaac, we see something quite remarkable: a prefigure of Jesus. Isaac was a beloved son, just as Jesus is the beloved Son of the Father. Isaac carried wood for the sacrifice, just as Jesus carried the wood of the cross for his execution. Isaac asked about the lamb for sacrifice. Prophetically, Abraham said God would provide the lamb. And he did—the Lamb of God, his beloved Son, the perfect victim who offered his life for all people.

The Patriarch Israel

Jacob, the second-born son of Isaac and his wife Rebecca, was able to secure the family's inheritance that typically went to the firstborn son. Isaac preferred the first son, Esau, while Rebecca favored Jacob. She and Jacob conceived a plan to secure the blind and aged Isaac's blessing, which would get him the family inheritance (Genesis 25:19–34). Esau, of course, was not happy about the outcome, so Jacob fled to the land of his uncle, where after years of labor he was allowed to marry Rachel.

Jacob sees Esau coming to meet him.

Jacob had two important experiences of meeting God. The first occurred when he was fleeing his brother. On the road at Bethel, he had a remarkable dream of angels ascending and descending a ladder to Heaven (Genesis 28:10–22). In this dream, God appeared to Jacob and repeated the terms of the covenant made with his grandfather, Abraham. Jacob would have many descendants. The nations of the world would be blessed through them. He would be given a land. And God would always protect him.

Years later, Jacob desired a reconciliation with Esau (Genesis 32—33). Before the meeting took place, Jacob had a strange meeting with a mysterious person who wrestled with him all night. Jacob persisted in a test of wills and refused to give up until he received a blessing from his opponent. Instead, Jacob received a new name from the stranger—Israel—meaning "one who contends with God." Though the mysterious stranger did not reveal his name, Jacob was sure that he met God face-to-face. This meeting blessed Jacob, transforming him from a crafty, deceptive person into an honorable man.

God did indeed fulfill his promises to Jacob. The newly named Israel found a home in Canaan, the Promised Land, and fathered a large and growing family. Included in Jacob's family were his twelve sons from whom came the **Twelve Tribes of Israel**. God was, and is, true to his word.

Joseph, the Favored Son

Some of the most dramatic Old Testament stories center on Jacob's favored son, Joseph (Genesis 37, 39–50). Jacob gave Joseph a long tunic as a sign of special esteem for him, and he freed Joseph from some of the work the other brothers were expected to do. Joseph also had dreams, one of which he reported to his brothers that they would be required to serve him. This did not go over well with the brothers, and they were naturally jealous of Joseph.

At first, the jealous brothers wanted to kill Joseph, but then they conspired to sell him into slavery. Eventually, Joseph was taken to Egypt, where he became the slave of Potiphar, the chief steward of the Egyptian pharaoh. Joseph's charm and intelligence won him favor with his new master, but that changed when Potiphar's wife tried to seduce Joseph. Joseph rebuffed her advances, and she falsely accused Joseph to her husband. Even when he was imprisoned, Joseph's skills and personality aided him; he successfully interpreted the dreams of some fellow prisoners, winning a reputation as an interpreter of dreams.

This gift of interpreting dreams came to the pharaoh's attention, and when Joseph correctly warned of an impending famine, he was made chief governor of Egypt and helped prepare the country to survive it. When the famine arrived, Joseph's brothers came to Egypt in search of grain. They did not recognize him, so Joseph played a cat-and-mouse game with them until he was convinced they were repentant for having sold him into slavery. He eventually revealed his identity to his brothers, forgave their betrayal, and convinced the pharaoh to allow his father and brothers and their families to come to Egypt during the famine. The pharaoh even granted his family land in Goshen in the delta region of the Nile River.

In many ways, Joseph prefigures Jesus. For example, like Joseph, Jesus is the beloved Son. Joseph's brothers were jealous of him; King Herod was jealous of Jesus. Joseph ended up in Egypt because of his brother's treachery; the Holy Family went to Egypt to flee the bloodthirsty Herod after Jesus' birth. Joseph's brother Judah, the namesake of the tribe from which Jesus would come, convinced his brothers to sell Joseph for twenty pieces of silver; Judas betrayed Jesus for thirty pieces of silver. Joseph was faithful to his master, falsely accused, and imprisoned. Jesus was faithful to his Father, falsely accused, and underwent his Passion, Death, and Resurrection on our behalf. Joseph forgave his brothers and saved them from famine. Jesus forgave his executioners and saved all humanity.

For Review

1. What was God's covenant with Abraham? What was its sign?

2. Discuss at least two ways Isaac prefigures Jesus Christ.

3. What did Jacob learn in his two encounters with God?

4. What is the origin of the names *Israelite*, *Hebrew*, and *Jew*?

5. Discuss three ways Joseph, the son of Jacob, prefigures Jesus Christ.

For Reflection

Read Genesis 37, 39–45. Find three specific verses in these chapters that remind you of something in the life of Jesus. Note them in your journal and explain the connection.

The Exodus and the Giving of the Law

The historical narrative of the Book of Genesis ends with the death of Joseph. The Book of Exodus returns to the story of the Chosen People around four centuries after the death of Jacob and Joseph. Their descendants were living in Egypt, probably intermarrying with other Semitic tribes who had come to Egypt. By 1500 BC, the new kings of Egypt had begun to enslave the foreign inhabitants in their country, including the Chosen People. During the reign of Egyptian pharaoh Ramesses II, perhaps around 1250 BC, the Hebrews fled Egypt, led by the prophet Moses. This event is known as the *Exodus*, foundational in the history of the Chosen People.

God's deliverance of the enslaved Israelites marks the beginning of the Chosen People's history as a separate nation. God uniquely singled out Israel

OLD TESTAMENT NAMES FOR GOD

Until God revealed his sacred name to Moses, the Chosen people called God by other names. Details of two of those names and the origins and meaning of YHWH are discussed below.

The Chosen People used a common Semitic name for the deity, *El*, to refer to God. Originally, the Canaanites had a god named *El*, the father of all other gods and of all creatures. *Elohim* is a plural form of El, thus suggesting divine majesty, similar to kings and queens who refer to themselves as "we."

No one knows the original meaning of *El*. The Chosen People typically spoke of God with names such as "the God of Abraham, of Isaac, of Jacob." God was known by what he meant to those who worshiped and developed a covenant relationship with him.

A popular designation of God in Genesis is *El Shaddai*, often translated as "God Almighty." This is a mistranslation. The title *Shaddai* probably came from Abraham's ancestors and may have meant "God of the mountain" or "God of the open wastes."

Although the J source author of Genesis used the name *YHWH* to refer to God from the beginning of time, the P and E traditions tell us that this name was only revealed to Moses on Mount Horeb. Its pronunciation is uncertain because, out of respect for Almighty God, the Jews never said the name aloud. Instead of reading or saying the divine name aloud, the Israelites substituted the word *Adonai* (translated "Lord").

The exact meaning of YHWH remains a mystery since the Chosen People understood God to be above all. It is most likely derived from some form of the Hebrew word "to be," thus underscoring God's majestic and mysterious presence. The Latin Vulgate translation is "I am who am," while the Septuagint renders the sacred name, "He who is." One further understanding of YHWH is "He who brings into being whatever comes into being," thus stressing God's role as Creator.

The patriarchs believed in the existence of one God. Only YHWH creates, reveals, judges, gets involved in human history, saves, and sets up the kingdom of which YHWH alone is Master.

to be a witness to him, the one true Lord. The Exodus event was sealed in the Sinai Covenant where God revealed himself amidst thunder and lighting. Delivering his message through Moses, God declared himself bound to the people, freed them from slavery, protected them in the desert, and promised them a land. For their part of the covenant, the Israelites solemnly promised that they belonged to God, that they were his special people.

The Prophet Moses

A central figure in the Exodus and the entire Old Testament is the prophet Moses, a name from the Hebrew *mashah* ("to draw"). Born an Israelite, Moses was rescued and drawn from a river and raised by an Egyptian princess who unknowingly hired Moses' mother as his nurse. Though raised as royalty, Moses knew his identity. When he killed an Egyptian official for attacking a fellow Hebrew, Moses fled Egypt to Midian, living there as a shepherd.

One day, God appeared to Moses in a burning bush that was not consumed by the fire. He instructed Moses to remove his sandals because he was on holy ground in God's presence. God instructed Moses to return to Egypt to lead the Chosen People to freedom. Moses complained that he was incapable of such a task, but God assured him of help. God even revealed the divine name YHWH to him. Entering into an intimate union with Moses, YHWH assured the prophet that he was the "God of Abraham, the God of Isaac, and the God of Jacob" who had always cared for his people. After Moses protested again about his inability to do such a task, God convinced Moses to obey by performing miracles and by appointing his brother, Aaron, to be Moses' spokesman.

Moses and Aaron returned to Egypt to convince the Israelites that God had heard their prayers for deliverance. The pharaoh, however, had other plans; he redoubled the workload of the Hebrew slaves. Only after God sent the ten plagues (see Exodus 7–11) was the pharaoh finally convinced to free the Israelites.

The Passover

The Passover event is central to both the Jewish and Christian faiths. "Every time Passover is celebrated, the Exodus events are made present to the memory of believers so they may conform their lives to them" (*CCC*, 1363). For Catholics, when the Church celebrates the Eucharist, we commemorate Christ's Passover, and it is made present. The last plague—the death of every firstborn—was a prequel of the Passover. For the Israelites to escape this plague, they had to kill an unblemished lamb and smear its blood on the doorposts and lintels of their houses. They were also to eat the lamb quickly with bitter herbs and unleavened bread—yeasted bread would take too long to rise. The blood on the doorpost was the sign for the Lord's avenging angel to pass over the house, thus saving the firstborn from destruction.

YHWH instructed Israel to celebrate this meal every year on the night of the fourteenth day of Nisan (corresponding to March or April on the Roman calendar). The Passover celebration reminded the Chosen People of God's deliverance, Salvation, fidelity, and love. Christians celebrate the suffering, Death, and Resurrection of Jesus Christ as the fulfillment of the Passover. Jesus is the unblemished Lamb who delivers us from the slavery and death of sin. We commemorate Jesus' sacrifice and saving actions every time we celebrate the Eucharist.

The first Passover struck fear into the Egyptian people and their pharaoh, who finally allowed the Hebrews to leave Egypt. After 430 years in Egypt (see Ex 12:40), the Lord led the people to freedom through the Reed Sea, a marshy area near the present-day Suez Canal. There were hardships in the desert, and the people complained to Moses about them. Moses in turn lamented to God. The Lord answered Moses and the Chosen People by providing them water, food in the form of quail and manna, and protection from the Amalekites, a nation who tried to destroy the wandering Israelites.

The Sinai Covenant

In the third month after fleeing Egypt, YHWH visited the Israelites in an overpowering **theophany** on Mount Sinai. There he made a covenant with the people through Moses. The prophets summarize this covenant in one simple line: "You shall be my people, and I will be your God" (Jer 7:23; Ez 11:20; Hos 2:25). This important covenant, known as the Sinai Covenant:

- bound God and the Chosen People in a personal, loving union.

- revealed God's special love and mercy for them.

- stipulated how God's People were to respond to his love by instructing them to follow the commandments and be faithful to God in obedience and worship.

The people agreed to the terms of the covenant, which Moses put into writing. He sealed it by building an altar with twelve pillars to represent the Twelve Tribes and by sacrificing some young bulls and splashing their blood (a symbol of life) on the people and the altar (a symbol of God). Through this ritual, YHWH and the Israelites joined in a common life, sealing their destiny for all time.

The Ten Commandments (Ex 20:1–17) summarize the Law, serving as its basic guide. Chapters 20–23 of Exodus report the duties the Chosen People must observe. The Law helped the Israelites live in conformity to God's will. Over the years, the Lord inspired other laws that were added to help the people adapt to new situations of worshiping God and treating others justly. There are 613 laws listed in the last four books of the Pentateuch.

Some of the laws may appear unnecessary or strange to us today, but Israel's laws reflected a major advance over their neighbors. Some of the laws of the Old Testament are similar to the famous Babylonian Code of Hammurabi (ca. 1700 BC). The Israelites, acting through divine inspiration, reshaped the borrowed laws to support belief in YHWH, the one true God who rescued and sustained the Chosen People.

The biblical authors attributed many of the later laws to Moses because they grew out of Mosaic foundations that began with the Sinai Covenant. They attempted to reform the Israelites and ignite the original

theophany
An appearance or manifestation of God, as when he "appeared" to Moses in a burning bush.

tabernacle
The portable sanctuary in which the Jews carried the Ark of the Covenant throughout their travels in the desert.

spark of enthusiasm at Sinai. For example, the Book of Deuteronomy was a restatement and further development of Mosaic Law. This biblical book resulted from a reform movement in the northern kingdom shortly before its conquest. It reflects the concerns of the prophets who wanted the leaders and people to be single-hearted in their devotion to the covenant.

Challenges in the Desert

Most of the remaining chapters of the Book of Exodus give instructions for building the Ark of the Covenant, which would contain the Law tablets, and the **tabernacle**, in which God would meet Moses. The tabernacle would serve as a symbol of God's presence with the people.

However, the people grew impatient with Moses and the frustrations that came with their time in the desert. With Aaron's help, they made a golden calf to worship. Thinking they could form God in an image like ones used by their neighbors, they ended up committing the sin of idolatry. This was a major breach of the covenant and an offense against the first commandment. It greatly disturbed Moses, who threw down and broke the tablets containing the Law, symbolizing the people's transgression. Moses desperately appealed to God to spare the people. Once again, YHWH was faithful, despite the sin and infidelity of his people. He renewed the covenant with these words:

"Here, then," said the LORD, "is the covenant I will make. Before the eyes of all your people I will work such marvels as have never been wrought in any nation anywhere on earth, so that this people among whom you live may see how awe-inspiring are the deeds which I, the LORD, will do at your side. But you, on your part, must keep the commandments I am giving you today." (Ex 34:10–11)

The Chosen People were in the desert a total of forty years before entering Canaan, the Promised Land. The Book of Numbers describes this period of wandering. It reports the way God cared for and directed the Israelites. He led them with a cloud by day and fire by night. He provided for all their needs.

The Book of Numbers also records the constant "murmuring" of the Hebrews—their complaints, discontentment, and rebellion against God's chosen leader, Moses. For example, they complained about the food God gave them and doubted that the Lord could help them defeat the powerful Canaanites. They even expressed a desire to return to Egypt. Despite their protests, God remained with the people. Their penance was to wander in the desert for forty years. And except for Joshua and Caleb, the Lord did not allow anyone of the first generation who came from Egypt to enter the Promised Land. Even Moses and Aaron were denied entry into the Promised Land for a sin they

EXPLAINING THE FAITH

What is the natural law? How is the natural law related to the Sinai Covenant?

The natural law is the expression of what a person knows in his or her own soul to be right or wrong. The basic principles of the natural law extend to the entire human race. Natural law corresponds to three basic human drives and needs: (1) preserving life; (2) developing as individuals and communities; and (3) sharing life with others. The Ten Commandments provide the principal commandments and ways to apply the natural law.

committed in connection to an instruction God gave them concerning providing water from a rock (see Numbers 20:2–13).

The message of Numbers remains applicable today. We may sin, misuse our freedom, and doubt God's presence. For this, we may deserve punishment, but God remains faithful. He does not abandon us. The Father has sent his Son to offer reconciliation to the world. The Holy Spirit remains with us, consoling us and bringing ongoing healing.

Other Themes from Leviticus and Deuteronomy

The Book of Leviticus gets its name from the priests of the tribe of Levi. They were in charge of Israel's official worship. Most of the 247 laws in this book deal with public worship, animal sacrifices, and ritual offerings.

Composed by the Priestly author, Leviticus stresses the theme of God's holiness and our need to worship him with respect and love. It also emphasizes the holiness of God's people because God chose them. Holiness requires respect for the sacredness of life and God's presence in ordinary life. Many of Leviticus' laws govern the various aspects of daily life, including sex, birth, disease, and death.

The Book of Deuteronomy is an update of the Law and was written toward the end of Israel's time as an independent kingdom. It reflects the appeals of northern prophets for the Chosen People to take to heart the requirements of the covenant. Deuteronomy centers on God's love of Israel and his unhappiness with the people for worshiping false gods and not responding wholeheartedly to his love. Deuteronomy also teaches that discipline is a sign of God's love. It exhorts the nation to choose between obedience to God and the Law, which bring life, and disobedience, which leads to death.

For Review

1. What is the meaning of the word *Adonai*? Why was it used in place of *YHWH*?

2. What is the purpose of the Passover celebration?

3. What were the terms of the Sinai covenant?

For Reflection

- Write a character sketch of Moses based on some of the things you've read in Exodus 32–34.

- List various ways people are unfaithful to God in today's world. What are "golden calves" the contemporary world worships?

Main Ideas

- Obedience was an important lesson learned by the Chosen People during the Exodus event (p. 74).

- Though Jesus referred to the Pentateuch as the "book of Moses," it is admitted that Moses was not its sole author (p. 75).

- The four major sources that make up the Pentateuch are known as Yahwist (Y), Elohist (E), Deuteronomist (D), and Priestly (P) (pp. 75–76).

- The two creation stories in the Book of Genesis reveal important truths about God, creation, and human beings (pp. 77–80).

- The first creation story comes from the Priestly tradition (p. 77).

- The second creation story—the older of the two accounts—comes from the Yahwist tradition (p. 78).

- The two creation stories reveal much about Jesus and help to connect the Old Testament with the New Testament (pp. 79–80).

- Adam and Eve were tempted by the devil and chose themselves over God. Their choice—the Original Sin—has impacted human beings ever since (pp. 80–83).

- The *Protoevangelium* is God's first announcement of a New Adam who would reconcile the world to God (pp. 82–83).

- God entered into a covenant with Abraham and promised that he and his descendants would be a great nation (pp. 83–85).

- Jacob, whose name was changed to Israel, fathered twelve sons from whom came the Twelve Tribes of Israel (pp. 85–86).

- Joseph, the favored son of Jacob, helped to save the Chosen People from famine through a number of providential occurrences (p. 86).

- The Exodus event, including the Passover, the escape from Egypt, and the giving of the Sinai Covenant, is central to the history of God's Chosen People (pp. 87–90).

- God appeared to Moses in a burning bush that was not consumed by fire and called him to lead the Chosen People (p. 88).

- God revealed his sacred name—YHWH ("I Am")—to Moses (p. 88).

- The Passover—central to Jews and Christians—reminded the Chosen People of God's deliverance, Salvation, fidelity, and love (pp. 88–89).

- The Sinai Covenant bound God to the Chosen People, revealed his special love and mercy for them, and stipulated how people were to respond to his love through the commandments (pp. 89–90).

- The Chosen People faced many challenges during their forty years in the desert, including the temptation to idolatry (pp. 90–91).

Terms, People, Places

Choose the italicized term in parentheses that best completes each sentence.

1. An anthropomorphic view of God involves describing God with (*animal/human*) characteristics.

2. Writings that used the term Elohim for God placed emphasis on the (*prophecies of Elijah and Elisha/the Sinai Covenant*).

3. The *Enuma Elish* was a (*Babylonian/Egyptian*) creation story.

4. The words "in the beginning" from the Book of Genesis point to the Incarnation, that is, the (*creation of the world in six days/the union of God and man in the person of Jesus Christ*).

5. Original holiness and justice refers to the state of men and women (*after the birth of Christ/before the Original Sin*).

6. Concupiscence refers to (*efforts to follow one's conscience/an inclination to sin*).

Chapter 4 Quick View

7. Prehistory is concluded with the (*creation stories/Tower of Babel passages*) of the Old Testament.

8. The Twelve Tribes of Israel were direct descendants of (*Jacob/Joseph*).

9. An example of a theophany in the Old Testament was (*the famine that struck Egypt/ YHWH's appearance in the burning bush*).

10. The tabernacle was used to (*carry the Ark of the Covenant/mark the houses during the Passover*).

11. *Yom Kippur* means (*Feast of the Harvest/ Day of Atonement*).

Primary Source Quotations

Modern Stewardship

God destined the earth and all it contains for all people and nations so that all created things would be shared fairly by all humankind under the guidance of justice tempered by charity.

— *The Church in the Modern World,* 69

Something Greater than Sin

But why did God not prevent the first man from sinning? St. Leo the Great responds, "Christ's inexpressible grace gave us blessings better than those the demon's envy had taken away." And St. Thomas Aquinas wrote, "There is nothing to prevent human nature's being raised up to something greater, even after sin; God permits evil in order to draw forth some greater good. Thus St. Paul says, 'Where sin increased, grace abounded all the more'; and the Exultant sings, 'O happy fault . . . which gained for us so great a Redeemer!'"

— *Catechism of the Catholic Church,* 412

The Face of God

When the LORD saw him coming over to look at it more closely, God called out to him from the bush, "Moses! Moses!" He answered, "Here I am." God said, "Come no nearer! Remove the sandals from your feet, for the place where you stand is holy ground. I am the God of your father," he continued, "the God of Abraham, the God of Isaac, the God of Jacob." Moses hid his face, for he was afraid to look at God.

— Exodus 3:4–3:6

Union with God

God wishes not to deprive us of pleasure; but he wishes to give us pleasure in its totality; that is to say, all pleasure. . . . What great pleasure is there than to find myself the one thing that I ought to be, and the whole thing that I ought to be? There is nothing pleasurable save what is uniform with the most inmost depths of the divine nature.

— Blessed Henry Suso

"God permits evil in order to draw forth some greater good." Write a short essay or poem using personal examples of why this statement is true for your life.

Ongoing Assignments

As you cover the material in this chapter, choose and complete at least three of these assignments.

1. Read Genesis 3. Based on the characteristics listed on pages 75–76, state which tradition—J, E, D, or P—probably produced this story. Offer some evidence for your choice.

2. Research and report on marriage customs in Old Testament times.

3. Locate any news website for the headlines of the day. Find three stories that attest to the existence of Original Sin and concupiscence.

4. Read Jacob's struggle with God (Gn 32:23–32). Rewrite this in a modern-day setting.

Then describe a time when you wrestled with God or his Word. What did you want to do? What did the Lord want you to do? Who won the struggle? What did you feel afterward?

5. Print a good quality map of Abraham's journey, the route of the Exodus, or the Twelve Tribes in Canaan. Use color highlights to emphasize points of interest. Glue to poster board. See Bible Maps: www.bible.ca/maps.

6. Read Exodus 23:14–17, which describes the requirement to observe the religious feasts of Passover, Pentecost, and Tabernacles. Using a biblical dictionary or a book on the Jewish faith, prepare a report on the history, practice, and rituals of one of these feasts.

7. With another student, write and perform a skit between God and Moses in which Moses tries to convince God not to destroy the disobedient Israelites. Use humor if you wish, but make sure that Moses wins the argument!

8. Create a PowerPoint presentation on the life and ministry of Moses. Select slides that depict his life in Egypt, Mount Horeb, the route of the Exodus, Mount Sinai, the Ark of the Covenant, the Tabernacle, and the place of his burial.

9. Prepare and give a short oral presentation on:

   • "the mark of Cain"

   • flood stories in the ancient world

   • Hebrew slavery in Egypt

   • the ten plagues of Egypt

   • ziggurats in the ancient Mesopotamian world (find an illustration)

10. Prepare a report on one of the great women described in the Pentateuch: Sarah, Rebekah, Rachel, or Leah.

11. Report on what three early Christian writers have said about the creation in Genesis at Catholic answers: www.catholic.com/library/Creation_and_Genesis.asp.

12. After researching one of the following, report on five major differences between the creation account you read and the two accounts given in Genesis.

   • Read *Enuma Elish*, the Babylonian creation myth, online at: www.ancienttexts.org/library/mesopotamian/enuma.html

   • Report on the Egyptian creation myth: www.egyptartsite.com/crea.html

13. Take several digital photos of favorite scenic areas near where you live. Be sure the scenes speak to you of God's wonderful creation. Develop a slide show with music and your own composition of a prayer or poem to accompany the presentation.

14. Report on the meaning of the name for god given by another religion—for example, Islam, Hinduism, or a Native American tribe.

15. Report on the meaning of Christian stewardship: http://catholiceducation.org/articles/environment/en0007.html

16. Report on the principles of Catholic environmental justice. Check out these websites:

   • http://conservation.catholic.org/background.htm

   • Pope John Paul II, "The Ecological Crisis—A Common Responsibility: Peace with God the Creator, Peace with All Creation": www.ncrlc.com/ecological_crisis.html

17. Read Leviticus 16. It tells of *Yom Kippur*, which purified the Israelites and their land of the sins and transgressions committed in the previous year. The ritual of the scapegoat (Lv 16:20–28) transferred the people's

sins to the animal. It was led to the desert, believed to be the home of Satan, to die. With the animal's death, the people's sins returned to the evil spirit, and their guilt was taken away. Report on the modern-day Jewish feast of *Yom Kippur*.

18. Read Deuteronomy 8:1–20; 11:8–17, 26–28; 28:1–69. Record the answers to the following in your journal:

    • What is obedience? What blessings follow obedience?

    • What is disobedience? What curses follow disobedience?

19. Memorize the words of *Shema, Israel* ("Listen, Israel") found in Deuteronomy 6:4–5. This prayer is the heart of the Jewish faith. Some Jews write this prayer (see also Deuteronomy 11:13–21 and Numbers 15:37–41) on a parchment scroll (called a *mezuzah*) and then fasten it to the doorposts of their houses. Others place the words in small leather boxes (*phylacteries*) worn on the left arm and forehead while praying. Thus, God's Word is close to one's mind and heart. Compose your own short prayer of faith in God and Jesus Christ. Print it out in a beautiful font on suitable bond paper and post it in a prominent place in your study area.

Prayer

In the Old Testament, YHWH reveals that he is a God who keeps his promises, despite the failings of his people. Staying close to God brings life; drifting away from God leads to disaster. Sacred Scripture teaches us to *choose life!* Reflect on these words from Deuteronomy:

Here, then, I have today set before you life and prosperity, death and doom. If you obey the commandments of the LORD, your God, which I enjoin on you today, loving him, and walking in his ways, and keeping his commandments, statutes and decrees, you will live and grow numerous, and the LORD, your God, will bless you. . . . Choose life, then, that you and your descendants may live, by loving the LORD, your God, heeding his voice, and holding fast to him.

—Deuteronomy 30:15–16, 19–20

• *Reflection*: How are you making a choice for God in your life *right now*?

• *Resolution*: For the next two weeks, review each day to see how well you are living the requirements of the fourth commandment: "Honor your father and your mother." If you fall short, ask for God's forgiveness and resolve once again to be a better son or daughter.

5

KINGS AND PROPHETS AWAITING THE MESSIAH

*You have been told, O man, what is good,
and what the L*ORD *requires of you: Only to do the right
and to love goodness, and to walk humbly with your God.*

—Micah 6:8

Qualities of Friendship

Through his experience with the Chosen People, the Lord taught that friendship includes qualities like loyalty, fidelity, and humility.

Conquest of the Promised Land

As the Israelites settled in Canaan, they were afflicted by the sin of apostasy only to discover time and again YHWH's merciful compassion.

The Monarchy of Israel

God answered Israel's request for a king even as they failed to recognize him as their sole King and Ruler.

God Sends Prophets

The basic message of the prophets both prior to and following the division of the kingdom was the necessity of repentance in order to be saved.

The Babylonian Exile

While living as captives, the Jewish exiles renewed their faith by study of the Law and their practice of prayer in synagogues.

Return and Recommitment

After returning to the Holy Land, Judaism was purified in part in preparation for the coming of the Messiah.

Qualities of Friendship

True friendship has many faces. Native Americans describe a friend as "one-who-carries-my-sorrow-on-his-back." Friends, it has been suggested, "know everything about you, but still like you anyhow." One key quality of friendship is loyalty.

The theme of friendship is prevalent in the Old Testament, especially in describing the relationship God had with his Chosen People. In many ways it may appear that the friendship God had with the Israelites was one sided on God's part. The Chosen People were not always faithful friends to the God who rescued them from slavery, who guided them with his Law, who gave them a land to live in, and who sent judges and kings to defend them from their enemies and prophets to correct them when they went astray. But the Lord God always remained faithful to Israel, fulfilled his promises to them, and, in due course, sent them a Savior.

In this chapter, we will survey the story of God's loyalty and friendship to his Chosen People. The history covered in this chapter stretches from the thirteenth century BC to the time approaching the birth of Jesus. The subjects include the conquest of

the Promised Land, the rise and fall of the monarchy, the division of the kingdom to north and south, the Babylonian Exile, and the return to Jerusalem along with a rededication to Judaism.

The Bible on Friendship

Read the qualities of friendship below that are described in the Old Testament. For each quality, share a personal anecdote of how you or a friend has put that quality into practice.

- *Putting the other first:* "Jonathan then said to David, 'I will do whatever you wish'" (1 Sm 20:4).

- *Confidentiality:* "A newsmonger reveals secrets, but a trustworthy man keeps a confidence" (Prv 11:13).

- *Dependability:* "He who is a friend is always a friend" (Prv 17:17a).

- *Humble:* "Do nothing out of selfishness or out of vainglory; rather, humbly regard others as more important than yourselves, each looking out not for his own interests" (Phil 2:3–4).

- *Positive influence:* "Some friends bring ruin on us, but a true friend is more loyal than a brother" (Prv 18:24).

For Reflection

- What is the most important quality of friendship for you? Write a paragraph describing how you've exhibited this quality in one of your friendships. Write another paragraph explaining how Jesus has shown this quality to you.

- Read John 15:13. Jesus described a willingness to lay down one's life for a friend as the greatest love. What would it take for you to be able to do this? Who is a friend who might give up his or her life for you?

Conquest of the Promised Land

The Old Testament books of Joshua and Judges cover the historical period of the Israelites from the time of Moses' death to the beginning of the monarchy, roughly from 1250 to 1030 BC. These books of the Bible tell how the Israelites moved into and settled the Promised Land and how they interacted with their Canaanite neighbors.

The Book of Joshua gives the impression that the conquest of the Promised Land was swift to highlight its major theological theme: the Lord fought for Israel, and without his help, the Israelites would never have settled in the "land flowing with milk and honey." The Book of Judges more accurately presents the historical record, namely, that the conquest spanned approximately two hundred years and involved several major battles that gave the Israelites a foothold in the land and served as the basis of further expansion.

Joshua led the Israelites into the Promised Land. The name *Joshua* means "savior." "Jesus" is a variation of the same name. Joshua prepared carefully for the invasion. For example, he sent spies to Jericho to judge the enemy's strength. Moreover, he stayed close to the Lord, celebrated a Passover Meal before the invasion, and always obeyed the Lord's commands. Obedience to God was the key to success: when the Israelites obeyed, they were victorious. When they ignored God and followed their own will, they failed.

We see this pattern of obedience leading to success in the famous story of the taking of Jericho and its collapsing walls at the sound of the ram's horns and a mighty war cry (see Joshua 5:13—6:27). We also learn of the great difficulty Israel had in defeating the city of Ai because of the greed of one of its leaders, Achan, who disobeyed God's command to destroy all the valuables the Israelites had taken from Jericho. Not until Achan was executed was the battle won (see Joshua 7:1–8:29). The lesson is clear: disobeying God leads to destruction, defeat, and death.

After the Israelites settled the Promised Land, Canaan was divided among the Twelve Tribes. This event is described in Joshua 13–21. The Book of Joshua concludes with a renewal of the covenant at Shechem and a farewell speech from Joshua.

Joshua told the Israelites:

> Today, as you see, I am going the way of all men. So now acknowledge with your whole heart and soul that not one of all the promises the Lord, your God, made to you has remained unfulfilled. Every promise has been fulfilled for you, with not one single exception. (Jos 23:14)

After Joshua's death, the Israelites still had work to do. The various tribes had to contend with the ongoing resistance of hostile neighbors. In the absence of a strong central authority

judges
In ancient Israel, judges were those who acted as temporary military leaders, as well as arbiters of disputes within and between tribes. Judges were also expected to remind the people of their responsibility to God.

like a king, God raised up various **judges**, that is, local, tribal leaders.

Chief among these judges were Deborah, Gideon, Jephthah, and Samson.

The history of the Israelites during the period of the judges involves a cycle of **apostasy**, which typically followed these stages:

1. The Israelites sinned by worshiping the false gods of the Canaanites, most notably the Baals, who it was believed controlled the land. The Israelites worshiped these gods in the hope of receiving abundant crops and livestock for themselves. YHWH forbade the worship of false gods and imposed a strict moral code on his people, outlawing many of the practices of the surrounding peoples.

2. False worship led to God's disciplining the Israelites by handing them over to their enemies.

3. The Israelites cried out to God to save them from their plight.

4. YHWH took pity on his people and appointed judges who saved them in their distress. Judges believed that the Israelites had to destroy the Canaanites in battle to eliminate the temptation to worship false gods.

5. Once a particular judge died, the cycle repeated itself.

This pattern showed how even though they were God's Chosen People, human inclination to sinfulness led them to want to go their own way. The miracle is God's faithful love. Time and again he rescued them, even raising up leaders who themselves were flawed individuals.

Deborah was one of the great judges. She was a prophetess who instructed the general Barak to lead the army in a successful holy war. Her story is told in the form of a poem in Judges 5, one of the Bible's oldest pieces.

God provided another judge—Gideon—after the Israelites were attacked by the Midianites. At first, the young Gideon objected that he was too weak and unworthy to lead, but an angel of the Lord gave him courage. God gave him a sign using a woolen fleece (see Judges 6:36–40) to show that YHWH would lead Israel to victory through him. Gideon did lead the people to victory, but his later years saw him abandoning his faith while fashioning an **ephod**, which was forbidden by the Law. Because of Gideon's infidelity, YHWH eventually punished his family.

Judges 14–16 details the exciting exploits of the famous judge Samson. Samson fought bravely against the Philistines, a sea people who had settled

SAMPLING SCRIPTURE

Read the following Scripture passages. Write your answers to each question.

- *Read Joshua 2-4, 6, 24.*
  1. What role did Rahab play in helping the Israelites inhabit the Promised Land?
  2. Describe the fall of Jericho.
  3. What symbolized Joshua's renewal of the covenant?

- *Read Judges 2, 6-8, 13-16.*
  1. Summarize Israelite behavior after Joshua's death and God's response to it.
  2. How did Gideon respond to God's call (Jgs 6:11-24)? What led to his ruin (Jgs 8)?
  3. What do you find most appealing about Samson's character? What do you find to be his greatest character flaw?

on the southern coast of Canaan and for whom Palestine got its name. Though a hero, Samson had many personal failings that led to infidelity and suffering, the same pattern followed by God's people throughout this and many other eras.

The Book of Judges ends by reporting how the nation fell apart without any strong leaders. Overall, Israel was lawless: "In those days there was no king in Israel; everyone did what he thought best" (Jgs 21:25). It was time for a new chapter in the history of Israel: the beginning of the monarchy.

🌐 For Review

1. What was the key to Joshua's success in the conquest of the Promised Land? Give an example.

2. What was "the cycle of apostasy" during the period of the judges?

3. Who were the judges? Name three important ones and list their accomplishments.

🌐 For Reflection

Gideon claimed that he was too weak and unworthy to lead Israel. Describe a time when you thought you were unable to do something asked of you, but you came through it "with flying colors."

The Monarchy of Israel

First and Second Samuel report the history of Israel from the end of the period of the Judges until the last years of King David's reign, a period of about one hundred years (1075–970 BC). The religious theme is familiar: fidelity to God leads to success; disobedience leads to disaster. Reports on the eras of three prominent leaders follow in the next sections.

Israel's Final Judge

Samuel, a priest and prophet, was Israel's last and most significant judge. He was different from other judges in that his rule covered a wider range of tribes rather than the localized tribes ruled by other judges. Samuel was a special gift from God from the time of his birth. When his barren mother, Hannah, gave birth, she praised God for helping the powerless, confounding the mighty, and lifting up the lowly (see 1 Samuel 2:1–10). In the New Testament, Mary's hymn of praise, the Magnificat, echoes Hannah's prayer (see Luke 1:46–55).

Samuel ruled wisely as a just judge, helping the people turn from the worship of false gods. Toward the end of his life, though, the people clamored for a king who would rule them like the kings of other nations. Samuel warned that this request insulted YHWH, who was the sole King and Ruler of Israel. Their desire to be like other nations was wrong because

Samuel annointing David.

apostasy
The denial of God and the repudiation of faith.

ephod
Typically in the Old Testament an ephod was a vestment worn by Hebrew priests; however in the example connected with Gideon, an ephod was likely an idol fashioned to worship as a false god.

Israel was special, God's own people. Further, a king would draft Israelite children into his army and court, tax the people, and treat them like slaves. Despite these warnings, Samuel, with God's approval, anointed Saul to lead the Chosen People.

Choosing a King

Samuel assembled the tribes to choose a king by lot (see 1 Samuel 10:17–27). Saul was selected, a sign of divine choice. At first, he was successful in his military exploits and in his efforts to unite the tribes. However, as happened so often in Israelite history, the leader became prideful. Saul took upon himself the privileges of priests and disobeyed certain commands from God as relayed by Samuel. Saul paid a steep prince for his sins: the loss of the kingship to David, the second and greatest of all Israel's kings.

David was anointed by Samuel to replace Saul while Saul was still king. David, a son of a shepherd named Jesse, was "ruddy, a youth handsome to behold" (1 Sm 16:12). From that day on, "the spirit of the LORD rushed upon David" (1 Sm 16:13). In contrast, God's spirit departed from Saul, who began to suffer psychological torments, including severe mood shifts. Because of David's reputation as a skilled harpist, he was called to Saul's court to help sooth his troubled soul. In gratitude, Saul made David his armor-bearer. David was also a brave warrior as evidenced by the famous story of how he killed Goliath, the powerful Philistine giant, armed only with a sling (see 1 Samuel 17:1–58). This event foreshadowed David's future career as a military genius and political strategist. It also demonstrated his strong faith in God, an even more important quality for a future king of Israel.

At first, Saul loved David, but jealousy soon set in. The latter chapters of 1 Samuel tell of Saul's many attempts to kill David (see, for example 1 Samuel 18:1–6). However, they all failed due to David's friendship with Saul's son, Jonathan, one of the great friendships in human history. Jonathan remained loyal to David to death, intervening on David's behalf and even renouncing his own claim to the throne. Saul pursued David as an outlaw. David had a couple of opportunities to kill Saul, but did not do so because of his respect for God's anointed one. Eventually, the Philistines besieged Saul, killed his sons, and wounded the tragic king. In despair, Saul fell on his sword.

Israel's Greatest King

At the time of Saul's death, Israel was in turmoil. David became king of Judah in the southern portion of the kingdom, while one of Saul's sons ruled in the north. After a period of political intrigue and assassinations, David became the sole king of Israel, uniting all the tribes into a single nation. He ruled seven years over Judah and thirty-three over a united Israel. This union lasted until the end of his son Solomon's reign, the golden age of the monarchy. It was during this time that David made Jerusalem Israel's capital. The city did not belong to any tribe. Therefore, it was an ideal site for a unified kingdom. David brought the Ark of the Covenant to Jerusalem to show YHWH's abiding presence to the new nation.

SAMPLING SCRIPTURE

Read the following Scripture passages. Write your answers to each question.

- *Read 1 Samuel 16:1-20:42.*
  1. What is the difference in judgment between God and human beings?
  2. Discuss with examples three qualities you learn about David from reading these chapters.
  3. Discuss the friendship between David and Jonathan.

- *Read 2 Samuel 11:1-12:15.*
  1. What were David's sins?
  2. How did he own up to them?
  3. What was his punishment?

He also tried to build a Temple to house the Ark, but the prophet Nathan, speaking for God, stopped him. Instead, Nathan told how YHWH would establish a royal dynasty through him. This promise led to the belief of a Messiah who would save the Chosen People from their enemies. The Messiah is Jesus Christ, the son of David, who came to save not only the Jews, but all of humanity. David joyfully thanked God for his mercy:

> Great are you, Lord GOD! There is none like you and there is no God but you, just as we have heard it told. What other nation on earth is there like your people Israel, which God has led, redeeming it as his people? (2 Sm 7:22–23).

Israel's enemies were subdued by David, and he built Israel into a powerful nation. Good administration, an experienced army led by an excellent general, and the decline of other powers contributed to the achievements of his kingship.

King David also had his faults, including his adulterous affair with Bathsheba, the wife of Uriah, who was one of his soldiers (see 2 Samuel 11:1–12:25). David eventually plotted to have Uriah killed in battle and, after a period of mourning, married Bathsheba. She gave birth to a son who died soon afterwards. Another son born to them, Solomon, eventually succeeded David as king.

When confronted by the prophet Nathan over his outrageous sins of adultery and murder, David repented, begging for God's forgiveness. God did forgive him, but David's sins led to punishment in the form of a troubled household: a son raping a half-sister, a revengeful murder by her brother, and a rebellious son, Absalom, who turned against his father. Eventually, he was killed by David's forces after becoming entangled in a tree, leading to great mourning from David: "My son Absalom! My son, my son Absalom! If only I had died instead of you, Absalom, my son, my son!" (2 Sm 19:1).

Absalom hanging on the Oak Tree.

Though he had reunited the rebellious tribes, David was less effective at the end of his reign. Tribal rivalry was on the increase, and David's judgments were clouded by favoritism. In his old age, he was frail and unable to keep warm. In a final act, he publicly anointed his son Solomon to be his successor and instructed him to keep the terms of the covenant.

Yet without a doubt, David was Israel's greatest king. He unified the tribes and established Jerusalem as Israel's capital. The covenant YHWH made enabled his dynasty to last for four hundred years, until the Babylonian conquest in 586 BC. Despite his sinfulness, David remained ever loyal to God. He repented of his sins, though the sins had consequences, just as our sins have their effects even after we are forgiven. Later generations would look to David as someone God used in a special way to work out his divine plan.

A Divided Kingdom

Chapters 1–11 of 1 Kings tell of King Solomon's reign. The son of David and Bathsheba, Solomon was a powerful and wealthy king with few rivals in the ancient Mediterranean world. Known as a great builder, he had a generally peaceful and prosperous reign. His greatest achievement was building the Temple in Jerusalem, which became the center of Israel's religious life.

Solomon has a well-deserved reputation for his wisdom. At the start of his reign, he prayed to the Lord for an understanding heart to judge the people and a spirit to discern right from wrong. "God gave Solomon wisdom and exceptional understanding and knowledge, as vast as the sand on the seashore" (1 Kgs 5:9).

Despite his wisdom, Solomon engaged in foolish behavior as power and the splendor of his office ended up corrupting him. For example, he overextended himself economically by keeping a large harem of wives that he had to support in luxury. Supplying his large army and various building projects led to severe taxation and forced labor among the people. Furthermore, his many foreign wives introduced their gods and priests into the land. This led to many Israelites turning to false religions.

Severe times for Solomon and all of Israel followed. Rebellions plagued Solomon's kingdom. After his death in 922 BC, the united kingdom was split in two. Rehoboam, Solomon's son, ruled the southern **kingdom of Judah**, commanding the loyalty of only the tribe of Judah and some descendants of Simeon. It was numerically smaller than the northern kingdom, but was more tightly united.

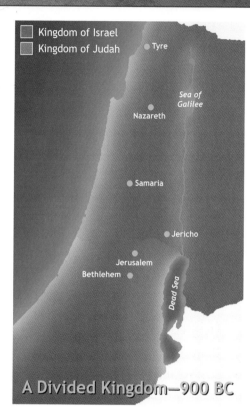

A Divided Kingdom—900 BC

Solomon's servant Jeroboam ruled the northern tribes. This was the **kingdom of Israel**, which included the ten tribes of the old alliance. Jeroboam centered worship at two ancient shrines—Dan and Bethel—not at the holy city of Jerusalem. Later Jews would explain Assyria's destruction of the northern kingdom by pointing to Israel's failure to worship God in Jerusalem. The weak King Ahab also allowed his wife, Jezebel, to erect altars to the pagan god Baal. This led to idolatry throughout the kingdom and the ultimate punishment of the northern kingdom, which was attacked and conquered by Assyria in 721 BC.

The history reported in the First and Second Books of Kings covers the period from the death of King David (ca. 970 BC), the split into two kingdoms in 922 BC, Assyria's destruction of the northern kingdom in

kingdom of Israel
The name of the northern kingdom that split with Judah after the death of Solomon. This revolt involved people and territory from ten of the twelve tribes.

kingdom of Judah
The name of the southern kingdom after the splitting of the monarchy. It included the territory originally belonging to just two of the twelve tribes, Judah and Benjamin.

721 BC, and the Babylonian captivity of the southern kingdom in 587–586 BC. This period of history shows that turning from true worship of God and neglecting and abusing the poor and helpless invite God's judgment. Yet, despite the sinfulness of the leaders and the people, the Lord never abandoned his people. He sent prophets to call Israel back to its true mission.

⊕ For Review

1. Why didn't Samuel think Israel should have a king?

2. Why was Saul jealous of David?

3. How did David's friendship with Jonathan help to preserve his life?

4. Name David's main accomplishments as king.

5. What did the Prophet Nathan say about David's sinful behavior?

6. Whom did David anoint as king?

7. What were some of the factors that led to the divided kingdom in 922 BC?

⊕ For Reflection

When God called out to Samuel in a dream, Samuel replied, "Speak, for your servant is listening" (1 Sm 3:10). Write a short reflection on how the Lord speaks to you in a personal way.

God Sends Prophets

Israel and Judah's decline as strong kingdoms, and the period of the Babylonian captivity, gave rise to Israel's greatest prophets. When the kings were unfaithful to the covenant, the people went astray. Everyone needed to hear the basic message of the prophets, that is, to repent and be saved. Failure to heed the words of the prophets would bring doom.

Who were the prophets? The basic Hebrew word for prophet was *nabi*, which means "one who speaks for another" or "mouthpiece." The first prophet of the Old Testament was Moses, who heard YHWH's message and then delivered it to the people.

Other prophets of the Old Testament are often classified in two groups: major and minor prophets. Those distinctions refer to the length of the books on which their names appear, not the importance of the message. Every prophetic message is important, and the basic message of the prophets is similar. The books of the major prophets—Isaiah, Jeremiah, Ezekiel, and Daniel—took up one scroll each. The twelve minor prophets were all written on the same scroll: Amos, Nahum, Hosea, Habakkuk, Micah, Zephaniah, Joel, Haggai, Jonah, Zechariah, Obadiah, and Malachi. Two additional short prophetic books—Lamentations and Baruch—traditionally have been associated with Jeremiah and placed in the Bible following the Book of Jeremiah.

The Basic Message of the Prophets

The prophets preached because they received an irresistible call from God, sometimes in dreams, visions, or internal inspiration. They preached their messages in many ways, often beginning with the formula, "Thus says the Lord." They also used stories, poetry, proverbs, satire, and other literary devices to share their message. In general, the message of the prophets proclaimed punishment if sins were not repented of, but prosperity if the people heeded God's warning. Typically the prophets went against the nation and the king, so they were often unpopular, and their lives were at times even threatened by the king. The prophet boldly prodded the people into repentance and "fear of the Lord" to avoid certain catastrophe. The sign of a true prophet was that his prophecy was fulfilled and his teaching was in line with doctrine about God. Old Testament prophets also preached the following themes:

1. *There is only one true God—YHWH*. God jealously loves his people. YHWH is the Creator of Heaven and earth; he is the Lord of all nations. There are no other gods.

2. *The one God is holy, and God demands that we renounce sin*. God's holiness goes beyond his creatures. Yet, the almighty God calls a special people to him and commands them to be holy. Sin, however, keeps people from God. Sin must be rooted out from the life of the nation and from individual lives. The covenant law guides Israel to holiness. It requires worship of God in truth *and* a passionate commitment to justice.

3. *The Messiah*. The prophets promised that God would not abandon the divine promises, even though the Chosen People deserved punishment. God would save a "remnant" of the People. He would set up an ideal kingdom ruled by an adopted son and royal vassal. This perfect earthly ruler would be the "anointed one," a descendant of David. Later prophets would see this earthly king as a Savior, a servant of YHWH. He would preach the law in truth and would even sacrifice his own life for the people. The messianic prophecies eventually converged in the life of Jesus of Nazareth. Jesus is the greatest prophet of all. As God's own Son, he reveals the Father's will perfectly.

The next sections provide brief background on the major prophets of the northern kingdom (Israel) and the southern kingdom (Judah).

Prophets of the Northern Kingdom

Elijah was an important ninth-century prophet of the northern kingdom. Elijah lived at the time the wicked King Ahab allowed pagan religion to take hold. Elijah called down a famine on the land in the hope that this would shock Israel back to fidelity. In a famous scene on top of Mount Carmel (see 1 Kings 18), he taunted the king's pagan prophets to ask their false gods to send down fire to consume a sacrifice. Predictably, their gods were powerless to do anything simply because they did not exist. YHWH, on the other hand, vindicated Elijah by sending fire to consume the sacrifice as well as the altar on which it lay. The people were awestruck, fell to their knees, and proclaimed, "The Lord is God! The Lord is God!" The famine ended, proving Elijah to be a true prophet.

Elijah had to flee for his life when the royal family tried to put him to death. God comforted and sustained Elijah, speaking to him in a "still small voice," assuring him that there would be a faithful remnant. Elijah was critical of the king's treatment of the poor and prophesied that his family would meet ruin, which it did.

Next to Moses, Elijah is the greatest of the Old Testament prophets. Because he was taken to Heaven in a whirlwind (see 2 Kings 2:9–18), the Jews believed that Elijah would, at the end of time, bring peace to the world. Elijah was viewed as the precursor and partner of the Messiah, interpreting properly the mysteries of the Law. The New Testament records the impact of this great prophet; for example, many people thought that Jesus himself was Elijah. The Gospels tell us that Elijah, along with Moses, was present at Jesus' Transfiguration. This symbolizes that Jesus fulfills the Law (represented by Moses) and the promises of the prophets (represented by Elijah). Jesus is God's covenant fulfilled. He is, in his person, the New Covenant.

The prophet Elisha succeeded Elijah. He is notable for the many miracles he performed, carrying on the work of Elijah. In fact, Elijah literally "threw his mantle" on the back of Elisha to transfer his power to his successor. Like Elijah, Elisha sided with the poor (see 2 Kings 4:1–2). The stories of Elijah and Elisha set the stage for two prophetic books that are likewise important to the Old Testament, the Books of Amos and Hosea. When King Jeroboam II and his successors came to power, they were religiously corrupt and morally bankrupt. They allowed the worship of the Baals and permitted the rich to exploit the poor. Amos and Hosea—two prophets of social justice—challenged them.

Though from the southern kingdom, Amos received God's call to preach in the north around 750 BC. His basic message was that the worship of God must show itself in concrete deeds of mercy and justice to the weak and the poor. Amos fearlessly warned that the many sins of the northern kingdom—sins like genocide, dishonesty, greed, sexual excess, robbery, violence, injustice, and pride—would lead to destruction. He called the nation to repent, saying:

> Hate evil and love good,
>   and let justice prevail at the gate;
> Then it may be that the LORD, the God of hosts,
>   will have pity on the remnant of Joseph.
> (Am 5:15)

Though Amos did not believe the people would repent in time to avert God's punishment, he still maintained hope. He foresaw that a small "remnant" would survive the impending destruction (Am 3:12). God would sift out the bad and raise up the kingdom of David (Am 9:11).

Predictably, Israel's leaders did not like Amos's message, so they banished him from the land (see Amos 7:12). His message remained to challenge Israel to repent before the day of doom would descend on the nation. Amos's message stands today to challenge all nations, especially rich ones, to serve the poor in their midst.

The prophet Hosea was a native of Israel, preaching from the last years of Amos' ministry (around 745 BC) until the fall of Israel. When his wife abandoned Hosea and became a temple prostitute, he drew on his painful relationship to describe YHWH's relationship with Israel. As his wife left him, so Israel became an unfaithful lover who ignored God's covenant love. Like Amos, Hosea saw Israel's worst crimes as idolatry and ruthless oppression of the poor.

Hosea's basic message was to accuse Israel of sin, infidelity to God, and crimes like perjury, lying, murder, theft, and adultery. Sin resulted from not truly knowing God and all the good he had done for the people. Not knowing God leads to false ritualism and exploiting the poor. Its antidote is clear:

> For it is love that I desire, not sacrifice,
> and knowledge of God rather than holocausts. (Hos 6:6)

Israel's crimes deserved punishment, so Hosea prophesied that the nation would perish. But God still loved the Chosen People with a steadfast love, like that of a husband to his wife, or a father to his son. God would never irrevocably abandon his people.

Assyria regained its former power, captured Babylon, and marched to Egypt. The Israelite kings foolishly tried to ally themselves with Egypt, leading to the northern kingdom's destruction in 722 BC. The king of Assyria deported over twenty-seven thousand Israelites into exile. These exiles were

Lost Tribes of Israel

The term "Lost Tribes of Israel" refers to the ten tribes from the northern kingdom that disappeared from history after being enslaved and exiled by the Assyrians.

Servant Songs

The name for four distinct poems accredited to Second Isaiah that deal with a specific individual, "the servant," whom God would use to usher in a glorious future.

SAMPLING SCRIPTURE

Write your answers to each question.

- Read 1 Kings 3, 6, 8.
  1. What is Solomon's request in 1 Kings 3:9?
  2. How does Solomon prove his wisdom in 3:16-28?
  3. How was the Temple decorated? What were some of the objects placed in the Temple?
  4. List three petitions Solomon prays for in his prayer of dedication.

- Read 1 Kings 17-19
  1. What does Elijah do for the widow?
  2. How did Elijah taunt the false prophets of Baal?
  3. Where did Elijah find the Lord God?

8   Read Amos 7-8; Hosea 1-3.
  1. What is the meaning of Amos's visions?
  2. List some of the sins of Gomer (Israel). Use biblical notes for more information.
  3. What does Hosea 3 say about the outcome of the unfaithful love affair between God and Israel?

the famous **Lost Tribes of Israel,** who eventually intermarried with the peoples of their new lands, thus losing their identity as God's Chosen People.

The fate of the northern kingdom was sealed. It had met its end. God had disciplined an unfaithful nation. The prophets of the southern kingdom, Judah, also warned of its dire fate.

Prophets of the Southern Kingdom

The prophets of Judah, the southern kingdom, preached to a smaller population than did the prophets of the north. Judah included the hills around Jerusalem and spread into the Negev desert. Politically, Judah found itself enmeshed in various struggles, alliances, and intrigues involving a series of kings who were little better than their northern counterparts. Solomon's son, Rehoboam, and grandson, Abijah, were unfaithful to the covenant. The next two kings were reformers who tried to keep the covenant alive. Their successors, however, married into the Ahab-Jezebel family, which led to murders and the same evils that befell the northern kingdom of Israel: idolatry, injustice, and religious worship marked by formalism rather than a godly spirit. God sent prophets to warn the nation. Prophets of this era were Isaiah, Micah, Jeremiah, and Ezekiel. Prophets known as "Second Isaiah" and "Third Isaiah" wrote at later times, both during and after the Babylonian Exile. Their works are also contained in the Book of Isaiah.

Isaiah

Isaiah was an influential Hebrew prophet. The book that bears his name is the largest of all prophetic books with sixty-six chapters. The Book of Isaiah is a collection of prophecies spanning 250 years. Chapters 1–39 come from the time of Isaiah the prophet himself, who preached from 742 to 700 BC. Chapters 40–55 are the work of a compassionate, anonymous prophet known as Second Isaiah, who wrote toward the end of the Babylonian captivity. Second Isaiah foretold the return of God's People to Jerusalem and that all the nations would come to recognize YHWH as the one, true God. These chapters contain the beautiful **Servant Songs** that meant so much to Jesus in his own ministry. Isaiah 55–66 is attributed to another prophet—Third Isaiah—and contains oracles from after the Exile.

The original prophet Isaiah is the one of whom the Scriptures tell some biographical details. He was the son of Amoz. Early in his life he had a vision of God in all his glory in the Jerusalem Temple. This vision convinced him that the Chosen People must imitate God's holiness by righteous living, true worship, and turning from the abuses that oppressed the poor. Repentance was a major theme preached by Isaiah during King Jotham's reign (742–735 BC). For example:

> Wash yourselves clean! Put away your misdeeds from before my eyes; cease doing evil; learn to do good. Make justice your aim: redress the wronged, hear the orphan's plea, defend the widow (Is 1:16–17).

Though repentance would help mend Judah's relationship with God, the prophet knew the people would not repent. In a beautiful story (see 5:1–7), the prophet compared the nation to a vineyard that God cultivated. Because the vines refused to bear fruit, the vinedresser (God) had to prune it so a future generation might bear fruit. This pruning was

 Promoting Justice

Complete the following project:

1. Select a current social justice issue in the news (e.g., poverty, prejudice, immigration reform, pollution of the environment, etc.). Read two recent articles on your topic, making sure that you reference at least one from a Catholic magazine, newspaper, or Web source.

2. Find the address of the "Letters to the Editor" section of your local newspaper or of a legislator or of a member of the executive branch of the government. Write a one-page letter to this person. Explain a few facts about the social justice issue you have chosen and why the problem concerns you as a young person. Suggest a course of action for the readers of the newspaper or the government official to whom you write.

3. Be sure to sign your letter and include your return address. If you write to a government official, you will probably receive a reply. If you write to a newspaper, your letter may be published. Share and discuss with your classmates any response you get as a result of this project.

Isaiah's image for the coming chastisement of both kingdoms.

When King Ahaz (735–715 BC) became a vassal to Assyria and even foolishly sacrificed his son to false gods, it looked like the Davidic covenant would end with Ahaz's death, but Isaiah promised a sign: "The virgin shall be with child, and bear a son, and shall name him Immanuel" (Is 7:14). This son would have many names: "Wonder-Counselor, God-Hero, Father-Forever, Prince of Peace" (Is 9:5). These titles call to mind the wisdom of Solomon, the valor and piety of David, and the many virtues of Moses and the patriarchs.

Isaiah's reference to *Immanuel* (meaning "God is with us") is really Jesus Christ, the Son of God, the promised Messiah. He was born of the Virgin Mary. Jesus Christ is the promised king who will rule forever, accomplishing God's will on earth as it is in Heaven.

During the reign of Hezekiah (715–687 BC), Judah was spared the fate of the northern kingdom when a plague struck the Assyrians as they were poised to attack Jerusalem. Even though Isaiah would prophesy that a new enemy—Babylon—would come into power after Hezekiah's death and sack Jerusalem and deport its people, he said the Lord would save a "remnant" of the nation after the time of judgment.

Micah

This message of hope was also preached by Isaiah's contemporary, the prophet Micah (see page 61). Although he warned of the coming judgment, Micah also told of a time when God would bring a universal reign of peace:

> They shall beat their swords
> into plowshares,
> and their spears into
> pruning hooks;
> One nation shall not raise the
> sword against another,
> nor shall they train for war
> again. (Mi 4:3)

Micah foretold a coming Messiah who would lead Israel to peace and justice. This anointed one would come from Bethlehem and would rule by the strength of the Lord. He would gather God's remnant—a righteous group who would survive the chastisement of the nation, the Babylonian captivity. This remnant would lead the nations to true worship of God.

SAMPLING SCRIPTURE

Read the following Scripture passage. Write your answers to each question.

- *Read Isaiah 1–7.*
  1. What will happen in the future age? (see Isaiah 2:4)
  2. To what does Isaiah compare the nation? (see Isaiah 3:16f)
  3. Interpret the allegory in Isaiah 5:1-7.

Jeremiah

Jeremiah was another Old Testament prophet who ministered to the southern kingdom. His message shouted the love of a God who desperately wanted the Chosen People to repent before catastrophe would strike the nation. Jeremiah's own life testified as forcefully as his spoken words. His life had its ups and downs, drama, faith and doubts, struggles with God, suffering at the hands of kings, and loneliness.

God's dramatic involvement in Jeremiah's life points out similarities between his life and the life of St. John the Baptist, forerunners of the Messiah. Both accomplished what many might have thought "impossible" if not for the grace of God (see Luke 1:37 and Jeremiah 32:27). The prophet Jeremiah also had much in common with the Lord himself:

- Jeremiah received his vocation and Jesus his mission in their mothers' wombs (compare Jeremiah 1:5 and Luke 1:26–38);

- their fellow citizens and family members rejected them and their message (compare Jeremiah 12:6 and Luke 4:24–29);

- both wept over Jerusalem (compare Jeremiah 8:23 and Luke 19:41); and

- both spoke of a new covenant (compare Jeremiah 31:31–33 and Luke 22:20).

An interesting feature of Jeremiah's teaching style was how he enacted in a living parable the messages he wished to deliver. A prime example was Jeremiah's never marrying, a rarity in the culture of his day. (This, also, was a similarity with Jesus.) Thus, Jeremiah became a living symbol of God's message that famine and slaughter would soon visit Jerusalem. This was no time to raise a family.

Another famous example was Jeremiah's comparing God to a potter (see Jeremiah 19). As a potter reshapes a flawed work, so YHWH would mold the nation in his hands. Unless the people would repent, God would break the nation through punishment. In a dramatic gesture, Jeremiah shattered a jug in front

SAMPLING SCRIPTURE

Read the following Scripture passages in the Book of Jeremiah. Write your answers to each question.

1. What evils does Jeremiah describe? Why does the nation deserve punishment? (see Jeremiah 5)
2. Why is God not happy with the way worship is taking place? (see Jeremiah 7)
3. Does Jeremiah prophesy good news or bad news? Explain. (see Jeremiah 31)
4. Interpret the following "living symbols" in these verses:
   * loincloth (Jer 13:1–11)
   * potter's vessel (Jer 18:1–12)
   * smashed clay pot (Jer 19:1–15)

of the elders and priests. This served to warn the nation that God would destroy those who had abandoned him.

Jeremiah consistently preached a message of repentance, warning that the people's sins would lead to sorrow and death. His message was ignored, and Jerusalem fell to Babylon. But he also offered hope. While the people were suffering in Babylon, he told of how God would make a new covenant with his people:

> "The days are coming," says the LORD, "when I will make a new covenant with the house of Israel and the house of Judah. It will not be like the covenant I made with their fathers. . . . I will place my law within them, and write it upon their hearts; I will be their God, and they shall be my people. . . . All, from least to greatest, shall know me," says the LORD, "for I will forgive their evildoing and remember their sin no more." (Jer 31:31–34)

This famous passage gave great hope to the suffering Chosen People. It told them that God would show the initiative, giving people a new heart so that they could be open to him. Knowledge of God would be from within; it would be personal. It would no longer be written on tablets of stone (as in Exodus) or in law books (as in Deuteronomy). God would touch a person's heart so the Lord may live within. God's forgiveness—an essential feature of the New

Covenant—would make everything new. Those words of Jeremiah are a prophecy of the covenant established by Jesus. The Savior's Life, Death, and Resurrection inaugurated the New Covenant.

The Book of Jeremiah describes many of his sufferings as God's messenger: his brothers attacked him; fellow citizens thought he was a traitor; the leaders wanted to kill him. Jeremiah begged the Lord for help. He criticized God for choosing him. But a fire burned in his heart that forced him to speak on God's behalf. His faith sustained him because he knew God would sustain him:

> But the LORD is with me,
> like a mighty champion:
> my persecutors will stumble,
> they will not triumph. (Jer 20:11)

Ezekiel

The life of the prophet Ezekiel overlapped with Jeremiah's, but from a different perspective. Ezekiel was deported to Babylon with the exiles while Jeremiah remained in Jerusalem until he was taken by force to Egypt by a group of Jews who were sympathetic to assistance being offered by the Egyptians in their attempt to free the exiles from Babylonian rule.

Ezekiel exhibited bizarre behavior, reported fantastic visions, and used symbolic actions to communicate his message. Born into a priestly family, he placed great value on the Temple and its worship.

The prophet's message is recorded in Leviticus 17–26 and the Book of Ezekiel—especially the need to keep the Sabbath and follow the law of holiness. He preached from Babylonian territory, where he was exiled before the Babylonian captivity. Ezekiel 1 tells how in 593 BC he had a fantastic vision of God involving a chariot and four winged creatures, each having four faces, representing the attributes of God: courage (lion), strength (ox), swiftness (eagle), intelligence (man). This vision struck Ezekiel dumb. A vision of God's glory was too much for him to take in. Eventually, God instructed Ezekiel to eat a scroll. The scroll (which contained God's Word) tasted as sweet as honey, but the message it held fell on the deaf ears of a stubborn people.

Before the fall of Jerusalem, Ezekiel censured the people of God and the nations for their sinful conduct. He engaged in symbolic actions to try to shock the people into turning from their sins. One involved cutting his hair and dividing it up as a sign of the fate of the people (see Ezekiel 6:1–4). He also pantomimed the actions symbolic of the exile (see Ezekiel 12:1–20). Nevertheless, Jerusalem did fall, the Temple was destroyed, and a demoralized, defeated nation joined Ezekiel in exile. The tone of his prophecies changed at that point from warning and despair to one of hope and consolation. For example, Ezekiel 33–39 tells of a new king, a shepherd who would make a covenant of peace with the people, of a time when God would restore the nation. In a famous vision, Ezekiel reported standing in a field of dry bones. His interpretation of the dream gave great hope to the nation:

> These bones are the whole house of Israel. . . . Thus says the Lord GOD: "O my people, I will open your graves and have you rise from them, and bring you back to the land of Israel. Then you shall know that I am the LORD, when I open your graves and have you rise from them, O my people! I will put my spirit in you that you may live, and I will settle you upon your land; thus you shall know that I am the LORD. I have promised, and I will do it, says the LORD." (Ez 37:11–14)

SAMPLING SCRIPTURE

Read the following Scripture passages in the Book of Ezekiel. Write your answers to each question.

1. Describe Ezekiel's vision of the Lord's chariot. What else happens to the prophet? What is his function supposed to be? (see Ezekiel 1-3)
2. Interpret the symbolic actions Ezekiel demonstrates. (see Ezekiel 4-5)
3. How does Ezekiel make a point on personal responsibility? (see Ezekiel 18)

He also prophesied the building of a new Temple, a New Jerusalem, and the nation's return. Ezekiel is often considered to be the "father of Judaism." His emphasis on God's holiness, and obeying the rules of the Holiness Code, greatly influenced the Judaism that emerged after the Exile.

🌐 For Review

1. Summarize the basic message of the prophets.

2. Describe Elijah's role in Jewish history, for example, his impact on New Testament times.

3. What was the important theme in the prophetic message of Amos?

4. Discuss two themes in the preaching of the original prophet Isaiah.

5. Define *Immanuel*.

6. What was the meaning of the promise by various prophets concerning "the remnant"?

7. List several ways the life of the prophet Jeremiah prefigured that of Jesus.

8. Explain the meaning of the prophet Ezekiel's visions of God and the dry bones.

🌐 For Reflection

- Which prophet described in this section most resonates with you? Why?

- In the large picture of Salvation History, how were the prophets necessary to prepare the way for Jesus?

- In what way is the Church a remnant of Israel?

The Babylonian Exile

Jerusalem and the Temple were destroyed in 586 BC, and the Babylonian King Nebuchadnezzar deported most of its residents to Babylon. Those left behind in Jerusalem were poor, weak, and leaderless; some of them fled to Egypt for safety. One tradition reports that Jeremiah was stoned to death there.

For pious Jews, living in a foreign land was difficult. Their religion was impacted when the Chosen People began to assimilate through intermarriage. This led to the loss of identify as God's special people. This is exactly what happened to the Israelites who were deported by the Assyrians in the eighth century BC. To distinguish themselves from their captors, the Jewish exiles studied the Law, observed the Sabbath, and continued the practice of circumcision. Without a Temple, there was no place for sacrifice, so they met in **synagogues** (prayer houses), where they studied and prayed together. Scribes gathered Israel's oral traditions and committed them to writing as a permanent record of God's love toward his people. Many of these texts became part of the Jewish Scriptures.

synagogues
Meeting places for study and prayer introduced by the Pharisees to foster study of the Law and adherence to the covenant code.

The Message of Second Isaiah

An anonymous author, Second Isaiah, writing in the spirit of the prophet Isaiah around 550 BC, encouraged the Jews in exile with a hope-filled message. He understood that the Babylonian Empire was on the verge of collapse and that the tolerant leader of the Persian Empire, Cyrus, would soon conquer the Babylonians. Perhaps then the Chosen People would be permitted to return. In fact, in 538 BC, this scenario played out, and God's remnant began to journey back to Jerusalem.

In the meantime, Second Isaiah offered great consolation to a suffering people. God instructed through the prophet that Israel had paid the price for its sins and that the Lord was coming to save his people:

> Comfort, give comfort to my people,
> says your God.
> Speak tenderly to Jerusalem,
> and proclaim to her
> that her service is at an end,
> her guilt is expiated. . . .
> A voice cries out:
> In the desert prepare the way of the LORD!
> Make straight in the wasteland
> a highway for our God!
> Every valley shall be filled in,
> every mountain and hill
> shall be made low. . . .
> Then the glory of the LORD shall be revealed.
> (Is 40:1–5)

The prophet reassured the people that God loved them. Second Isaiah wrote of the love of God as that of a mother for her child:

> Can a mother forget her infant,
> be without tenderness for
> the child of her womb?
> Even should she forget,
> I will never forget you.
> See, upon the palms of my hands I have
> written your name. (Is 49:15–16a)

Cyrus of Persia was the Lord's instrument to free the exiles in a new exodus, but Second Isaiah made it clear that it was the all-powerful, Creator God, the source of everything, who was the true deliverer. This one, true God chose the Israelites for a specific task: to serve as a beacon of light to attract other nations to the one true God: "I will make you a light to the nations, that my Salvation may reach to the ends of the earth" (Is 49:6).

Second Isaiah contains four distinct poems that deal with a specific individual, "the servant," whom God would use to usher in a glorious future. They are known as the Suffering Servant songs. In these songs, the servant's identity is not clearly revealed. Some hold that the servant represents the nation of Israel itself, a picture of an ideal people who embody the true values of the nation. Another theory suggests the servant is the prophet himself or someone like Jeremiah. Christians, however, see in these servant passages prophetic images of Jesus, the Servant whose sufferings redeemed all people. Jesus uniquely interpreted the Messianic way to Salvation as the path of

SAMPLING SCRIPTURE

Read the following Scripture passages. Write your answers to each question.

Read Isaiah 40-44; 52:13-53:12.

1. Transcribe at least five verses that speak of God's mercy and tenderness to the Chosen People. What will happen in the future age (2:4)?
2. Note three ways the Servant Song applies to Jesus.

suffering and service and not the easy road of glory and domination. Some main themes of the Suffering Servant songs are as follows:

1. The first song (Is 42:1–4) speaks of God's chosen one who will bring justice to the world and treat the bruised reed, Israel, tenderly.
2. The second song (Is 49:1–6) tells how God chose the servant before his birth. The servant's strength is his prophetic word—"a sharp-edged sword"—that will bring spiritual light and Salvation to the nations.
3. The third song (Is 50:4–9) describes how God's special messenger runs into resentment. People beat and spit on him and pluck his beard. Yet the servant suffers quietly. He knows that God will vindicate him and that his enemies will disintegrate, like moth-eaten cloth.
4. The final song (Is 52:13–53:12) has remarkable parallels to Jesus Christ's suffering, Death, and Resurrection. The servant, perhaps representing Israel, is brutally treated. He is like a lamb led to slaughter, the one God chose to bear the guilt of the world's sins. Without complaint, the servant accepts a painful, humiliating death so that through him the world can be saved.

EXPLAINING THE FAITH

Why should Catholics bother reading the Old Testament?

The Old Testament is important to Catholics for several reasons. The books are divinely inspired. They are heard in the liturgy and contain many beautiful prayers. The books of the Old Testament are a testimony to the entire story of our Salvation, including a prophecy of the coming of Jesus Christ, our Redeemer. Also, there is unity to the Old and New Testaments. The New Testament has to be read in light of the Old Testament. An old saying put it this way: "the New Testament lies hidden in the Old and the Old Testament is unveiled in the New."

These magnificent servant songs stress God's love for all people. Second Isaiah delivered one of the Old Testament's most important messages: our God is a saving God, a Lord who forgives and forgets our sins.

For Review

1. Identify Second Isaiah and discuss two themes in his preaching.

2. Who is the Suffering Servant?

3. List three Messianic prophecies treated in this chapter. Discuss how they apply to Jesus Christ.

For Reflection

Isaiah 49:15-16 compares God's love to that of a mother. Write a short reflection on what a mother's love means to you and how God's love mirrors that love.

Return and Recommitment

The Exile taught the Chosen People an important lesson: God would not tolerate idolatry and pagan worship. After the return to the Holy Land, a purified Judaism was more faithful to its vocation of witnessing to the nations by keeping the Law. Led by Zerubbabel, a descendant of King David, and the priest Joshua, the returning Jews rebuilt the Temple and Jerusalem, reestablished the worship of YHWH, and renewed the covenant. In rebuilding the Temple, they refused the help of the **Samaritans**, a mixed population of Israelites and Assyrians who continued to worship God at Dan and Bethel. Mutual distrust between the Jews and Samaritans festered for centuries and was evident in the time of Jesus.

Many exiles freely decided to remain in Babylon, Egypt, and elsewhere. Though they looked to Jerusalem for leadership, paid taxes to the Temple, and made pilgrimages to the Holy City, they were more open to **Gentile** ideas. In fact, because more Jews lived outside Palestine than within, the synagogue became an even more important institution. **Rabbis** and **scribes** became increasingly important religious roles both within and outside the Holy Land.

Postexilic Judaism

Back in Jerusalem, the decades after the return were a time of consolidation, reflection, and recommitment. Prophets like Haggai, Zechariah, and Malachi wrote about issues such as the rebuilding of the Temple, the role of priests, and proper worship. Strong personalities like Nehemiah, the Persian-appointed governor of Judah, and Ezra, the reformer-scribe, helped create postexilic Judaism. Their basic tasks were to rebuild the Temple and renew the covenant in the hearts of the people. The Old Testament took on its present form as scribes compiled and edited earlier texts and oral traditions. The Pentateuch was completed, and

Samaritans
Descendants of a mixed population of Israelites who survived the Assyrian deportations and various pagan settlers imported after the northern kingdom fell. They worshiped YHWH on Mt. Gerizim but only considered the Pentateuch inspired. Ordinary Jews of Jesus' day despised the Samaritans.

Gentile
A term for non-Jews.

rabbi
Hebrew word for a Jewish master or teacher of the Torah.

scribes
People trained to write using the earliest forms of writing before literacy was widespread.

the historical books reached their final form. The works of the prophets were organized. This period also produced some of its own writings like the historical books of Chronicles, Ezra, Nehemiah, and various other prophetic books.

Ezra was a priest and religious reformer of this period who likely came to Jerusalem around 398 BC. He helped solidify Jewish identity by forbidding mixed marriages and unnecessary mingling with foreign nations. He also promulgated the Torah, making it the constitution of Judaism. Fidelity to the Torah set the spiritual tone of the postexilic Jewish community and helped Judaism survive to our own day.

The postexilic prophets in Judah included Zechariah, Haggai, Third Isaiah, Joel, and Malachi. Zechariah predicted a Messianic age to come. Third Isaiah (the author of the Book of Isaiah 56–66) looked to a future day when God's light would shine on the Jewish nation and attract all people to God. The vocation of a restored Jerusalem was to bring glad tidings to the lowly, heal the brokenhearted, proclaim liberty to captives, release to prisoners, and comfort to those who mourn (see Isaiah 61:1–3). This is as a reference to Jesus Christ who did all of this and more: the Salvation of all peoples.

The prophet Joel preached a message of repentance, believing that a locust plague that devastated the country was a sign of God's punishment on the people (see Joel 1). But he also told of a future "day of the LORD," when God will battle all the evil forces (see Joel 2). This Day of Judgment will mark an entirely new beginning, a fresh creation of the world when God's Spirit will be poured out on all humanity. The Church understood that this prophecy was fulfilled with the Descent of the Holy Spirit on Pentecost.

Fidelity to the covenant and its teachings are hallmarks of the Book of Malachi. The prophet criticized priests who offered blemished animals instead of clean ones as the Law required. He also denounced Jewish men who divorced their wives to marry wealthy Gentile women. It is fitting that the Book of Malachi is the last book in the Old Testament canon. In the last two verses of the Old Testament, Malachi prophesied a coming messenger (Elijah the prophet) who would announce the Day of the Lord on which God will usher in his reign. John the Baptist, often called the last Old Testament prophet, announced the coming of Jesus Christ, the Messiah and Savior who would usher in God's Kingdom.

Jewish History Prior to the Birth of Christ

Under the Persians, the Jews were not required to practice the official Persian religion, **Zoroastrianism**. By the end of the second century BC, some of the revealed matters of faith like angels and fallen angels (demons), and Satan could also be found in Persian writings. In the Book of Daniel and the Second Book of Maccabees, references are made to the

 Power and Majesty

The promises of Israel's restoration are expressed in Isaiah 43:1-28. Read the entire chapter, and pick out verses that express God's power and majesty. Then do one of the following:

1. Write a poem or song that describes God's glory.
2. Design a collage or PowerPoint presentation that illustrates the passage from Isaiah 43.
3. Report on a contemporary group of people or an individual who has rebounded from pride and sinfulness to reclaim the righteousness God intends for them.

resurrection of the dead and divine punishment or reward for an evil or good life lived on earth.

Alexander the Great toppled the Persian Empire in 334 BC. In his conquered territories, he established a cultural union of East and West known as **Hellenism**. He wished all his conquered people to be one, with classical Greek culture serving as the unifying force. Thus, he introduced common (*koine*) Greek as the official language. The Septuagint was the *koine* Greek translation of the Old Testament that took place around 275 BC in Alexandria, Egypt.

After Alexander's death, two competing families fought over his empire: the Ptolemies of Egypt and the Seleucids of Syria. The Ptolemies ruled Palestine from 323–198 BC. Their rule was generally benevolent with no concerted effort to impose Hellenistic culture. However, while most Jews in Egypt remained loyal to the Law and the Jerusalem Temple, some did change their Jewish names to Greek ones and adopted Greek forms of government and other Greek customs. The Book of Wisdom, written in Alexandria in Greek, was influenced by Greek philosophers. Back in the Holy Land, some Jews also adopted Greek customs while others deplored any assimilation as a desertion of the faith of their ancestors.

The Seleucids ruled Palestine from 198–63 BC. In general, the Seleucid rulers, especially Antiochus IV (175–164 BC), tried to impose unity on their subjects. He wanted to build a mighty army and force Greek culture on the people. He twice robbed the Temple and forbade Jews to engage in religious practices central to their faith: circumcision, Sabbath observances, Temple sacrifices, and abstinence from pork. Worst of all, he engaged in what the Jews termed "the abomination of desolation" by installing a statue of Zeus on the altar of holocausts in the Temple (167 BC).

His cruel rule led to a revolt by the Maccabee family, headed by Mattathias and his five sons. Judas Maccabaeus (meaning "hammer") was a remarkable leader who recaptured Jerusalem and rededicated the Temple in 164 BC. The December Feast of **Hanukkah**, the festival of lights, commemorates this event in Jewish history.

Under the Maccabees, the **Hasmonean Dynasty** formed. It gov-

erned the Jews until 63 BC, the time of the Roman conquest under General Pompey. The dynasty brought glory and political freedom to the Jews. It extended the nation's borders and led to conversions and the founding of Jewish communities. Unfortunately, the regime became corrupt. When Palestine fell to the Romans, the Hasmoneans were deposed and a puppet

Zoroastrianism
The official religion of the Persian Empire, which understood the universe to be caught in a constant struggle between light and darkness.

Hellenism
The diffusion of Greek culture throughout the Mediterranean world after the conquest of Alexander the Great.

Hanukkah
The Jewish Feast of Dedication, which celebrates the recovery and purification of the Temple from the Syrians in 164 BC. It is an eight-day feast that takes place during December near Christmas. Also known as the Feast of Lights, Hanukkah is normally celebrated with gift giving.

Hasmonean Dynasty
Descendants of the Maccabees who ruled in Judea after the ousting of the last of the Syrians in 141 BC until the establishment of Roman authority in 63 BC. John Hyrcanus was the first ruler of this dynasty and ruled until 128 BC.

SAMPLING SCRIPTURE

Read the following Scripture passages. Write your answers to each question.

- *Read Zechariah 8:1-23.*
  1. Note five things that will take place in the Messianic age.

- *Read either the Book of Joel or the Book of Malachi.*
  1. Read the introduction to the book that appears in your Bible.
  2. Briefly summarize what the book is about.
  3. Copy at least five verses that speak a powerful message to you.

king was appointed. Herod the Great served as the king of Judea from 37–4 BC. He was in some ways a brilliant ruler who was known for his great building projects, including the rebuilding of the magnificent Jerusalem Temple. He was also a bloodthirsty ruler who called for the execution of male Jewish children. Some time toward the end of his reign, perhaps between 6 and 4 BC, one of the young boys who escaped Herod's wrath, Jesus Christ, was born in Bethlehem. The birth of the Messiah fulfilled all the Old Testament prophecies. The details and meaning of Christ's life on earth is the subject of the remaining chapters of this book.

For Review

1. Identify Ezra. Discuss two of his accomplishments.

2. What is meant by the "abomination of desolation"?

3. Who were the Maccabees? What did they accomplish for the Jewish nation?

4. What was the Hasmonean Dynasty? When did it fall?

5. Name both a positive and negative characteristic of Herod as a leader.

For Reflection

How does your religion contradict the ruling government and society? In what ways have you been assimilated by the government and society in opposition to your religion? In what ways have you opposed them?

The Maccabean Revolt

The Maccabean Revolt lasted for a total of three years. After that time the Temple was cleansed, and the Jews gathered to celebrate its rededication with the Feast of Hanukkah. Also, Judas Maccabeus was successful in negotiating a peace treaty with the Syrians. Because of the revolt, the Jews remained an independent nation until 63 BC.

Read the cited Scripture passages from the First Book of Maccabees. Answer each of the questions below.

1. What was the pact the Jewish Hellenizers initiated with the Gentiles? (Read 1 Maccabees 1:11-15.)

2. What were some of the crimes Antiochus committed against the Jews? (Read 1 Maccabees 1:20-62.)

3. Describe the incident that led to Mattathias's revolt. (Read 1 Maccabees 2:15-30.)

4. What led to Mattathias's decision to fight against the Gentiles? (Read 1 Maccabees 2:31-41.)

Main Ideas

- God's friendship with the Chosen People models the type of relationship we should have with God and others (p. 100).

- Joshua led the Israelites into the Promised Land; the historical record of this is provided in the Book of Joshua and the Book of Judges (p. 101).

- Judges were local tribal leaders who took special military roles when their tribes were threatened by hostile neighbors (pp. 101–103).

- A cycle of apostasy affected the Israelites while always revealing God's faithful love for them (p. 102).

- Israel's final judge, Samuel, ruled wisely and reluctantly agreed to help choose a king (pp. 103–104).

- Saul, Israel's first king, was affected by the sin of pride (p. 104).

- Israel's greatest king was King David, uniting the tribes into a single nation (pp. 104–105).

- Though David was plagued by sinfulness himself, the prophet Nathan foretold that God would form a royal dynasty through David, leading to a belief that a Messiah would come to save the Chosen People (p. 105).

- Solomon succeeded King David; though known for his wisdom, he engaged in foolish behavior as the power and splendor of his office ended up corrupting him (pp. 105–106).

- After Solomon's death, the kingdom was divided in two: the kingdom of Judah and the kingdom of Israel (pp. 105–106).

- God sent prophets with the basic message: repent and be saved. Other themes were that there is only one true God, God is holy and demands that we renounce sin, and a Messiah would save the Chosen People (pp. 107–108).

- Prophets like Elijah, Elisha, Amos, and Hosea warned the people of the northern kingdom of their sinfulness (pp. 108–110).

- Assyria deported many of the Israelites into exile, effectively ending the Lost Tribes of Israel's identity as God's Chosen People (pp. 109–110).

- The prophets of the southern kingdom, especially Isaiah, Micah, Jeremiah, and Ezekiel, warned of doom that would eventually come with the impending Babylonian exile (pp. 110–116).

- Micah foretold a coming Messiah would lead Israel to peace and justice; he would come from Bethlehem and gather God's remnant would survive Babylonian captivity (p. 112).

- During the Babylonian Exile, the Chosen People rededicated themselves to study and prayer, especially in synagogues (p. 116).

- Second Isaiah consoled the people and foretold a Suffering Servant who would come to save the people (pp. 117–119).

- In Postexilic Jerusalem, the people rebuilt the Temple as well as renewed the covenant in the hearts of the people. The Old Testament took on its present form (pp. 119–120).

- Zoroastrianism and Hellenism both influenced the Jews in the centuries prior to the birth of Christ (pp. 120–121).

- The Maccabean Revolt brought a brief period of Jewish independence (pp. 121–122).

Chapter 5 Quick View

Terms, People, Places

Complete each sentence by choosing the correct answer from the list of terms below. You will not use all of the terms.

judges   ephod
kingdom of Judah   kingdom of Israel
Lost Tribes of Israel   Servant Songs
synagogues   Samaritans
Gentile   rabbis
scribes   Zoroastrianism
Hellenism   Hanukkah
Hasmonean Dynasty   idolatry

1. The Israelites' worship of false gods can be defined by the sin of _____.
2. The diffusion of Greek culture throughout the world after the conquests of Alexander the Great is called _____.
3. The incident surrounding the deportation of Israelites by the Assyrians led to the Israelites' permanent loss of identity or to what is called the _____.
4. Without a Temple for worship, the Israelites met, prayed, and studied in _____.
5. The _____ was a period of time when the Jews were in governance of the Holy Land.
6. _____ was the official Persian religion that influenced Judaism near the second century BC.
7. The _____ was the name for the southern kingdom.
8. The _____ of Second Isaiah spoke of a Messiah who would usher in God's glorious Kingdom.
9. _____ were a mixed raced of people who worshiped God at Dan and Bethel, not Jerusalem.
10. The term _____ is used to describe a person who is not Jewish.

Primary Source Quotations

Restoration in the Lord

God foresaw that the Temple would be destroyed, and he said, "While the Temple exists, and you bring sacrifices, the Temple atones for you; when the Temple is not there, what shall atone for you? Busy yourselves with the words of the Law, for they are equivalent to sacrifices, and they will atone for you."

—Tanhuma (from the Jewish Talmud)

Return, O Israel, to the LORD your God:
    you have collapsed through
    your guilt.
Take with you words,
    and return to the LORD;
Say to him, "Forgive all iniquity,
and receive what is good, that we
may render
    as offerings the bullocks from
    our stalls.
Assyria will not save us,
    nor shall we have horses to mount;
We shall say no more, 'Our god,'
    to the work of our hands;
for in you the orphan finds compassion."

—Hosea 14:2–4

The Suffering Servant Who Offers Redemption

Who would believe what we have heard?
To whom has the arm of the LORD been revealed?
He grew up like a sapling before him,
    like a shoot from the parched earth;
There was in him no stately bearing to make us look at him,
    nor appearance that would attract us to him.

He was spurned and avoided by men,
    a man of suffering, accustomed to
    infirmity,
One of those from whom men hide their
faces,
    spurned, and we held him in no
    esteem.

Yet it was our infirmities that he bore,
    our sufferings that he endured,
While we thought of him as stricken,
    as one smitten by God and afflicted.
But he was pierced for our offenses,
    crushed for our sins,
Upon him was the chastisement that
makes us whole,
    by his stripes we were healed.

—Isaiah 53:1–5

The Promulgation of the Feast of Christ the King

It has long been a common custom to give to Christ the metaphorical title of "King," because of the high degree of perfection whereby he excels all creatures. So he is said to reign "in the hearts of men," both by reason of the keenness of his intellect and the extent of his knowledge, and also because he is very truth, and it is from him that truth must be obediently received by all mankind. He reigns, too, in the wills of men, for in him the human will was perfectly and entirely obedient to the Holy Will of God, and further by his grace and inspiration he so subjects our free-will as to incite us to the most noble endeavors. He is King of hearts, too, by reason of his "charity which exceedeth all knowledge." And his mercy and kindness which draw all men to him, for never has it been known, nor will it ever be, that man be loved so much and so universally as Jesus Christ. But if we ponder this matter more deeply, we cannot but see that the title and the power of King belongs to Christ as man in the strict and proper sense too. For it is only as man that he may be said to have received from the Father "power and glory and a kingdom," since the Word of God, as con-substantial with the Father, has all things in common with him, and therefore has necessarily supreme and absolute dominion over all things created.

—Pope Pius XI, December 11, 1925

Who or what do you pledge allegiance to in your life? How strong is your allegiance to Christ the King?

Ongoing Assignments

As you cover the material in this chapter, choose and complete at least three of these assignments.

1. Prepare a PowerPoint presentation of some famous Old Testament persons who have been depicted in major works of art through the ages. Consult the following website for resources: www.textweek.com/art/art.htm.

2. Read Matthew 1:1–6. What connection does Rahab have with Jesus? Read Joshua 2 and James 2:24–25. Why is she praised?

3. Report on various theories as to what happened to the Ark of the Covenant at the time of the Babylonian conquest of Jerusalem and the destruction of Solomon's Temple in 586 BC.

4. Read and report on one of the following:

   • Thomas Storck's, "The Old Testament Messianic Hope," at www.ignatius insight.com/features2005/tstorck_ otmessiah_dec05.asp

   • Virginia Smith's, "Israel vs. Judah: The Chosen People Divided," at www .americancatholic.org/Newsletters/SFS/ an0600.asp

5. Read the section in chapter 2 of the United States Catholic Bishops' Pastoral Statement *Economic Justice for All* (www .usccb.org/sdwp/international/Economic JusticeforAll.pdf), which cites biblical perspectives on the issue. Write out ten Old Testament quotations cited by the bishops.

6. Prepare a report, including illustrations, on the design of Solomon's Temple.

7. Report on what happened to the walls of Jericho at the time of Joshua's invasion of the Holy Land. Use the following website to get started: www.bibleplaces.com/ jericho.htm.

8. Write a profile of one of the prophets.

9. Compose your own version of the "Vineyard Song" (Is 5:1–7). Create an image for our nation and God in relationship to it. Does our nation need punishment? Why or why not?

10. In the style of Jeremiah or Ezekiel, create a small pantomime or skit that prophetically calls attention to the immorality of a contemporary social issue like abortion, consumerism, poverty, pollution, or war.

11. On poster board, create a list of kings of both the northern and southern kingdoms. Write a short profile on one of the kings. Helpful links include:

   - www.infoplease.com/ipa/A0197620 .html

   - www.geocities.com/thekingsofisrael/ kings.html

Prayer

The Book of Psalms was the hymnbook of ancient Israel since most of the Psalms were poems meant to be sung, typically as part of the Temple's worship service. Over a period of almost a thousand years, many anonymous poets were responsible for the writing of the Psalms. Seventy-three Psalms are attributed to David himself, a gifted poet and musician. King David was the individual responsible for introducing music into the sanctuary and likely did compose some of the Psalms. However, many ascribed to him were composed by poets who were active during the rule of other kings in David's line.

The Psalms include hymns of praise and thanksgiving. Others petition God directly, either individually or communally. Still others are prophetic oracles or take up problems of human living. A special category of Psalms sings of a coming Messiah, for example, Psalms 2, 72, and 110, the ones the New Testament quotes most frequently.

Prayerfully reflect on these verses of Psalm 54, which appeal to God for justice. Its message is timeless.

O God, by your name save me.
By your strength defend my cause.
O God, hear my prayer.
Listen to the words of my mouth.
The arrogant have risen against me;
the ruthless seek my life;
they do not keep God before them.
God is present as my helper;
the Lord sustains my life.

—Psalm 54:3–6

- *Reflection*: In what area of your life do you most need the Lord's help?

- *Resolution*: Reflect on how you treat your classmates, family members, and coworkers. Do you treat them with respect and give them what they deserve? If not, do something in the coming weeks to help right any wrong you might have committed against someone.

THE SYNOPTIC GOSPELS

*When Jesus went into the region of Caesarea Philippi
he asked his disciples, "Who do people say that the Son of Man is?"
They replied, "Some say John the Baptist, others Elijah,
still others Jeremiah or one of the prophets." He said to them,
"But who do you say that I am?" Simon Peter said in reply,
"You are the Messiah, the Son of the living God."*

—Matthew 16:13-16

Putting Others First

It is important to put others ahead of our own wishes and desires, just as Jesus did.

Introducing the Synoptic Gospels

The Gospels of Matthew, Mark, and Luke have much in common and differ significantly from the Gospel of John.

Important Events in the Early Life of Christ

Many of the mysteries of Christ's life were revealed at his birth and through his hidden family life in Nazareth.

Followers of Jesus

Jesus' life-giving words and saving deeds drew many people to him as followers; he chose Twelve Apostles to assist him in his work.

Important Events in Jesus' Public Life

Each event in Jesus' public life—from his Baptism through his Passion, Death, and Resurrection—teach great meaning of a Father's love for his Son and for all of humanity.

Jesus Proclaims the Gospel

Jesus taught in words and deeds a message centered on the Kingdom of God.

Putting Others First

Western Oregon softball player Sara Tucholsky had never hit a home run over the fence in all her many years of playing the game. Central Washington player Mallory Holtman had hit many home runs; in fact, she held her school's all-time record.

When the teams played in a conference tournament game in 2008, it was easily the biggest game of the season. When the diminutive Tucholsky came to the plate in the second inning, no one expected her to hit a ball over the fence, but she did. "The first pitch I took, it was a strike. And then I really don't remember where the home run pitch was at all; I just remember hitting it, and I knew it was gone."

In her excitement to round the bases, Tucholsky missed first base. Her coach told her to come back and touch it. That's when an unusual set of circumstances began. Tucholsky tripped and fell. Her right knee gave out and she lay on the ground in pain, unable to move, much less get up on her own.

When her coach, Pam Knox, surveyed the scene, she realized that if she touched her or had one of her teammates help her to her feet, the home run would be disallowed. Instead it would only be scored as a single and the memory of her only home run would have been ruined.

"And right then," Knox said, "I heard, 'Excuse me, would it be okay if we carried her around and she touched each base?'"

The voice belonged to Holtman, the opposing first baseman. "Honestly, it's one of those things that I hope anyone would do for me," Holtman said. "She hit the ball over the fence. She's a senior; it's her last year. I think anyone who knew that we could touch her would have offered to do it, just because it's the right thing to do."

Holtman, with help from other Central Washington players, carried Tucholsky around the bases. When they reached home plate, they handed her to her Western Oregon teammates.

The heartwarming show of solidarity led to a standing ovation for the contestants. Something special had taken place. In a world that promotes "me first," Holtman and the Central Washington players had demonstrated that it is more important to help others get ahead than to put oneself first.

The life of Jesus Christ is the perfect illustration of putting others first. He is the Good Shepherd who gave his life for his flock. He stoops down, picks us up, and carries us to eternal life. The heavenly choirs sing songs of praise for his goodness and love.

The four Gospels are our primary source of information about Jesus. We cannot get to know Jesus without knowing the Gospels. St. Jerome, who translated the Bible into Latin, once wrote, "Ignorance of Scripture is ignorance of Christ." In this chapter, the life of Christ is presented as told in the three synoptic Gospels: Matthew, Mark, and Luke. Key events in the life of Jesus Christ that will be considered are the infancy narratives, Jesus' baptism and temptations, some events in Jesus' public life, Jesus' teachings and miracles, and the call of the Apostles.

Using My Gifts for Others

Read the descriptions of the following talents. Then, search for and watch the YouTube coverage of the Central Washington players helping Sara Tucholsky around the bases. Write a short essay explaining how each of these gifts is represented in what happened. Next, write about an incident from your own experience in which you have witnessed some or all of these gifts in action.

- *Service*: I sense when others need help and often respond to them.
- *Teaching*: I am good at explaining things to others. I can help others learn.
- *Encouraging*: I can see the good in others and know what to say to spur them on.
- *Generosity*: I have the ability to share my time, possessions, and friendship.
- *Leadership*: I can organize people to get things done. I am also dependable when put in charge of things.
- *Compassion*: I sense when others are hurting and can respond in a loving, supportive way.

For Reflection

- How would you and your peers react to the sportsmanship exhibited by the Central Washington players?
- Whom have you helped to reach a goal?

Introducing the Synoptic Gospels

The Gospels of Matthew, Mark, and Luke are closely related and are collectively known as the "synoptic Gospels." The synoptic Gospels have much in common and differ significantly from the Gospel of John. For example, there are 661 verses in Mark's Gospel; 80 percent of these appear in Matthew's Gospel, and 65 percent show up in Luke's Gospel. Matthew (1,068 verses) and Luke (1,149) are considerably longer than Mark, but they follow the general outline of Mark's Gospel in reporting the events of Jesus' life. When lined up in parallel columns, the synoptic Gospels exhibit many similarities. They can be looked at together (the Greek *synoptikos* means "seen together"). Note the following example:

MATTHEW 5:13	MARK 9:50	LUKE 14:34-35
"You are the salt of the earth. But if salt loses its taste, with what can it be seasoned? It is no longer good for anything but to be thrown out and trampled underfoot."	"Salt is good, but if salt becomes insipid, with what will you restore its flavor? Keep salt in yourselves and you will have peace with one another."	"Salt is good, but if salt itself loses its taste, with what can its flavor be restored? It is fit neither for the soil nor for the manure pile; it is thrown out. Whoever has ears to hear ought to hear."

Until the nineteenth century, Matthew's Gospel was believed to be the first Gospel written. Mark's Gospel was believed to be an abridged, later version of Matthew. The traditional order might have resulted because ancient Church writers like Papias, Irenaeus, and Origen all told how the Apostle Matthew, writing for his fellow Jews, originally wrote the first Gospel in the language Jesus spoke—Aramaic. The Gospel of Matthew is a well-ordered work with detailed lessons, especially in the area of Christian morality. Thus, it became popular in worship services and for teaching new Christians. It also emphasizes the fulfillment of Old Testament prophecies, thus beautifully linking the Old and New Testaments.

However, later biblical scholarship led to the understanding that Mark's Gospel is the oldest and that Matthew and Luke used it in composing their own Gospels. This conclusion is based on a number of factors, including how Matthew and Luke both "improve" on some difficult passages found in Mark. For example, Mark 10:35–44 reveals that Jesus' disciples James and John request to be able to sit at Jesus' right hand in the coming Kingdom. This revealed their lack of understanding of Jesus' model of humility and service. Matthew's Gospel includes the same story (see Matthew 20: 20–28), but has the mother of James and John request the favor. By the time these Gospels were written and read, James and John were well-known and well-respected Church leaders. Their mother likely had passed on by that time and her reputation was not as important to preserve.

What Is Meant by "Gospel"

Drawing on the oral tradition, the lived faith of his own community, and other written sources available to him, the author of Mark was the first to write the literary form we term *gospel*. This unique form of literature is primarily a faith summary of the Good News of Jesus Christ. *Gospel* means "Good News." The term is used in three distinct but interrelated ways:

1. Primarily, *the very life* of Jesus Christ is the Good News of God's love and Salvation for all humanity.

2. *Preaching* about Jesus is also Good News. To proclaim to others the Gospel of Jesus and what he accomplished for our Salvation is a message that is always "news" and is always good.

3. Finally, there are the *four written versions* of the Good News, what we term the four Gospels. Written by the Evangelists under the inspiration of the Holy Spirit, the Gospels were composed for specific reasons for first-century communities. They proclaim in their own unique way the story of the Good News of Jesus Christ.

A second-century bishop, Papias, held that the author of the Gospel of Mark was John Mark, a disciple of Peter, and that his writing includes some themes of Peter's preaching. Whatever his identity, the date of authorship of the Gospel of Mark is placed between AD 67–73, that is, either shortly before or after the destruction of the Jewish Temple by the Romans in AD 70.

Sometime in the AD 80s, the authors of Matthew and Luke wrote their Gospels, using the following sources:

- The Gospel of Mark, including its basic narrative outline.

- "*Q.*" Matthew and Luke also have in common another 220–235 verses (in whole or part).

Scholarly opinion holds that the authors of Matthew and Luke drew on a common source, which they designate "Q" (from the German word *Quelle*, meaning "source"). This hypothetical document was probably a collection of Jesus' sayings that came down to the Evangelists in written or perhaps oral form.

- "*M*" and "*L*." Finally, the authors of Matthew and Luke used materials that were unique to each of them, designated "M" and "L" respectively.

The following diagram gives a bird's-eye view of the relationship among the first three Gospels.

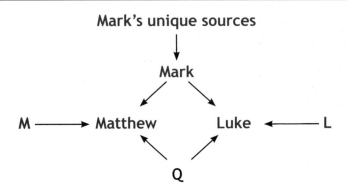

Some examples of how Matthew and Luke used their sources when they wrote their Gospels are highlighted below. Remember, Q is material common to Matthew and Luke, M is unique to Matthew, while L is unique to Luke.

Q	M	L
Beatitudes (Mt 5:3, 4, 6, 11–12; Lk 6:20–23)	The Infancy Narratives: Joseph's dreams, Jesus' birth, Magi, Flight into Egypt, Massacre of the Infants of Bethlehem, Return from Egypt (Mt 1:18–2:23)	The Infancy Narratives: Announcement of John's and Jesus' births, Mary's visitation of Elizabeth, Magnificat of Mary, John's birth, Zechariah's Canticle, Jesus' birth, shepherds, circumcision and naming of Jesus, presentation in the Temple, return to Nazareth, Jesus in the Temple (Lk 1:5–2:52).
The Lord's Prayer (Mt 6:9–13; Lk 11:2–4)	Peter trying to walk on water (Mt 14:28–31)	Parable of the Good Samaritan (Lk 10:29–37)
Parable of the Lost Sheep (Mt 18:12–14; Lk 15:4–7)	The Parable of the Sheep and the Goats (Mt 25:31–46)	Zacchaeus the tax collector (Lk 19:1–10)

Overview of the Gospel of Mark

As noted, the author of Mark's Gospel, writing about AD 67–73, might have been Peter's interpreter or secretary. The Gospel does indeed seem to have some connection to Peter's preaching. It highlights Jesus' deeds, rather than his words, presenting a vivid, human, and down-to-earth portrait of Jesus.

Mark likely wrote his Gospel for a non-Jewish, Gentile-Christian audience, which was undergoing persecution, perhaps in Rome. A central theme is that following Jesus often means that a Christian must suffer like Jesus did. Theologically, Mark portrays Jesus Christ as a Suffering Messiah for Christians to imitate. Some other main themes of the Gospel are discussed in the sections that follow.

The Son of God Became Man

In the Gospel's very first verse, Mark clearly tells the readers who Jesus is: "The beginning of the gospel of Jesus Christ (the Son of God)" (Mk 1:1). Jesus is God's unique Son, but Mark also stresses Jesus' humanity throughout his Gospel. For example, consider when Jesus met the skepticism of his critical countrymen before curing a man with a withered hand: "Looking around at them *with anger* and grieved at their hardness of heart . . ." (Mk 3:5,

italics added). Matthew and Luke do not mention that Jesus was angry.

Matthew and Luke also toned down other details that Mark included, especially if these details might cast Jesus in an unfavorable light. For example, Mark minces no words when he reports that Jesus' family said of him, "He is out of his mind" (Mk 3:21). Matthew and Luke drop this quote from their report of what Jesus' kinsmen thought of him. Mark also pointedly reports of Jesus' hometown that Jesus "was not able to perform any mighty deed there, apart from curing a few sick people by laying his hands on them" (6:5) because people in Nazareth lacked faith. Luke drops this story altogether, perhaps because he didn't want his readers to get the wrong idea about Jesus' power. Matthew, on the other hand, changes Mark's "was not able" to "And he *did not* work many mighty deeds there because of their lack of faith" (Mt 13:58, emphasis added).

Mark's portrait of Jesus is written more as a historical narrative. In Mark's Gospel, Jesus curses a fig tree (see Mark 11:12–14), a scene Luke changes to a parable. Jesus also warmly embraces children who approach him. And at the calming of the storm, Mark gives us a vivid detail: "Jesus was in the stern, asleep on a cushion" (Mk 4:38). The Gospel of Mark teaches that Jesus is the Son of God who assumed human nature. Jesus has real emotions like anger and compassion and, as any other human, needs to sleep.

Titles for Jesus in Mark's Gospel

Three titles for Jesus are revealed in this critical passage from Mark 8:27–34:

> Now Jesus and his disciples set out for the villages of Caesarea Philippi. Along the way he asked his disciples, "Who do people say that I am?" They said in reply, "John the Baptist, others Elijah, still others one of the prophets." And he asked them, "But who do you say that I am?" Peter said to him in reply, "You are the Messiah." Then he warned

them not to tell anyone about him. He began to teach them that the Son of Man must suffer greatly and be rejected by the elders, the chief priests, and the scribes, and be killed, and rise after three days. He spoke this openly. Then Peter took him aside and began to rebuke him. At this he turned around and, looking at his disciples, rebuked Peter and said, "Get behind me, Satan. You are thinking not as God does, but as human beings do." He summoned the crowd with his disciples and said to them, "Whoever wishes to come after me must deny himself, take up his cross, and follow me."

In this passage, we find that Jesus accepts the title *Christ* that Peter gives to him, but then we find that Jesus immediately begins to use the title *Son of Man* to describe himself. He also teaches that he will be a *Suffering Servant* for his people.

Christ (from the Greek word *Christos*) translates the Hebrew word *Messiah*, meaning "anointed one." Many of the various Jewish sects of Jesus' time had different ideas of what the Messiah would be. For example, the Pharisees thought the Messiah would be a religious leader who would endorse their way of interpreting the Law; the Essenes expected two Messiahs, one a priest, the other a king; the Zealots looked for a revolutionary who would remove Roman oppression through military means. Probably many of the people, and even the disciples themselves, pictured the coming Messiah as an earthly king, the prophesied descendant of King David. Mark's Gospel points out that Jesus accepted this important title, but that he was reluctant to let people know of his identity. There is no doubt he did this because his concept of the "anointed one" was radically different from that of his people and disciples.

After Jesus accepted Peter's proclamation of his true identity, Jesus warned Peter not to tell anyone. Jesus revealed to his Apostles that he is the Son of Man who would suffer and die for his people. The title *Son of Man* comes from a prophecy in Daniel where the glorious Messiah is called "Son of Man" (Dn 7:14). Many times throughout the Gospels Jesus refers to himself with this title. However, he also understood this title in light of the prophecies of Second Isaiah, who portrayed the Messiah as a *Suffering Servant* (Is 42–53). For Jesus, the Son of Man is both a Messiah who will come in glory (Daniel), but only after he has suffered and sacrificed his life for his people (Isaiah).

Peter had difficulty accepting Jesus' interpretation of the Messiah. He argued with Jesus. Jesus

Reading Mark

Mark is the shortest Gospel, written in a simple style. It helps us understand the other synoptic Gospels. Read the entire Gospel of Mark in one sitting (this should take about an hour or so). If you want to break your reading into two segments, then first read to Mark 9:1. Read for the big picture. Note in your journal the following:

1. Ten favorite quotes or sayings of Jesus.

2. A list of ten key events in the Gospel.

3. Five passages that raise questions in your mind, passages that you want to revisit for further discussion or study.

Emmanuel
A name for Jesus that means "God is with us." This is the name given to Jesus as foretold in the Old Testament (see, for example, Isaiah 7:14 and 8:8) and recounted to Joseph, the foster father of Jesus, in a dream.

realized that Peter was tempting him away from his true mission, so Jesus positioned Peter in front of his Apostles and compared him to Satan. Peter was judging by human standards, not divine ones.

Mark's Gospel tells us that Jesus is indeed the Messiah, but not an earthly, kingly Messiah. His leadership is the way of the cross. Not until the Resurrection and Ascension of Jesus Christ would the early Church begin to understand Jesus' way. A key message of Mark's Gospel is that to follow Jesus means to pick up our daily cross in imitation of him. Suffering for the Lord leads to Salvation and our participation in his glorious Resurrection. In conclusion, Mark proclaims that even *suffering* Christians can *celebrate* the Good News of Jesus because Jesus brings eternal life.

Overview of the Gospel of Matthew

The author of the Gospel of Matthew was most likely a Jewish scribe who had a thorough knowledge of Palestine and Jewish customs. Writing sometime in the 80s, he may have drawn on a source of sayings in Aramaic, as well as Mark's Gospel and Q, the source of Jesus' sayings that he had in common with Luke's Gospel.

Matthew's Gospel was written at a time when there was increasing tension between Jews and Christians. Most early Christians were also Jews. But after the destruction of the Temple in Jerusalem (AD 70), Gentile converts to Christianity were quickly outpacing Jewish Christians. A major theological emphasis of Matthew's Gospel is to show Jewish-Christian readers, as well as new Gentile converts, that Jesus Christ—**Emmanuel**—is indeed the Messiah prophesied in the Old Testament. For example, Matthew uses the title "Son of David" (a clear reference to the Messiah) more than any other Gospel. He also quotes many Old Testament prophecies to proclaim Jesus' identity as the promised Messiah.

Jesus as the New Moses

Matthew also presents Jesus as the new Moses. Moses gave the Torah (Law) to the Chosen People; Jesus gave the New Law to all people. To show this connection, the author of Matthew divided his Gospel into five books, plus the infancy and the Passion narratives. This five-book arrangement, centered on five important sermons, parallels the Pentateuch, which presents the Old Testament Law.

The sermons in Matthew's Gospel reveal Jesus as a great Teacher. In his Sermon on the Mount (Matthew 5–7), the most important collection of Jesus' moral teaching, he preaches about the "Kingdom of God" or "the Kingdom of Heaven." In it, Jesus instructs us on what is necessary to become his followers. Other sermons instruct the Apostles on how to spread the reign of God (Matthew 10), give vivid parables about God's Kingdom (Matthew 13), teach Church leaders how to be faithful servants (Matthew 18), and tell of the coming of God's reign (Matthew 24–25).

Throughout his Gospel, Matthew strives to show that Jesus Christ fulfills all of God's promises to the Chosen People and through them to all people. The Gospel ends with Jesus instructing his disciples to go to the ends of the earth to preach the Good News, to "make disciples of all the nations, baptizing them in the name of the Father, and of the Son, and of the holy Spirit, teaching them to observe all that I have commanded you" (Mt 28:19–20).

Overview of the Gospel of Luke

Tradition identifies Luke as a Gentile Christian (who might have been attracted to Judaism) as the author of the Gospel of Luke. He also wrote the Acts of the Apostles, thus making him responsible for writing about one-fourth of the entire New Testament. A second-century Church Father, St. Irenaeus, also identified Luke as a doctor and a traveling companion and friend of St. Paul.

Luke wrote about AD 75–90, perhaps around 85, to a largely Gentile-Christian audience. His writing style was highly polished. For example, he highlighted the city of Jerusalem as an important symbol in both of his works. His Gospel reports that the Messianic age begins in Jerusalem, and that the second part of Jesus' ministry centers on his journey to the Holy City. The drama of Salvation unfolds

COMPARING PROPHECIES

Read the following passages from Matthew's Gospel and its corresponding Old Testament prophecy. In parallel columns in your notebook, note what each passage says.

Matthew	Event	Old Testament
1:22-23	Jesus born of a virgin	Isaiah 7:14
2:5-6	Born in Bethlehem	Micah 5:1
2:15	Flight into Egypt	Hosea 11:1
2:18	Slaughter of the Innocents	Jeremiah 31:15
4:15-16	Ministry in Galilee	Isaiah 8:23-9:1
12:18-21	Serving by leading	Isaiah 42:1-4
13:14-15	Spiritual blindness	Isaiah 6:9-10
13:35	Teaching in parables	Psalm 78:2
21:5	Entry into Jerusalem on a donkey	Isaiah 62:11; Zechariah 9:9
27:9-10	Judas betrays Jesus	Zechariah 11:12-13

there. Acts of the Apostles takes the message of Jesus Christ to the end of the world, starting from Jerusalem, where the Apostles received the Holy Spirit. Luke highlights two major themes throughout his literary masterpiece:

1. The Gospel of Jesus Christ is truly Good News and thus a cause of celebration.
2. Jesus is a universal Savior who brings Salvation to Jew and Gentile alike.

These messages are highlighted in more detail below.

Jesus Offers a Message of Joy

Luke 15 is the heart of the Gospel. It includes the parables of the lost sheep, the lost coin, and the Prodigal Son. These parables, which are covered in more depth in Chapter 7, announce God's forgiveness of sinners, a true cause for celebration. Jesus proclaims, "I tell you, there will be rejoicing among the angels of God over one sinner who repents" (Lk 15:10).

Through his actions and through his message, Jesus is God for the world. His gentleness, his compassion, his sensitivity are all divine signs of healing love. Luke writes, "The whole crowd rejoiced at all the splendid deeds done by him" (Lk 13:17).

Jesus Is for Everyone

In the Gospel of Luke, we repeatedly see how Jesus sought out people who were considered "outcasts." For example, he cured lepers, who were avoided by people out of fear of contamination. He praised one

leper for returning to thank him (see Luke 17:11–19). This leper also happened to be a Samaritan, a hated enemy of Jews. Jesus made a point to praise this traditional enemy by making a Samaritan the hero of a parable, a true model of love toward neighbor.

Jesus also associated with tax collectors and Pharisees, even accepting dinner invitations from them. Luke's Gospel also highlights Jesus' treatment of women, considered revolutionary for its day. They came to him for cures, anointed his feet, and were his constant companions. Mary and Martha were his friends. His pity for the widow of Nain moved him to raise her son from the dead. Jesus' Mother is also singled out as the model believer. Only in Luke do we find Mary's beautiful Magnificat (see Luke 1:46–55), a prayer of deep faith and submission to God's will.

Jesus' compassion is evident throughout the Gospel, symbolized perfectly in his dying moments. While he was being crucified, taunted and tormented by his executioners, our Lord said, "Father, forgive them; they know not what they do" (Lk 23:34). With his last ounce of energy he thought of the good thief hanging in misery next to him, promising him paradise.

Jesus is *everyone's* compassionate Savior. His love has no limits. The message of Luke is clear: We should allow Jesus to live in us so we can love everyone—saint and sinner—in imitation of our Lord.

 Canticle of Joy

Read the verses of Zechariah's canticle from Luke 1:68-79. Design an artistic prayer card with the canticle or choose instrumental music to accompany the canticle and lead a recitation with your classmates or younger students (e.g., in a parish religious education program).

For Review

1. What are the synoptic Gospels? Where do they get their name?
2. Explain the relationship between and among the synoptic Gospels.
3. Give an approximate date and identify the probable author of each of the synoptic Gospels.
4. What is the meaning of the term *gospel*? In what ways do we use it?

Compassionate Touch

Jesus' compassion in Luke's Gospel is highlighted through the healing power of touch. Read the following passages in the Gospel and note in your journal how Jesus touched people literally and figuratively.

- 4:40-41
- 5:12-16
- 7:11-17
- 8:40-56
- 13:10-13
- 18:15-17

For further application, determine a list of people who need the healing touch of compassion. (For example, consider the elderly who may be lonely and yearn for visitors.) Make a list of at least ten categories of people. Then, decide what you can do as an individual to show God's compassion to someone who needs your loving presence. Follow through, and then report on what you *felt* by sharing your love.

5. Identify *Q, M,* and *L.*

6. Identify the audience for whom each of the synoptic Gospels was written.

7. What is a central theme of Mark's Gospel?

8. How does Mark's Gospel explain that the Son of God took on human nature?

9. Briefly explain an important theological theme in each of the synoptic Gospels.

10. Discuss the meaning of these titles: Christ, Son of Man, Suffering Servant. How did Jesus apply these to himself?

11. What does the Gospel of Matthew mean when it refers to Jesus as the Son of David and the New Moses?

12. What is the meaning of *Emmanuel*? Why is it an appropriate designation for Jesus Christ?

13. List five Old Testament prophecies that the Gospel of Matthew shows are fulfilled in the coming of Jesus.

14. Discuss several examples of the compassion of Jesus reported in Luke's Gospel.

For Reflection

- What does it mean to pick up your cross and follow Jesus?

- In what ways do you feel connected to your ancestors in faith?

- Explain your need for Jesus as your Savior.

- How do you imitate the Lord?

- What does it mean to you to say that Jesus is "for everyone"?

Important Events in the Early Life of Christ

The synoptic Gospels present the mysteries of Christ's life. The term *mystery* refers to God. God is a mystery because his infinite greatness, omnipotence, and perfect love are beyond human understanding. In the New Testament, the Greek word *mysterion* also refers to God's saving plan ("the mystery of Salvation") that he gradually unfolded in human history.

Both understandings of the word are intimately connected. The God who is mystery is the very same God who revealed himself in human history. God's fullest Revelation took place when he assumed human nature and became man in order to accomplish our Salvation in that same human nature. Therefore, everything about Jesus—his words, deeds, teachings, Passion, Death, and Resurrection—all reveal God as infinitely loving and merciful. The next sections describe the early years of Christ's life, including those that are hidden from Gospel coverage.

Birth of Jesus

Mark's Gospel begins with John the Baptist announcing the advent of the Messiah. It does not contain stories about Jesus' birth, but Matthew 1:1–2:23 and Luke 1:1–2:52 do contain records of the **Nativity**. Although drawing on different traditions (M and L) about the Lord's birth, each Evangelist agrees on many important facts. For example, both Matthew and Luke highlight Jesus, Mary, and Joseph, the foster father of Jesus. We also learn the following:

- Mary, Jesus' Mother, was a virgin. She freely consented to God's action in her life and so became the Mother of God and the spiritual Mother of all of us. She was open to God and thus serves as a model for all Christians who are to bring Christ to others.

- Mary conceived Jesus by the Holy Spirit.

- Jesus was born during the reign of King Herod the Great in the town of Bethlehem, as it had been prophesied.

- Jesus received his name before his birth. The name *Jesus* comes from the Hebrew word *Yehoshua* (Joshua). It means "God saves," "God is Salvation," or simply, "Savior." This most appropriate name points to both Jesus' identity and to his mission. From the moment of his conception, God had destined Jesus to save the world from sin and death.

- Jesus was descended from King David, as had been prophesied.

- The Holy Family settled in the town of Nazareth.

- The infancy narratives that begin the Gospels of Matthew and Luke reveal more about Jesus and his mission. For example, Jesus was born in poverty, entering the world humbly. Luke tells us how the shepherds were the first to see him. Pious Jews looked down on shepherds because their occupation did not allow them to keep faithfully the ritual precepts of the Law. Yet, from the beginning, we see that Jesus came to call people such as these.

Circumcision and Presentation in the Temple

Jewish Law required males to be circumcised as a sign of the covenant. Jesus' circumcision incorporated him into the Chosen People. His submission to Jewish Law was another example of his humility. Similarly,

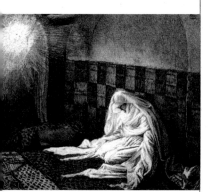

Nativity
The Nativity of Jesus is the story of our Savior's birth in Bethlehem. Two different accounts of the Nativity are given in the New Testament, one in the Gospel of Matthew, the other in the Gospel of Luke.

Epiphany
The feast that celebrates the mystery of Christ's manifestation as the Savior of the world.

Jesus' presentation in the Temple (see Luke 2:22–38) shows how the firstborn son belongs to God. In the Lord's case, this is literally the truth: Jesus is God's only Son. The old prophets Simeon and Anna recognized him as the long-awaited Messiah, thus fulfilling the Old Testament promises. They blessed God for the privilege of seeing him and predicted the perfect sacrifice that the Lord would endure for our Salvation (the sword of sorrow that will pierce Mary's heart).

The Magi, Flight into Egypt, and Herod's Slaughter of the Innocents

The Christian feast of the **Epiphany** celebrates the mystery of Christ's manifestation as the Savior of the world. This feast commemorates the visit of the magi from the East, revealing from the very beginning that the Christ came for all people, not just Jews. In Matthew's Gospel, the treachery of King Herod is brought to light. When he learned of the birth of the new King, he felt threatened. The Holy Family's flight into Egypt and the killing of the innocent children in Bethlehem reveal how the forces of evil were gathered against Jesus from the very beginning, yet these stories also show how God protected his Son who came to save all persons.

Hidden Years

Luke's Gospel tells how the boy Jesus lived a life of humble obedience in the Galilean town of Nazareth. Jesus' submission to his Mother and foster father contrasts sharply with Adam's disobedience to God in the Garden. It points to Jesus' obedience in all things to his heavenly Father.

As a child growing up, Jesus learned the trade of carpenter from Joseph. He also grew in knowledge of his Jewish faith from both of his parents, learning from their example. As a young man, he regularly participated in the religious festivals in Jerusalem. At one of them, he astounded his teachers with his superior knowledge. The mystery of the finding in the Temple represents Jesus' total consecration to his mission as the Father's Son. Luke concludes his second chapter by simply saying, "Jesus advanced [in] wisdom and age and favor before God and man" (Lk 2:52). His humility in living as an obedient and observant son during his "hidden" years teaches us, his followers, how to pray, live, and witness to our faith.

EXPLAINING THE FAITH

Why are the Gospels the most important books of the Bible?

The Second Vatican Council taught that "the Gospels have a special place, and rightly so, because they are our principal source for the life and teaching of the incarnate Word, our Savior." The four Gospels faithfully hand on what Jesus "really did and taught for their eternal Salvation." The Gospels have the purpose of confirming the truth about Jesus Christ. St. Luke, writing in the prologue of his Gospel, explains that "I too have decided, after investigating everything accurately anew, to write it down in an orderly sequence for you, most excellent Theophilus, so that you may realize the certainty of the teachings you have received" (Lk 1:3-4).

⬤ For Review

1. In what way is the word *mystery* linked to God and to his plan of Salvation?

2. Discuss four facts the infancy narratives in Matthew and Luke have in common.

3. What is the meaning of the name *Jesus*? Why is it an appropriate name for our Lord?

⬤ For Reflection

Read the infancy narratives in Matthew 1:1-2:23 and Luke 1:1-2:52. Focus on either Mary or Joseph. Then, based on what you discover, write a three-paragraph profile on either one of them.

Followers of Jesus

Jesus' ministry took him throughout Galilee and, at times, into Judea. His life-giving words and marvelous deeds inevitably drew **disciples** to him. Jesus had many disciples, including a special group of seventy described in Luke 10:1–17. There were also women disciples, very unusual for its time. Some of these women helped Jesus with financial support, traveled with him and his other followers, supplied meals and lodging, witnessed the Crucifixion, and visited his tomb on Easter Sunday. To be a disciple of Jesus required sacrifice, such as leaving one's home or occupation to be with Jesus. In the end, true disciples of Jesus even suffered martyrdom for believing in him and proclaiming the Gospel.

Jesus spoke of the meaning of discipleship several times in the synoptic Gospels. For example, he said of his disciples:

Behold, I am sending you like sheep in the midst of wolves; so be shrewd as serpents and simple as doves. (Mt 10:16)

You are the light of the world. A city set on a mountain cannot be hidden. Nor do they light a lamp and then put it under a bushel basket; it is set on a lampstand, where it gives light to all in the house. Just so, your light must shine before others, that they may see your good deeds and glorify your heavenly Father. (Mt 5:14–16)

If anyone wishes to come after me, he must deny himself and take up his cross daily and follow me. (Lk 9:23)

Call of the Twelve

From among his disciples, Jesus selected the Twelve Apostles to assist him in his work. The number twelve brings to mind the twelve tribes of Israel. Thus, the Apostles represent a renewed Israel. The term *apostle* comes from the Greek word for "send." Jesus commissioned the Twelve to preach to the Chosen People the coming of God's Kingdom. Their main job was to become fishers of people (see Mark 1:17), that is, to evangelize by preaching the Gospel.

Jesus selected the Twelve after a night of silent prayer on the mountain. Most of the Apostles were from humble backgrounds, though they were skilled

at some craft or trade. Several were fishermen; one was a tax collector. Their relationship to Jesus was similar to students of the day to their teacher or rabbi. He expected them to learn carefully from his words *and* actions so that they could pass his message on to others.

However, the Lord's relationship to his Apostles differed in two ways from that of the rabbis of his day. First, Jesus *chose* the Apostles; rabbinical students, on the other hand, chose which teacher they wanted to study under. Second, Jesus taught unlike any other rabbi. He taught on his *own authority*, directly interpreting the will of his Father. Rabbis of his day were rigorously trained by other rabbis to interpret the Law. They based their opinions on the teachings of others. Jesus was unique.

The Twelve Apostles as listed in Luke 6:13–16 are:

1. *Peter*. Originally he was named Simon bar Jonah, a fisherman, but Jesus renamed him Peter, a name that means "rock." He was the leader and spokesman of the Apostles and the first to declare Jesus' identity. Jesus confided in a special way with Peter (along with James and John). Take, for example, the Transfiguration. Peter was impulsive and headstrong. He betrayed Jesus by three times denying that he knew him. However, Peter repented and became a great saint. Tradition tells us that Nero crucified him upside down in Rome.

2. *Andrew*. A fisherman and brother of Peter. Both came from the town of Bethsaida. John's Gospel tells us that Andrew was Jesus' first disciple and that he encouraged his brother to come to Jesus. Early Church tradition holds that Andrew was put to death on an X-shaped (Saint Andrew's) cross.

3. *James, Zebedee's Son*. He and his brother, John, were both fishermen. They must have had a fiery temperament because Jesus nicknamed them "sons of thunder." They wanted Jesus to destroy a Samaritan village because it refused to show Jesus hospitality (see Luke 9:54). James became the leader of the local church in Jerusalem after the Resurrection. Herod Agrippa beheaded him in AD 44.

4. *John, Zebedee's Son*. Many scholars believe John was the so-called "beloved disciple" of John's Gospel. He had a privileged place at the Last Supper. Jesus entrusted his Mother to him while he hung on the cross. He was the source of the Fourth Gospel, Revelation, and the Epistles named after him. Tradition tells us that he lived to an old age and preached Jesus' message of love to the very end of his life.

5. *Philip*. He was also from Bethsaida. Jesus asked Philip where they could purchase bread before he performed the miracle of the loaves. At the Last Supper,

disciple
A follower of Jesus. The word means "learner."

Philip asked Jesus to show the apostles the Father, to which Jesus replied, "Whoever has seen me has seen the Father" (Jn 14:9).

6. *Bartholomew.* This Apostle was probably the same as the *Nathanael* in John's Gospel. *Bartholomew* means "son of Thalmai" and may have been Nathanael's surname. When hearing from his friend Philip that Jesus was the Messiah, Nathanael asked, "Can anything good come from Nazareth?" (Jn 1:46). Imagine his surprise when Jesus met him for the first time and told him where he was sitting when he said his unkind words! Tradition holds that Bartholomew preached in India and was flayed alive and then beheaded for his faith.

7. *Matthew. Levi* and *Matthew* were probably the same person. He was a tax collector by profession, a job that pious Jews loathed because it meant cooperation with the Romans. Tradition holds that in the 40s he wrote a Gospel in Aramaic, Jesus' own language. Some scholars believe that the New Testament's Gospel according to Matthew used it as one of its sources.

8. *Thomas.* John's Gospel calls Thomas "the Twin." He eagerly professed faith in Jesus, saying that he would gladly go to Jerusalem to die with Jesus. However, when told of the Lord's Resurrection, "doubting Thomas" said he would not believe until he saw the Risen Lord for himself. Tradition also holds that he preached in India, where he was martyred.

9. *James, Son of Alphaeus.* Mark's Gospel calls him James the Younger, perhaps to distinguish him from James Zebedee's son. Not much else is known of this particular Apostle. He is probably *not* the so-called "brother of the Lord" who took over the leadership of the Christians in Jerusalem after Peter. This James was stoned to death in 62.

10. *Simon the Zealot.* We don't know much about this Apostle. The Zealots were a group of revolutionaries who worked to overthrow Roman rule in Palestine through violent means. By following Jesus, Simon had to give up these notions since Jesus was opposed to violent solutions and is the "Prince of Peace."

11. *Judas son of James.* This Judas is also known as *Jude.* Matthew and Mark call him *Thaddeus*, a probable surname so as not to confuse him with Judas Iscariot, the traitor. At the Last Supper, he asked Jesus why he revealed himself to them and not to the rest of the world. Tradition states that he and Simon the Zealot preached together in Persia, where they were martyred.

12. *Judas Iscariot.* Each of the Gospels calls Judas a traitor. His surname may mean "from Kerioth," which was a small town in Judea. This would have set him apart from all the other Apostles, who were from Galilee. It might also be derived from the Greek word *sikarios,* which came from the Latin word for "daggerman" or "assassin," a name given in Jesus' day to outlaws who worked to overthrow Roman rule. He was the treasurer for the disciples; John's Gospel tells us that he was dishonest. He criticized Mary for anointing Jesus at Bethany, an anointing that prefigured Jesus' Death and burial. Judas betrayed Jesus for thirty pieces of silver, and when he realized the magnitude of what he did, he hanged himself.

⬤ For Review

1. What is the meaning of *disciple? Apostle?*

2. How did Jesus' relationship with his apostles differ from the rabbi-disciple relationships of his day?

3. Who were the Twelve Apostles?

For Reflection

Which Apostle do you most identify with? Why?

Important Events in Jesus' Public Life

Because Jesus Christ is God-made-flesh, everything about his life carries great meaning. Learning about the events of our Lord's public life can teach us about the Father's love for us through his Son. Jesus is our model. His humility, his gentle interactions with people, his forceful teaching of the truth, his compassion, his love for all (including his enemies), his patient suffering, and his many other human qualities can teach us how to live as God's children.

Baptism by John the Baptist (CCC, 535-537; 565)

In all three synoptic Gospels, Jesus' public life begins with his baptism by John the Baptist. John, the son of the priest Zechariah and his wife Elizabeth, was a distant relation to Jesus. Isaiah had prophesied that there would be one sent to announce the coming of the Messiah:

> A voice of one crying out in the desert:
> 'Prepare the way of the Lord.' (Lk 3:4)

John the Baptist preached the need for repentance for the forgiveness of sin. By his submission to John's baptism, Jesus, the sinless one, displayed great humility. He also showed that he was accepting the mission that he was to begin, that of serving all humanity as God's Suffering Servant.

At his baptism, the Holy Spirit descended on Jesus in the form of a dove and a heavenly voice proclaimed Jesus to be the beloved Son. Thus, in this important scene at the beginning of Jesus' public life, all Three Persons of the Blessed Trinity—Father (the heavenly voice), Son (Jesus), and Holy Spirit (dove)—are present. It is clear what is being proclaimed here: Jesus is the Messiah. Jesus is God. Jesus is God's only Son.

Jesus' baptism revealed his perfect obedience to his Father's will. It also foreshadowed the baptism of his Death for the remission of our sins. Finally, it serves as a model for our own Baptism.

Temptations in the Desert (CCC, 538-540; 566)

Luke's Gospel reports how the Holy Spirit, after Jesus' baptism, led him into the desert to pray, fast, and prepare himself for the difficult mission ahead. During this forty-day retreat, Satan tempted Jesus. The number *forty* recalls the forty years the Chosen People wandered in the desert after the Exodus from Egypt. They, too, were tempted to turn away from God and his Law and, sadly, all too often they fell, turning to the worship of false gods. But by being faithful, Jesus showed himself to be the New Israel.

A temptation is a test. The Letter to the Hebrews (see Hebrews 4:15–16) explains that Jesus underwent testing to sympathize with our human weaknesses. He was tested in every way, but did not sin. This is why, when we are also tempted to do wrong, we can turn to our Lord for help and strength. He knows well the weaknesses of human nature and wants to give us his grace and mercy.

The Gospels report that Satan tempted Jesus three times: to turn stones into bread, to worship him instead of God, and to jump from the top of the Temple. The first temptation was for Jesus to take care of his own needs, in this case, that of hunger. Jesus' response was, "One does not live by bread alone" (Lk 4:4). Unlike the Chosen People in the desert, who often gave in to their sensual appetites, Jesus had his mind fixed on doing the Father's work, not self-gratification. Throughout his ministry, he always put others first.

In the second temptation, Jesus was given the opportunity to gain all worldly power and glory if

COMPARING ACCOUNTS OF JESUS' BAPTISM

Note the similarities and differences of each Gospel account of Jesus' baptism. Note, for example, that John's Gospel never clearly mentions that it was John the Baptist who baptized Jesus:

	Mt 3:13-17	Mk 1:9-11	Lk 3:21-22	Jn 1:29-34
Who sees the sky opened?				
Who sees the dove descending?				
Who hears the voice of the Father?				

Create a similar chart and compare the following three passages about Jesus' temptations in the desert: Matthew 4:1-11, Mark 1:12-13, and Luke 4:1-13.

- Note three differences that you found in these accounts.
- What is the likely source of the stories of the three temptations? State your reasons.

ing victory over sin, Satan, and death, won by his Passion, Death, and Resurrection.

Jesus' time in the desert affirmed his identity as God's Son and his future mission. Jesus refused the easy way out. Facing temptation as all humans do, Jesus fought evil through a life of gentle, compassionate service of others. He embraced the suffering his fidelity to the Father brought. The devil always tempts us to take the easy way out. In contrast, Jesus gave us the example of true love. It is sometimes tough and requires sacrifice, but it is the only way to God and to true happiness.

For Review

1. What is celebrated in the Christian feast of the Epiphany?

2. What important lessons do we learn from the baptism of Jesus?

3. What is the meaning of each of the temptations of Jesus in the desert?

For Reflection

- What is the value of learning to obey God and other proper authority?

- How can conquering temptations make a person stronger?

he would worship Satan. This temptation would surface throughout Jesus' ministry as the people wanted to make him a king. Even his own Apostles thought the Messiah should be a worldly ruler, but Jesus rejected this temptation. He came to serve, not to be served. His reply to Satan: "You shall worship the Lord, your God, and him alone shall you serve" (Lk 4:8).

The third temptation was for Jesus to test God by jumping off the top of the Temple. Such a spectacular deed would attract people to him, proving his identity and furthering the aims of his ministry. Jesus' response was, "You shall not put the Lord, your God, to the test" (Lk 4:12). Jesus always trusted his Father. Even as he hung dying on the cross, abandoned by many of his friends and hearing the taunts of the bystanders to save himself, Jesus had confidence in his heavenly Father.

The temptations of Jesus bring to mind Satan's temptation of Adam and Eve. Then, Satan triumphed over Adam. But Jesus is the New Adam. He decisively conquered the devil and sent him away. Jesus' victory in the desert foreshadowed his last-

Jesus Proclaims the Gospel (*CCC*, 541)

After Jesus emerged from the desert, he began his teaching ministry. The Gospel of Mark summarizes the message Jesus came to deliver. It is centered on the **Kingdom (or reign) of God**. Jesus' words of announcement are key:

This is the time of fulfillment. The kingdom of God is at hand. Repent, and believe the gospel. (Mk 1:15)

Jesus came to proclaim that God's Kingdom was coming in his very person. Jesus is the Good News. He is the Gospel. He is the Revelation of the Father. This essential announcement requires two things: that we repent and that we believe in him.

Jesus proclaimed the Good News in short sayings known as aphorisms, for example, "But many who are first will be last, and the last will be first" (Mt 19:30). He also taught his message in important sermons like the Sermon on the Mount. Finally, many of his teachings are found in short stories known as parables, for example, the Parable of the Good Samaritan.

Jesus taught in words, but his deeds were powerful messages, too. He lived the message he preached. His unconditional love for the poor and needy, the sick, women, foreigners, children, sinners, marginalized people—indeed every single human being—reveals the presence of God's Kingdom in him, God's only Son. More about Jesus' rich message of God's Kingdom will be covered in Chapter 7.

Miracles of Jesus

Among Jesus' most important deeds were his miracles. These mighty works, wonders, and signs revealed that God's Kingdom was present in his very person. They helped prove that Jesus is the Messiah, the Son of God.

The miracles of Jesus were signs of the messianic age. They freed some people from earthly problems and evils, but they did not abolish all human sufferings. Their purpose was to show Jesus' power over sin. The Gospel miracle stories are explained in more detail in Chapter 8.

Transfiguration (CCC, 554-556; 568)

Jesus proclaimed the Good News in a dramatic way through his **Transfiguration**. During this event, which occurred on a high mountain, Jesus revealed his divine glory before Peter, James, and John. "His face shone like the sun and his clothes became white as light" (Mt 17:2). Through this manifestation, Jesus was foreshadowing God's Kingdom.

Pope Benedict XVI points out that the Transfiguration took place while Jesus was praying.

[I]t displays visibly what happens when Jesus talks with his Father: the profound interpenetration of his being with God, which then becomes pure light. In his oneness with the Father, Jesus is himself "light from light."

At the Transfiguration, two Old Testament figures—Moses and Elijah—also appear. Their presence recalls how the Law (given to Israel through Moses) and the Prophets (Elijah was a great prophet) had announced the sufferings of the coming Messiah. This vision also reveals all Three Persons of the Blessed Trinity: the Father (in the voice), the Son (Jesus), and the Holy Spirit (in the shining cloud).

Jesus instructed Peter, James, and John not to spread word of this vision until after the Resurrection. They were to withhold news of this remarkable event "until the Son of Man has been raised from the dead" (Mt 17:9). Though the Son of God, Jesus came not as an earthly king—he came to preach the Good News of God's love. This preaching led him to Jerusalem and his own Death at the hand of the authorities.

Paschal Mystery

Jesus most clearly proclaimed the Gospel through the **Paschal Mystery**, that is, his Passion, Death, Resurrection, and Ascension. This mystery of total love reveals to everyone over all ages that Jesus Christ is the way to Salvation. His Paschal Mystery rescued humanity from sin and death. This is the story the synoptic Gospels and John's Gospels want us to know: Jesus, the Christ, the Son of God, has risen from the dead! Reality is different now. Believe this Good News. Be baptized, and accept the Lord and Holy Spirit into your lives. Share the truth of faith with others. The Paschal Mystery will also be studied in greater detail in Chapter 8.

⬤ For Review

1. How did Jesus proclaim the Kingdom of God?

2. What was the purpose of Jesus' miracles?

3. What took place at the Transfiguration?

⬤ For Reflection

• Finish this sentence in your own words: "The Kingdom of God is like . . ."

• Why do you think Jesus appeared before Peter, James, and John in a transfigured state?

Kingdom (or reign) of God

The Kingdom of God (also called the reign of God) was proclaimed by Jesus and began in his Life, Death, and Resurrection. It refers to the process of the Father's reconciling and renewing all things through his Son, to the fact of his will being done on earth as it is in Heaven. The process has begun with Jesus and will be perfectly completed at the end of time.

Transfiguration

The mystery from Christ's life in which God's glory shone through and transformed Jesus' physical appearance while he was in the company of the Old Testament prophets Moses and Elijah. Peter, James, and John witnessed this event.

Paschal Mystery

Christ's work of redemption, accomplished principally by his Passion, Death, Resurrection, and glorious Ascension. This mystery is commemorated and made present through the sacraments, especially the Eucharist.

Main Ideas

- Jesus is the Good Shepherd who gave his life for his flock; we are called to a similar life of putting the needs of others before our own needs (pp. 130–131).

- Matthew, Mark, and Luke are called the "synoptic Gospels" because they have several common verses and can be "seen together" (p. 131).

- Mark's Gospel is likely the first Gospel written; Matthew and Luke drew from Mark as a source in compiling their own Gospels (pp. 132–133).

- Gospel means "Good News" (p. 132).

- The term gospel is used in three interrelated ways: as the very life of Christ, as the preaching about Christ, and as the four written versions of the Good News (p. 132).

- Besides drawing from the Gospel of Mark, Matthew and Luke also have in common another 220–235 verses from a common source called "Q." They also used materials unique to their Gospels, designated "M" and "L" (pp. 132–133).

- Mark's Gospel portrays Jesus Christ as the Suffering Messiah or Suffering Servant, a role intended for Christ's disciples as well (pp. 134–136).

- Matthew's Gospel was intended for Jewish Christians to show that Jesus Christ was indeed the Messiah prophesied in the Old Testament (pp. 136–137).

- Luke's Gospel, intended for Gentile Christians, portrays the celebratory aspect of the Gospel and defines Jesus Christ as the universal Savior of all (pp. 136–139).

- The synoptic Gospels present the mysteries of Christ's life (pp. 139–141).

- Important events in the early life of Christ are the Nativity, the circumcision and presentation in the Temple, the magi, flight into Egypt, and Herod's persecution, and the hidden years in Nazareth (pp. 140–141).

- Jesus had many disciples, including a special group of seventy. He also had women disciples which was unusual for that time and culture (p. 142).

- Jesus chose Twelve Apostles whose main job was to evangelize by preaching the Gospel (pp. 142–144).

- Important events in the public life of Jesus are his baptism in the River Jordan and being tempted by Satan in the desert (pp. 145–147).

- Jesus, the Revelation of the Father, came to deliver the essential message that the Kingdom of God is at hand (pp. 147–148).

- Jesus used powerful signs called miracles to share the Good News (p. 148).

- The Transfiguration of Jesus revealed the Good News in a dramatic way (pp. 148–149).

- Jesus most clearly proclaimed the Gospel through the living of his Paschal Mystery (p. 149).

Terms, People, Places

Match the following terms with the definitions below.

A. Emmanuel
B. Nativity
C. Epiphany
D. disciple
E. Kingdom (or reign) of God
F. Transfiguration
G. Paschal Mystery

___ 1. The process that was started with Jesus and that will be perfectly completed at the end of time.

___ 2. The Passion, Death, Resurrection, and Glorification of Jesus Christ.

___ 3. Jesus specially chose seventy of these.

___ 4. Only Matthew's and Luke's Gospels record this event.

___ 5. "God is with us."

___ 6. Occurred in the presence of Old Testament prophets Moses and Elijah and Jesus' companions Peter, James, and John.

___ 7. The feast that celebrates the mystery of Christ's manifestation as the Savior of the world.

Primary Source Quotations

Apostolic Origins of the Gospels

The church has always and everywhere maintained, and continues to maintain, the apostolic origins of the four Gospels. The apostles preached, as Christ had charged them to do, and then, under the inspiration of the holy Spirit, they and others of the apostolic age handed on to us in writing the same message they had preached, the foundation of our faith: the fourfold Gospel, according to Matthew, Mark, Luke, and John.

—*Dei Verbum*, 18

There Is One Gospel

While the New Testament contains four writings called "gospels," there is in reality only one gospel running through all of the Christian scriptures, the gospel of and about Jesus Christ.

—Introduction to the New Testament of the *New American Bible*

The Importance of Grounding Oneself in the Gospels

But above all it's the Gospels that occupy my mind when I'm at prayer; my poor soul has so many needs, and yet this is the one thing needful. I'm always finding fresh lights there, hidden and enthralling meanings.

—St. Thérèse of Lisieux

Anyone who is well grounded in the testimonies of Scripture is the bulwark of the Church.

—St. Jerome

• Read Mark 10:45. In what way does this passage summarize Jesus' mission?

• How does this passage encourage your mission as a Christian?

Ongoing Assignments

As you cover the material in this chapter, choose and complete at least three of these assignments.

1. Create a comprehensive chart of Q, M, or L. This can be done on a poster board or in an Excel document. Refer to this site for help: http://catholic-resources.org/Bible/Synoptic_Outlines.htm.

2. Carefully read the Beatitudes as they appear in the Gospels of Matthew (Mt 5:1–11) and Luke (6:20–26). In your journal, note how particular Beatitudes differ.

3. Write a profile of one of the Apostles. Consult some of the following websites for ideas:

   • www.goarch.org/en/ourfaith/articles/article7065.asp

   • Catholic Encyclopedia: www.newadvent.org/cathen/index.html

   • Patron Saints: www.catholic-forum.com/saints/indexsnt.htm

4. Report on women in the ministry of Jesus. Articles to start your research include:

   • www.wcg.org/lit/church/ministry/women6b.htm

   • Daniel J. Harrington, S.J., "The Truth about Jesus and Women": www.americancatholic.org/Newsletters/JHP/aq0906.asp

   • www.wcg.org/lit/jesus/andwomen.htm

5. With one or more classmates, write and enact a skit of Peter's recognition of Jesus as the Messiah on the road to Caesarea Philippi. Base your skit on one of the following passages: Mark 8:27–33 or Matthew 16:13–23.

6. Create a PowerPoint presentation on biblical scenes from Jesus' hidden life. Include scenes from Bethlehem, Nazareth, and Jerusalem. You can download images from sites such as these:

   - Holy Land Photos: www.holy landphotos.org

   - Bible Places: www.bibleplaces.com

7. Create a collage or a PowerPoint presentation illustrating the Hail Mary.

8. Create a two-page (with graphics) newsletter that covers the events of the infancy narrative reported in Matthew's Gospel (Mt 1:18–2:23).

9. Write a short history of the Christmas crèche. Use appropriate illustrations.

   - www.catholictradition.org/Children/creche.htm

   - www.friendsofthecreche.org/historyCreche.html

   - www.catholiceducation.org/articles/religion/re0238.html

   - www.livingcatholicism.com/archives/2006/12/a_short_history.html

10. After your reading of Mark's Gospel, locate a difficult passage that caused some confusion. Consult two biblical commentaries. Then, write a two-paragraph explanation of what you learned about the meaning of the verses.

11. Read one of the following sermons in Matthew's Gospel: Matthew 10 or Matthew 18. Write a profile of good Christian leadership based on what Jesus taught in these passages.

12. View the film *The Nativity Story* (www.thenativitystory.com). Write a short report discussing how faithfully the film represents the Gospel accounts.

13. Read Acts 1:15–26. Note in your journal: How does Acts record the death of Judas? What happened to the money Judas got for betraying Jesus? Who replaced Judas Iscariot? How was he chosen?

Prayer

When Mary heard that she was to be God's Mother, she prayed the Magnificat, a prayer of praise to God. This famous Christian prayer teaches the true meaning of humility and doing God's will. God is the source of all that we are and all that we have. He deserves our praise and gratitude. Mary, our Blessed Mother, shows the way. Pray the Magnificat with Mary, confident of, and believing in, God's goodness.

> My soul proclaims the greatness
> of the Lord;
> my spirit rejoices in God my savior.
> For he has looked upon his
> handmaid's lowliness;
> behold, from now on will all ages
> call me blessed.
> The Mighty One has done
> great things for me,
> and holy is his name.
> His mercy is from age to age
> to those who fear him.
> He has shown might with his arm,
> dispersed the arrogant of
> mind and heart.
> He has thrown down the rulers
> from their thrones
> but lifted up the lowly.
> The hungry he has filled
> with good things;
> the rich he has sent away empty.

He has helped Israel his servant,
remembering his mercy,
according to his promise to our fathers,
to Abraham and to his descendants
forever.
—Luke 1:46–55

- *Reflection:* Through our Baptism and the
gift of the Holy Spirit, the Lord has exalted
us, too. He has done great things for us by
making us his friends and disciples.

- *Resolution:* Spend five minutes each day
in the coming week thinking of the many
things the Lord has done for you. Thank and
praise him for his goodness by praying the
Magnificat each day.

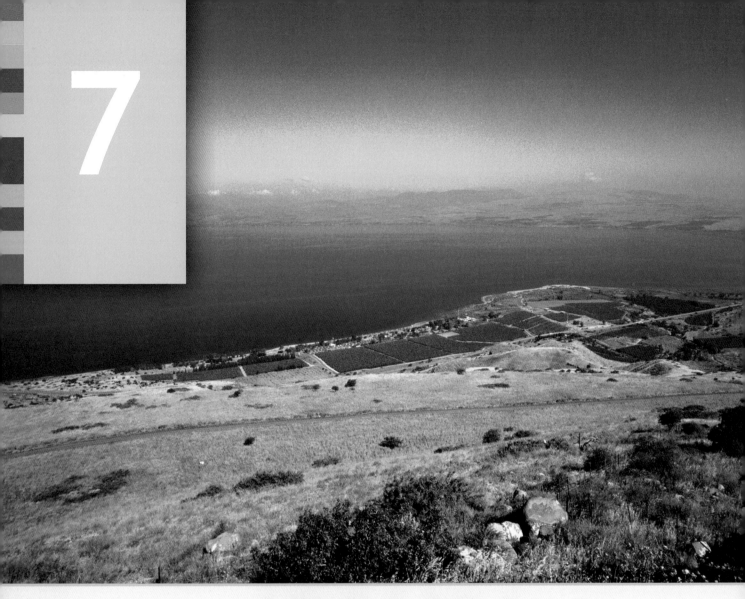

7

JESUS' TEACHING

There will be more joy in Heaven over one sinner who repents than over ninety-nine righteous people who have no need of repentance.

—Luke 15:7

Only for Today

What counts most in life is Jesus Christ, his Church, the gospel, truth, and goodness.

Jesus the Teacher

Jesus is a one-of-a-kind Teacher who used several unique and creative means to reveal God's Kingdom.

The Regions Where Jesus Taught

Understanding the cultural, political, and religious backgrounds of the particular regions of the Holy Land where Jesus taught can help us to better understand his message.

Jesus Preached the Kingdom of God

The Kingdom of God—which won't reach fullness until the end of time—was initiated by Jesus in his life and words and was most revealed in his Paschal Mystery.

Jesus' Sermon on the Mount

Chapters 5-7 of Matthew's Gospel reveal the Beatitudes, Jesus' instruction on how to live, and the Lord's Prayer.

pontiff

A term with roots from the Latin *Pontifex*, which translates "bridge-builder." Originally the term was associated with the highest leaders of any religion; now the term is reserved almost exclusively for the pope.

beatified

From the word for "blessed," this term refers to a person who has been declared by the Church to have the ability to intercede for those who pray in his or her name. Beatification is a step toward canonized sainthood.

Only for Today

One of the most influential people of the twentieth century was Pope John XXIII (1881–1963), who convened the Second Vatican Council in 1962. Loved by Catholics and non-Catholics alike, John XXIII strongly believed that the Church should be like a "welcoming mother," open to everyone, and in a special way to the poor. He lived a simple life even as **pontiff** and drew inspiration from a set of rules for living a Christlike life. Here are six of his rules:

1. Only for today, I will take the greatest care of my appearance: I will dress modestly; I will not raise my voice; I will be courteous in my behavior; I will not criticize anyone; I will not claim to improve or to discipline anyone except myself.
2. Only for today, I will adapt to circumstances, without requiring all circumstances to be adapted to my own wishes.
3. Only for today, I will devote ten minutes of my time to some good reading, remembering that just as food is necessary to the life of the body, so good reading is necessary to the life of the soul.
4. Only for today, I will do one good deed and not tell anyone about it.
5. Only for today, I will do at least one thing I do not like doing; and if my feelings are hurt, I will make sure that no one notices.
6. Only for today, I will firmly believe, despite appearances, that the good providence of God cares for me as no one else who exists in this world.

Inspired by the teachings and life of Jesus Christ, Pope John XXIII was **beatified** in 2000 by another holy pope, Pope John Paul II. Blessed Pope John XXIII's Christ-centered life is evident in his final testament: "What counts the most in life is blessed Jesus Christ, his holy Church, his Gospel, truth and goodness."

What counts most in life is Jesus, his Church, his Gospel, truth, and goodness! Truer words have never been spoken. This chapter examines more closely the teachings of Jesus Christ as they come to us in the synoptic Gospels. The material focuses on the qualities of Jesus as Teacher, background on the locations of where Jesus taught, the parables of Jesus, and his famous declarations in the Sermon on the Mount.

⚫ Jesus Success Stories

St. Jerome said, "He is rich enough who is poor with Christ." Reflect on the meaning of this statement by completing the following exercise.

- List the names of people (famous or not so famous) you believe have found fullness of life by following Jesus. Don't get stuck solely on "church-types." Think of friends, relatives, neighbors, teachers, and acquaintances that reflect a spirit of having found life in Christ.

- Write a wise quotation about faith in Jesus or life in general that you have heard someone on your list say.

- Write one quotation of your own that represents your faith in Jesus.

For Reflection

For the next six days, put into practice each of the six rules of Blessed Pope John XXIII that were described on page 156. Focus on one per day. Note in your journal the progress of what you did to accomplish your goal.

Jesus the Teacher

The Gospel of Luke reports that when Jesus came out of the desert after his forty-day retreat, he returned to Galilee in the power of the Holy Spirit. He then began to teach in the synagogues throughout the whole region, and people began to praise him for his message.

On the Sabbath, he came to his hometown of Nazareth and went to the synagogue, a typical practice for Jesus. On this particular day, he did the public reading of Scripture. He was handed the scroll that contained the writings of the prophet Isaiah. Jesus unrolled the scroll until he found the following passage, which he read aloud:

> The Spirit of the Lord is upon me,
> because he has anointed me
> to bring glad tidings to the poor.
> He has sent me to proclaim liberty
> to captives
> and recovery of sight to the blind,
> to let the oppressed go free,
> and to proclaim a year acceptable
> to the Lord. (Lk 4:18–19)

This was a remarkable text because it prophesied the coming of the Messiah. His listeners were struck by Jesus' dramatic reading and looked intently at him after he sat down. He looked back at them and said, "Today this scripture passage is fulfilled in your hearing" (Lk 4:21). At first, Jesus' neighbors admired him, but then the full impact of what he proclaimed struck them. Jesus was claiming that in him Isaiah's prophecy about the Messiah was taking place, that in him, God's Kingdom was present. In fact, Jesus of Nazareth is the Messiah. He had come to preach the Good News to the poor, to help people live freely, to perform acts of mercy and work for justice, and to celebrate God's presence in the world.

Jesus' explanation astonished his fellow citizens. When they realized the full impact of his claim, they showed outrage, saying things like, "Who is Jesus? Isn't he the son of Joseph? How can he be the Promised One?"

Luke's Gospel explains that Jesus defended himself by relating that no prophet ever received honor in his own hometown. He pointed to the examples of Elijah and Elisha, prophets of Israel, who also ministered to Gentiles, and were rejected by their contemporaries. By mentioning them, Jesus strengthened his own claim to be a prophet. Like Old Testament prophets, Jesus called on people to repent. Like them, he used creative teaching methods (e.g., teaching with parables) to get people to pay attention. He also engaged in symbolic, attention-grabbing actions (e.g., the cleansing of the Temple in Luke 19:45–48), warned of God's judgment at the end of time, and performed healings and other miracles. His teachings and actions revealed his identity. For example, when he raised the dead son of the widow of Nain (see Luke 7:11–17), witnesses to the marvelous event proclaimed, "A great prophet has arisen in our midst," and "God has visited his people" (Lk 7:16).

But on that occasion at the beginning of Jesus' ministry in the synagogue, his own neighbors were critical of him, enraged on this particular Sabbath to the point where they tried to throw him down a hill. Jesus escaped this first attempt on his life.

Jesus had much work to do after that day in Nazareth. This work involved preaching, teaching, and performing mighty works to reveal who he was and the coming of God's Kingdom. People would respond one way or another to Jesus because of his mighty message, his marvelous deeds, and his engaging personality. Jesus definitely was a one-of-a-kind teacher.

How Jesus Taught

The philosopher Aristotle said that teachers are to be more honored than one's parents. His point was that while parents give us physical life, teachers show us how to live well. If this observation is true, then we should revere Jesus above all teachers. His message and his person bring eternal life.

Jesus was an exceptional teacher, easy to learn from and good to be around. He had many qualities that made him an outstanding teacher, worth listening to. For example:

Jesus was genuine. Like all superb teachers, Jesus' deeds backed up his words. A prime example is how he taught that the greatest love we can show another is to lay down our lives for that person. Jesus did what he preached when he freely gave up his life for all of us.

Jesus was available. Jesus met people where they were. A wandering preacher and teacher, he taught everywhere—on hillsides, on dusty roads, at the tables of the rich and poor, as well as in the synagogues and in the Temple. To keep the attention of so many different types of people, Jesus surely was interesting, attention getting, and entertaining.

Jesus was understandable. Jesus used down-to-earth, picturesque language. For example, instead of giving a high-blown maxim like "Charity should not be ostentatious," Jesus said, "But when you give

alms, do not let your left hand know what your right is doing" (Mt 6:3). Or Jesus could have said, "Hypocrisy is unbecoming for my disciples." Instead he taught, "Why do you notice the splinter in your brother's eye, but do not perceive the wooden beam in your own eye?" (Mt 7:3).

Jesus' metaphors and similes created vibrant images that made his listeners take notice. For example, Jesus told us that the Son of Man would appear very quickly. "For just as lightning comes from the east and is seen as far as the west, so will the coming of the Son of Man be. Wherever the corpse is, there the vultures will gather" (Mt 24:27–28).

Jesus also appealed to our senses. He used vivid images to teach about our vocation: "You are salt for the earth. But if salt loses its taste, with what can it be seasoned? It is no longer good for anything but to be thrown out and trampled underfoot. You are light for the world" (Mt 5:13–14).

Jesus spoke Aramaic, a poetic language. Aramaic was the language spoken by his contemporaries. This language was vivid and poetic. For example, Jesus spoke in *parallel statements*, that is, he repeated thoughts a second time in a slightly different form to drive home an idea. Here's an example: "Give to the one who asks of you, and do not turn your back on one who wants to borrow" (Mt 5:42).

Jesus also used *hyperbole*, or exaggeration, to make a point. This speech pattern was also common in Aramaic. A parallel example in English is, "I have a ton of homework," or "It's raining cats and dogs." Hyperbole drives home a point, but we should not take it literally. Jesus said, "If your right eye causes you to sin, tear it out and throw it away. . . . And if your right hand causes you to sin, cut it off and throw it away. It is better for you to lose one of your members than to have your whole body go into Gehenna" (Mt 5:29–30). Jesus' point is clear: Fight temptation rather than risk eternal loss. He does not want us to mutilate ourselves. He exaggerated to drive home his message.

Jesus taught with authority. When rabbis of Jesus' day taught, they typically quoted prominent teachers to back up their positions. Jesus quoted no other rabbi, and when he quoted Scriptures, he gave novel, penetrating, and profound interpretations. As God's Son, he spoke on his own authority.

We can see this clearly in the way Jesus used the simple little word *Amen*. *Amen* is a Hebrew word that comes from the same root as the word "believe." It carries the sense of "Yes, certainly, I believe." It was used at the end of an oath or blessing or a curse or some similar saying. It showed agreement with the words of another.

Jesus used this simple word *to introduce* (not end) and *to strengthen* his own words. The *Catechism of the Catholic Church* states, "Our Lord often used the word 'Amen,' sometimes repeated, to emphasize the trustworthiness of his teaching, his authority founded on God's truth" (*CCC*, 1063). No one but Jesus taught in this manner. He spoke with unusual authority. He quoted no other teacher.

Jesus was a brilliant debater. Jesus' opponents sometimes tried to catch him in one of his teachings, but he would have none of their tricks. One incident involved the coin of tribute Jews were expected to give to the Roman emperor. Pious Jews hated paying the tax. One day the Pharisees' disciples approached Jesus with the question, "Is it lawful to pay the census tax to Caesar or not?" (Mt 22:17).

If Jesus said no, his opponents would then claim that he was preaching rebellion against Rome, a crime punishable by death. If he said yes, he would

lose face with zealous Jews who hated the Roman tax. Jesus understood clearly the malice of the question. He asked his opponents to show him a coin. This was a clever move on his part because his opponents produced a Roman coin, something they should not have been carrying if they hated the Romans as much as they claimed. Their hypocrisy was immediately clear to everyone. Jesus' response: "'Then repay to Caesar what belongs to Caesar and to God what belongs to God.' When they heard this they were amazed, and leaving him they went away" (Mt 22:21–22). Jesus saw through their ploy, revealing to everyone their true intentions.

Jesus challenges his listeners. Good teachers stretch their students' minds, challenging them to grow. An example from Jesus' ministry involved a rich aristocrat who asked Jesus what he must do to gain eternal life. Jesus reviewed the commandments. When the man assured Jesus that he had kept all the commandments, Jesus challenged him to sell everything he owned, distribute his money to the poor, and come follow him. The rich man sadly turned from Jesus and walked away. Jesus looked at the departing man and said, "How hard it is for those who have wealth to enter the kingdom of God! For it is easier for a camel to pass through the eye of a needle than for a rich person to enter the kingdom of God" (Lk 18:24–25).

This saying demands that Jesus' followers examine their consciences.

grace
God's gift of friendship and life that enables us to share his life and love. Grace introduces us to the intimacy of life with the Blessed Trinity.

JESUS AND PARADOX

A paradox is defined as "a comparison that appears to contradict" or "something that leads to a situation that defies intuition." For example, consider the paradox of Petronius: "Moderation in all things, including moderation." Jesus used thought-provoking paradox in his teaching. Often this took the form of short, memorable sayings of great significance. Here are three examples:

For whoever wishes to save his life will lose it, but whoever loses his life for my sake will save it. What profit is there for one to gain the whole world yet lose or forfeit himself? (Lk 9:24-25)

For the one who is least among all of you is the one who is the greatest. (Lk 9:48)

For everyone who exalts himself will be humbled, but the one who humbles himself will be exalted. (Lk 14:11)

- Write the meaning of each of these paradoxes of Jesus. Also, write about one or more experiences from your life when these have been true.

What is the meaning of Jesus' saying? Is this hyperbole? After all, a camel cannot pass through the eye of a needle and, by comparison, a rich man cannot be saved. This saying does involve some hyperbole as well as a *paradox* (see page 160), an apparent contradiction. He gave his own solution to the problem when his disciples questioned him: "What is impossible for human beings is possible for God" (Lk 18:27).

Jesus warned against a person trying to earn or merit the gift of God's **grace**. We enter God's Kingdom only through the miracle of God's grace. We need to be humble and to have faith and trust in God alone. The danger of having too much wealth is the belief that money can buy Salvation. In reality, material possessions can blind us to think that we don't need anyone, including God. Owning many things and hoarding money can make us miss the humble workings of God in our midst. Jesus warns us and challenges us just like he did in the Sermon on the Mount: "Blessed are the poor in spirit, for theirs is the kingdom of Heaven" (Mt 5:3).

⬥ For Review

1. What significant event took place when Jesus began to preach in Nazareth? How did Jesus' neighbors react? Why did they react this way?

2. Discuss some qualities of Jesus as a teacher.

3. What language did Jesus customarily speak?

4. What is the meaning of the word *Amen*? How and why did Jesus use it in a unique way?

⬥ For Reflection

Create a list of four more qualities that you believe make for a great teacher. How did Jesus exhibit that quality in his own ministry in the Gospel of Matthew?

The Regions Where Jesus Taught

The Gospels report that Jesus limited his teaching ministry to the Holy Land, especially in Galilee and Jerusalem. Piecing together the regions of the Holy Land and the cultural, political, and religious situations in each provides further background information for understanding the Gospel message. Galilee, Samaria, and Judea were the three important regions of the Holy Land that figured prominently in Jesus' ministry.

Galilee

Jesus and most of his Apostles were from Galilee, a region in the north with fertile land and rolling hills watered by the Jordan River and the Sea of Galilee. Jesus grew up in Nazareth, a small town of perhaps no more than five hundred people at the time he lived there. It was about an hour's walk from the Hellenistic city of Sepphoris, a former capital of Galilee. Sepphoris might have provided work for Joseph and Jesus, though Jesus probably avoided it during his public life since Herod Antipas and others who opposed Jesus were centered there.

Herod Antipas (4 BC to AD 37), the son of Herod the Great, ruled Galilee during Jesus' lifetime. Farmers and shepherds were relatively prosperous because of the fertility of the land. The Sea of Galilee provided a living for fishermen. Most of the population was Jewish, though some Gentiles (non-Jews) could be found in the area. Jews from Judea sometimes doubted the religious fervor of Galilean Jews because of their relationships with Gentiles. Galilean Jews also spoke with a distinctive Aramaic accent. However, many Galileans were zealous about their religion and greatly disliked foreign rulers. It was from this area that the religious group known as the Zealots (see Chapter 8) first formed and held great influence.

Many of the colorful details of Jesus' parables come from his keen observation of Galilean life: birds, flowers, farmers at work in the fields, fishing nets straining under a heavy load. Cana (the site of Jesus' first miracle), Bethsaida (the home of Peter, Andrew, and Philip), and Capernaum (the headquarters of Jesus' Galilean ministry) were all located in Galilee.

Samaria

Samaria was the region to the south of Galilee, north central in relation to the entirety of the Holy Land. The Samaritans descended from foreigners who intermarried with the old northern Israelite tribes at the time of Assyria's conquest of the northern kingdom. The Samaritans accepted the Mosaic Law, but did not accept the prophetical or wisdom writings. They rejected the Jerusalem Temple because they believed that God chose **Mount Gerizim** as the proper place to worship. The Judeans destroyed the Mount Gerizim temple in 128 BC, leading to hostility between Jews and Samaritans. On pilgrimages to Judea, Galileans would try to avoid Samaria if they could for fear of being attacked by Samaritans.

Though Jesus did not allow his Apostles to preach to the Samaritans (see Matthew 10:5), he showed only love to them. He made one a hero of a parable (see Luke 10:30–35), was kind to a Samaritan woman (see John 4:1–42), and praised a leper from Samaria for being the only one to thank him for a cure (see Luke 17:16). Some of Jesus' enemies insulted him by calling him a Samaritan (see John 8:48).

Judea

Bethlehem, the birthplace of Jesus, was located in Judea, as was Bethany, the home of Jesus' friends Lazarus, Martha, and Mary. Another notable Judean town was Jericho, where Jesus healed a blind man and met a famous tax collector, Zacchaeus.

The region was in the southern part of the Holy Land. It was a dry, barren, craggy land where most of its inhabitants were Jews who returned from the Babylonian captivity. Jerusalem was the principal city. Lofted on two hills 2,255 to 2,400 feet above sea level, Jerusalem was Judea's religious, political, and economic center. Life centered on the Temple located there.

Most of the Judean population lived in or near Jerusalem. In Jesus' day, the city may have had a population of 55,000 to 70,000 people with as many as another 120,000 swelling the population during the Jewish festivals. Jews in Jerusalem worked at many various trades. The city also attracted scribes whose job it was to interpret the Law.

A barren wilderness was located in southernmost Judea, the place where Jesus retreated after his baptism. Also found there was the fifty-three-mile-long Dead Sea, which, at 1,300 feet below sea level, is the lowest point on earth.

Mount Gerizim
One of the two mountains in the immediate vicinity of the West Bank city of Nablus. The mountain is sacred to the Samaritans, who believe it to be the location chosen by YHWH for a holy temple. The mountain continues to be the center of Samaritan religion to this day.

WHERE WAS IT?

Read the following Scripture references from the synoptic Gospels. Locate on the map where each event took place.

- Where did Jesus cast out a demon? (see Mark 1:21)
- To which city was the traveler in the parable of the Good Samaritan going? (see Luke 10:30)
- On the road to which city does Jesus predict his Passion and Death? (see Mark 8:27-33)
- To what does Jesus compare Chorazin and Bethsaida? (see Matthew 11:20-22)
- Where did Jesus dine with Zacchaeus? (see Luke 19:1-10)
- Where did Jesus instruct two disciples to find a colt for him? (see Matthew 21:1)
- Where did the resurrected Jesus eat a meal with two disciples? (see Luke 24:13)

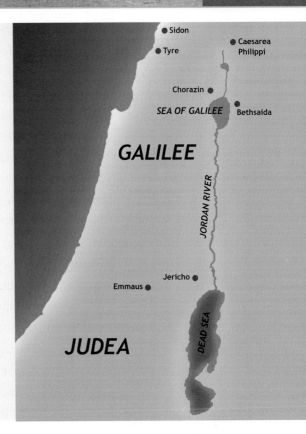

For Review

1. Describe each of the regions of the Holy Land that figured in the public life of Jesus.

2. Who were the Samaritans? What were some of their beliefs?

3. When were times that the population of Jerusalem would swell?

For Reflection

Write a journal entry describing what you imagine one day of travel with Jesus would have been like in any of the regions described.

Jesus Preached the Kingdom of God

From the beginning of his public ministry until his Death on the Cross, Jesus preached the coming of God's Kingdom. "This is the time of fulfillment. The kingdom of God is at hand. Repent, and believe in the gospel" (Mk 1:15). In doing so, Jesus accomplished the will of his Father. The Father's will is to share his divine life with all human beings. He accomplishes this by gathering all persons around his Son Jesus Christ. The Church is, in fact, this gathering, "on earth the seed and beginning of the kingdom" (*Lumen Gentium*, 5, *CCC*, 541).

The "Kingdom of God" (or "Kingdom of Heaven," used by Matthew) is not a place. Rather, it is the active presence of God's love, justice, truth, and Salvation working in the world. Jesus Christ is God's presence in the world, the one who brings the Kingdom. He is the one who gathers all people into the unity of the Blessed Trinity—Father, Son, and

Holy Spirit—through his preaching and miracles. Ultimately, it is the event of the Paschal Mystery—Christ's work of redemption, accomplished principally by his Passion, Death, Resurrection, and glorious Ascension—that brings about the Kingdom. It is the saving event that unites us to our Savior Jesus Christ and makes it possible for us to be adopted into God's family.

One prominent way that Jesus used to help people understand the mystery of God's Kingdom growing in our midst was the use of parables. While his miracles confirmed the truth of his words, his parables helped his contemporaries, and help us today, to understand the meaning of his message.

What Are Parables?

The English word *parable* comes from the Greek word *parabole,* which means "placing two things side by side in order to compare them." The parables that Jesus told were simple, vivid picture stories drawn from ordinary life. They compare something very familiar—like seeds, wheat, yeast, sheep, farmers, and nets—to an unfamiliar truth, usually about some aspect of God's Kingdom. Jesus told these stories to challenge his listeners to use their imaginations, emotions, and minds to grapple with the truth he wants to teach.

By using parables, Jesus again demonstrated his brilliance as a teacher. His stories revealed truth in an interesting way. They are easy to remember. This was important because Jesus' disciples did not take notes when he taught them; they had to commit his teaching to memory. Jesus' stories were so vivid that his hearers could easily recall them.

Consider the parable of Lazarus and the Rich Man (see Luke 16:19–31). The message of the parable is that wealthy people must share their riches with poor people. If they don't, God will punish them in eternity. In the story, Jesus tells how Lazarus was poor and sick. He was so poor that he longed to eat the scraps that fell from the tables of the rich man, and he was so sick that he was covered with

sores. The rich man never even noticed Lazarus, who eventually died and went to Heaven.

Before long, the rich man also died. He was buried and went to hell. There he suffered every torment. He saw a vision of Lazarus in Heaven who was totally happy in the company of Abraham, the father of the Jews. The rich man begged Abraham to allow Lazarus to dip the tip of his finger in water to cool his tongue, for he was in agony burning in the flames. Abraham refused the rich man his request, nor could the rich man appear to his five brothers to warn them what was in store for them if they didn't change their selfish ways. Abraham replied that the rich man's brothers had the Sacred Scriptures to tell them what to do; even if a man came back to life, they wouldn't pay attention.

Principal Parables of Jesus in the Synoptic Gospels

Read at least five parables from the list. Be sure to select at least one from each Gospel. Summarize the interpretation of the parable found in one biblical commentary. Write your own interpretation of the meaning of parable drawing on the information you read in the commentary.

	Matthew	Mark	Luke
Lamp under a bushel	5:15-17	4:21-22	8:16-18
New cloth on old garments	9:16	2:21	5:36
New wine in old wineskins	9:17	2:22	5:37
The Sower	13:3-23	4:2-20	8:4-15
Mustard seed	13:31-32	4:30-32	13:18-19
Wicked tenants of the vineyard	21:33-45	12:1-12	20:9-19
Budding fig tree	24:32-35	13:28-32	21:29-33
House built on a rock	7:24-27		6:47-49
Wayward Children	11:16-19		7:31-35
Leaven	13:33		13:20-21
Lost sheep	18:12-14		15:3-7
Weeds among the wheat	13:24-30		
Treasure hidden in a field	13:44		
Pearl of great value	13:45-46		
Dragnet	13:47-50		
Unmerciful servant	18:23-25		
Laborers in the vineyard	20:1-16		
Father and two sons	21:28-32		
Marriage feast for the king's son	22:1-14		
Wise and foolish maidens	25:1-13		
The servants and their talents	25:14-30		
Separating sheep from goats	25:31-46		
Seed growing silently		4:26-29	
Doorkeeper on watch		13:34-37	
Two debtors			7:41-43
Good Samaritan			10:25-37
Friend at midnight			11:5-10
Rich fool			12:16-21
Watchful servants			12:35-38
Wise steward	24:45-51		12:42-48
Barren fig tree			13:6-9
Dinner guests			14:16-24
Lost coin			15:8-10
Prodigal son			15:11-32
Dishonest steward			16:1-13
Rich man and Lazarus			16:19-31
Useless servants			17:7-10
Persistent widow			18:1-8
Pharisee and tax collector			18:9-14
Ten pounds			19:11-27

How could anyone forget this story once they heard it? How could they forget the religious message Jesus was trying to teach?

Another reason Jesus' spoke in parables was to force his listeners to look at reality in a fresh way. Parables stretch the mind into active thought. If people are not willing to change their preconceptions, they will fail to understand Jesus' point: "They look, but do not see and hear but do not listen or understand" (Mt 13:13). Jesus' parables are windows into the mystery of God's reign. They help to uncover the marvelous work of God in our midst. Their teaching is often surprising and usually clear, but the original listeners or today's readers has to look at the story with open eyes to discover what Jesus means. Consider, for example, the short parable of the pearl. Jesus said:

> The kingdom of Heaven is like a merchant searching for fine pearls. When he finds a pearl of great price, he goes and sells all he has and buys it. (Mt 13:45–46)

The meaning of this story is clear, yet urgent. So valuable is the man's discovery of the perfect pearl that he surrenders his entire fortune to buy it. When we discover God's Kingdom, we should do what the merchant did. God's Kingdom is so valuable that we should stake our whole life on it.

The Meaning of the Parables (CCC, 543-546)

There are several important messages to be gleaned from the parables of the synoptic Gospels. For example, the Kingdom of God is for all; sinners are welcome; Salvation has arrived in the person of Jesus; repentance is a prerequisite for entering the Kingdom; the Kingdom is for the poor and lowly; and the Kingdom should be rejoiced over. More information on these meanings follows.

God's Kingdom Is for All (see the Mustard Seed, Luke 13:18-19; the Sower, Mark 4:1-20)

God's Kingdom has arrived in his Son Jesus Christ who came to reconcile and renew all things. God is near because Jesus is near. Salvation is taking place right now. YHWH's justice is bringing peace to the land, justice to the poor, and comfort to widows and orphans. Jesus is the Promised One, the Messiah, who came to usher in God's reign. He is the principle sign of the Kingdom, of God's will being accomplished on earth, even as it is in Heaven.

The growth of the Kingdom is steady, but sure. Jesus says it begins small like a mustard seed, but it will grow large. It spreads in its own mysterious way, like yeast working in dough or seeds secretly unleashing their power. Its harvest will be greater than we can possibly imagine.

The parable of the Sower tells us that the Kingdom, despite all the obstacles in may encounter, will flourish. This parable also teaches that everyone is invited to accept the Kingdom but people must first accept Jesus' Word. The word of the Lord is compared to seed sown in a field, seed that must fall on receptive ground to take root and flourish. Followers of Jesus are the fertile ground that receives the Lord's word, letting it sprout and grow until the harvest at the end of time. It is at the end of time that the Kingdom of God will come in fullness so that "God may be all in all" (1 Cor 15:28). The just will reign with Christ forever, glorified in body and soul, and the material universe will itself be transformed.

Sinners Are Welcome (see the Lost Sheep, Luke 15:1-7; the Lost Coin, Luke 15: 8-10; the Lost Son, Luke 15:11-32)

Jesus preached forgiveness and mercy. He associated with all kinds of people, especially those who needed God's love and forgiveness: tax collectors, the poor, prostitutes, and the sick. His invitation to the Kingdom was open to all sinners to sit at the table of the Lord.

Those who self-righteously believed in their own holiness severely criticized Jesus for associating with the outcast. They believed that if you associated with bad companions then you yourself must be evil. Jesus replied, "Those who are well do not need a physician, but the sick do. I did not come to call the righteous but sinners" (Mk 2:17).

On one occasion, when certain Pharisees and scribes complained about Jesus' association with sinners, Jesus told three important parables of forgiveness. In the parable of the Lost Sheep, Jesus tells of the shepherd who goes out of his way to rescue the lost sheep. In a world where shepherds might quietly accept the loss of one percent of their flock, and not risk abandoning the rest of the flock, Jesus' example would have surprised his audience, but Jesus wanted to show us the depth of the Father's love, especially for the lost sinner. God's love is beyond what we can comprehend, and it is intended for everyone.

God's love is also tender. Note how the shepherd places the lost sheep on his shoulders. Why? Simply because a lost sheep will lie down and refuse to move. The tender care and loving concern of the shepherd is a glimpse of the immense love God has for us.

The Lost Coin paints a vivid picture of a woman sweeping the whole house to retrieve a lost coin and then announcing to her friends and neighbors that she has found it. Besides this happy outcome, note, too, how Jesus compared God to a woman, something no rabbi of his day ever did. God's love is like that of a persistent woman who would not give up. God will not give up on sinners. The love of Jesus' Father—our Father—greatly exceeds the expectations of the learned men of Jesus' day. God's mercy is something to rejoice about.

Finally, a careful reading of the parable of the Lost, or Prodigal, Son reveals a compassionate father and his two sons. (Pope Benedict XVI suggests

that we should name the parable "The Two Brothers and Good Father.") Certainly, the younger son threw away his father's patrimony and was foolish, ending up his miserable spending spree by dining with swine. For his Jewish audience, who considered pigs unclean animals, Jesus could not have painted a more desolate picture.

When the son realized how low he had sunk, he repented and returned to his father. His father was waiting all the time, to rush out to him, embrace him, and throw a welcome-home party. It is the father's love that is prodigal, spendthrift, beyond all our expectations; and so is the father's attitude toward the second son, who complained about his father's generosity. Like those who were criticizing Jesus for mingling with sinners, the second son is self-righteous, not even calling his brother "my brother," rather referring to him as "this son of yours." But the father, always loving and wise in his ways, assured his elder son that one day he would inherit all of his father's possessions, but the time at hand was a time to rejoice because his lost brother "was dead and has come to life again; he was lost and has been found" (Lk 15:32).

The father in this parable is lavish in his love. Jesus tells this story to teach that his Father's love is similar. He stands ready to unconditionally accept his children back into the family and with great love. Such is God's love and mercy. Since Jesus is the Father's unique Son, the one who reveals the Father, he associates with sinners to bring them the Good News of God's mercy and compassion.

Be a Good Samaritan

The parable of the Good Samaritan, one of the most popular of all parables, is recorded in Luke 10:25-37. It has often been turned into an allegory throughout Christian history. Here is a popular interpretation of the parable of the Good Samaritan as an allegory.

Parable Elements	Allegorical Meaning
Traveler	Adam (who represents all humanity)
Jerusalem	the heavenly city, our goal
Jericho	the fallen world
Robbers	demons who strip Adam of immortality
Priest	the Law
Levite	Prophets
Samaritan	Jesus Christ (who heals humanity with oil and wine—comfort and admonition)
Inn	the Church
Innkeeper	Apostles: Peter and Paul
Samaritan's return	Second Coming of Christ

Complete this project with a classmate:

- After carefully reading the parable, share your own allegorical interpretation. Who are the victims of violence in *your* world? Who fails to take notice? What kinds of aid can you and your classmates give? What would correspond to the inn? Write a short report summarizing your and your partner's responses.

- Devise a short service project where you can respond to someone in your school who might be neglected or hurting. Follow through on the project, and write a summary of its results.

Salvation (see the Workers in the Vineyard, Matthew 20:1-16; the Great Feast, Luke 14:15-24)

Jesus emphasized time and again in his teaching that a new age had dawned, that the day of Salvation had arrived. He spoke of new wine being poured into new wineskins, of a new harvest, of the need to put on new robes. His vivid image of a wedding feast especially announces that the Lord is among his people. (The wedding banquet was a familiar symbol for Jews of Heaven and God's presence among his people.) Nothing can be the same again. The divine physician has come.

Jesus came to assure us that Salvation is taking place. Jesus is the Savior of everyone. The wedding feast is open to all—Jew and Gentile alike. It is a pure gift, something we cannot earn. God gives it as he pleases, just like the landowner dispensed wages freely and generously to workers who only labored for an hour. God's Salvation is great news.

Jesus announced Salvation, and he brought it. It comes through repentance and forgiveness of sin. In speaking to the wealthy tax collector Zacchaeus, Jesus said, "Today Salvation has come to this house . . . For the Son of Man has come to seek and save what was lost" (Lk 19:9–10). Jesus is the Savior. It is he who makes us whole, who heals the alienation between us, the Father, and other people. Jesus' miracles reveal his identity, show forth Father's power, and demonstrate that the Good News is taking place.

Belief and Repentance (see the Two Foundations, Matthew 7:24-27; the Two Sons, Matthew 21:28-32)

The English word *repent* (Greek *metanoia*) literally means "change one's mind," a radical way of thinking and doing things. Because Jesus is here, reality and life are now radically different. It is time to stop living selfishly and bitterly toward our neighbor. God's justice is breaking into our world. We should accept this new order of things first by believing it to be true, then by living justly and lovingly. Saying we are going to change and not following through is empty lip service. The one who obeys God's Word is the one who does God's will.

After announcing the coming of the Kingdom, Jesus called for repentance and faith in the Gospel. Repentance and faith go hand in hand. Jesus expects us to respond to his announcements that God's Kingdom is happening now, that God is a loving and forgiving Father, and that Salvation is happening in our midst. What are we called to do? First, we should repent, that is, change our lives, and then we should believe the Good News of Salvation. Listening to, and acting on Jesus' words is like the wise man who built his house on a foundation of rock. Nothing can destroy the foundation of the Gospel!

Preparation for God's Judgment (see the Ten Virgins, the Talents, the Sheep and Goats, Mt 25:1-46)

The Kingdom belongs to the poor and lowly, that is, to those who accept Christ in humility. Jesus came to preach to the poor, and he blesses them. He shared their life, experiencing hunger, thirst, and privation. He identified himself with all poor people, and he requires that we love them as a condition of entering his Kingdom. In fact, when Christ comes to judge us, he will separate the sheep from the goats based on this criterion: "Whatever you did for one of these least brothers of mine, you did for me" (Mt 25:40). Oppositely, those who ignore the needs of the least ones will be asked to depart from the Lord to the "eternal fire prepared for the **devil** and his angels" (Mt 25:41). This warning of Christ, echoed by the Church, is of the eternal punishment of **Hell** for those who die separated from God in the state of mortal sin.

Entering God's Kingdom requires faith, but it also demands action. Love is faith-in-action. Because God is love, we, as Jesus' disciples, must also be loving. We help Jesus in his work of Salvation by being instruments of God's mercy and love. For one

devil

The name for a fallen angel who refused to accept God or his Kingdom. Another word for the devil is Satan, or the "Evil One." The devil and other demons were at first good angels, but became evil due to their own choices and actions.

Hell

Eternal separation from God that results in a person's dying after freely and deliberately acting against God's will (that is, not repenting of mortal sin).

Mount Sinai, Sinai, Egypt.

Sermon on the Mount

A section in Matthew's Gospel (Mt 5:1—7:29) in which Jesus delivers the first of five discourses recorded in the Gospel. The Sermon on the Mount begins with the sharing of the Beatitudes. The Beatitudes are also found in the Sermon on the Plain in Luke 6:20—26.

thing, we must use the talents he gave to us for the benefit of others (see Matthew 25:14–30). And we must serve as he served. To follow Jesus, and to love in imitation of him, takes sacrifice and commitment. Jesus' invitation is a challenge: "Whoever wishes to come after me must deny himself, take up his cross, and follow me" (Mk 8:34). This means service:

> Rather, whoever wishes to be great among you will be your servant; whoever wishes to be first among you will be the slave of all. For the Son of Man did not come to be served, but to serve and to give his life as a ransom for many. (Mk 10:43–45)

Rejoice (see Weeds among the Wheat, Matthew 13:24-30; Hidden Treasure, Matthew 13:44; Rich Fool, Luke 12:16-21)

The Good News Jesus came to preach met with resistance. Perhaps in some ways Jesus' words were so good they were almost impossible to accept. Jesus' enemies saw him as a threat to their power over people. They worked to get rid of him. Jesus knew the Kingdom would be opposed, but he assures us that it will triumph in the end. This is the point of the parable of the Sower. Even amidst apparent setbacks in working for God's Kingdom and Salvation, we should be happy, joyful people. We know there will be suffering and evil in our world. There will be forces working against God's

plan, but in the end, things will work out. The weeds will be separated from the wheat on harvest day.

Those who accept God's Kingdom and Jesus, who proclaimed it, have found the hidden treasure. We should stake everything on it. Jesus has revealed to us his Father's goodness, his generosity, his forgiving love, and Salvation. Jesus announces that good triumphs over evil. Therefore, we should accept this Good News with joy and deep conviction. We should not wait for tomorrow because it might be too late. This was the lesson a foolish man did not learn. He tore down his old barns, and he built new ones to store his riches. Unfortunately, he did not count on dying that night. The time to choose Jesus and his Father's Kingdom is *right now.*

The Lord wants us to believe in him and his message because he needs us to share it with others. We have his joy to share with others; we have the Good News of Salvation to give others. We are instruments of his love. "Repent, believe the Good News of Jesus and live his life of love—this is the message of Christ our Savior!"

◉ For Review

1. What is meant by the expression "Kingdom of God"?

2. What is a parable? Why did Jesus tell parables?

3. What is the meaning of the following parables?

   • Lazarus and the Rich Man

   • Pearl

- Mustard Seed
- Sower
- Lost Sheep, Lost Coin, Lost Son (Good Father and Two Brothers)
- Sheep and Goats
- Rich Fool
- Good Samaritan

4. Discuss five points of Jesus' message.
5. What does it mean to repent?

For Reflection

Write or share a parable that expresses your belief in the presence of God's Kingdom.

Jesus' Sermon on the Mount

The Gospel of Matthew records Jesus' **Sermon on the Mount**, an occasion when Jesus went up on a mountainside to speak to a great crowd of his followers. Recall that the Evangelist Matthew wrote his Gospel for a Jewish-Christian audience. The scene of Jesus' teaching on the mountain brings to mind Moses, who delivered the Law from a mountain, Mount Sinai. A message of the Sermon on the Mount is that Jesus is the New Lawgiver. His instructions guide those who have accepted the Good News and wish to live as his faithful followers.

The Sermon on the Mount is recorded over three chapters in Matthew 5–7 and contains over one hundred verses. It begins with Jesus' blessings, the Beatitudes, and then it treats Jesus' instructions on how to live and how to pray. It concludes with additional reflections on what is important in life. Luke's Gospel contains a shortened version (32 verses) of this teaching in the "Sermon on the Plain" (Lk 6:17–49). The missing verses in Luke mainly concern sayings specifically related to Jewish-Christian problems. Luke, remember, wrote for a predominately Gentile-Christian audience. The following sections provide more detail on Jesus' teachings from the Gospel of Matthew.

The Beatitudes (CCC, *1716; 1725-1727*)

The moral teaching offered in the Sermon on the Mount is a roadmap to eternal happiness. Another word for happiness is *beatitude*. In the Beatitudes, Jesus' blessings reveal how to fulfill our desire for happiness and teach us the final end to which God calls us: the Kingdom, the vision of God, participation in divine nature, eternal life, life as children of God, and rest in God. The life-giving words of the Beatitudes show us how to love God and others in imitation of our Lord. (For comparison, see Lk 6:20–26.) The Beatitudes also complete the promises that God made to Abraham, the father of the Jewish faith.

A summary of the Beatitudes follows.

Blessed are the poor in spirit, for theirs is the kingdom of Heaven.

Jesus associated with poor, weak, and vulnerable people and expects that his followers should also. This beatitude is not intended to condone the condition of material poverty, which is an evil that should be eradicated. Rather, Jesus wants us to recognize our spiritual poverty—that everything we are and everything we have are gifts from God. We show our gratitude for what we have been given by sharing what we have and what we are with others.

Blessed are they who mourn, for they will be comforted.

Jesus blesses those who mourn over injustices and evils committed against God and his children, that is, the sufferings of needy and innocent people. The hearts of those close to God ache for the sins of the world and for their own sins, too. The Lord tells us not to lose heart, though, because he promises that he will eventually console us. Through deep mourning, we receive comfort that only God can provide.

Blessed are the meek, for they will inherit the land.

Meek people are humble and patient with others. Jesus exemplified meekness when he treated others with gentleness and compassion. He also forgave others when they hurt and taunted him. His heavenly Father also treats each of us with patience, forgiveness, and gentleness when we sin. We should imitate God our Father and Jesus our Savior by being patient with the shortcomings of others. We should work to solve disagreements with gentleness and goodwill and never give in to hate or violence.

Blessed are they who hunger and thirst for righteousness, for they will be satisfied.

Our restless hearts cannot find true happiness until they find God. Jesus blesses those who know that only God's righteousness can fulfill us. God made us so our hearts seek divine justice, the holy Father, and the loving, forgiving friendship of Jesus Christ, our Savior. The Lord Jesus comes to us in the Eucharist to help us grow in holiness, to satisfy our spiritual hunger, and to unite with us so we can take him to others.

Blessed are the merciful, for they will be shown mercy.

When we pray the Our Father, we petition God to "forgive us our trespasses as we forgive those who trespass against us." God shows his great love for us through his Son Jesus Christ, who forgives our

 ## How Well Are You Living the Beatitudes?

Examine how well you are putting the teachings of the Beatitudes into practice. Read each statement below and rate your own behavior. Write a short summary of how well you are doing and in what ways you need to improve. Then answer the questions that follow.

- I thank God for all that I am, and I share my gifts with others.
- I fight the evil influences that tempt me and ask for God's forgiveness for my own sins.
- I am a gentle, humble person who works to build others up.
- I am growing in holiness—for example, I receive the Eucharist at least once a week.
- I am a forgiving person.
- My priorities are God is number one, family is number two, and friends are number three.
- I am an instrument of God's peace in my family and school.
- I am willing to suffer criticism for doing the right thing. I resist peer pressure.

Questions

1. Which Beatitude does the world most need to see practiced? Why?
2. What are practical examples of how today's teens might put into practice each of the Beatitudes?
3. Read Luke's version of the Beatitudes in Luke 6:20-26. What are some differences between Luke's and Matthew's versions?

sins and makes it possible through the Holy Spirit and Baptism to become members of the divine family. As a sign of our gratitude, we should share with others the love, mercy, and forgiveness that we have been given. Forgiving others, especially our enemies, is a sign to others that our merciful God loves everyone.

Blessed are the clean of heart, for they will see God.

A person with a clean heart has a single-hearted commitment to God. School, money, possessions, family, sports, friends, and everything else should come after a total commitment to accomplish God's will. The clean of heart are honest, sincere, and unselfish.

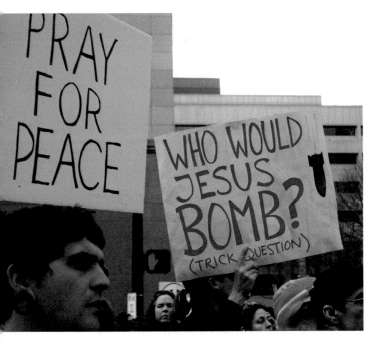

Blessed are the peacemakers, for they will be called children of God.

Adopted children of God must be loving and peaceful and never cause conflict with others. They will work hard to end strife that leads to violence. A Christian is a peacemaker, a disciple of the Prince of Peace, one who treats others as brothers and sisters in the Lord.

Blessed are they who are persecuted for the sake of righteousness, for theirs is the kingdom of Heaven.

Suffering for faith in Jesus is a great sign of love for him. He himself suffered misunderstanding and abuse when he preached the truth. Our Christlike words and actions will at times bring us ridicule and rejection. Some brave Christians even suffered martyrdom. When we remain faithful to the Lord, he will reward us with eternal happiness in Heaven. There is no greater reward.

Sayings on How to Live

The next section of the Sermon on the Mount offers more sayings of Jesus that form the central part of Matthew's Gospel. The source for many of these sayings is Q and the material unique to Matthew. As you proceed through the subsections of what follows, begin your study by first reading each referenced passage from the Bible.

Salt of the Earth and Light of the World (see Matthew 5:13-16)

Jesus shares the beautiful image of Christians as salt and light. He teaches that if we put into practice each of the Beatitudes, they will make a compelling difference in the world. Just as salt flavors food, committed disciples flavor the world with Christ's love. This means that the world should be a better place because Christians are in it. Salt also preserves food, saving meat for future consumption. Our presence as Jesus' disciples should bring the world closer to eternal Salvation.

Christians are also like light. Light dispels darkness. It shows the way and dispels fear of the unknown. Jesus tells us that our good works should be like a beacon of light that leads others to God. The Good News is only good and newsworthy if people can see it in action.

BREAKING OPEN THE LORD'S PRAYER

(CCC, 2759-2865)

As with the Beatitudes, there are also two versions of the Lord's Prayer in the synoptic Gospels. In the Gospel of Matthew (6:9-13), Jesus teaches the Lord's Prayer in the context of instructing his disciples to be authentic when they pray, to trust in God without using a lot of empty words, and to pray with forgiveness in their hearts. Directed to a Jewish-Christian audience, the Lord's Prayer in Matthew's Gospel has been described as "the gospel in miniature."

In Luke's Gospel, the Lord's Prayer appears in Luke 11:2-4, right after Jesus is discovered praying by himself. His disciples then ask him how they should pray. The context in this case is that Luke was writing for a Gentile-Christian audience who did not have a strong heritage of prayer. Thus, Luke presents the Lord's Prayer as a formula, the model prayer for followers of Jesus. The Gospel then relates two of Jesus' parables that emphasize the need to be persistent when we pray because God will surely answer our prayers. This may have been a new a message for Gentile Christians since they did not grow up with the Jewish experience of YHWH, who indeed answered the prayers of his Chosen People.

A brief explanation of the various petitions of the Lord's Prayer follows. The wording given is traditional, based most closely on Matthew's version.

OUR FATHER

Jesus invites us to address God as Abba. This intimate term is roughly equivalent to our word "daddy" or "dad," a sign of intimacy and childlike trust. Jesus teaches us that God is good, gracious, loving, and one we can address with confidence. Jesus' Father is our Father, too. Moreover, we share the same God the Father with our fellow human beings, meaning we should treat each other as brothers and sisters with understanding, compassion, and love.

WHO ART IN HEAVEN

"In Heaven" refers to God's transcendence, his way of being, and his majesty above all his creatures. Through Jesus, God lives in the hearts of the just. We profess that we are God's people who are united to Christ in Heaven. We wait for the day when our heavenly reward will be fully ours.

HALLOWED BE THY NAME

"Hallowed be thy name" is a petition that everyone will regard God as holy (as he is in Heaven). God is the source of all holiness. We hallow (make holy) God's name when we accept his love and act like his Son, Jesus Christ. When we live up to our name as Catholics, we lead others to come to know and praise God because they can see his image reflected in us.

THY KINGDOM COME; THY WILL BE DONE ON EARTH AS IT IS IN HEAVEN

Jesus inaugurated God's Kingdom in his earthly ministry and through his Paschal Mystery. But God's Kingdom will be fully established only at the end of time. Until then, we should live, experience, and work for the Kingdom now, in the present. Praying for God's Kingdom to come is to ask for Christ's return, the final coming of God's Kingdom, when there will be perfect righteousness, peace, and joy. It requires that we join in Jesus' ongoing work by loving others and responding to the least in our midst.

GIVE US THIS DAY OUR DAILY BREAD

Bread represents all that sustains our lives. When we ask for bread, we are requesting what bread represents: physical life (food, shelter, clothing); psychological life (friendship, love, companionship); and spiritual life (the Eucharistic Jesus, the Word of God accepted in faith, and the Body of Christ we receive in Holy Communion).

Praying for *our* daily bread also challenges us to remember the needs of others, especially our obligation to share with poor people.

In this petition, we are also praying for the fullness of God's material and spiritual blessings that will be ours in Heaven.

AND FORGIVE US OUR TRESPASSES AS WE FORGIVE THOSE WHO TRESPASS AGAINST US

Here, we admit that we are sinners and need the Holy Spirit to help us repent of our selfishness and turn to a life of love and service. In humility, we confess that we need Jesus' help and forgiveness on our way to the Father.

Jesus teaches that there is an intimate link between God's forgiveness of us and our forgiveness of others. The forgiveness we have received must be shared with others. Forgiving others is a great sign of love and understanding of the human condition; it invites others to love in return.

AND LEAD US NOT INTO TEMPTATION

We pray to God to spare us the path that leads to a sinful life and for strength to remain in his grace until the very end of our lives and to conquer against the test of Satan. Temptation translates as "test." To defeat Satan requires our picking up the cross of suffering. We petition God for the strength to overcome difficulties in living a Christian life. We ask for the assistance of the Holy Spirit to give us gifts like fortitude, watchfulness, perseverance, and a heart that can tell the difference between trials that strengthen us spiritually and temptations that lead to sin and death.

BUT DELIVER US FROM EVIL

In union with the saints, we ask God to manifest the victory that Christ has already won over Satan. We pray that the Father will deliver us from Satan's snares, the temptations of a godless society. We petition God to keep us from the evil of accidents, illness, violence, and natural disasters. We pray that God will keep us from cooperating with the evils of injustice, prejudice, and selfishness. Finally, we pray with the Holy Spirit, and all God's people, for the Lord's Second Coming. On that day, humanity will be forever free from the snares of the Evil One.

AMEN

When we recite the Lord's Prayer in private, we end it with "Amen," thus affirming our belief and agreement with what we have just prayed. When we say our amen with conviction, the Lord's Prayer becomes our prayer, too.

transcendence
A trait of God that refers to his total otherness and being infinitely beyond and independent of creation.

lust
The "disordered desire for or inordinate enjoyment of sexual pleasure" (*CCC*, 2351).

oaths
Oaths are solemn, formal declarations of promise. They are false when an oath is contrary to a person's dignity or communion with the Church.

Golden Rule
The Golden Rule is described by Jesus and recorded in Matthew 7:12: "Do to others whatever you would have them do to you."

New Standard of Law (see Matthew 5:17-48)

The Old Law is a preparation for the Gospel of Jesus Christ. Jesus said that he did not come to abolish the Law and the Prophets of the Old Testament, but to fulfill them. He came to fulfill all the promises of the Old Covenant. Jesus shows us the way to greatness by amplifying six examples from the Law to emphasize the importance of a changed heart, an interior attitude of love of God and neighbor. He teaches with authority using the formula, "You have heard that it was said . . . but I say this to you." Jesus stresses that mere external observance of the Law is not enough:

- We must not murder, but we should not even be angry with our neighbors or harbor evil thoughts about them. Anger and resentment lead to action. Rather, if we have an enemy, we must reconcile with him or her before we approach God in worship. Jesus seems to be saying that we should not go through the motions of worshiping the God we *can't* see if we harbor negative feelings toward the neighbor we *can* see.

- Jesus affirms the sixth commandment against adultery, but he also tells us we should avoid **lust**, the disordered, unrestrained sexual craving that leads to sin. Jesus also teaches fidelity in marriage and forbids the divorce of lawfully married couples.

- True disciples of the Lord do not need to take idle **oaths**, swearing to back up their word. Catholics

should be persons of integrity, that is, truthful in everything they say or do.

- Finally, two of the most difficult teachings of all: love of one's enemy and the injunction not to seek revenge. The Old Law introduced strict justice into the legal system of its day by teaching that one should limit one's justice to "an eye for an eye and a tooth for a tooth," but Jesus tells us more is expected of Christians. We should be forgiving of our enemies by breaking the chain of violence and by not seeking revenge. Why? Because everyone is our brother and sister; everyone is our neighbor, even our enemies.

The New Law is difficult to put into practice. Jesus set high standards for his followers, calling them to "be perfect, just as your heavenly Father is perfect" (5:48). From a human point of view, Jesus seems to be demanding the impossible. What he is calling us to do is to stretch, to be more loving and responsive to others. What is impossible for us to achieve on our own efforts is possible when

we surrender to God's love and allow his Kingdom to rule our lives.

Have a Right Attitude (see Matthew 6:1-34)

Having good intentions or a right attitude is essential for moral living. Jesus instructed his followers to examine their attitudes when they perform virtuous works. For example: Is our motive to seek the approval of others? Or is it to give glory to our loving Father? Jesus tells us that his way to holiness is the path of humble love. This means that when we give money to the poor, we should do it in a way that does not draw attention to ourselves. When we pray, we should do so simply and sincerely. (The Lord's Prayer is the model prayer for Christians.) When we fast, we should do so without calling attention to ourselves. God loves us with an everlasting love and has already rewarded us. Why should we be motivated by what others think?

Jesus said to trust his Father. God will watch out for us. If the Father takes care of the birds in the sky and the flowers of the field, how much more will he watch over us, his children. Worrying about things we can't control is empty and leads nowhere. If we make doing God's will our priority, then he will lead us and provide what we truly need.

Requirements for Christian Living (see Matthew 7:1-29)

The last chapter of the Sermon on the Mount shares several requirements for Christian living, beginning with Jesus' admonition not to judge others. Jesus does not approve of those who think they are morally superior to others. Just as God will forgive us as we forgive others, so he will judge us as we judge others. Thinking ourselves better than others, making them live up to our idea of what is holy, is arrogant. Jesus wants humility and gentleness in his followers. He teaches the **Golden Rule**, the summary of his Law of Love: "Do to others whatever you would have them do to you" (Mt 7:12).

Jesus instructs us to trust God always, especially when we pray. The Father knows what is good for us, and if we ask for it, he will grant it. He warns us about false prophets, perhaps a problem in the community for whom Matthew wrote. But even today, many false prophets vie for our attention, making deceitful promises of happiness. These voices come from many directions, but Jesus says we can judge a tree by its fruits. Check out the lives of the people making promises. Are they credible? Do they love? Do they bring joy, peace, and true happiness? If not, reject them.

The Sermon concludes by encouraging us to take Jesus' words to heart and build our lives on them. It is not enough to mouth them; *we must put them into action!* These teachings are a solid foundation for a Christian life, a foundation that nothing can shake.

Jesus asks much of us in the Sermon on the Mount. Catholics should live differently than the rest of the world because we have accepted the message of his Good News. We are special to Jesus, and the Lord will always care for us. We must pray to our Father sincerely and forgive others. If we do so, the Father will send goodness our way and enfold us in his love. The Sermon on the Mount is the charter statement of our Christian life. If we want to know what it means to be a disciple of Jesus Christ, we need to study and live out the Beatitudes.

EXPLAINING THE FAITH

Is God male? If not, then why do we address God as "Father"?

God is not distinctly male. God is a pure Spirit who is beyond biological distinction. God has both feminine and masculine characteristics, as evidenced by the fact that both men and women are created "in the image and likeness of God." With that said, we are called by Jesus himself to address God as Father and to turn to him as the children he loves. The name Jesus most clearly referred to for God is *Abba* ("Daddy"). That he would refer to God as Daddy or Father when he could have used a number of other words and titles from Hebrew Scriptures is significant. It showed clearly that Jesus had come to earth to tell us about God, his Father and our Father.

For Review

1. What are the Beatitudes? What does each mean?

2. How are practicing Christians like "salt" and "light"?

3. In the Sermon on the Mount, what does Jesus have to say about almsgiving, praying, and fasting?

4. What is the Golden Rule?

5. What does Jesus say about judging others?

6. Discuss the meaning of each of the elements in the Lord's Prayer.

For Reflection

Write a practical and contemporary definition of what it means to be "poor in spirit."

Main Ideas

- Pope John XXIII taught that Jesus, the Church, and the Gospel represent the greatest truths in life (p. 156).

- Jesus taught with authority and prophesied that the Messiah had come (pp. 157–158).

- Many people in Jesus' hometown of Nazareth could not accept the authority of his teaching (p. 158).

- Jesus was an exceptional teacher who used many teaching skills: he was genuine, available, understandable, dramatic, authoritative, a brilliant debater, and challenging (pp. 158–161).

- Jesus used paradox to help him dramatize his message (p. 160).

- The regions where Jesus taught—Galilee, Samaria, and Judea—had different political, religious, and cultural agendas (pp. 161–163).

- Jesus taught that the Kingdom of God was at hand and that the Kingdom was the active presence of God's love, justice, truth, and Salvation working in the world (pp. 163–164).

- Parables are story devices employed by Jesus, which use ordinary events while comparing them to spiritual matters (pp. 164–166).

- Among the messages of the parables are that the Kingdom of God is for all; sinners are welcome; Salvation has arrived in the person of Jesus; the Kingdom is for the poor and lowly; and the Kingdom should be rejoiced over (pp. 166–170).

- Jesus' Sermon on the Mount resembles Moses' giving the Law on a Mountain (p. 171).

- The Sermon on the Mount includes Jesus' blessings, the Beatitudes; instructions on how to live and pray; and additional stories (pp. 171–177).

- The Beatitudes fulfill our desire for happiness. Another word for Beatitude is happiness (p. 171).

- The Lord's Prayer is included in the Gospel of Matthew (pp. 174–175).

Terms, People, Places

Use a vocabulary word from the list below to help rewrite the following sentences to make them true.

pontiff	beatified
Mount Ararat	Sermon on the Mount
lust	oaths
Golden Rule	transcendence

1. The Sermon on the Plain begins a section in Matthew's Gospel in which Jesus delivers the first of five discourses recorded in that Gospel.

2. Pope John XXIII was canonized by Pope John Paul II in 2000.

3. In themselves, laws are not evil. However, they are false when they are contrary to a person's dignity or communion with the Church.

4. The term "lord" was originally associated with the highest leader of any religion, now it is most exclusively for the leader of the Roman Catholic Church.

5. Jesus went beyond the demands of the sixth commandment and extended its prohibitions to include the sin of swearing.

6. The Beatitudes summarize the main standard for behavior: "Do to others whatever you would have them do to you."

7. The line "in Heaven" in the Lord's Prayer is a reference to God's power.

8. Mount Ararat was a place sacred to Samaritans because they believed it to be the place YHWH chose for his holy temple.

Primary Source Quotations

Love Your Neighbor as Yourself

In our neighbor, we should observe only what is good.

—St. Jeanne de Chantal

We Are Christ for the World

Christ has no body now on earth but yours, no hands but yours, no feet but yours; yours are the eyes through which Christ's compassion looks out at the world, yours are the feet with which he is to go about doing good, and yours are the hands with which he is to bless us now.

—St. Teresa of Avila

We Are Poor in Spirit

In our more honest moments, we recognize our profound neediness, our intellectual limitations, our spiritual inadequacy, our moral failures. In our helplessness, we turn to God. Our response of gratitude and trust, itself a grace, means that the kingdom of Heaven is ours.

—Bishop Robert F. Morneau

Jesus Is the Parable

The real novelty of the New Testament lies not so much in new ideas as in the figure of Christ himself, who gives flesh and blood to those concepts—an unprecedented realism. In the Old Testament, the novelty of the Bible did not consist merely in abstract notions but in God's unpredictable and in some sense unprecedented activity.

This divine activity now takes on dramatic form when, in Jesus Christ, it is God himself who goes in search of the "stray sheep," a suffering and lost humanity. When Jesus speaks in his parables of the shepherd who goes after the lost sheep, of the woman who looks for the lost coin, of the father who goes to meet and embrace his prodigal son, these are no mere words: They constitute an explanation of his very being and activity.

—Pope Benedict XVI

Research the meaning of the term *anawim*. How are the *anawim* another way to describe the poor in spirit? Who are the *anawim* in your community? How can you serve them? Write a short essay that answers these questions.

Ongoing Assignments

As you cover the material in this chapter, choose and complete at least three of these assignments.

1. Many of Jesus' sayings are great guides for living. Read through the Gospel of Matthew or the Gospel of Luke to discover ten good rules for living that you find especially meaningful. Reproduce them in an attractive format, such as a poster board.

2. Create a PowerPoint presentation on places that factored into Jesus' ministry. Check sites like these:

   • Nazareth: www.bibleplaces.com/ nazareth.htm

   • Bethsaida: www.bibleplaces.com/ bethsaida.htm

   • Jerusalem: www.bibleplaces.com/ index.htm (check index)

3. Prepare an illustrated report on at least three aspects of daily life in the time of Jesus. Consult biblical dictionaries or Internet sites like the following:

   • www.jesuscentral.com/ji/ historical-jesus/jesus-firstcentury context.php

   • For a video presentation, see: www .firstcentury.tv/video/DailyLife.htm

4. Visit a Jewish synagogue or interview a rabbi to discover how a synagogue service is conducted today. If permitted, take

pictures or tape your interview with the rabbi. Report your findings.

5. Report on a woman who played a role in the ministry of Jesus. The following website can give you some ideas:

   - http://gbgm-umc.org/umw/jesusand women/index.html

6. Draw your own map of the Holy Land in the time of Jesus. Do an Internet search for ideas.

7. Create a PowerPoint presentation that illustrates the different elements of the Lord's Prayer. Select appropriate background music.

8. With a partner, write a script of a conflict between two teens. Illustrate how it can be resolved in a creative way by employing the teachings of the Sermon on the Mount.

9. Do one of the following activities on the parables:

   - Write an original parable to exemplify one theme in the teaching of Jesus. Use pictures or create your own artwork to illustrate your story.

   - Rewrite the parable of the Good Samaritan in a modern urban setting.

   - After choosing a parable from one of the synoptic Gospels, research three commentaries to discover more about its meaning. Write a one-page report using appropriate footnotes. Conclude the paper with your own interpretation of the parable.

   - With several other students, enact a skit of the Prodigal Son or Good Samaritan in a contemporary setting.

10. Prepare a short report on J. Brent Bill's "Happy Hunger: Revisiting the Sermon on the Mount," a Youth Update article found online: www.americancatholic.org/ Newsletters/YU/ay1291.asp.

11. Compose your own short prayer in imitation of the Lord's Prayer with petitions that fit your needs.

Prayer

Here is the Lord's Prayer as it is found in the Gospel of Luke. Pray it slowly several times, meditating on each phrase:

> Father, hallowed be your name,
> your kingdom come.
> Give us each day our daily bread
> and forgive us our sins
> for we ourselves forgive everyone in debt to us,
> and do not subject us to the final test.

—Luke 11:2–4

- *Reflection*: How do you make God's name holy? How do you bring the Good News of Jesus to others?

- *Resolution*: Extend forgiveness to someone who has hurt you. Ask for forgiveness of someone whom you have hurt.

Chapter 7 Quick View

JESUS' MIRACLES AND THE PASCHAL MYSTERY

*Then [Jesus] opened their minds to understand
the scriptures. And he said to them,
"Thus it is written that the Messiah would
suffer and rise from the dead on the third day
and that repentance, for the forgiveness of sins,
would be preached in his name to all the nations,
beginning from Jerusalem. You are witnesses of these things."*

—Luke 24:45-48

Famous Last Words

The saving life, Passion, Death and Resurrection, and glorious Ascension of Jesus allow us to face our own death with hope of eternal life.

Jesus, the Miracle Worker

Jesus' words were accompanied by many "mighty works and wonders and signs" that allow us to experience God's presence and accept the invitation to believe.

People Who Encountered Jesus

Understanding more about the religious, cultural, and historical background of Jesus' contemporaries help us to better put into context his words and actions.

The Paschal Mystery

The Life, Passion, Death, and Resurrection of Jesus are central to our Salvation and are experienced today in the living sacraments.

Resurrection of Jesus

The Resurrection is the crowning truth of our faith; without a belief that Jesus is raised from the dead our faith is empty.

Famous Last Words

People are always fascinated by the last words spoken by a person who is approaching death. A person's "final words" often help us glimpse beyond this world to the next. Here are some examples of what some famous people have said in their last moments:

"It is very beautiful over there."
—Thomas Alva Edison, inventor (1847–1931)

"All my possessions for a moment of time."
—Elizabeth I, Queen of England (1533–1603)

"Oh, do not cry—be good children and we will all meet in Heaven."
—Andrew Jackson, seventh president of the United States (1767–1845)

"For the name of Jesus and the protection of the church I am ready to embrace death."
—St. Thomas Becket, martyred by King Henry II of England (1118–1170)

"Go on, get out! Last words are for fools who haven't said enough!"
—Karl Marx, atheist philosopher, father of Communism (1818–1883)

"Lord, help my poor soul."
—Edgar Allan Poe, American author (1809–1849)

"So little done, so much to do."
—Cecil John Rhodes, British imperialist, mining magnate, and politician (1853–1902)

Looking at her crucifix: "Oh! . . . I love him. . . . My God. I . . . love . . . you!"
—St. Thérèse of Lisieux, the beloved saint known as the Little Flower, who died painfully of tuberculosis at the age of twenty-four (1873–1897)

"Father, into your hands I commend my spirit."
—Jesus Christ, Savior of the World (4/6 BC–AD 30)

None of us knows what words will come to mind at the time our own death. However, we believe that Jesus Christ allowed death to touch him so that he could destroy death and the power of sin once and for all. The Death and Resurrection of Christ enable us to face our final hours with the firm hope that our dying is the transition into an eternal life of union with our loving God.

This chapter provides more information about the Paschal Mystery, that is, the saving events of Christ's Passion, Death, Resurrection, and glorious Ascension that have won for us the forgiveness of sin and eternal life. In connection with the Paschal Mystery, more details are offered of Jesus' earthly ministry help to reveal his identity, including his miracles and the cultural, religious, and historical background of the people he interacted with.

For Reflection

What would you hope your dying words to be?

What I Want from Life

Read the following quotation. Answer the following questions about how you imagine your life and death.

Life is uncertain and, in fact, may be very brief. If we compare it with eternity, we will clearly realize that it cannot be but more than an instant. A happy death of all the things of life is our principal concern. For if we attain that, it matters little if we lose all the rest. But if we do not attain that, nothing else will be of any value.

—Blessed Junipero Serra

- What does Serra mean that "a happy death" should be our principal concern?

- What do you imagine Heaven to be like?

- How does understanding that life on earth is just "an instant" in comparison with eternity help you to live your life now?

- What five things would you like to accomplish in your life?

- Write a one-paragraph obituary of your life.

Jesus, the Miracle Worker (*CCC*, 547-550)

The Gospels report how Jesus' words were accompanied by many "mighty works and wonders and signs." These signs highlighted Jesus' ministry: "When it was evening, after sunset, they brought to him all who were ill or possessed by demons. The whole town was gathered at the door. He cured many who were sick with various diseases, and he drove out many demons" (Mk 1:32–34). Jesus' miracles served many purposes. They show how the Kingdom of God is present in him. They prove that he is the Messiah. His miracles confirm that he was sent by God the Father. They invite us to believe in him. They also strengthen our faith in Jesus Christ as God's only Son.

Types of Miracles

Jesus' **miracles** are often grouped in the following way: as physical healings, nature miracles, exorcisms, and raisings from the dead. In each of these categories, Jesus addresses a particular problem and provides a solution. Sometimes he accompanies the miracle with an explanation of its meaning. These categories of miracles are described in the next sections.

Physical Healings

Jesus was a healer *par excellence*. He caused blind people to see, deaf people to hear, and lame people to walk. He cured many dreaded skin diseases, healed a woman who bled for twelve years, and relieved the sufferings of many others.

An example of a physical healing is Jesus' cure of a leper in Mark 1:40–45. This miracle follows a typical pattern for miracle stories that we find in the Gospels:

- First, there is an *introduction*. In this case, a leper approaches Jesus and kneels down.

- Second, there is a *display of faith*. The leper begged Jesus, "If you wish, you can make me clean" (Mk 1:40).

- Third, there is the *cure*. "Moved with pity, he stretched out his hand, touched him, and said to him, 'I do will it. Be made clean'" (Mk 1:41). Note here the compassion of Jesus in touching the man with the skin disease, something that people simply feared to do for fear of catching the disease.

miracles
Powerful signs of God's Kingdom worked by Jesus.

exorcism
The public and authoritative act of the Church to liberate a person from the power of the devil in the name of Christ.

- Next, there is the *result of the miracle*. "The leprosy left him immediately, and he was made clean" (Mk 1:42). Jesus' word and his touch result in the healing.

- Finally, we learn the *people's reaction* to the mighty deed. In this example, Jesus instructed the man not to tell anyone of his cure but simply to go to a priest, who would certify that the man was cured, and then to offer the proper sacrifices as the Law required in Leviticus 14. But the man simply could not keep what happened to himself. He spread the great news wide and far. As a result, Jesus' reputation grew so much that he could not enter a town openly. Even though he remained in deserted places, "people kept coming to him from everywhere" (Mk 1:45).

Nature Miracles

Jesus demonstrated mastery over the elements. For example, he calmed a storm and walked on water. His cursing of a fig tree caused it to wither. He changed water into wine.

In another famous example, Jesus fed five thousand people on the shores of Lake Galilee. This miracle is reported in all four Gospels. (The Gospels of Matthew and Luke also tell of Jesus' feeding four thousand people on another occasion.) According to the accounts in Matthew 14:15–21 and Luke 9:12–17, Jesus had gone to the Sea of Galilee to be by himself, but the people followed him there. Jesus was moved by their faith, so he healed the sick among them. He also taught them about the Kingdom of God. When evening came, the disciples approached Jesus and realized that the people would be hungry if they didn't eat soon. They told Jesus: "This is a deserted place and it is already late; dismiss the crowds so that they can go to the villages and buy food for themselves" (Mt 14:15).

However, Jesus wanted the people to stay, and he told his disciples to feed the crowd. The disciples were confused; the only food for the whole crowd was five loaves of bread and two fish. Jesus instructed them to bring him the food. He took it, looked up to Heaven, blessed and broke the loaves, and gave them to the disciples who in turn gave them to the crowds. "They all ate and were satisfied, and they picked up the fragments left over—twelve wicker baskets full" (Mt 14:20).

This miracle has great meaning. For example, the twelve baskets represent the twelve tribes of Israel under the Twelve Apostles, who helped Jesus distribute the food. The actions of Jesus—blessing, breaking, and giving—point to the Last Supper, where Jesus instituted the Eucharist. The

crowd learned that Jesus is the Bread of Life who gives his very self in Holy Communion. This sacrament, foreshadowed in the miracle of the loaves and fishes, is a marvelous sign of Christ's love for us on our earthly journey. The Holy Eucharist is the food that will sustain us until we reach the messianic banquet in God's Kingdom at the end of time.

Exorcisms

An **exorcism** is the expulsion of an evil spirit that possesses a person or sometimes a place or object. In Jesus' day, these spirits tormented people and sometimes drove them crazy. Among Jesus' exorcisms was his expulsion of a legion of spirits from a crazy man. The spirits went into a herd of swine, which then ran off a cliff. The Lord also healed epileptics and a possessed man who was both blind and mute.

Luke 4:31–37 records an occasion when Jesus cured a man possessed by an unclean spirit. Jesus was teaching in a synagogue in Capernaum on the Sabbath. People were astonished at his teaching because he spoke with authority. The possessed man cried out, "Ha! What have you to do with us, Jesus of Nazareth? Have you come to destroy us? I know who you are—the Holy One of God!" (Lk 4:34). Jesus rebuked the demon and ordered him to be quiet and come out of the man. "Then the demon threw the man down in front of them and came out of him without doing him any harm" (Lk 4:35). The people who observed this powerful deed were amazed, saying, "What is there about his word? For with authority and power he commands the unclean spirits, and they come out" (Lk 4:36). Jesus has the power to make whole. He has power over evil. Jesus is truly God's Holy One. A secondary lesson to learn from the incident is the close proximity between good and evil. While many humans, including Jesus' disciples, do not recognize him or his mission, Satan does recognize and name the source of goodness, that is, Jesus.

Raisings from the Dead

Finally, the Gospels report several examples of Jesus bringing a dead person back to life: the widow's son at Nain; the daughter of Jairus; and his friend, Lazarus, whose corpse lay rotting in the grave.

The raising of Jairus' daughter is found in all three of the synoptic Gospels. Jairus, the head of a local synagogue in Galilee, sought Jesus out, fell at his feet, and begged Jesus to come to his house to cure his dying daughter. Before reaching the house, word came that the daughter had indeed died. Jesus told the synagogue official, "Do not be afraid; just have faith" (Mk 5:36). When Jesus reached the official's house, he found people weeping and wailing over the death of the child. Jesus said to them, "Why this commotion and weeping? The child is not dead but asleep" (Mk 5:39). Jesus' words were met with ridicule.

Jesus was not deterred. He took the child's father and mother with him, as well as Peter, James, and John, and entered the child's room. Taking her by the hand, he said, "'*Talitha, koum*,' which means, 'Little girl, I say to you, arise!'" (Mk 5:41). Immediately, the twelve-year-old girl got up and started to walk around. This incredible deed of power over death "utterly astounded" those who witnessed it. Jesus instructed them to give her something to eat. As is typical of Mark's Gospel, Jesus also ordered the witnesses to the miracle not to spread word about it. Jesus did not want people to approach him with misunderstandings of who he was and what his mission was. He was the Messiah, but not an earthly king intent on earthly power. He was the Suffering Servant who would die to save the people.

This miracle of the raising of the child, like all Jesus' miracles that brought people back to life, clearly points to the resurrected life of Jesus and those who have faith in him.

How Jesus' Contemporaries Understood Miracles

Many people who encountered Jesus took offense at him because he would not work miracles to satisfy their curiosity or to prove himself to possess the powers of a magician. Others refused to believe in him in spite of his great deeds. For example, John's Gospel reports of a man Jesus cured of his blindness (see John 9:1–34). Jesus' opponents simply claimed that the man was never blind to begin with. On other occasions, people admitted Jesus could heal, but they gave credit to Satan, a charge that Jesus claimed was ridiculous. Satan works against our good; why would he heal someone? "Every kingdom divided against itself will be laid waste and house will fall against house" (Lk 11:17).

Many people in today's secular society deny the reality of supernatural events. They think it is impossible that God would suspend the laws of nature to get directly involved in the natural universe. In this way of thinking, there is a verifiable scientific reason to explain away what appears to be a miracle. Other skeptics hold that Jesus was nothing more than a clever healer who could diagnose people's mental disorders and say the right words to make them heal themselves. Other non-believers explain away a nature miracle like the multiplication of the loaves by saying what really happened is that Jesus inspired the people to share their food with one another. Still others claim that Jesus' did not really raise anybody from the dead, but simply used a form of artificial respiration that revived an apparently dead person.

In all these interpretations, note how skeptics limit the power of God. Jesus is the Second Person of the Blessed Trinity, both truly God and truly man. He is able to do *anything*. At root, many modern disbelievers are denying the divinity of Jesus or simply not understanding the nature of a biblical concept of Jesus' miracles.

There were other healers in Jesus' time in both the Jewish and Roman world. Jesus' contemporaries believed that God-inspired men had the ability to perform some healings. Even the New Testament itself mentions certain people who had the power to heal.

However, Jesus' miracles are unique among those performed by other wonder-workers of his day. First, there is no record that anyone else cured such a variety of problems—blindness, paralysis, severed ears, leprosy, and death. Second, Jesus did not engage in any bizarre rituals to bring about the cures, as did so many of his contemporaries. He healed on his own authority, using his own power, often stressing the need for the afflicted to have faith. Finally, Jesus did not perform miracles for pay. He did his works out of the goodness of his heart and to further the will of God.

New Testament Understanding of Miracles

To appreciate Jesus' miracles, an understanding of miracle from the biblical perspective is needed. The Scriptures assume that God continues to work in human history. God cares for us, demonstrated perfectly by God's sending his Son. This is the real miracle of God's love—that God became man in Jesus Christ. The miracles that Jesus performed are a powerful sign of God's compassionate love for us.

The New Testament uses three different but related words to express the concept of miracle. The synoptic Gospels use the word *dynamis,* which means, "act of power." Note how the English words *dynamic* and *dynamite* are derived from this Greek word. On the other hand, John's Gospel uses the Greek words *ergon* ("work") and *semeion* ("sign") for miracle. In John's Gospel, Jesus' "works and signs" reveal Jesus' glory, purpose, identity, and relationship to his Father. Jesus' mighty works were both *power*ful and *sign*ificant. These adjectives tell us two important things about Jesus' miracles:

1. Jesus' miracles reveal God's power.
2. Jesus' miracles are signs of God's Kingdom.

In and through Jesus, God's power has broken into human history. God is the ruler of nature. When Jesus calms the storm, for example, he is demonstrating that he is closely identified with YHWH, who is the Master of the universe. The miracles help show who Jesus is and where he comes from.

Jesus also mastered Satan and the forces of darkness. When Jesus drove out demons, he was proclaiming that God has power over sickness and the evil it brings upon people. When he raised someone from the dead, Jesus showed that he has power over the worst evil of all—death. In performing miracles, Jesus was crushing Satan's power.

The miracles also show that Jesus has power to forgive sins. Sin separates people from God and others. It makes us hate God, other people, and ourselves. It leads to death. When Jesus forgives sin, he is speaking for God. He helps free people from the alienation that causes spiritual suffering and death. A dramatic example of Jesus' power to forgive sins appears in Mark 2:1–12. A paralyzed man wanted to get close to Jesus, but the only way he could do so was for his friends to lower him through the roof of a crowded room. Jesus was moved by the man's faith and said to him, "Child, your sins are forgiven" (Mk 2:5). The scribes who were present were upset by this proclamation. They accused Jesus of blasphemy because only God can forgive sins. Jesus could read their accusing thoughts. So, to demonstrate that he had the authority and power to forgive sins, he instructed the paralytic to get up and go home. The man immediately did what he was told. Everyone was astounded. They glorified God and said, "We have never seen anything like this"

(Mk 2:12). What they were seeing was, in fact, God in their midst!

Thus, miracles reveal Jesus' identity. Anyone who has God's power over nature, over sickness and death, over Satan and the forces of evil, over sin itself must be God himself. The miracles help show that Jesus is God's Son.

Additionally, Jesus' miracles are *signs* of the coming of God's Kingdom. With Jesus, God's Kingdom is here; Satan's kingdom is ending. Sin, sickness, and death entered the world when Adam sinned. Jesus is the New Adam who inaugurates God's reign over human hearts. The miracles are the signs of the advent of God's Kingdom. Satan's reign ended at the coming of Jesus.

The miracles prompted people to put their faith in Jesus. Faith plays a major role in Jesus' miracles. On two occasions in Mark (5:34 and 10:52) and one in Luke (17:19), Jesus says, "Your faith has saved you." In some cases, the miracle increases faith to a remarkable degree, as in the case of exorcism of the Gerasene demoniac, who begged Jesus to permit him to remain with him. One of the most dramatic of all Jesus' miracles appears in John's Gospel, where Jesus taught that he is the Way, the Truth, and the Life. Speaking to Martha, the sister of Lazarus, who was mourning the death of her brother, Jesus said:

> "I am the resurrection and the life; whoever believes in me, even if he dies, will live, and everyone who lives and believes in me will never die. Do you believe this?" She said to him, "Yes, Lord. I have come to believe that you are the Messiah, the Son of God, the one who is coming into the world." (Jn 11:25–27)

Jesus raised Lazarus from the dead in one of his most significant miracles of all. This miracle was a powerful sign that Jesus has power to conquer death; it symbolizes that through Jesus our own resurrection takes place. Our ultimate Salvation—the conquering of our own death—comes through Jesus

Christ through the Church. He is the resurrection and the life. Without him we are dead.

John's Gospel reports that many Jews believed in Jesus after witnessing this miracle, but some went to the Pharisees, who along with the chief priests plotted Jesus' Death. Miracles force people to ask some basic questions: "Is Jesus the sign we have been looking for? Is he the promised one? Is he the Messiah? If he is, then we will have to change our lives and follow him."

Jesus' miracles compelled his contemporaries, as they do us, to face and answer the question "Who do *you* say that I am?"

For Review

1. What were the four kinds of miracles Jesus performed? Give an example of each.

2. What is the meaning of the miracle of the multiplication of the loaves and fish?

3. What is the significance of the exorcisms Jesus performed?

4. Why was it ridiculous for Jesus' opponents to claim that Jesus' power to heal came from Satan?

Reading and Interpreting Jesus' Miracles

A complete list of Jesus' miracles in the Bible is found below. Work through the following steps to learn more about the miracles of Jesus:

1. Read all versions of the miracles that are listed in boldface type.

2. Briefly summarize what has taken place and why it is a miracle.

3. Assign this particular miracle to one of the four categories of miracle discussed in this section: physical healing, nature, exorcism, or raising from the dead.

4. Interpret the deeper meaning of the miracle. How does it show God's *power*? What *significance* does it have, that is, what is it a sign of?

Miracle	Matthew	Mark	Luke	John
Changing water into wine				2:1-11
Healing of the nobleman's son				4:46-54
Disciples' catch of fish			5:1-11	
Stilling of the Storm	**8:23-27**	**4:35-41**	**8:22-25**	
Demoniacs of Gerasenes	8:28-34	5:1-20	8:26-39	
Raising Jairus's daughter	9:18-26	5:21-43	8:40-56	
Healing the bleeding woman	9:20-22	5:24-34	8:43-48	
Healing of the two blind men	9:27-31			
Healing of possessed mute	9:32-34			
Healing of the paralytic	**9:1-8**	**2:1-12**	**5:17-26**	
Cleansing of the leper	8:1-4	1:40-45	5:12-16	
Healing of the centurion's servant	8:5-13		7:1-10	
Demoniac at Capernaum		**1:23-27**	**4:33-36**	

5. What is unique about the miracles Jesus performed?

6. How does the New Testament understand the concept of miracle?

7. What role did faith play in Jesus' miracles?

⬤ For Reflection

- How are miracles possible today?
- Give an example of a modern-day miracle.

People Who Encountered Jesus

Judaism in Jesus' day had several religious parties or sects who were influential among the common people. Some members of some of these sects did not approve of Jesus or his message. It is helpful to be familiar with the names and background of each of the sects as a way to better place Jesus' message in context.

Miracle	Matthew	Mark	Luke	John
Healing of Simon's mother-in-law	8:14-15	1:29-31	4:38-39	
Raising of the widow's son			7:11-17	
Healing at the pool of Bethesda				5:1-15
Healing of blind and deaf mute	12:22			
Feeding of the five thousand	14:15-21	6:34-44	9:12-17	6:5-14
Walking on water	14:22-23	6:45-52		6:14-21
Opening the eyes of the man born blind				9:1-41
Healing the man's withered hand	**12:9-13**	**3:1-5**	**6:6-11**	
Healing the woman on the Sabbath			13:10-17	
Healing the man with dropsy			14:1-6	
Cleansing the ten lepers			17:11-19	
Healing the Syrophoenician woman's daughter	**15:21-28**	**7:24-30**		
Healing the deaf man with a speech impediment		7:31-37		
Healing of the suffering	15:29-31			
Feeding the four thousand	15:32-39	8:1-9		
Healing the blind man at Bethsaida		8:22-26		
Healing of the lunatic child	17:14-21	9:14-29	9:37-42	
Finding the coin in the fish's mouth	17:24-27			
Raising of Lazarus				**11:1-54**
Healing the two blind men at Jericho	20:29-34	10:46-52	18:35-43	
Cursing the barren fig tree	21:18-22	11:12-24		
Healing of Malchus's ear			22:49-51	
Second miraculous catch of fish				21:1-14

Sadducees

The Sadducees' name comes from Zadok, the priest Solomon appointed to care for the Ark of the Covenant (see 1 Kings 2:35). In Jesus' time, the Sadducees were mostly priests and aristocrats who cared for Temple practices and worship in Jerusalem. They collaborated with the Romans to keep their positions. The Sadducees believed that only the Torah was inspired. They did not accept the resurrection of the dead, immortality, or the existence of angels.

Sanhedrin
The seventy-one member supreme legislative and judicial body of the Jewish people. Many of its members were Sadducees.

proselytes
From a Greek word for "stranger," the term refers to a convert to Judaism.

Many Sadducees made up the seventy-one-member **Sanhedrin**, the major law-making body and supreme court of Judaism. It was this group that judged Jesus a threat and accused him of blasphemy. Therefore, the Sadducees were Jesus' main opponents at the time of his trial. They saw Jesus as a threat to their power and influence over people.

Pharisees

The total number of Pharisees in Jesus' time was about 6,000. They believed in resurrection, divine judgment, and the value of spiritual practices like prayer, almsgiving, and fasting. Unlike the Sadducees, they opposed cooperation with the Romans.

Pharisees means "separated ones" in the sense of those who strictly observe the Law to distinguish themselves from lukewarm religious practice and Gentile influence. Many fellow Jews found the religious devotion of the Pharisees to be admirable. However, when some Pharisees tried to apply the Torah to daily life, they developed an elaborate system of oral interpretation held to be almost as sacred as the Law itself. At times these oral interpretations missed the spirit of the Law. Jesus respected the Law and in no way sought to abolish it, but he distinguished between what God meant by the Law and man-made interpretations that conflicted with the needs of people. This brought him into conflict with some Pharisees.

The Pharisees were influential in the synagogues that were found in every Jewish neighborhood. Their presence in the synagogue, their scholarly study of the Law, and their pious attempts to live it gained for them influence over the common people. Many Pharisees were also scribes—that is, experts in Jewish Law—who did not like how Jesus taught on his own authority. In contrast, they looked to their own scholarly interpretation of the Law as a sure way to holiness.

The Gospels show how at times Jesus criticized certain Pharisees because they thought they could earn Heaven by keeping all their religious customs. Jesus taught that God's love and Kingdom are unmerited gifts. Conflict between these two approaches to God's goodness was inevitable.

Although the Pharisees have a relatively poor reputation in the New Testament, many of them were very good Jews. Some Pharisees, like St. Paul, later became staunch followers of Jesus. The Pharisees preserved the Jewish religion after the Roman general Titus destroyed of the Temple in the year AD 70.

Essenes

The Essenes were an apocalyptic group, believing God would usher in his Kingdom through a dramatic, even catastrophic, event. In Jesus' day, many Essenes withdrew to the desert community of Qumran near the northwest shore of the Dead Sea. The members of this community did not marry, lived a communal life, and engaged in many ritual washings throughout the day. Other Essenes lived in tight-knit religious groups in towns and villages, but most probably did not marry, a fact that helped in ensure their eventual demise.

The Gospels make no mention of the Essenes. Like the Sadducees, they disappeared from Jewish history after the destruction of the Temple. They hid their sacred writings in the caves in the Judean desert around the time the Romans came through their area in AD 67–68. Their writings—the Dead Sea Scrolls—were discovered in 1947 by an Arab shepherd boy when he was tossing rocks into the caves and heard a jar smash.

Zealots

Begun as a group in Galilee to protest foreign taxation and occupation, the Zealots were active as Jesus grew up and during his public ministry. They eventually fomented the revolt against the Romans (AD 66–70). One of Jesus' Apostles, Simon, was a Zealot. The Zealots despised Roman rule and believed in violence to overthrow their enemies. Barabbas (see Matthew 27:17), the prisoner whom Pilate freed during Jesus' trial, was probably a Zealot.

A symbol of Jewish pride today is the famous stand of the Zealots at Masada, a fortress near the southeastern shore of the Dead Sea. Although the Romans defeated the Jews in AD 70, a pocket of Zealots resisted until AD 73 at this mountaintop fortress. Rather than surrender and be taken in chains to Rome, the Zealots at Masada took their own lives.

Jesus resisted the tactics of the Zealots by preaching a message of peace and forgiveness of one's enemies.

Other Contemporaries of Jesus

There were several other people who encountered Jesus as he ministered in and around Galilee. These people heard and responded in different ways to the Good News. Most of Jesus' contemporaries were the common people who lived their daily lives removed from the intellectual disputes of the major sects. Typically they tried to follow the Law, pray, and participate in the synagogue services. Jesus greatly appealed to these simple people who were open to his message of conversion, repentance, and Salvation. The Galileans were often called "people of the land." This was a derogatory term when it was used by the Pharisees, who thought the common people's ignorance kept them from holiness. By extension, some Pharisees characterized Jesus and his disciples this way because they did not strictly follow the oral law in regards to fasting (see Luke 5:33) and washing (see Matthew 15:2).

Another class of people described in the New Testament is tax collectors. They were hated for cooperating with the Romans and for lining their own pockets at the expense of their fellow Jews. Jesus associated with this despised group of people and even called one of them—Levi (Matthew)—to be an Apostle (see Mark 2:14–15).

The Jews themselves divided people into two classes: Jews and Gentiles (the nations of people who were not circumcised). Some Gentiles, known as **proselytes**, converted to Judaism. Others, known as "God-fearers," accepted many Jewish beliefs but did not undergo circumcision. Pious Jews avoided contact with Gentiles. The Acts of the Apostles tells how the early Christian missionaries turned to the Gentiles after many Jews rejected the Gospel.

During Jesus' life, men looked on women as property. They were also considered too weak to follow the religious requirements of the Law. A Jewish man was allowed to divorce his wife for any reason as long as he gave her a legal document saying she was free to remarry. In contrast, it was much more difficult for a woman to divorce her husband.

Women were segregated during synagogue and Temple worship and had few political rights. Their domain was the home, where they played a central role in child rearing. Motherhood was esteemed, while a childless woman was scorned and pitied. It was especially tough to be a widow, left alone in the world. In most every way, Jews considered women inferior to men. Jesus did not live by these standards for treating women. Jesus elevated the position of women, treated them as equals, and instructed husbands to cherish them as persons. Many women were his disciples and were the most faithful to him at the end of his life. Mary and Martha were his friends, and Jesus appeared first to Mary Magdalene. Mary, the Mother of Jesus, is the perfect Christian role model. Jesus' attitude and treatment of women was revolutionary.

◉ For Review

1. Identify some important beliefs of each of the following first-century Jewish groups: Sadducees, Pharisees, Essenes, and Zealots.

2. What was the Sanhedrin?

3. Who were "the people of the land" in Jesus' day?

4. What status did women have in Jesus' day? What was Jesus' attitude toward women?

✿ For Reflection

- How do you identify with the contemporaries of Jesus?

- How does your family and cultural background impact how you hear the Gospel?

The Paschal Mystery (*CCC*, 571-594)

The Paschal Mystery is at the center of the Gospel that the Apostles, and the Church after them, must proclaim to the world. Recall one meaning of *mystery* is something concealed, or a truth that is hidden. More importantly, it also refers to the mystery of God's Kingdom, that is, the divine plan in action. The divine plan is God's saving plan that was accomplished for all time by the redemptive Death and Resurrection of Jesus Christ.

The word *paschal* comes from the Jewish word for Passover, *pasch*. Passover goes back to the Exodus experience when God spared the firstborn of the Hebrews and chose Moses to lead them out of slavery in Egypt to freedom in the Promised Land. A paschal (or Passover) experience, therefore, is a journey from slavery to freedom. Jesus' life, his suffering, his Death on the cross, and his Resurrection were also a Passover experience. His Sacrifice was a passing from the slavery of sin and its greatest effect—death—to the greatest freedom of all: Resurrection.

The Church remembers in a special way the events of Jesus' Passion, Death, and Resurrection during Holy Week. Easter, the most important feast on the Church calendar, celebrates the Resurrection of Christ. The sacraments enable us to live the Paschal Mystery. In Baptism we are initiated into the mystery of Christ's saving events. Baptism is the first and chief sacrament of forgiveness of sins because it unites us with Christ. Jesus, himself, affirmed that

Baptism is necessary for Salvation. The Eucharist re-presents (makes present) the Paschal Mystery, enabling us to enter into the saving events of our Lord's Death and Resurrection.

The Paschal Mystery of Christ's sacrifice repairs the broken relationship between God and humans. It bestows God's blessings, grace, and life on humanity and adopts us into God's family. Jesus is our Savior. He is the Head of the Body of Christ, the Church. We are members of the Body. His Salvation through the Church brings forgiveness for our sins and redeems us from sin, evil, and death.

Historical Background of Jesus' Death

Jesus came to fulfill, not abolish, the Law. For example, he honored the Temple by celebrating the major Jewish feasts there. Despite this, Jesus met with resistance from certain Pharisees, supporters of Herod Antipas, and some scribes and priests. Jesus' opponents felt threatened by some of Jesus' words and actions, including:

- exorcisms
- the forgiveness of sins
- healing on the Sabbath, even claiming to be Lord of it
- unique interpretations of the Law "as one who taught with authority"
- disregard of cleanliness and dietary laws
- association with sinners and tax-collectors

- teaching that God is bounteously merciful toward all repentant sinners
- cleansing of the Temple and his prophecy that it would one day be destroyed

These led some of the religious authorities to judge that Jesus was a **false prophet** who claimed to be God. As a result, out of ignorance and the "hardness" of their unbelief, members of the Sanhedrin accused Jesus of **blasphemy**, a crime under Jewish law punishable by stoning to death. However, under Roman occupation, only Romans could exercise the death penalty. Thus, these Jewish authorities turned Jesus over to Pilate for execution as a political criminal and a threat to Caesar.

Theological Background of Jesus' Death (CCC, 595-598)

Responsibility for Jesus' Death is historically assigned to Pontius Pilate, the Roman prefect of Judea, Samaria, and Idumea from AD 26 to 36. He sentenced Jesus to death, probably in April of AD 30 (or 33). He knew Jesus to be innocent, and hence violated his conscience in doing the politically expedient thing.

Unfortunately, some in history have blamed Jesus' Death on the Jewish people as a whole. This is wrong. The Passion narratives reveal that Jesus' trial was complex. Only a few Jewish leaders opposed Jesus and

false prophets
Jesus said of false prophets: "By their fruits you will know them" (Mt 7:16). Jesus said to be aware of people who claimed to speak in the name of God without being inspired by him.

blasphemy
Any thought, word, or act that expresses hatred or contempt for God, Christ, the Church, saints, or holy things.

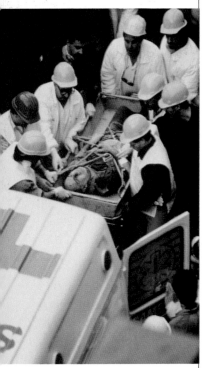

The result of an anti-Semitic attack in Buenos Aires.

anti-Semitism
Unfounded prejudice against the Jewish people.

collaborated with Pontius Pilate to crucify Jesus. In fact, some Pharisees (like the leading figure of Nicodemus) and a prominent ally in the Sanhedrin (Joseph of Arimathea) were Jesus' strong supporters. In addition, other secret followers may have voiced their support for Jesus during the various deliberations over what they should do with him.

The real authors and instruments of Jesus' crucifixion are sinners—that is, each of us—because Jesus died for our sins. It is not right to blame the Jews as a people for the Death of Jesus. Remember that all of Jesus' Apostles, disciples, and early converts were Jews. We must always remember how Jesus, while dying on the cross, forgave his executioners, saying that they acted out of ignorance. Holding the Jewish people responsible for Jesus' Death is a form of **anti-Semitism** and contrary to the love of Christ. The Second Vatican Council declared the following:

> [N]either all Jews indiscriminately at that time, nor Jews today, can be charged with the crimes committed during his Passion. . . . [T]he Jews should not be spoken of as rejected or accursed as if this followed from holy Scripture. (*Declaration on the Relationship of the Church to Non-Christian Religions*, No. 4, *CCC*, 597)

Why Jesus Died (CCC, 599-609)

Because of his immense love for us, Jesus *freely* chose give up his life for us. He did so out of obedience to the Father and according to his Father's definitive plan. Jesus' Death and Resurrection have won for us Salvation, making us, through the Holy Spirit, partakers of the divine nature (see *CCC*, 460). As John the Baptist predicted, Jesus' Death was a perfect sacrifice undertaken by the Lamb of God for our benefit (see John 1:29). Early Christian theology taught that this sacrifice was a "ransom" or a "redemption" that defeated the powers of evil. By substituting for each human being, Jesus took on our guilt and died a Death we deserve. With it, he bought our freedom.

Jesus Christ died for all human beings. In his unique and definitive sacrifice, Jesus took our sins to the cross and, like a New Adam, represented us to the Father. In his suffering and Death, Jesus' humanity became the free and perfect instrument of divine love, a self-surrendering gift of love on our behalf. It opened eternal life to us, a supreme gift that we sinners do not deserve. Anyone who reflects on Jesus' Death must be drawn to Jesus as the perfect man. He is the ultimate example of love, the gracious Lord who gave his life that we might live.

The Passion Narratives (CCC, 610-618)

The Passion of Jesus is described in the Gospel accounts and in response to God's plan foretold in the Old Testament: "Christ died for our sins in accordance with the Scriptures" (1 Cor 15:3). Mark's account of the Passion recounts how the leaders plotted Jesus' Death in a way that would not cause an uprising. Helping them in the cause was Judas Iscariot, one of the Twelve, who agreed to hand Jesus over to the authorities. He acted out of greed. Before Jesus entered Jerusalem, a sympathetic woman anointed him at Bethany. This foreshadowed the anointing of Jesus' dead body after his Death. Fully in control of the situation, Jesus then prepared for the Passover meal. The Passion narratives unfold with the following events.

Last Supper

Jesus celebrated a Last Supper with his Apostles "on the night he was betrayed." Jesus changed this Passover meal into the memorial of his voluntary offering to the Father for our Salvation. At this meal, Jesus instituted the Eucharist. In this sacrament of love, we celebrate Jesus' Passover from Death to new life and the gift of himself under the forms of bread and wine. Jesus' Passion, Death, and Resurrection are God's new covenant with us, his new way of delivering his people. The Eucharist is the memorial of Christ's sacrifice. The Apostles (and later the bishops they chose and ordained) serve as priests of the New Covenant. At the Last Supper, Jesus told how one of the Twelve would betray him. And after the meal, on the way to the Mount of Olives, Jesus predicted how Peter would three times deny knowing him.

Gethsemane

We learn how Jesus looked into the horror of death and recoiled. He prayed, "Abba, Father, all things are possible to you. Take this cup away from me, but not what I will but what you will" (Mk 14:36).

Always faithful and obedient, Jesus courageously accepted his destiny. He did not flee when his sleeping Apostles could not stay awake to be with him in his agony, nor did he flee when Judas betrayed him with a kiss, usually a sign of friendship. The soldiers used this sign to arrest Jesus at night. Darkness is the realm of Satan.

Jesus did not use violence to resist, though one of his followers did by cutting off the ear of the high priest's servant. In Matthew's Gospel, Jesus said, "Put your sword back into its sheath, for all who take the sword will perish by the sword" (Mt 26:52). Jesus could easily have called down legions of angels to help him, but until the end, he took the path of peace. Simply, the Prince of Peace refused to be a political or military Messiah.

Before the Sanhedrin

The Gospel accounts all testify to a hearing Jesus had before the Sanhedrin where he was interrogated by the high priest, Joseph Caiaphas, and other priests. False witnesses testified against him. In Mark's Gospel, Jesus acknowledged that he was the Christ, the Son of the Living God, predicting that the Son of Man will come in glory. This led the Jewish authorities to judge that Jesus committed the sin of blasphemy, a crime punishable by death under Jewish Law. They then spat on, struck, and ridiculed him.

Out in the courtyard, Peter, identified as a Galilean by his accent, denied knowing Jesus three times.

When the rooster crowed the second time, Peter realized what he did, broke down, and wept. Peter, the one who had acknowledged Jesus to be the Messiah and Son of God, out of fear had turned his back on his Lord, but unlike Judas, who eventually committed suicide, Peter repented and became a great saint. Tradition tells us that he himself was crucified (on an inverted cross) under the emperor Nero in AD 64 or 67.

Pilate Condemns Jesus to Death

Under Roman occupation, only the Roman prefect had the authority to inflict the death penalty. The religious sin of blasphemy would not have been a crime under Roman law, but claiming to be a king in competition to Caesar was sedition, a capital offense. This was the charge the Jewish authorities took to Pontius Pilate.

The historical record reveals that Pilate might have been a relatively competent ruler, but also a harsh and arrogant one. He realized that Jesus was innocent, but he tried to escape personal responsibility by invoking a Passover custom of freeing a prisoner of the citizens' choosing. He thought they would choose Jesus. However, he miscalculated when the people, inflamed by the Jewish leaders, asked for Barabbas, a murderer who had been involved in a rebellion. Pilate then caved in to crowd pressure, pronounced Jesus guilty, and had him viciously scourged. He then turned Jesus over to the soldiers who mocked and hailed him as "King of the Jews." Without knowing it, they had spoken the truth because Jesus is not only king of the Jews but the entire universe.

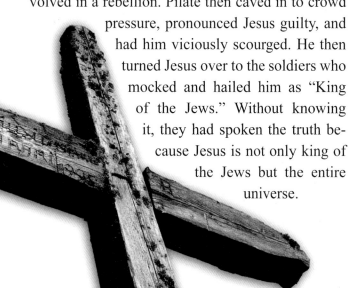

Crucifixion

Jesus' scourging severely weakened him so that he was unable to carry the horizontal crossbeam. (The vertical beam was fixed in the ground at Golgotha, a small, elevated, skull-like hill.) The soldiers enlisted a bystander, Simon of Cyrene, to help carry the crossbeam.

In Jesus' day, crucifixion might have included nailing or tying the extremities to the cross and stretching the arms on the crossbeam. Crucifixion could have taken place in an inverted position, with the victim's head pointed to the ground. At other times, victims might be impaled or hung from a wooden stake.

The traditional image of Jesus' wrists and feet nailed to a cross in an elongated plus sign is historically plausible. Whether Jesus' cross had a support for his feet or a seat for his buttocks is hard to determine. The purpose of these supports was to aid breathing and thus prolong the agony. Ultimately, crucifixion resulted in a horrible death, usually by dehydration, loss of blood, shock, and respiratory arrest. Typically, crucified victims died by suffocation. When their tired muscles could no longer support their bodes, the chest muscles would be stretched, making it difficult and then impossible to exhale. John's Gospel tells how the Romans would sometimes break a victim's legs after some time so they could not support their weight and thus hasten death.

While on the cross, Jesus refused to take the wine mixed with myrrh—a drug to help ease pain. Our Lord experienced the full effect of his suffering. He was crucified between two thieves, showing the indignity that befell him, the Innocent One. An inscription written in Hebrew, Greek, and Latin ironically advertised his crime—"King of the Jews." Jesus was mocked and taunted as the people dared him to save himself. Among the last words he spoke were a quotation from Psalm 22:1, "My God, my God, why have you abandoned me?" These heart-wrenching words represent Jesus' utter agony and pain as a human

EXPLAINING THE FAITH

Why do some crucifixes have the letters INRI at the top of the cross?

The letters INRI are related to the custom of Roman authorities of posting the crime of condemned criminals on their crosses. The idea was to advertise the crime to deter others from doing something similar. In the Holy Land, Romans would have affixed a sign in three languages: Greek, Hebrew, and Latin. Visitors to Jerusalem during the religious festivals could understand at least one of these languages.

INRI abbreviates the Latin words that would have been posted: *Iesus Nazarenus Rex Judeorum,* which translates to "Jesus of Nazareth, King of the Jews."

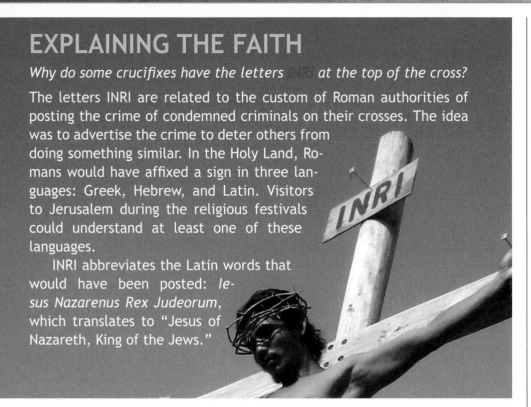

INRI

INRI is an abbreviation of Jesus' crime in the Latin language: I=Jesus, N=Nazareth, R=King, I=Jews.

being who cries out to God. Observers thought he was calling on Elijah for help, thus showing how they continued to misunderstand him.

Jesus' Death

According to Mark's Gospel, Jesus let out a loud cry just prior to expiring (see Mark 15:37). The veil in the Temple sanctuary was torn in two, thus symbolizing that the days of the Old Covenant were over. Jesus' Death began a new age when everyone can now worship God directly, in truth and spirit.

Jesus' Death removed the barrier separating us from God. His sacrifice is unique, completing and surpassing all other sacrifices. His Death fulfilled the atoning mission of the Suffering Servant. A Roman centurion was moved to profess, "Truly this man was the Son of God!" (Mk 15:39).

A lone Gentile understood Jesus and recognized his true identity.

Jesus' Burial

Not everyone abandoned Jesus at the end. His Mother, Mary, stood under the cross, as well as John, the **"beloved disciple."** Also present were Mary Magdalene and other women. Joseph of Arimathea, a member of the Sanhedrin and secret follower of Jesus, asked Pilate for permission to bury the Lord. Pilate was surprised that Jesus had died so quickly (after six hours according to the synoptic Gospels and in just three hours as reported in John's Gospel). Due to Jesus' severe scourging, and the terrible shock his body endured, he died quickly. After a centurion assured him that Jesus was indeed dead, Pilate released the body to Joseph.

Among those who assisted at Jesus' burial was Nicodemus, a Pharisee

"beloved disciple"

Since the term is not found in any of the other Gospels, it is understood to refer to John the Evangelist, the author of the Gospel.

JESUS' LAST WORDS

The Gospels report several examples of Jesus' last words. Each example in some way typifies the way he lived.

"Father, forgive them, they know not what they do." (Lk 23:34)

In his dying moments, Jesus showed the loving forgiveness that characterized his entire ministry. He died as he lived. His forgiveness extends not only to those who crucified him, but also to everyone because we, too, are sinners and implicated in the Death of Christ.

"Amen, I say to you, today you will be with me in Paradise." (Lk 23:43)

Jesus assures the "good thief" of Salvation on the very day it is accomplished for everyone. In his own moment of suffering, Jesus' thoughts were on others.

"Woman, behold, your son . . . Behold, your mother." (Jn 19:26,27)

Jesus showed concern for his Mother in his dying moments. He also entrusted his Mother to the Church, represented by the beloved disciple, believed to be John. Thus, by Jesus' desire, Mary is Mother of the Church.

"Eli, Eli, lema sabachthani?" . . . "My God, my God, why have you forsaken me?" (Mt 27:46)

Here Jesus prayed Psalm 22, not despairing as some of the bystanders thought. These lines suggest that he prayed the entire Psalm, which ultimately proclaims God's mercy to his Suffering Servant.

"I thirst." (Jn 19:28)

John includes these words to show that Jesus fulfilled the prophecy about the Messiah, "For my thirst, they gave me vinegar" (Ps 69:22). Jesus accepted the agony of death until the divine plan was fulfilled.

"It is finished." (Jn 19:30)

The plan of Salvation has been accomplished: Jesus' work of preaching the Good News, working miracles, and bringing Salvation to all was now complete. Jesus allowed sin and Death to overcome him, but by his Resurrection, he overcame both. God's will for Jesus included his death on the cross, but it also included the magnificent Resurrection to superabundant life and the remission of sin through his Son.

"Father, into your hands I commend my spirit." (Lk 23:46)

Jesus quoted Psalm 31 here. He entrusted his life to his Father in an act of supreme faith and love. With these words, Jesus Christ stands for us all; he feared death, but trusted his Father to rescue him out of the depths. He gave to his Father his very life on our behalf. Thus, his Death

and member of the Sanhedrin. According to the Gospel of Matthew, Pilate even stationed a guard at the tomb to prevent the disciples from stealing Jesus' body.

While in the grave, Jesus' corpse was preserved from corruption because his human soul and body were still linked to the Divine Person of the Son. The Apostles' Creed professes that the dead Christ went to the abode of the dead to proclaim the Good News to the just who were awaiting the Messiah.

Then, on the third day following his Death, the first day of the week, the most important event in human and Salvation History took place: Jesus rose from the dead!

For Review

1. What does the Paschal Mystery mean?
2. What were some of the things that Jesus did that led some religious authorities to judge that he was a false prophet?
3. What crime was Jesus accused of committing under Jewish law? Under Roman law?
4. Who is responsible for the Death of Jesus?
5. Why did Jesus die for us?
6. Outline the main events in the Passion Narrative of one of the synoptic Gospels.
7. Identify: Barabbas, Caiaphas, and Joseph of Arimathea, Mary Magdalene, Nicodemus.
8. What were the seven last words or sayings of Jesus as he hung on the cross? What do they mean?

For Reflection

- When have you felt abandoned by someone who really loves you?
- How did you resolve that feeling?

Resurrection of Jesus (*CCC*, 638-658)

Without the Resurrection of Jesus, you wouldn't be reading this book. There would be no New Testament. There would be no Catholic Church. St. Paul put it this way: "If Christ has not been raised, then empty too is our preaching; empty, too, your faith" (1 Cor 15:14). As the *Catechism of the Catholic Church* puts it, "The Resurrection of Jesus is the crowning truth of our faith in Christ, a faith believed and lived as the central truth by the Christian community; handed on as fundamental by Tradition; established by the documents of the New Testament; and preached as an essential part of the Paschal Mystery along with the cross" (638).

Christ's Resurrection is the fundamental event of Salvation History, a real event that was totally unexpected by Jesus' followers. Fearful of being arrested and persecuted themselves, the Apostles were hiding in Jerusalem when the women in their company reported they had seen the tomb empty. At first, they did not believe, for while the empty tomb points to a concrete historical event—toward belief that the Father brought the Son back to life—it does not by itself produce faith.

Scriptural Accounts of the Resurrection

The Apostles and other disciples came to believe in the Resurrection when they actually *saw* Jesus. The Gospels of Matthew and Mark tell how Mary Magdalene, another Mary, and Salome (in Mark) went to the tomb on Sunday morning to anoint Jesus' body. Matthew reports that guards were posted at the tomb. A sudden earthquake took place, and an angel appeared. The guards were terrified. The angel then told the women that "Jesus is risen" and that they should go to Galilee to meet the other Apostles. In Galilee Jesus gave them the great commission to teach the Gospel to the ends of the earth and to baptize in his name.

In Luke's Gospel, two men in "dazzling garments" told Mary Magdalene, Joanna, and Mary, the mother of James, that Jesus had risen. They told the Apostles this news but were met with disbelief. Peter, however, ran to the tomb to see for himself and was amazed when he found the burial cloths there. Jesus then appeared to two followers on the

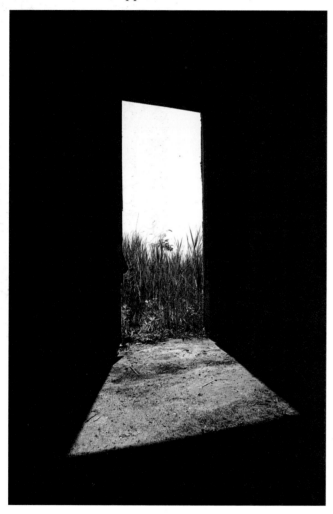

road to Emmaus. Jesus discussed with them the events of the recent days when Jesus joined them and explained to them the meaning of Sacred Scripture. After they arrived at their destination, the Lord shared a meal with them. When he took bread that he blessed, broke, and gave to them, they recognized him. He then vanished from their midst. When the excited disciples reported to the Apostles what took place, Jesus appeared to them and invited them

to touch him. He also ate some food and then explained to them how the Scriptures had prophesied about his Resurrection.

John's Gospel recounts how Mary Magdalene went to the tomb and found it empty. When she told Peter, he and John ran to the tomb and saw the burial clothes. Jesus then appeared to Mary Magdalene. At first, she thought he was the gardener. When Jesus addressed her, she recognized him and wanted to cling to him, but Jesus told her not to, for he had to ascend to the Father. He instructed her to report to the Apostles what she had seen. Later, Jesus appeared to the disciples in the locked room where they were hiding. This was the same Upper Room where the Last Supper had taken place. He extended his peace to them and showed them his wounds. The Lord then breathed on them, giving them the gift of the Holy Spirit and commissioning them to forgive sins in his name.

John's Gospel includes the incident with the Apostle Thomas, who was not present at this appearance and did not believe the others when he heard about it. Thomas wanted to see the nail marks for himself and put his hands into them and into Jesus' side. A week later, the Lord appeared when Thomas was present and invited him to touch him. Thomas answered, "My Lord and my God!" the first scriptural record of anyone addressing Jesus as God. The last appearance reported in John's Gospel took place when Jesus met the disciples on the shores of the Sea of Tiberias. He cooked them breakfast there and commissioned Peter to feed his flock.

Writing around AD 56, in his First Letter to the Corinthians, St. Paul quoted an early creed in which he tells how Christ died for our sins, was buried, and then was raised on the third day. Most remarkably, Paul then lists various people to whom Jesus appeared. These people included Peter, the Twelve Apostles, five hundred other disciples (some of whom were still living when Paul wrote his letter), St. James, and to all the Apostles yet again. Finally, he appeared last to Paul himself, someone who had once persecuted Christians when he was a strict Pharisee (1 Cor 15:1–11).

Theological Meaning of the Resurrection

Real meetings with the Risen Lord transformed the frightened and disillusioned disciples into bold eyewitnesses who would spread the Good News of Jesus Christ far and wide. Their testimony, aided by the Holy Spirit's gifts of faith and fortitude, led many of them to suffer martyrdom for their firm conviction and belief that Jesus Christ rose from the dead.

Down through the ages, and even in our own day, some have tried to deny or explain away Jesus' Resurrection. Some misconceptions of the Resurrection are that it was a

- *reanimated corpse* like that of Lazarus who was brought back to life to die once again;

- *metaphor*, a poetic way of saying that Jesus' soul was immortal;

- *reincarnation*, a belief that the human soul is reborn time and again in new bodies or

- *psychological explanation* created by the Apostles who were trying to say that the *cause* of their teacher would live on.

All these explanations limp in face of the scriptural evidence and the remarkable history of the early Church. Jesus actually died. Jesus appeared to the Apostles and others in a bodily form after death. The *Catechism* puts it this way: "In his risen body he passes from the state of death to another life beyond time and space" (646). Jesus' human body was gloriously transfigured, filled with the Holy Spirit, into an incorrupt, glorious, immortal body "seated at the right hand of the Father." The event of the Resurrection is historical; at the same time, it goes beyond human experience:

> Faith in the Resurrection has as its object an event which is historically attested to by the disciples, who really encountered the Risen One. At the same time, this event is mysteriously transcendent insofar as it is the entry of Christ's humanity into the glory of God. (*CCC,* 656)

The Resurrection proves that Jesus is divine. It shows how the Father responded to the false condemnation and execution of Jesus with the witness that Jesus is indeed the true Son of God and the Lord God himself. The Resurrection further reveals the unending loving communion of God as Trinity: the Father who glorifies the Son, the Son whose sacrifice merits his exaltation, and the Holy Spirit who is the Spirit of life and resurrection. Raised to a glorious body and filled with the power of the Holy Spirit, our Lord has definitively conquered sin and death.

The effect of Christ's Resurrection on humanity is tremendous. As part of the Paschal Mystery of God's love, Christ's Death frees us from slavery to sin, death, and suffering while his Resurrection opens the way to a new life. Jesus' Resurrection also gives us

reincarnation
A false teaching that holds that people return to earth after they die. Instead, death is the end of our earthly pilgrimage and the beginning of eternal life.

hope for our own rising on the last day and a future of eternal life with the Blessed Trinity.

No longer limited by space and time, Christ our Lord lives and reigns forever. He lives in his Body, the Church, and in a special way in the powerful signs of love he has given his Church—the sacraments. For example, by the power of the Holy Spirit, the Lord comes to us at Baptism, forming us into his own image. In the Sacrament of Confirmation, the Holy Spirit strengthens us with spiritual gifts to live like Christ, and we experience the Lord's forgiveness in the Sacrament of Penance and his healing touch in the Sacrament of the Anointing of the Sick. We also receive his help to live loving lives of service in the Sacraments of Holy Orders and Matrimony.

In a very special way, we meet Jesus Christ in the Eucharist, the sacrament of unity and love. At Mass, he continues to speak to us in his holy word proclaimed in the readings. More importantly, the Risen Lord comes to us under the forms of bread and wine. We receive the great gift of Christ to become other Christs, especially for poor people, victims of discrimination, the powerless, the suffering, and the lonely.

"Christ has died, Christ is risen, Christ will come again." Because he is risen, he remains with his Church, the Body of Christ, and continues to lead us with teachers (the pope and bishops) to guide us in his truth. Jesus Christ, our Savior, remains close to us and is alive and present in all believers and in the world that he created. All believers wait for his glorious Second Coming.

RESURRECTION APPEARANCES

The fact that the four Gospels report different events concerning Jesus' appearances should not surprise us. Such diversity is normal in genuine accounts of such a remarkable, one-of-a-kind miraculous event. The differences in the accounts support the reality of the actual Resurrection appearances and argue against their fabrication. If the Resurrection were mere fiction, wouldn't the Evangelists have taken great care to report about it in the exact same way?

Listed below are the appearances of Jesus recorded in the New Testament. Read and summarize at least six of these references. Then, imagine yourself to be one of the persons to whom Jesus appeared. Write a few paragraphs describing the following: what you feel about your Master's now being alive; what he looks like; what he says to you.

The Resurrection Appearances

- Disciples on the road to Emmaus (Lk 24:13-35)
- Women (Mt 28:9-10)
- Mary Magdalene (Jn 20:11-18)
- Peter (Lk 24:34; 1 Cor 15:5)
- Four separate appearances to the Eleven and some other disciples (Jn 20:19-23; Jn 20:24-29; Mt 28:16-20; Acts 1:6-9)
- Seven disciples (Jn 21:1-14)
- More than five hundred brethren (1 Cor 15:6)
- James (1 Cor 15:7)
- Paul (Acts 9:3-8)

The Ascension of Jesus (CCC, 668-682)

The Ascension of Jesus refers to the time when Jesus stopped appearing to the disciples in visible, human form. Christ's body was glorified at the moment of his Resurrection, but when he appeared to his disciples, his glory remained hidden under the appearance of ordinary humanity. When the Ascension took place, Jesus took his rightful place at the right hand of the Father. The Ascension "indicates a difference in manifestation between the glory of the risen Christ and that of the Christ exalted to the Father's right hand" (*CCC*, 660).

The Ascension of Jesus is another part of the Paschal Mystery, which includes Christ's suffering and Death (Good Friday), his descent to the dead (Holy Saturday), and his glorification. Jesus' glorification consists of the Resurrection (Easter Sunday) and his Ascension into Heaven (forty days after Easter). The Descent of the Holy Spirit on Pentecost (fifty days after Easter) flows from this glorification.

The Gospel of Mark does not describe the Ascension of Jesus. John's Gospel reports how Jesus told Mary Magdalene that he would soon be ascending to his Father. Matthew's Gospel suggests the Ascension in its final verses that tell how Jesus took the Apostles to a mountain where he gave them his final instructions.

Luke, however, gives the fullest account of the Ascension, which he locates near Bethany (see Luke 24:50–52). In the Acts of the Apostles, also written by Luke, it is reported that Jesus appeared to the disciples over a period of forty days. He also promised to send them the Holy Spirit. While he finished telling them this, he was lifted up and taken from their sight. Two messengers in white garments were standing there with them and told the Apostles that Jesus would return one day the same way he went into Heaven (see Acts 1:6–12). The text continues with a report of the glorious day of Pentecost (see Acts 2) when the Holy Spirit descended on the Apostles and gave them the power to preach with conviction the message that Jesus is risen and is the Lord of the universe.

Jesus came from the Father and went back to the Father. He makes it possible for human beings to also enter his Father's house because he has gone before us. Now seated at the right hand of the Father, Jesus Christ glorifies the Father as the incarnate Son of God. Furthermore, he continually intercedes for us before the Father. This is the beginning of the Messiah's Kingdom, one without end.

The Second Coming of Christ (CCC, 668-682)

At Jesus' Ascension, the angels told the Apostles that the Lord would come again. They were referring to a future event known as the **Parousia**, that is, the

Parousia
The Second Coming of Christ when the Lord will judge the living and the dead.

Being Hospitable

Jesus welcomed everyone and challenges us to do the same. This is done by practicing the virtue of **hospitality**, a virtue that extends a friendly and generous welcome to strangers and guests.

Today, there are both "shut-ins" and "shut-outs." Shut-ins are housebound because of age or sickness or some other inability to get around. Shut-outs are people who are ignored and not included in certain groups simply because of who they are.

"I was . . . a stranger and you welcomed me" (Mt 25:35). When we are welcoming, Jesus promises us the gift of eternal life.

- With a partner, devise some practical strategies to show hospitality to shut-ins and shut-outs. Create a list of ten concrete things you can do. (For example, you can befriend a classmate who is lonely, invite a lonely classmate to join your extracurricular activity, engage in a conversation with a neighbor with whom you have never spoken, or visit a sick person who is bedridden.) Then, put at least one of your strategies into effect during the coming week. Report on what happened.

hospitality
The act of welcoming, receiving, or hosting.

Maranatha
An Aramaic phrase that means "Come, O Lord."

arrival of Jesus in all his glory. It is also called the Second Coming. Christians look forward to that day and proclaim belief in it in the Creed. On that glorious day, the world we know will end. All of God's creatures everywhere will acknowledge that Jesus is Lord. The glorious Lord Jesus will then fully bring about the Father's Kingdom of justice, love, and peace. Jesus said that the time and date when this will take place is already hidden in God's almighty plan. However, we should be ready at all times "Be watchful! Be alert! You do not know when the time will come" (Mk 13:33).

According to Matthew 25:31–46, at the Parousia the Son of Man will judge the living and the dead based on whether we were loving toward others. Did we feed the hungry and give drink to the thirsty? Did we welcome strangers and minister to the poor, the sick, prisoners? If we can answer yes to his questions, then

Christ, our compassionate Judge, will reward us beyond what we can possibly imagine. Jesus' instructions to us are simple:

> I give you a new commandment: love one another. As I have loved you, so you also should love one another. This is how all will know that you are my disciples, if you have love for one another. (Jn 13:34–35)

The second to last verse of the New Testament is a prayer to the Triumphant Lord that he might return right away: "Amen! Come, Lord Jesus!" (Rv 22:20). **Maranatha** is a most appropriate prayer for Christians. In faith, we know who Jesus really is and what he has done for us. Who would not want him to come soon?

For Review

1. What is the crowning truth of our faith in Jesus Christ?

2. Explain why it is reasonable to believe that Jesus rose from the dead.

3. List various witnesses to the resurrected Jesus.

4. What are four wrong interpretations of the Resurrection of Jesus that non-believers have held through the ages?

5. Discuss three points in the theological meaning of Christ's Resurrection.

6. What does the Ascension of Jesus mean?

7. Identify *Parousia*.

For Reflection

Imagine that our Lord is going to return tomorrow. What would you do differently today? Which people would you absolutely want to see? What would you tell them?

Main Ideas

- Jesus was a miracle worker who performed these signs to show how the Kingdom of God is present in him, to prove that he is the Messiah, to show that he was sent by God the Father, and to invite us to believe in him (p. 185).

- Jesus' miracles are grouped as physical healings, nature miracles, exorcisms, and raisings from the dead (pp. 185–187).

- The physical healing miracles are described in five steps: an introduction, display of faith, cure, result, and the reaction of the people (pp. 185–186).

- In nature miracles Jesus showed his mastery over the elements; the feeding of the thousands is a primary example of this type of miracle (pp. 186–187).

- In his exorcisms, Jesus expelled evil spirits from people who were affected by them (p. 187).

- Jesus brought several people back to life (p. 187).

- Jesus' miracles revealed God's power and are a sign of God's Kingdom (pp. 188–190).

- Jesus encountered many people in his ministry, including many common people and those in Jewish sects (Sadducees, Pharisees, Essenes, Zealots) (pp. 191–193).

- Women were treated with respect and dignity by Jesus and many of his closest followers were women (p. 194).

- The events of the Paschal Mystery are at the center of the Gospel (p. 194).

- All sinners are responsible for the Death of Jesus (p. 196).

- Jesus was found guilty of blasphemy, turned over to Pontius Pilate by the Jewish Sanhedrin, and accused as a political criminal in the Roman court (pp. 197–198).

- It is wrong to hold the Jewish people responsible for Jesus' Death; it is a form of anti-Semitism (pp. 195–196).

- Jesus died for all human beings (p. 196).

- The Passion Narratives of the Gospels describe how the events of our Salvation unfolded (pp. 197–201).

- Jesus' Death removes the barrier separating us from God (p. 199).

- The Resurrection of Jesus is the central truth of the Church; it is the fundamental event of Salvation History (p. 201).

- The Apostles and others came to believe in Jesus from both the empty tomb and his appearances to them (pp. 201–203).

- The Resurrection proves that Jesus is divine. Its effects are that it repairs our friendship with God and frees us from slavery to sin, death, and suffering (pp. 203–204).

- Luke's Gospel describes in most detail Jesus' Ascension and his promise to return again (p. 205).

- At a future event known as the Parousia, Jesus will come again to judge the living and the dead (pp. 205–206).

Terms, People, Places

Choose the term from the numbered column that best describes a word or phrase from the lettered column.

1. false prophets
2. miracles
3. Maranatha
4. Sanhedrin
5. hospitality
6. exorcism
7. Parousia
8. proselytes
9. INRI
10. "beloved disciple"
11. reincarnation
12. anti-Semitism
13. blasphemy

A. The statement of Jesus' crime

B. Powerful signs worked by Jesus

C. Known by their "bad" fruits

D. "Come, O Lord"

E. They sent Jesus to Pilate.

F. The Second Coming of Christ

G. A Gentile convert to Judaism

H. Welcoming, receiving, or hosting

I. As performed by the Church, liberation from the power of the devil

J. A false teaching about what happens after we die

K. Prejudice against the Jews

L. Likely John the Evangelist

M. A thought, word, or action that expresses hatred of God, Christ, the Church, saints or holy things

Primary Source Quotations

More Final Words

What a beautiful thing I see.

—St. Dominic Savio

I am not afraid. I have been waiting for my Lord for a long time. He is the one who has made me love death and now my one desire is to go and be with him.

—Blessed Rafka al-Rayes

Signs of the Kingdom

The signs worked by Jesus attest that the Father has sent him. To those who turn to him in faith, he grants what they ask. So miracles strengthen faith in the One who does his Father's work; they bear witness that he is the Son of God.

—*Catechism of the Catholic Church*, 548

Salvation through the Paschal Mystery

For the love of Christ impels us, once we have come to the conviction that one died for all; therefore, all have died. He indeed died for all, so that those who live might no longer live for themselves but

for him who for their sake died and was raised.

—2 Corinthians 5:14–15

Ongoing Assignments

As you cover the material in this chapter, choose and complete at least three of these assignments.

1. Visit the following websites related to the devotion of the Way of the Cross:

   • Via Crucis: http://198.62.75.1/www1/jsc/TVCcenac.html

   • Creighton University's Collaborative Ministry: www.creighton.edu/CollaborativeMinistry/stations.html

   • Catholic online: www.catholic.org/prayers/station.php

   • EWTN: www.ewtn.com/devotionals/Stations/face.htm

   Then, do one of the following:

   • Pray the Way of the Cross.

   • Write your own short reflections and prayers for each station.

   • Create a PowerPoint presentation using some of the images you find on the Internet.

2. Compose an imaginative guided meditation from the viewpoint of someone who experienced the miracle of the loaves and fishes.

3. Report on how crucifixion took place in ancient times. Check out these websites:

   • Joe Zias, "Crucifixion in Antiquity: The Evidence": www.centuryone.org/crucifixion2.html

   • www.wcg.org/lit/booklets/risen/risen3.htm

   • www.orlutheran.com/html/crucify.html

4. Prepare a report on Pontius Pilate from one or more of the following websites:

Chapter 8 Quick View

- http://ecole.evansville.edu/articles/ pilate.html
- www.newadvent.org/cathen/12083c.htm
- www.livius.org/pi-pm/pilate/ pilate01.htm
- www.bibleinterp.com/articles/ Carter-Pontius_Pilate_Roman_ Governor.htm

5. Report on Caiaphas and the archaeological find of his ossuary. See:

- www.kchanson.com/ANCDOCS/ westsem/caiaphas.html
- www.newadvent.org/cathen/03143b.htm
- www.law.umkc.edu/faculty/projects/ ftrials/jesus/jesuskeyfigures.html
- www.abu.nb.ca/courses/NTIntro/ images/CaiaphasOss.htm
- www.bibleinterp.com/articles/Bond_ Joseph_Caiaphas.htm

6. Report on what the Jewish historian Josephus says about the Sadducees and Pharisees using this website: http://virtual religion.net/iho/pharisee.html#sects

7. Read more about the Dead Sea Scrolls and the Essenes at one of these sites. Prepare a short report related to topics you discover.

- Scrolls from the Dead Sea: www.ibiblio .org/expo/deadsea.scrolls.exhibit/intro .html
- The Essenes and the Dead Sea Scrolls: www.pbs.org/wgbh/pages/front line/shows/religion/portrait/essenes.html
- Orion Center for the Study of the Dead Sea Scrolls: orion.mscc.huji.ac.il/
- Dead Sea Scrolls at the West Semitic Research Center: www.usc.edu/ dept/LAS/wsrp/educational_site/ dead_sea_scrolls

- The Dead Sea Scrolls: http:// virtualreligion.net/iho/dss_2.html

8. Retell the Passion story from the point of view of one of the Apostles.

9. Use the following website to report on the Zealots and their stand at Masada during the First Jewish Revolt:

- www.jewishvirtuallibrary.org/jsource/ Judaism/masada.html

10. Read the article "Women in the Synoptic Gospels" by Fr. Felix Just, S.J. at http:// catholic-resources.org/Bible/Synoptics_ Women.htm. Read five passages, and report on the role the woman or women had in the particular passages.

11. Rewrite one of the miracles by putting it into a modern-day setting. Be sure to follow the outline of a typical miracle story that you read about on pages 185–186.

12. Read the following passages and answer the questions in your journal.

- Matthew 23:1–5: What does Jesus criticize?
- Luke 13:30–31: What is admirable about the Pharisees in this passage?
- Mark 7:1–23: According to Jesus, from where does evil come?

13. Read the Passion Narrative in Mark 14–15. List the main events in your journal. Then read the account of either Luke 22–23 or Matthew 26–27. Note any new facts you learn from reading one of the other accounts.

14. View a modern-day reading of the Resurrection (see John 20:1–31), produced by the American Bible Association and starring the Catholic actor Jim Caviezel at www .newmediabible.org/Default.htm. Write a short review of the film.

Prayer

Then the king will say to those on his right, "Come, you who are blessed by my Father. Inherit the kingdom prepared for you from the foundation of the world. For I was hungry and you gave me food, I was thirsty and you gave me drink, a stranger and you welcomed me, naked and you clothed me, ill and you cared for me, in prison and you visited me."

— Matthew 25:34–36

Meditate on Jesus' words in Matthew's Gospel concerning the Last Judgment. Follow these steps:

1. Assume a comfortable position. Relax, and get ready for your time with Jesus.
2. Become aware of the Lord's presence. Feel his love surround you.
3. Slowly, meditatively, read Matthew 25:31–46. Put yourself into the scene. Engage all your senses: What do you see? Hear? Taste? Smell? Feel? The Lord is separating the sheep from the goats. Listen carefully once again to his words.
4. Reflect by reviewing your life right now. What if you were to meet our Lord tonight at midnight? What could you say to him?
5. Thank the Lord for his time with you.

- *Reflection*: Who in your life needs your love right now?

- *Resolution*: Respond with a specific act of kindness to the person who needs you.

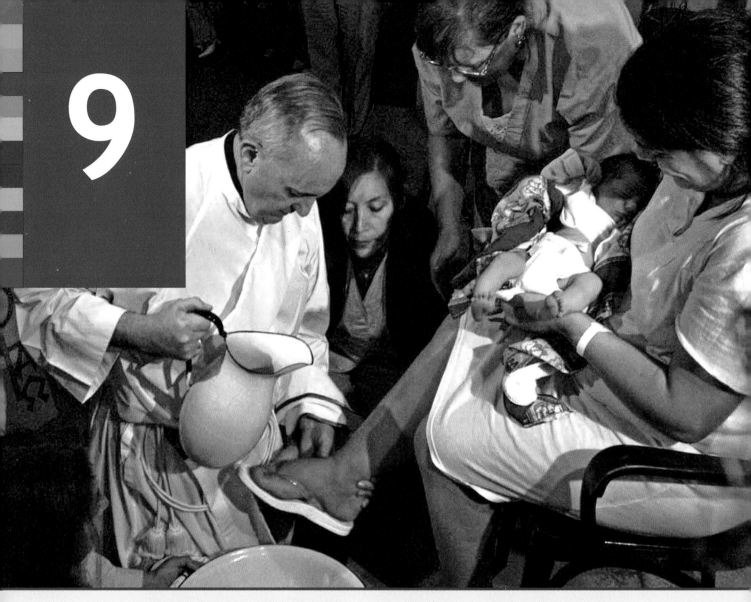

9

JESUS IN THE GOSPEL OF JOHN

For God so loved the world that he gave his only Son, so that everyone who believes in him might not perish but might have eternal life.

—John 3:16

God's Love for Us

John's Gospel clearly reveals the love God has for the world: that he gave us his only Son for our Salvation.

Background of the Gospel of John

The author of the Gospel of John was an eyewitness to Jesus' life; he is named John, the "Beloved Disciple of the Lord."

Prologue to John's Gospel: The Word Became Flesh (John 1)

The first eighteen verses of the Gospel introduce the major themes: Incarnation and descending Christology.

The Signs in John's Gospel

Seven signs or miracles are included in John's Gospel that reveal Jesus' identity, his mission, and his glory.

The Book of Glory

The messages in the second part of John's Gospel are about service, love, and the promise of the Holy Spirit.

Passion, Death, and Resurrection of Jesus in the Gospel

The Passion narrative reveals that Jesus is in control of those events; the Resurrection account reveals his glory and the need for his disciples to give testimony.

God's Love for Us

"God sees everything." You may have heard this lesson of faith from the time you were young, but did you think its meaning was that God watches you so he can catch you doing something wrong? This is not really the reason God constantly watches over us.

As the famous passage from John 3:16 teaches, God loves us so much that he sent his Son to live with us so that we can have eternal life. He watches us because he loves us. St. Irenaeus, a second-century Church Father, stated it this way: "For this is why the Word became man, and the Son of God became the Son of man: so that man, by entering into communion with the Word and thus receiving divine sonship, might become a son of God."

The Gospel of John helps us to learn the incredible love God showed us through his Son, Jesus Christ. Besides some main themes of the Gospel, including the Bread of Life discourse, this chapter reviews the authorship of the Gospel, the prologue, the miraculous signs of Jesus, and the Last Supper discourse leading to the Passion, Death, and Resurrection of Christ.

For Reflection

What does the statement "God is always with you" mean to you?

Focusing on the Organization of John's Gospel

The Gospel of John is organized into four main sections:

I.   Prologue (1:1–18)

II. The Book of Signs (1:19–12:50)

III. The Book of Glory (13:1–20:31)

IV. Epilogue: Resurrection Appearance in Galilee (21:1–25)

Read the following synopsis, and complete the assignments for each section:

- The prologue highlights Jesus' divinity and states the main themes in the Gospel: life, light, truth, world, testimony and the preexistence of Jesus as the incarnate **Logos**, that is, the substantial image of the Father and the only Son of the Father. Read John 1:1–18, replacing "the Word" with "Jesus."

- The Book of Signs contains seven "signs" or miracles of Jesus, beginning with the wedding at Cana and ending with the raising of Lazarus. Each of the signs is followed by a teaching. Find and name each sign and the main teaching expressed in each.

- The entire Gospel is meant to reveal Jesus' glory. In the Book of Glory, Jesus' hour arrives, and he explains the meaning of the Passion, Death, and Resurrection in the dialogue that takes place in the Upper Room. What does Jesus say about the meaning of these events?

- The Gospel ends with Resurrection appearances of Jesus. What are the differences between Jesus' newly resurrected body and his former one?

Background of the Gospel of John

St. Irenaeus, writing around AD 180, was the first to attribute the fourth Gospel to John, the "beloved disciple" of the Lord. Church tradition has identified the beloved disciple as the Apostle John son of Zebedee. Along with his brother James son of Zebedee and Peter, John was one of Jesus' specially chosen Apostles who witnessed the Transfiguration and the raising of Jairus's daughter.

Further study of the Gospel reveals its complex nature. The Gospel of John may have been written in several stages and edited by different people. For example, some material appears twice with only slight changes in the wording (see John 6:35–50; 6:51–58). John 21 reads like an appendix that someone other than the original author added to the end of the Gospel.

The understanding of the meaning of authorship was different in the ancient world than it is today. Often authorship was attributed more to the one who inspired a particular work than to the one who actually wrote it. If this were the case with John's Gospel, it would mean that the witness of the beloved disciple is the foundation of the Gospel. A solid tradition places him in Ephesus (in present-day Turkey), where he likely gathered around him a community of followers. One of these followers was a certain priest, called Presbyter John by Papias, a Church bishop who wrote of meeting him. This John was a close associate of John son of Zebedee, the beloved disciple, and was probably the author of the Second and Third Letters of John. It could be that disciples like Presbyter John took the beloved disciple's testimony, meditated on his words, and later produced in stages a Gospel that addressed the concerns of their own Christian communities.

The Evangelist who wrote the Gospel of John was certainly an eyewitness to Jesus' public life. As he wrote at the end of the Gospel, "It is this disciple who testifies to these things and has written them, and we know that his testimony is true" (Jn 21:24). Pope Benedict XVI takes this same view on the authorship of the Gospel. He wrote,

> This Gospel ultimately goes back to an eyewitness, and even the actual redaction [editing] of the text was

Logos
The Greek term for "Word." In the Old Testament, Logos referred to creation, the Law, God's Revelation through the prophets and his presence among the people. John's Gospel reveals that Jesus is the Word of God who has existed forever.

THE BELOVED DISCIPLE IN THE GOSPEL

Read the following passages from the Gospel of John about the beloved disciple: 13:23; 19:26; 20:2-10; 21:7, 21-23. In your journal, answer the following:

- How do we know that Jesus favored this disciple?
- Describe the beloved disciple in relationship to Peter. What might his stepping aside to allow Peter to enter the tomb first signify?
- Read John 18:15-16, a likely reference to the beloved disciple. What do you find interesting about this passage?

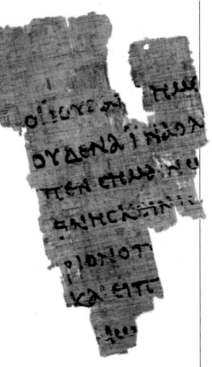

John Rylands Greek papyrus

Generally accepted as the earliest record of a New Testament text, it is a fragment that measures 2.5 x 3.5 inches that includes lines from John 18:31—33. It is kept at the John Rylands Library in Manchester, United Kingdom.

mystical

Inspiring a sense of mystery; the word also refers to having direct communication with God.

substantially the work of one of his closest followers within the living circle of his disciples.[3]

The Gospel of John was likely composed between AD 90 and 100. The earliest fragment of any New Testament writing is a short piece of papyrus with a verse from John's Gospel found in Egypt. Known as the **John Rylands Greek papyrus**, it dates to around AD 130. Thus, it remarkably proves that John's Gospel was widely circulated throughout the Mediterranean world only a few decades after its composition.

John wrote for a diverse audience, including Samaritan converts to Christianity (see John 4:4–42), Gentile Christians, and Jewish-Christians who were expelled from synagogues after the Roman Revolt of 66 that led to the destruction of the Jerusalem Temple. Many Christians had fled the city and did not fight alongside their compatriots. This persecution caused some of John's community to leave Palestine and emigrate to Ephesus.

The Evangelist drew on written and oral traditions that he shared in common with Mark and Luke's Gospels. The final editor of the Gospel probably was familiar with the synoptic Gospels, though he did not greatly rely on them. One of John's major sources included seven miracles, three of which appear only in his Gospel: the changing of water into wine, the cure of a man born blind, and the raising of Lazarus. A second major source was a version of the Passion and Resurrection narratives that would have been in circulation for many years before any of the Gospels were written.

Two major themes of John's Gospel are to strengthen the faith of the believers and to win new converts. The Gospel teaches clearly that faith leads to eternal life:

> Now Jesus did many other signs in the presence of (his) disciples that are not written in this book. But these are written that you may (come to) believe that Jesus is the Messiah, the Son of God, and that through this belief you may have life in his name. (Jn 20:30–31)

Another objective the Gospel fulfilled was to fight false ideas about Jesus' full humanity or even his divinity. Finally, the Gospel challenges certain followers of John the Baptist who, even as late as the last decade of the first century, wrongly believed that John the Baptist was the Messiah. In contrast, the Gospel of John insists that Jesus is superior to John the Baptist, who proclaimed that there was one coming "whose sandal strap I am not worthy to untie" (1:27).

The Uniqueness of John's Gospel

The Gospel of John is more **mystical** than any of the synoptic Gospels. Recall that "mystery" is a word that points to something hidden as well as to the plan of God's saving action in human history, that is, "the mystery of Salvation." To describe John's Gospel as mystical highlights both aspects

Reading Assignment on John's Gospel

Though theologically sophisticated, the outline of John's Gospel is simple (see page 214). Chapter 21 contains an Epilogue dealing with Jesus' appearances to his disciples in Galilee.

John's Gospel contains a great deal of theological insight that is often presented in simple, contrasting images that convey profound meaning. Examples of some of the more important images are death and life, light and darkness, flesh and spirit, and glory and eternal life. Major themes in John's Gospel include the following:

Theme	Explanation	Application
Jesus Christ, Word of God, Son of God	Jesus is the Word of God, God's total self-communication. He is both the revealer and the revealed. As God's eternal Son, true God and true man, in the unity of his divine person, Jesus is the only mediator between God and humans.	Jesus is most trustworthy. Listening to Jesus puts us on the path to the "way, truth, and life."
Faith	Look to the signs Jesus performs and believe. Belief leads to eternal life.	Response to Jesus means believing in him—his life, his words, his deeds, and his Death and Resurrection.
Love	Jesus embodies God's love, represented through his Paschal Mystery.	Follow the command Jesus gave to us: "This is my commandment: love one another as I love you" (Jn 15:12).
Holy Spirit	Jesus promised another Paraclete who would guide, comfort, and counsel the world. Through the Spirit, the Lord will be present in believers.	The Spirit enables us to believe and understand Jesus' teaching. Allowing the Spirit to live within us helps us experience the love of the risen Lord.
Resurrection	Jesus lives! On the third day, he rose from the dead, a fact testified by the Apostles and others. It is the basic fact of Christian faith.	Believe in Jesus! He is the Resurrection and the Life. If we die united to him, we also will live forever.

Do the following:

1. Read John 1. In your journal, note the reactions of John the Baptist toward Jesus. How did Jesus choose the Apostles?

2. Read John 2-12, the Book of Signs. Briefly describe and explain what took place in each sign, and then summarize the main points of any dialogues given. Note how people react to Jesus.

of this definition: the God who is mystery and his plan of Salvation come together in Jesus Christ. The Gospel of John emphasizes that Jesus Christ is the One who mediates between God and humanity, because he is true God and true man, in the unity of his divine person.

There is other material and points of emphasis that differentiate the Gospel of John from the synoptic Gospels. These include:

- New characters appear (for example, Nicodemus, Lazarus, a man born blind, and a Samaritan woman).

- Jewish feasts are highlighted in the course of Jesus' three-year ministry. John's Gospel reports that Jesus attended three Passover festivals, not just one as in the synoptics. John 2–4 describes a first Passover where he chose the Apostles. John 6 mentions a second Passover. The third and final Passover feast is described in John 11:55. This was the time of Jesus' crucifixion. John 5 details how Jesus cured a crippled man on the Sabbath during "a feast of the Jews." John 7–9 reports that Jesus went to Jerusalem for the **Feast of Tabernacles**, where he taught and the authorities wanted to arrest him. Jesus also attended the **Feast of Dedication** as described in John 10. This was the feast where he proclaimed, "The Father and I are one" (Jn 10:30), a claim that led his opponents to want to stone him.

- Due in part to Jesus' attendance at the religious feasts, the center of his ministry in John's Gospel is Jerusalem in contrast to Matthew, Mark, and Luke, who stress his ministry in Galilee.

- There are no demonic possessions mentioned.

- Jesus gives long, extended discourses in the Gospel of John. This contrasts with the short sayings and parables of the synoptic Gospels.

- Jesus is clearly portrayed as the focus of God's Revelation. He shows the way to the Father. We learn of Jesus' great "I AM" statements, which reveal who he is in relationship to God and who he is in relationship to us.

Consequently, the Kingdom theme receives less attention.

Either a thorough or casual read of the Gospel of John reveals a great emphasis on God as love and the disciples as friends of Jesus. In writing style, the Gospel of John is very poetic. Literary techniques like irony (where opponents often say things about Jesus that have deeper meanings than they realize), plays on words, metaphors (implied comparisons), figurative language to help clarify the many misunderstandings people have of Jesus, and similar techniques are used throughout.

For Review

1. Transcribe John 3:16 from memory. Explain its meaning.

2. Who wrote the Gospel of John? Identify the beloved disciple.

3. Where and when was the Gospel of John composed? What is its purpose?

4. Discuss three major aspects of John's Gospel that sets it apart from the synoptic Gospels.

5. Discuss three major themes in John's Gospel.

For Reflection

If you could write or say only one sentence to express your belief in Jesus, what would that be?

Prologue to John's Gospel: The Word Became Flesh (John 1)

The first eighteen verses of John serve as a prologue or introduction to some of the major themes of the entire Gospel. They tell us who Jesus is and understand the meaning of his life and ministry. This study is known as **Christology**.

The Incarnation (CCC, 456-463)

The Incarnation of Jesus Christ is an essential dogma of our faith, that is, a teaching of the highest authority. It means that Jesus Christ, the Son of God, "assumed a human nature in order to accomplish our Salvation in it" (*CCC,* 461). The Word of God took on human flesh from his Mother Mary by power of the Holy Spirit. Thus, Jesus is true God and true human.

The Prologue to the Gospel of John provides the scriptural basis for the Church's belief in the Incarnation:

> In the beginning was the Word, and the Word was with God, and the Word was God. He was in the beginning with God. All things came to be through him, and without him nothing came to be. What came to be through him was life, and this life was the light of the human race; the light

shines in the darkness, and the darkness has not overcome it . . . And the Word became flesh and made his dwelling among us, and we saw his glory, the glory as of the Father's only Son, full of grace and truth. (Jn 1:1–4, 14)

The Evangelist makes it clear that the Word of God (*Logos* in Greek) became a real human being by using the word *flesh* (from the Greek word *sarks*, translated *carne* in Latin). Incarnation means "enfleshment." We are not human beings without bod-

ies, without flesh. John chose *flesh* to counteract a first-century heresy known as **Docetism**. Docetists did not believe that the almighty God became human, so they taught that Jesus only *seemed* to be a man. They could not accept that God would demean himself by becoming like humans with all their weaknesses and limitations. Therefore, they claimed that Jesus was a ghostly figure who *appeared* to instruct people about godly things.

Feast of Tabernacles
Also called Sukkot, or the Feast of Booths, it commemorates the forty years the Jews spent in the desert when they had to protect themselves by constructing huts or booths. It begins five days after Yom Kippur and lasts for eight days.

Feast of Dedication
Commonly known as Hanukkah ("Festival of Lights"), it marks the time when the Temple was rededicated in the days of the Maccabees.

Christology
The study of Jesus Christ; that is, trying to understand who he is.

Docetism
An early heresy that was associated with the Gnostics that taught that Jesus had no human body and only appeared to die on the Cross.

Glory of God
The visible Revelation of the power of the invisible God.

Docetism is heretical based on this point: If Jesus Christ only seemed to be human, then he could not have really died and risen from the dead. The Paschal Mystery would not have taken place. Therefore, we have not really been saved, nor would there be any hope for our own future resurrection from the dead. The Gospel of John combated this heresy in advance by recording the truth that Jesus was *really* human and *really* divine.

There are several other truths that are related to the truth of the Incarnation. For example, Christ brings us life. He has reconciled us with God. Because of Original Sin of Adam and Eve, humans inherited a fallen nature and are prone to sin, sickness, and death. Jesus' great sacrifice heals our human nature, overcomes sin, and wins for us everlasting life.

Also, as the Word of God, Jesus is God himself. "In the beginning was the Word, and the Word was with God, and the Word was God" (Jn 1:1) echoes the opening verses of the Book of Genesis. The Old Testament understanding of "Word of God" included God's activity at the creation of the world. When God speaks, creatures come into existence. In Salvation History, "the Word of God" also referred to God's Wisdom, which is associated with creation, the Law, God's Revelation through the prophets, and his close presence among his people. These are rich ideas that reach their climax in the Prologue of the Gospel. The eternal Word of God, the only Son of the Father, who is creative and the source of wisdom and knowledge, became incarnate:

> And the Word became flesh,
> and made his dwelling
> among us,
> and we saw his glory,
> the glory as of the
> Father's only Son,
> full of grace and truth.
> (Jn 1:14)

In Jesus, we can perceive God's glory. The **Glory of God** refers to the visible Revelation of the power of the

EXPLAINING THE FAITH

Was Jesus really human in the same way we are humans?

"Jesus became truly man while remaining truly God" (*CCC*, 464). Jesus Christ is true God and true man. Jesus was a real man who was born of a woman and who lived and walked on the same earth that we live on now. He lived in a place where we can still travel today—Nazareth, a town in Israel nearly two thousand years ago. Christ is like us in all things except sin. In his human nature, Christ also had the immediate knowledge of the Father and of the secret thoughts of people he encountered. Jesus Christ has two wills, divine and human. His human will is always conformed to his divine will.

invisible God. In and through Jesus, God's glory—his power, radiance, and love—shines forth for us to perceive.

In the Incarnation, Jesus reveals God the Father; at the same time, he is the Revelation of God. In his book *Jesus of Nazareth*, Pope Benedict XVI stressed that only the Son of God has seen God. Only the Son of God can reveal God perfectly. The prophet Moses spoke to God as a friend, but was never able to see God's face. Although Moses could speak for God, and God used him to reveal the terms of the Sinai Covenant, Moses was a man with human limitations. Jesus is the last and greatest of all prophets. John's Prologue ends this way: "No one has ever seen God. The only Son, God, who is at the Father's side, has revealed him" (Jn 1:18). Pope Benedict XVI wrote:

> Jesus' teaching is not the product of human learning, of whatever kind. It originates from immediate contact with the Father, from "face-to-face" dialogue—from the vision of one who rests close to the Father's heart. It is the Son's word. . . . Jesus is only able to speak about the Father in the way he does because he is the Son.

Additionally, when we study the Incarnation and its meaning for our Salvation, we must also focus on Mary, the Mother of God. The Second Vatican Council taught that "this union of the mother with the Son in the work of Salvation is made manifest from the time of Christ's virginal conception up to his death." By responding "yes" to God's invitation to the Incarnation at the Annunciation, Mary was already collaborating with the whole work her Son was to accomplish. Mary is the first and best example of the heights to which any person can be elevated by God.

The Incarnation has several implications for our lives today. Because Jesus Christ is God-made-man, he is our perfect model of holiness. Later in John's Gospel, Jesus is described as "the way and the truth and the life" (Jn 14:6) who teaches that the path to holiness is for us to give ourselves to others in imitation of him. "Love one another as I love you" (Jn 15:12). Finally, by becoming human, the Word of God makes it possible for us to share in God's nature. "For the Son of God became man so that we might become God" (St. Athanasius, quoted in *CCC,* 460). As John's Prologue states, "But to those who did accept him he gave power to become children of God" (Jn 1:12).

Christology

The Prologue reveals a different emphasis between the Gospel of John and the synoptic Gospels, namely in the area of Christology. John's Gospel focuses on the heavenly origins of Christ and his fundamental identity as God's only Son, the preexistent Word of God. The divinity of Jesus shines forth in almost every verse of John's Gospel. Its pattern shows how Christ the Savior comes to us first from above (see John 1:1–13); he next reveals the Father to us and then takes us to him (see John 1:14–18).

The Synoptic Gospels provide a narrative of Jesus of Nazareth, details of his ministry, and his impact on people. They then develop his story as an ascent to heavenly glory through his Passion, Death, and Resurrection.

The remaining verses in the Gospel's prologue reveal even more about Christ. John the Baptist explains that he is not the Christ, Elijah, or the Prophet spoken of in Deuteronomy 18:15. Rather, he came to prepare for the one who "existed before me" (Jn 1:30), "whose sandal strap I am not worthy to untie" (Jn 1:27). John testified that he saw the Spirit come down on Jesus and that Jesus is "the Lamb of God, who takes away the sin of the world" (1:29). In him, the Spirit dwells. "He is the Son of God" (1:34).

John the Baptist prefigures all the others who will testify for Jesus later in the Gospel. He also bridges the message of hope that had been offered by the Old Testament prophets. John the Baptist is followed in the Gospel by people including the Samaritan woman, the crowd at Lazarus's raising, the

Titles of Jesus in John's Gospel

The prologue of the Gospel identifies Jesus as the Word of God, the Son of God, the Christ, the greatest Prophet, the Lamb of God, Teacher, King of Israel, and the Son of Man.

Later in the Gospel, other designations for Jesus are recorded. In the titles listed below, Jesus reveals himself by first proclaiming "I am," a reference to the name YHWH (I AM) revealed to Moses (see Exodus 3:14). Jesus' divine nature shines through these self-designations. In John 8:58, Jesus clearly states his true identity, "Amen, amen, I say to you, before Abraham came to be, I AM." His opponents knew exactly what he was claiming. They picked up stones to throw at him because they thought he had blasphemed, "but Jesus hid and went out of the temple area" (Jn 8:59).

Read the references below. Note in your journal which title means most to you and why. Write a prayer to Jesus using your favorite title. Design the prayer using a form of creative media (e.g., PowerPoint, collage, prayer card). Share and pray your prayer with others.

Verse	Title	Meaning
6:35f.	Bread of Life *Sign*: Jesus feeds five thousand (6:5–14)	Jesus gives true life, eternal life. By receiving him in the Eucharist, he lives in us.
8:12	Light of the World *Sign*: Jesus cures the man born blind (9:1–41)	Jesus is the beacon of truth who points us to his Father. Living in the light brings true life.
10:7	Sheep gate *Words*: "I am the gate."	Jesus is the way into God's Kingdom, Heaven.
10:11	Good Shepherd *Words*: "I am the good shepherd. A good shepherd lays down his life for his sheep."	Jesus tenderly loves each of us and has surrendered his life for us. He is the Messiah who watches out for his flock.
11:25	Resurrection and the Life *Sign*: Jesus raises Lazarus from the dead (11:1–44)	Jesus has power over death. Believe in him, live in his light, and you will have eternal life.
14:6	Way, Truth, Life *Words*: "I am the way and the truth and the life. No one comes to the Father except through me."	This summarizes the Word's purpose for joining us: He is the Way to God; he proclaims the message of Salvation; he bestows on us eternal life.
15:5	True Vine *Words*: "I am the vine, you are the branches. Whoever remains in me and I in him will bear much fruit, because without me you can do nothing."	Jesus is the source of life; we must remain attached to him.

Twelve, and the "beloved disciple," who all testify for Jesus. God the Father, the Holy Spirit, and Jesus himself also testify to his identity as God's only Son. The seven signs recorded in the Gospel of John also point to his mission and identity.

The prologue teaches even more. Two disciples address Jesus as "Rabbi," the Hebrew word for "Teacher." One of them, Andrew, proclaims to his brother Simon Peter, "We have found the Messiah" (1:41). And Nathanael, personally invited by Jesus himself to be a disciple, is astounded by Jesus' extraordinary knowledge. Nathanael boldly proclaims, "You are the Son of God; you are King of Israel" (1:49). Jesus responds that Nathanael has not seen anything yet: "Amen, amen, I say to you, you will see the sky opened and the angels of God ascending and descending on the Son of Man" (1:51). For John, "Son of Man" is not simply a title of a mere human being like all others. It is a title to describe a unique mediator, a go-between for Heaven and earth.

🌐 For Review

1. What lessons about the Incarnation are taught in the Prologue to John's Gospel?

2. What is Docetism? What follows from its false teachings about Jesus?

3. What does the Incarnation mean for humanity?

4. How is Jesus the Word of God?

5. Discuss the meaning of three of the "I AM" titles Jesus used of himself. What is the meaning of his proclamation in John 8:58?

🌐 For Reflection

In your own words, explain how you understand the different emphases of Christology between John's Gospel and the synoptic Gospels.

The Signs in John's Gospel

In John's Gospel, Jesus' miracles (called works or signs) reveal his identity, his reason for coming to us, his heavenly glory, and his relation to his heavenly Father. As his first onlookers did, we too need faith to grasp the deeper meaning of his signs. After performing a miracle, Jesus often gave a long discourse to explain its significance. These discourses teach more about Jesus' identity and the necessity for faith in order to achieve eternal life. The following sections detail the events of each sign and explain the meaning of the discourses that also make up this part of the Gospel.

Sign 1: The Wedding at Cana (John 2:1-12)

This sign at a wedding feast is the first public event where Jesus revealed his glory with a miracle. Wedding feasts symbolized a new life begun in this world and the future Messianic banquet in God's Kingdom. Jesus' attendance at a festive wedding feast shows how he enjoyed and celebrated ordinary life. Jesus' attendance at this wedding blessed marriage as a sacrament of divine love.

Mary, the perfect model of faith, had an important role to play at Cana. Hospitality was important in our Lord's society, so it would have been shameful for the wedding hosts to run out of wine. Mary's concern for others moved her to intercede. She had faith in her son's compassion, even though his time to manifest himself openly had not yet come. When he mentioned, "My hour has not come" (Jn 2:4), Jesus was referring to his Passion, Death, Resurrection, and Ascension, when his real glory would be manifested. All the signs in John's Gospel point to his Paschal Mystery, the climax of his heavenly mission of giving up his life so that all humanity might gain eternal life (3:16). Additionally, this sign

intercessory prayer
To intercede means to "come between" or "mediate" between two parties. Jesus is our model intercessor, one who mediates between us and God the Father.

teaches that Mary is a Mother who will also intercede on our behalf with her Son.

That Jesus provided superior wine for this occasion represents the rich wisdom and revelation he brings from God. As Jesus changed water to wine, we believe that the Lord can change us. Also, the water in this miracle is a symbol of the baptismal waters that purify us. The wine represents the Eucharist, which brings us spiritual life—communion with Jesus, the Lord.

Jesus' first sign helped the disciples to believe, manifested his power over nature, and foreshadowed his ministry of helping others by acting with authority.

After the Wedding at Cana

Related to this first sign, Jesus left Cana for Jerusalem where he cleansed the Temple and met the Jewish leader Nicodemus, a Pharisee and secret follower (see John 2:13–25). Jesus

told Nicodemus that no one can enter God's Kingdom "without being born of water and Spirit" (Jn 3:5), which leads to faith, living the truth, and living in the light (see John 3:16–21). In Judea, Jesus also met John the Baptist again. John testified that he is like a bridegroom whose role is to serve the groom, Jesus.

Next, Jesus headed back to Galilee by way of Samaria. It is in Samaria where, thirsty and tired, he met a woman at a well in the town of Sychar. What Jesus did was unheard of for a self-respecting, first-century Jewish man: speak in public to a woman, and even more dramatically, to a hated Samaritan who was also a notorious sinner. This behavior would have scandalized his contemporaries.

The conversation reveals that the woman had spiritual needs that "living water" of new life given by the Messiah could meet. The woman thought literally and wondered aloud how Jesus could provide this special water from an underground river when the old well collected only ground runoff. Jesus patiently explained. When he revealed that she had five husbands, she proclaimed, "You are a prophet" (4:19). Jesus satisfied the woman's thirst for true knowledge: He is the Messiah, the source of eternal life, the one who refreshes and renews and brings life. He also told her that his life enables a person to worship God in spirit and truth. We can meet God everywhere, not just on Mount Gerizim, as the Samaritans believed, or the Jerusalem Temple, as the Jews believed. "God is Spirit, and those

who worship him must worship in Spirit and truth" (4:24).

The woman told the people in her town of her meeting with Jesus. Many came, listened to him, and believeed for themselves that he "is truly the savior of the world" (4:42).

Sign 2: Cure of the Official's Son (John 4:46-54)

Jesus' second sign also occured in Cana. The power of Jesus' word was enough to heal the son of a court official from Capernaum, perhaps a Gentile. The father's faith moved Jesus to act. A lesson from this sign is that believing in Jesus can rescue us from spiritual death. Prayer for others—**intercessory prayer**—has power. Our Lord will respond to our concern for others as he did for the father who wanted health restored for his boy.

Sign 3: Cure on a Sabbath (John 5:1-47)

Jesus' third sign teaches that Jesus is the source of life. He healed a man on the Sabbath who had been lame for thirty-eight years. Some observers thought that healing a non-life-threatening illness on the Sabbath was work forbidden by the Torah, but Jesus said that God does indeed work on the Sabbath: "My Father is at work until now, so I am at work" (Jn 5:17).

Note how Jesus boldly claimed to be equal to God. The unique Son, like the Father, actively works on the Sabbath. Like the Father, the Son also gives life to whomever he wants. Finally, the Father gives his Son the right to judge. Jesus' clear claim of divine authority enraged his opponents: "For this reason the Jews tried all the more to kill him, because he not only broke the sabbath but he also called God his own father, making himself equal to God" (Jn 5:18).

This sign also points out how the Evangelist uses the expression the "Jews" in a hostile way.

Several times throughout John's Gospel the antagonism between Jesus and "the Jews" is so intense that it appears anti-Semitic (prejudicial against the Jews). Remember, though, that Jesus and all his early disciples were Jews. John was writing for a largely Jewish-Christian community that had undergone the Jewish Revolt in AD 70, was later expelled from synagogues, and met continual nonacceptance from Jewish nonbelievers in the communities in which they lived. For the Evangelist, "the Jews" represent those who persist in not accepting Jesus while at the same time persecuting Jewish Christians. The term also symbolized anyone who stubbornly refused to accept Jesus or who engaged in lifeless religious practices and missed out on a vital relationship with Jesus. The Church condemns prejudice against the Jews and all people. Recall from Chapter 8 that it is wrong to assign responsibility for the Death of Jesus to the Jews of Jesus' time or Jews today (see *CCC*, 597).

Signs 4 and 5: Multiplication of Loaves and Walking on Water (John 6:1-14, 16-24)

These signs are grouped together because they each recall Moses' miracles in the Book of Exodus after the first Passover (manna in the desert, walking through the Red Sea). Thus, it is appropriate that the setting for these signs is close to the time of the Passover feast. Jesus is the New Moses and the true Passover. In the first miracle, Jesus feeds the hungry crowd that follows him because of the signs he was performing for the sick. After the miracle, they wanted to make him king, so he withdrew from them to the mountain.

Jesus' walking on the water revealed that he was indeed God's Holy One. Jesus' words to his disciples, "It is I. Do not be afraid" (6:21), reveal his true identity. "It is I" refers to the name God revealed to Moses—YHWH—which means "I AM." Therefore, Jesus pointed to his identity as God by using that term. A message of this sign is that despite the storms that come our way in life, we should never fear. Jesus, God himself, is with us and will never leave us.

Bread of Life Discourse (John 6:25-70)

Following the signs of feeding the thousands and walking on water, the Gospel records a long dialogue between Jesus and his disciples in which he explains the meaning of the multiplication of the loaves. Speaking in a synagogue in Capernaum, Jesus said *he* replaces the manna of the Exodus. He is the new bread God has given to them, their source of eternal life. Through him, we will pass over from death to new life.

> I am the bread of life; whoever comes to me will never hunger, and whoever believes in me will never thirst. . . . I will not reject anyone who comes to me. . . . For this is the will of my Father, that everyone who sees the Son and believes in him may have eternal life, and I shall raise him [on] the last day. (Jn 6:35, 37, 40)

Jesus taught the necessity of eating the flesh of his Body and drinking his Blood, a clear reference to the Eucharist. The Eucharist

brings about an intimate relationship between Jesus and his Church, those who believe in him. He lives in us, and we in him. As the Father is the source of Jesus' life, so Jesus is the source of our life.

This shocking teaching about his Body and Blood caused many to abandon Jesus. But Peter and the Apostles put their trust in him:

> Master, to whom shall we go? You have the words of eternal life. We have come to believe and are convinced that you are the Holy One of God. (Jn 6:68–69)

Sign 6: Cure of a Man Born Blind (John 9:1-41)

This sign contrasts a blind man who was given sight with those who had physical sight yet were spiritually blind. The man born blind received sight after Jesus smeared clay on his eyes and after he obeyed the Lord's instructions to wash in the **Pool of Siloam**. When questioned by the authorities about the cure, the physically cured man grew in spiritual insight as well. At first, he refered to Jesus as "the man called Jesus" (Jn 9:11); then he called him a prophet (Jn 9:17); next he testified that Jesus is a man from God who was able to perform the unheard-of deed of giving sight to one born blind (Jn 9:33). Finally, the cured man confessed that Jesus is the Son of Man and began to worship him (9:38). Severely challenged by the authorities, he refused to criticize

Pool of Siloam

A rock-cut pool located outside of the walls of the old city of Jerusalem. The pool is mentioned other times in the Bible (e.g., Isaiah 8:6; 22:9).

Jesus, even though he was thrown out of the synagogue, a fate shared by the community for which the Gospel was written. This community would have learned an important lesson from the example of the blind man: remain faithful to Jesus and your faith will also deepen.

In contrast to the blind man are those who have physical sight but who are spiritually blind. This included some Pharisees who refused to see the source of Jesus' power or acknowledge who he is. Rather, they called him "a sinner" (Jn 9:24). This message recalls a theme from the Prologue: Jesus is the light that has come into the world. His truth dispels the darkness of ignorance. His light directs us and overcomes the darkness of sin. He asks for faith in him to overcome spiritual blindness. Their human interpretations of the meaning of the Law blinded some Pharisees. Believing that Jesus violated the Sabbath law of rest made them blind to God's presence in their midst. The Lord teaches that spiritual blindness is worse than physical blindness (9:41).

Sign 7: Raising of Lazarus (John 11:1-44)

This most important sign prefigures Jesus' own Death and Resurrection. On his way to Jerusalem, Jesus learned that his friend Lazarus is ill and near death. Jesus waited two days before going to Lazarus. His waiting allowed God the Father to glorify him through a marvelous sign.

Once he arrived, Lazarus's grieving sister Martha tells Jesus that Lazarus would not have died had Jesus been there with him. Jesus responded:

I am the resurrection and the life; whoever believes in me, even if he dies, will live,

THE GOOD SHEPHERD

Like sheep that trust the shepherd, believers can feel safe and secure with Jesus, the Word of God. Jesus chose the beautiful image of the Good Shepherd (John 10:1-21) to emphasize the close, personal relationship he has with those who believe in him. A shepherd's sheep know and belong to him; he knows and belongs to them. He guides and protects them. Jesus also said: "I am the gate for the sheep" (Jn 10:7). Here we can imagine the shepherd sleeping across the entrance to the sheepfold to protect his flock from enemies like wolves. This Shepherd loves greatly—to the point of giving up his life for his flock. "I lay down my life in order to take it up again" (Jn 10:17) is a clear reference to the Cross and Resurrection.

Jesus also teaches that he wishes to gather all people into his flock. Pope Benedict XVI wrote, "However widely scattered they are, all people can become one through the true Shepherd, the Logos [Word] who became man in order to lay down his life and so to give life in abundance."

- Read Psalm 23 and Ezekiel 34, both of which image God as the true Shepherd. Write a brief explanation of how any three verses apply to Jesus, the Good Shepherd.

and everyone who lives and believes in me will never die. Do you believe this? (Jn 11:25–26)

Deeply moved by his death, Jesus wept for his friend Lazarus. Jesus also prayed to his Father, thanking him for answering his prayer. Then, he called Lazarus out of the grave. The dead man came out and was freed of his burial clothes.

Lazarus's raising caused many to believe. However, some of Jesus' enemies decided to eliminate him because they feared his popularity among the people would lead to Roman reprisals. Not realizing the truth of what he was saying, Joseph Caiaphas, the high priest, said, ironically, "It is better for you that one man should die instead of the people, so that the whole nation may not perish" (Jn 11:50). Jesus' Death indeed has saved the Jewish people and all nations.

This seventh sign sums up all the other signs in John's Gospel and highlights important theological themes:

- Jesus is the way to life
- he is the Resurrection
- he is God ("I AM")

Also, the raising of Lazarus summarizes that faith is essential for us to gain eternal life with him in union with the Father and the Holy Spirit.

For Review

1. Explain the meaning of any three of the signs of Jesus reported in John's Gospel.

2. What can we learn from Mary's role in the miracle at Cana?

3. Why did so many of Jesus' followers leave him after the sign of the multiplication of the loaves?

4. How is Jesus the Good Shepherd?

For Reflection

- The Samaritans came to listen to Jesus for themselves. This highlights another theme in John's Gospel: *Each of us must come into personal contact with Jesus.* Write about times in your life when you personally met Jesus.

- Also, reflect on what you most thirst for in your life right now. How can Jesus help quench that thirst?

- How do the seven signs reveal Jesus' presence and mission for you?

The Book of Glory

The second part of John's Gospel is known as the Book of Glory. Jesus' Last Supper discourse is the setting and subject of John 13–17. Other messages in this part of the Gospel pertain to service, love, and the promise of the Holy Spirit. The Lord also prays a moving prayer to his Father for unity for his followers. John 18–21 is concerned with Jesus' Passion, Death, and Resurrection, where Christ's glory is revealed, marking his triumph and the victory of Salvation he won for us.

The Last Supper (John 13:1–16:4)

Differing from the synoptic Gospels, John reports that the Last Supper occurred a day earlier than the Passover; it was the day on which the Jews killed the lambs for the Passover meal. This is an important connection, because Jesus is the Lamb of God whose sacrifice frees us from the slavery of sin. This sacrifice is commemorated in the Eucharist, a memorial of Christ's Passover (*CCC*, 1362). Every Eucharist re-presents in an unbloody manner the one, single sacrifice Christ made for us.

At the Last Supper, in an act of profound humility, Jesus washed the feet of his disciples. When Peter objected, Jesus explained that he did this as an example of humble service. We must serve as he serves.

After Judas Iscariot left the meal to go into the night (a symbol for the darkness of Satan), Jesus offered a new commandment:

> Love one another. As I have loved you, so you also should love one another. This is how all will know that you are my disciples, if you have love for one another. (Jn 13:34–35)

Jesus showed his great love through his Death and Resurrection. He calls on his followers to likewise die to selfishness and to attend to the needs of others. A follower of Jesus must be on the frontline of service, not on the sidelines as an observer.

John 14–17 offers Jesus' last testament or discourse. He encourages his followers to stay close to him because:

> I am the way and the truth and the life. No one comes to the Father except through me. . . . Whoever has seen me has seen the Father. (Jn 14:6, 9)

Jesus promises that he will give anything we ask for in his name. Our way to the Father is through him since Jesus and the Father are one.

Jesus also promises to send the Holy Spirit, another **Paraclete**, that is, a Helper, Counselor, and Advocate. The Spirit will open our minds and hearts, helping us understand and live Jesus' teaching.

Jesus also instructs us to keep his commandments, especially his command to love. Love unites us to the Lord. Among its fruits are peace and joy.

John 15 tells of Jesus' great love for us. He is the vine, we are the branches whose life comes from him. As the Father loves him, so Jesus loves us. We must remain attached to him. We must believe God the Father and his Son and love God and one another. Loving as he loved is the principle of life that keeps Jesus' life in us.

In John 15:13–17, Jesus calls us his friends, teaching us to keep his commandments and to love one another. This is the heart of the Good News. Jesus has chosen us, his friends, to continue his work of love. The Holy Spirit allows Jesus to dwell in us and protects, guides, and empowers us to

Paraclete
A name for the Holy Spirit. In John 14:26, Jesus promised to send an Advocate, a Helper, who would continue to guide, lead, and strengthen the disciples.

FRIENDSHIP

No one has greater love than this, to lay down one's life for one's friends. You are my friends if you do what I command you. (Jn 15:13-14).

Write or Discuss:

- What are some demands of being a good friend?
- How do friends figuratively and literally lay down their lives for one another?
- What does it mean to you personally to have Jesus call you his friend?

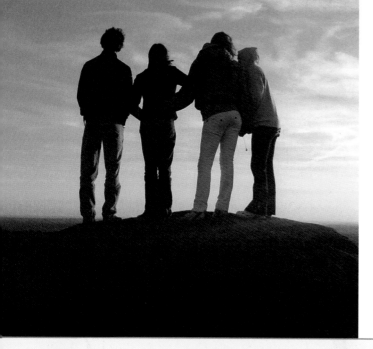

witness to the Lord. The Holy Spirit enables us to love.

The High Priestly Prayer of Jesus (John 17)

The Last Supper ends with the "High Priestly Prayer" of Jesus. Jesus is the High Priest, the one who intercedes for us by praying to the Father on our behalf. Jesus begins the prayer saying that his work is done and the hour of his glory has come, the hour when through his sacrifice he will give eternal life to us. Jesus' Passion, Death, and Resurrection will bring glory to the Father and Salvation to all.

Because his followers will be left in a hostile world, Jesus prays that the Father will watch over them and protect them from the evil one. This prayer is made on our behalf as well. Jesus prays that we will remain united to him, our friend and Savior, and to each other. Jesus prays that our lives will be shaped by the truth of God's Word and that we will remain one, in union (communion) with the Father, Son, and Spirit. Jesus prays:

> Holy Father, keep them in your name that you have given me, so that they may be one just as we are. . . . Consecrate them in the truth. Your word is truth. As you sent me into the world, so I sent them into the world. . . . I pray not only for them, but also for

 Serving as Jesus Served

In John 13:1-20, Jesus teaches the disciples of the importance of serving others. He washed the feet of his disciples—a task that even slaves were not required to do—to teach them that leaders must serve and that love requires humility.

In your journal, write a short reflection on how you are currently making service a part of your life. How helpful are you at home, at school, with your friends? Do you participate in a parish or school service program? Do you share some of your "time, talent, treasure" with the needy? In the past couple of months, have you helped someone without expecting to be repaid?

Take stock and judge how well you are doing. Then, write up three practical suggestions on how you might be of service to others in the coming month. Set up a timetable and then follow through.

those who will believe in me through their word, so that they may all be one, as you, Father, are in me and I in you, that they also may be in us, that the world may believe that you sent me. (Jn 17:11, 17–18, 20–21)

Jesus wants his followers to cherish the truth and witness to it. Staying united to him allows him to continue his work of Salvation through us by power of the Holy Spirit. St. Teresa of Avila (1515–1582) echoed Christ's words when she wrote what is expected of Jesus' friends:

Christ has no body now, but yours. No hands, no feet on earth, but yours. Yours are the eyes through which Christ looks compassion into the world. Yours are the feet with which Christ walks to do good. Yours are the hands with which Christ blesses the world.

Toward the end of the High Priestly Prayer Jesus says, "Father, they are your gift to me. I wish that where I am they also may be with me, that they may see my glory that you gave me" (Jn 17:24). How extraordinary that Jesus calls his followers the Father's gift to *him!* We are his friends and his gifts.

Also, the Lord's gentle touch is our touch. His forgiving words are heard on our lips. His compassionate concern for the lonely, the poor, the sick, and victims of injustice shows up in our kind deeds. His acceptance of others is seen in our eyes. In short, this High Priestly Prayer teaches us that the Lord greatly desires to live in us, Christians united to him. As Jesus revealed the Father to us, our task is to reveal Jesus to others by the power of the Holy Spirit. The world can only know Jesus through disciples who remain attached to him, through Christians who love. What an enormous responsibility, but what an extraordinary privilege!

For Review

1. Discuss two elements of Jesus' message given to his followers at the Last Supper.

2. What does it mean to be a friend of Jesus?

3. In what way does Jesus fulfill a priestly role in our Salvation?

For Reflection

Answer the following questions posed by St. Ignatius of Loyola: What have you done for Christ? What are you doing for Christ? What will you do for Christ?

Passion, Death, and Resurrection of Jesus in the Gospel

The discourses in John 13–17 serve as a prologue to the traditional narratives of the Passion and Resurrection in John 18–20. In the Resurrection account, Jesus reveals his glory and confesses the need for testimony to the Resurrection. More information follows in the next sections.

Passion Narrative (John 18-19)

Jesus is in control of the events of his Passion as described in the Gospel of John. He reveals his and the Father's glory every step of the way, willingly accepting his Death as an atoning sacrifice for all humanity. For example, there is no anguished prayer in the garden. When the soldiers arrested Jesus, they fell to the ground in fear of the divine majesty (Jn 18:6) when he identified himself as "I AM." Though Jesus could have easily escaped from his impending Death, he admonished Peter, who came to his defense by attacking one of the servants, "Put your sword into its scabbard. Shall I not drink the cup that the Father gave me?" (Jn 18:11).

At his trial, Jesus remained in control. He questioned Pilate about the meaning of truth (Jn 18:38). The soldiers' division of his clothing according to Scripture's prophecies illustrates how Jesus chose to go along with the divine plan; he was still in charge. John also highlights the Old Testament prophecies concerning the crucifixion—the persecuted just man of Psalms 22 and 69. The soldiers gamble for his seamless tunic (see Psalm 22:18), sour wine is offered (se Psalm 69:21), and his legs are not broken in reference to the paschal lamb of Exodus 12:46. All these prophecies fall into the pattern of Jesus' being "lifted up" on the cross for our Salvation. God is in charge. Jesus freely obeyed his Father's will.

While hanging on the cross, Jesus continued to minister to others, carrying on his Father's work. For example, he entrusted his Mother to the beloved disciple, and symbolically, to the whole Church (see John 19:26–27). Thus, he teaches what a disciple should be: compassionate, loving, and concerned for others. Finally, Jesus freely gave up his spirit only when he decided to do so (see Jn 19:30).

Resurrection of Jesus (John 20-21)

Nothing exemplifies the glory of Jesus and his Father as does the Resurrection, the central event of our Salvation. Together, the four Gospels provide fourteen stories describing the Resurrection. Mark emphasizes the empty tomb. Matthew stresses God's power and majesty. Luke highlights the Risen Jesus alive in the Word of God and the breaking of the bread. Finally, John focuses on Jesus' commission to the leaders to continue his work of reconciliation and love. The resurrection accounts in John's Gospel are contained in a series of single stories.

Recall from Chapter 8 that John's Gospel reveals that Jesus appeared first to a woman, Mary Magdalene. At first, she did not recognize the transformed, glorified Lord, but when he called her by name, Mary knew it was the Lord. "Rabbouni [Teacher]" (Jn 20:16), she exclaimed. A personal encounter with Jesus, not an empty tomb, brings about faith. Faith and love mark true discipleship, not rank, wealth, position, prestige, one's sex, or power. Mary Magdalene, like Martha earlier (11:27), exhibited faith and love in great abundance. Perhaps this is why she was the first to see and believe in the Risen Lord.

COMPARING THE RESURRECTION NARRATIVES

Read Mark 16:1-8, 9-20; Matthew 28:1-20; Luke 24; John 20-21.

All four Gospels proclaim the Resurrection as a real event, with historically verifiable elements. As mentioned, there are some differences in the descriptions. However, all four Gospels agree on the following essentials:

1. The Resurrection took place early in the morning on the first day of the week.

2. Women were present at the tomb, definitely including Mary Magdalene.

3. The stone had been rolled away and the tomb was empty. This fact did not cause faith. For example, in John's Gospel, Mary Magdalene was weeping because she thought someone stole Jesus' body. In Luke, the Apostles first thought the women's report about the empty tomb was sheer nonsense. Even after they saw for themselves, they were amazed, but nothing was said about belief. However, an empty tomb is important to the Resurrection stories. It was an essential sign of his Resurrection, a first step in acknowledging God's work in bringing the Son back to life. It corroborates that *something happened*. The enemies of the early Christians were never able to produce Jesus' corpse, though they probably tried to do so.

4. A messenger or messengers who spoke to the women were at the tomb; a message was given for the women to tell the disciples what took place.

Most importantly, Jesus appeared to his disciples on several occasions. These appearances were decisive, convincing frightened disciples that the crucified Jesus was alive, that he was Lord, and that he was God's Son. These appearances were life changing for them. Strengthened with the Holy Spirit's gifts of faith and fortitude, frightened, confused, and disappointed followers were transformed into bold, courageous witnesses. They willingly lived and died proclaiming, "Jesus Christ is Lord."

An important point to note is that Jesus appeared only to his disciples. Sometimes they were slow to recognize him. One reason was that they were not expecting the Lord to come back to life. Second, Jesus' resurrected body shone with the glory of God's life. They needed the Lord's own words of peace, instruction, and reassurance to help them come to Resurrection faith.

The Gospel accounts teach that Jesus was not a ghost. Luke, for example, reports that the resurrected Jesus ate fish, while John's Gospel tells how Jesus ate breakfast with his disciples. Furthermore, Jesus asked Thomas to touch his wounds. The resurrected Jesus is *not* a ghost; but neither is he a corpse that is breathing again. He is alive in a transformed, glorified body that still has an aspect of "bodiliness" to it.

One of the most significant testimonies about the Resurrection is St. Paul's account in 1 Corinthians 15:1-19. Besides testifying that the Lord appeared to him, St. Paul mentions several other appearances, including a most significant one to more than five hundred people. At the time of his writing in the early 50s, St. Paul assured his readers that many of these eyewitnesses were still alive! They could easily be called on to verify that the Lord rose from the dead and appeared to them.

Jesus prepared the disciples for his Ascension and the Descent of the Spirit. Jesus instructed the Apostles to wait for him (see Mark 16:7) or he helped them reflect on Scriptural prophecies concerning him (see Luke 24:25-27). He commissioned them to preach (see Matthew 28:18-20) and forgive sin (see John 20:21-23). He told them to wait for the Spirit who would empower them to accomplish marvels in his name (Lk 24:49).

The Resurrection of Jesus is the heart of the Gospel. It gives new meaning to our lives. Death does not have the last word. Superabundant, eternal life with Jesus in community with the Father and the Holy Spirit and all others who love the Lord has the last say.

Jesus also appeared to the Apostles locked behind a bolted door. We learn how the Risen Jesus, not bound by the laws of ordinary physics, suddenly appeared in their midst. The Apostles rejoiced "when they saw the Lord" (20:20). The Lord wished them peace and commissioned them to continue his work, to be **missionaries**. Breathing on them, signifying the giving of the Holy Spirit, he instructed them to forgive sins in his name.

The Risen Jesus' next appearance came eight days later to the doubting Thomas, who was absent when Jesus appeared to the others. By showing him his hands and side, Jesus taught Thomas that he is the same Jesus who lived and died. Thomas acknowledged Jesus' divinity—"My Lord and my God!" (20:28)—the highest proclamation of faith in Jesus made in any of the Gospels. In answer to Thomas, Jesus blessed all of us who believe, yet do not see him.

Originally, John's Gospel ended with Chapter 20. However, its final edition includes Chapter 21, which reports Jesus' appearance to the Apostles in Galilee. There Jesus helped the disciples catch fish, symbolic of their future role as fishers of people. He also prepared a breakfast for them, suggesting on a deeper level his communion with them at Eucharistic celebrations. Finally, he recommissioned Peter, who three times had denied knowing Jesus. This time the Lord elicited from Peter a threefold promise of his love (see John 21:15–19).

missionaries
People who are "sent" to share the Good News of Jesus Christ with others. St. Paul was the Church's greatest missionary.

For Review

1. Discuss three elements of the Passion Narrative in the Gospel of John.

2. Explain the reason for the different stories about the Resurrection of Jesus in the four Gospels.

3. What is the meaning of Jesus' Resurrection for Christians?

For Reflection

- "Blessed are those who have not seen and have believed" (Jn 20:29). What does Jesus' Resurrection mean to you?

- In what ways do you personally find the Lord today?

Main Ideas

- The Fourth Gospel is attributed to John, the "beloved disciple" of the Lord (p. 214).

- The Gospel may have been written in several stages with John providing its foundation (pp. 214–215).

- Two major themes of the Gospel are to strengthen the faith of the believers and to win converts (p. 216).

- To describe the Gospel of John as mystical highlights both that God is mystery and that his plan of Salvation is fulfilled in Jesus Christ (pp. 216–218).

- The Gospel emphasizes that God is love and the disciples are friends of Jesus (p. 218).

- The prologue of the Gospel serves as an introduction to major themes of the entire Gospel, including the Incarnation and ways to understand Christology (pp. 219–223).

- There are seven signs or miracles in John's Gospel that reveal Jesus' identity, his reason for coming to us, his heavenly glory, and his relationship to the Father (pp. 223–228).

- The second part of the Gospel is known as the Book of Glory; it is the setting and subject of the Last Supper and is concerned with the events of the Paschal Mystery (pp. 228–231).

- Jesus is in control of the events of his Passion as described in John's Gospel (pp. 231–232).

- In the Resurrection accounts, John's Gospel focuses on Jesus' commission to the leaders to continue his work of reconciliation and love (pp. 232–234).

Terms, People, Places

Write your answers to the following questions.

1. Besides Jesus, who are other saints, family members, or other Catholics you rely on for intercessory prayer on your behalf?

2. In what country can the John Rylands Greek papyrus be found?

3. How would you respond against the heresy of Docetism?

4. Why is Sukkot also called the Feast of Tabernacles?

5. Besides St. Paul, name two other famous Catholic missionaries.

6. Where can the Pool of Siloam be found?

7. What is the emphasis on Christology in the Gospel of John?

8. Why is Jesus the Logos?

Primary Source Quotations

Why John's Gospel begins with "the Word was made flesh"

I will now tell you what the reason of this is. Because the other Evangelists had dwelt most on the accounts of His coming in the flesh, there was fear lest some, being of groveling minds, might for this reason rest in these doctrines alone, as indeed was the case with Paul of Samosata. In order, therefore, to lead away from this fondness for earth those who were like to fall into it, and to draw them up towards Heaven, with good reason he commences his narrative from above, and from the eternal subsistence. For while Matthew enters upon his relation from Herod the king, Luke from Tiberius Cæsar, Mark from the Baptism of John, this Apostle, leaving alone all these things, ascends beyond all time or age.

—St. John Chrysostom,
Homilies on the Gospel of John

We are part of Jesus, the Logos

He is also called the Logos, because he takes away from us all that is irrational, and makes us truly reasonable, so that we do all things, even to eating and drinking, to the glory of God, and discharge by the

Logos to the glory of God both the commoner functions of life and those which belong to a more advanced stage. For if, by having part in him, we are raised up and enlightened, herded also it may be and ruled over, then it is clear that we become in a divine manner reasonable, when he drives away from us what in us is irrational and dead, since he is the Logos (reason) and the Resurrection.

—Origen

Our natural will is to have God, and the good will of God is to have us, and we may never cease willing or longing for him until we have him in the fullness of joy. Christ will never have his full bliss in us until we have our full bliss in him.

—Blessed Julian of Norwich

I know Christ dwells within me all the time, guiding me and inspiring me whenever I do or say anything. A light, of which I caught no glimmer before, comes to me at the very moment when it is needed.

—St. Thérèse of Lisieux

Paraphrasing the words of the doxology of the Eucharistic prayer, how do you live "through Jesus, with Jesus, and in Jesus" to bring glory and honor to God the Father? Write a short essay explaining how.

Ongoing Assignments

As you cover the material in this chapter, choose and complete at least three of these assignments.

1. Create a modern-day skit of the story of the Woman Caught in Adultery (John 8:1–11).

2. Find different passages on the theme of light in John's Gospel. Examples include John 3:19–21; 8:12; 11:9–10; 12:35–36, 46. Do one of the following:

   - Write a short report on how this image is used in the Gospel.

   - Report on the customs of lighting candles that Catholics use to show their faith. Examples: votive lights, the Paschal Candle, baptismal candle, Christmas candles, luminaria.

3. Report on shepherding in the days of Jesus. Write a short report on some implications of what it means for Jesus to call himself the Good Shepherd.

4. Jesus promised to send the Holy Spirit, an Advocate who will defend us from evil, guide us in the Truth, help us understand the teaching of Jesus, and live in us. Prepare a short report on some of the images of the Holy Spirit used in the Bible.

5. Jesus entrusted Mary, his Mother, to the Beloved Disciple (see John 19:25–27). She is our Mother, too, the Mother of the Church. Catholics in many countries have a strong devotion to Mary under various titles. For example, in the United States, Mary is honored as the Virgin of the Immaculate Conception. In Mexico, Mary is honored as Our Lady of Guadalupe. Check one of the websites below to gather information on one of the popular devotions to the Blessed Virgin. Prepare a short report.

   - Mary Page: http://campus.udayton.edu/mary/marypage21.html

   - Our Lady's Page: www.christusrex.org/www1/CDHN/ourlady.html

   - Our Lady of Guadalupe: www.sancta.org

6. Report on wedding customs in our Lord's day.

7. See "New Testament Proofs" in the following *Catholic Encyclopedia* article for a list of New Testament passages: www.newadvent.org/cathen/07706b.htm

8. Choose ten of your favorite quotations by Jesus from the Gospel of John. Assemble

them into a prayer booklet with suitable artistic work to illustrate each quote.

9. Create a PowerPoint presentation depicting several of the archaeological sites or discoveries associated with John's Gospel. For example, you might find illustrations for:

- The "Galilee Boat"—the type of boat the Apostles might have used.
- The Garden of Gethsemane
- Excavations at Cana
- The Sea of Galilee
- Jacob's Well in Samaria
- The Pool of Bethesda
- The Pool of Siloam
- Ossuary of Joseph Caiaphas

Use this website to get a start on this assignment:

- http://catholic-resources.org/John/Archaeology.html

10. Do a one-page report on Mary Magdalene. Use one of the following websites to aid you in your research:

- www.catholic.org/saints/saint.php?saint_id=83
- www.newadvent.org/cathen/09761a.htm

11. Choose an artwork from the following website that depicts a scene from John's Gospel. Download the image with the name of the artist and its date of composition. Include it in a short paper that describes what details from the Gospel show up in the work of art. Describe how the painting depicts them. Then discuss what details from the Gospel do not appear there or any other elements added by the artist.

- Fr. Felix Just, S.J.'s, website: http://catholic-resources.org/John/Art.html

Prayer

We have a desire to pattern our lives on Jesus. Pray the following prayer frequently to grow into the likeness of our Savior.

Prayer to Become More Like Jesus

God, our Father, You redeemed us and made us Your children in Christ. Through Him You have saved us from death and given us Your Divine life of grace. By becoming more like Jesus on earth, may I come to share His glory in Heaven. Give me the peace of Your Kingdom, which this world does not give. By Your loving care protect the good You have given me. Open my eyes to the wonders of Your Love that I may serve You with a willing heart.

- *Reflection*: What quality of Jesus do you most admire? (Examples: his compassion, his loving friendship, humility, his gentleness, his sacrificing love, etc.) What do you need to do in your life *right now* to grow in this quality?

- *Resolution*: Put into practice this week one of the qualities of Jesus that you most admire.

WHO DO YOU SAY THAT I AM?

He is the image of the invisible God, the firstborn of all creation.
For in him were created all things in Heaven and on earth,
the visible and the invisible, . . .
all things were created through him and for him.
He is before all things, and in him all things hold together.
He is the head of the body, the church.
He is the beginning, the firstborn from the dead.

—Colossians 1:15-18

Who Is Jesus to You?

It is important for each person to clarify what he or she personally believes about Jesus.

Gospel Portrait of Jesus

The Gospels reveal many appealing human qualities about Jesus: he was a faithful friend, possessed gentle strength, modeled humility, and treated women with dignity.

Some Titles of Jesus in the Gospels

Beyond the name Jesus—which means "God saves"—the Gospels share other meaningful titles: Christ, Son of God, Lord, and Son of Man.

The Early Church Preaches the Good News

The Acts of the Apostles reports how the Holy Spirit descended on the early Church and inspired the sharing of the *kerygma*, Jesus is Risen!

Making a Commitment to Really Know Jesus

It is not enough to know about Jesus Christ; rather, it is important to develop a personal relationship with him.

Who Is Jesus to You?

One of the most important questions Jesus asked of his followers occurred on the road to Caesarea Philippi: "Who do you say that I am?" (Mk 8:29). The disciples had a ready answer. They knew he was the Messiah. Further, Peter said that he was the Son of the living God (see Matthew 16:16).

Today, some people hold that Jesus was a great teacher, but nothing more. Others hold that he was a prophet like John the Baptist. Still others admit that he was a historical figure—but only a good-hearted if not misguided philosopher—whose teachings led to a tragic death.

But the question remains: who do *you* say Jesus is? The Christian author C. S. Lewis wrote that there are only three reasonable possibilities He is either a liar, lunatic, or Lord. In *Mere Christianity*, Lewis wrote:

> A man who was merely a man and said the sort of things Jesus said would not be a great moral teacher. He would either be a lunatic —on the level with the man who says he is a poached egg—or else he would be the Devil of Hell. You must make your choice. Either this man was, and is, the Son of God: or else a madman or something worse. You can shut Him up for a fool, you can spit at Him and kill Him as a demon; or you can fall at His feet and call Him Lord and God. But let us not come with any patronising nonsense about His being a great human teacher. He has not left that open to us. He did not intend to.

C. S. Lewis had it right: Each person must make his or her own decision about Christ, answering the question, "Who is Jesus to me?" This chapter presents how early Christians, empowered by the Holy Spirit, clearly saw Jesus as the Lord. For close to two thousand years, untold millions of believers have been convinced that Jesus is the world's most important person, not only because he is a great philosopher, teacher, or wonder worker, but because he is God. But who do *you* say he is?

For Reflection

Why is it important for you to come up with a personal response to Jesus' question: "Who do you say that I am?"

Christian Advice

St. Paul is one of the Church's greatest **theologians**. His letters to various local communities developed some important theological themes about Jesus and encouraged early Christians to live upright lives.

Read Romans 12. Focus on the verses that follow.

- Do not conform yourself to this age but be transformed by the renewal of your mind (Romans 12:2).

Write a Letter

Take St. Paul's advice: "Love one another with mutual affection; anticipate one another in showing honor" (Rm 12:10). Write a letter (not an e-mail) to a grandparent, a friend who has moved away, or to a sibling at college. Besides sharing personal news, be sure to tell the person how special he or she is to you.

- Do not think of yourself more highly than you ought to think (cf. Romans 12:3).
- Exercise hospitality (Romans 12:13).
- Be concerned for what is noble in the sight of all (Romans 12:17).
- Live at peace with all (Romans 12:18).

For each verse reflect and then write how well you are living in this way. Also write how you can improve in these areas.

Gospel Portrait of Jesus

Everyone who reads the Gospels comes away with a distinct impression of what a remarkable person Jesus is, so much so that more books, articles, and films have been produced about Jesus than for any other human being. What is so special about this man, the one Christians believe to be the Son of God? How do you answer this question? What do *you* find attractive about Jesus? Listed in the following sections are some qualities about Jesus that many have found appealing.

Jesus the Faithful Friend

Jesus had many different kinds of friends. Consider, for example, his Apostles. Peter was headstrong and impetuous. The brothers James and John—Zebedee's sons—had such hot tempers that Jesus nicknamed them

"sons of thunder." Jesus chose a hated tax collector—Matthew—to be one of his closest associates. Ordinary fishermen were part of his inner circle. Sick, maimed, undesirable, and sinful people flocked to him, trying to touch him and be at his side. For this, Jesus was often criticized by Jewish leaders, yet Jesus numbered among his friends leading members of the Sanhedrin like Joseph of Arimathea and Nicodemus. Jesus must have attracted such a diverse collection of followers because they saw in him not only an exemplary human being, but a source of life and acceptance. He told them of their eternal destiny and what they had to do to achieve it. He did so in a loving, unselfish way.

Jesus showed true human emotion to his friends. He was especially close to John, the Beloved Disciple, and Lazarus, over whose death he wept. Jesus' love ran deep. His devotion to his friends, and his willingness to sacrifice his very life for them, exemplifies the very meaning of friendship—"to give and not to count the cost," as St. Ignatius Loyola once described.

The Gospels also point to Jesus' personal invitation to each of us to accept his friendship: "I have called you friends. . . . It was not you who chose me, but I chose you. . . . This I command you: love one another" (Jn 15:15–17). Jesus' love for us is immense. He sees in each of us something so worthwhile that he chooses us to continue his work ("I . . . chose you . . . to go and bear fruit" [Jn 15:16]). With his Father and the Holy Spirit, he has given us everything we

theologians
People who study the nature of God and religious truth.

need to do his work: the gift of life itself, parents, friends, intellectual gifts, individual talents, health, and so forth.

As the saying goes, "What a friend we have in Jesus!" He is always faithful and will never take away his invitation to friendship. We may sin and deny his love (see Peter). We may misuse our gifts (consider the Samaritan woman). We may hurt others and turn from God (consider those who put Jesus to death). Nevertheless, Jesus always invites us to accept his friendship. Nothing in this life can compare to Jesus' astounding invitation, "I call you friends."

The Gentle Strength of Jesus

Jesus exhibited a dramatic show of strength when he cleared the Temple precinct of money changers (see John 2:13–23). He criticized them for turning his Father's house from a place of prayer to one of crass business transactions. Jesus also stood up boldly to some teachers of his day who laid heavy religious burdens on people while not always practicing what they preached. Jesus loathed their hypocrisy, calling them blind fools and whitewashed tombs, even though he knew his strong words would lead to their plotting his Death.

Jesus had passionate convictions, but at the same time he was tender, loving, and sensitive to others. Picture the little children coming to Jesus. He warmly accepted them over the objections of his disciples (see Mark 10:13–16). Jesus tenderly embraced them and made them feel welcome and loved.

Jesus comforted Peter, James, and John when they became frightened at the time of his Transfiguration (see Matthew 17:7). His loving touch healed repulsive lepers as well as countless other sick people. His sensitivity extended to the woman with an incurable blood flow who merely touched the tassel of his cloak. In the midst of the many who were reaching out to him, he sensed her need and cured her (see Luke 8:47–48). Jesus had compassion for others, yet was strong in confronting evil.

Jesus Modeled Humility and Truth

Jesus both modeled and taught humility and honesty. For example, he instructed his disciples not to parade good deeds in public just to attract notice. He said to give alms discreetly without drawing attention to individual charity. Jesus taught humility and service when he washed the feet of his disciples at the Last Supper. He said, "I have given you a model to follow, so that as I have done for you, you should also do" (Jn 13:15).

Jesus modeled everything he taught: He said we should forgive others, even our enemies; he did so on the cross when he was dying in excruciating pain. He taught us to love: "No one has greater love than this, to lay down one's life for one's friends" (Jn 15:13). Jesus' own Passion and Death testify to his courageous honesty and heartfelt love for each human being. He practiced what he preached.

Jesus Elevated the Status of Women

Jesus was revolutionary in the way he treated women. Although his fellow Jews respected women more than most people of the first century, they still considered women to have an inferior status. For example, women were not allowed to study the Torah (Law), and only rarely were they taught to read or write. They were not required to recite morning prayers, prayers at meals, and other Jewish prayers. They had no official part in the synagogue and were only permitted to sit behind a screen or on a balcony.

So lowly were women regarded that in public men were not supposed to even speak with their wives, daughters, or sisters. Only rarely were women allowed to testify in court, and they could not divorce their husbands, though it was very easy and common for men to divorce their wives for almost any reason. A general attitude toward women in Jesus' time was exposed in a daily prayer recited by men: "Praised be God that he has not created me a Gentile; praised be God that he has not created me a woman; praised be God that he has not created me an ignorant man."

Oppositely, Jesus demonstrated that women were equal to men. He allowed women to follow him as disciples. He instructed them contrary to the practice of any rabbis of his day.

Women were also instrumental in the three resurrection miracles Jesus performed during his public ministry: He raised the daughter of Jairus and the son of the widow of Nain. He also compassionately responded to the heartfelt emotion of Mary and Martha when their brother Lazarus died. Moreover, the Gospels tell us that Jesus appeared first to Mary Magdalene, a fact that the Eleven refused to believe, likely because they mistrusted women, as did most men of the day.

Jesus associated freely with women, for example, with the Samaritan woman at the well, both to the surprise and consternation of his Apostles. On another occasion, Jesus' enemies wanted to trap Jesus into condemning a woman caught in adultery, but Jesus forgave her and told her to sin no more. On still another occasion, his enemies criticized him for allowing a sinful woman to anoint his feet. Jesus refused to judge her negatively; rather, he forgave her sins and told her to go in peace.

Jesus' teachings showed high regard for women. For example, when his enemies wanted him to take sides on the conditions under which a man may divorce his wife, Jesus simply forbade divorce altogether. He also told men to treat women with respect: "Everyone who looks at a woman with lust has already committed adultery with her in his heart" (Mt 5:28).

Jesus also used women to illustrate his stories and sayings, something the rabbis of his day rarely did. His images of women were always positive. Take the important example of the woman in Luke's parable of the Lost Coin. Just as the woman rejoices when she finds the missing coin, how much more will God rejoice over a repentant sinner. The

Portrait of Jesus' Character

Read the following Gospel passages that help to reveal Jesus' character. Use these Scripture passages to help you. Write an essay describing what you think Jesus was like as a person. Share your essay in class.

- Matthew 15:32-39
- Matthew 23:1-36
- Mark 1:40-45
- Mark 14:43-65
- Luke 7:36-50
- Luke 23:27-43
- John 8:1-11
- John 13:1-5

point is made: Jesus compares God to a woman! How this message must have jolted Jesus' enemies. They certainly could not miss the significance of his teaching.

In sum, Jesus' attitude toward women gives us a wonderful insight into his character. He was revolutionary in his thinking and public behavior in every way. He challenged people of his day—and our own day—to treat women as equals to men in dignity, worthy of the utmost respect. You might wonder why Jesus did not choose women as Apostles. While there is no reason given in the New Testament, it is known that Jesus had every opportunity to do so if had wanted to. Also, the Apostles did not choose a woman to replace Judas Iscariot. However, it is important to remember that Jesus reserved the premier position of discipleship for a woman. Mary, the Mother of Jesus, is the Mother of God and Mother of us all. She is the disciple *par excellence.*

Jesus' example reminds us that, in God's Kingdom, there are no second-class citizens. The way he treated others—with love, gentleness, strength, sensitivity, honesty and humility—shows us how best to live as *his* brothers and sisters.

🌐 For Review

1. List and discuss three character traits revealed about Jesus in the Gospels. Give scriptural evidence to illustrate your choices.

2. How did Jesus treat women? What does this reveal about his character?

🌐 For Reflection

- What do you find most special about Jesus?

- Discuss what it might mean for someone to have Jesus call that person *his* friend.

- Select three passages from the Gospels that you believe capture the essential character of Jesus. Explain what they reveal about him.

Some Titles of Jesus in the Gospels (*CCC*, 430-455)

The human qualities of Jesus are certainly worth emulating in our own lives, but Jesus is much more than just a great *human* being. His identity as God's only Son with the divine mission of Salvation comes across in every chapter of every Gospel. The very name *Jesus*, a late form of the Hebrew name *Joshua* (Yehoshua), means "God saves" or "YHWH is Salvation." This name is to be revered above all others, as St. Paul wrote in his letter to the Philippians:

> God greatly exalted him and bestowed on him the name that is above every name, that at the name of Jesus every knee should bend, of those in Heaven and on earth and under the earth, and every tongue confess that Jesus Christ is Lord, to the glory of God the Father. (Phil 2:9–11)

Listed in the sections that follow are some other important titles of Jesus found in the Gospels with a brief note of explanation for each.

Christ

The word *Christ* derives from the Greek word *Christos*, which, in turn, translates the Hebrew word *Messiah*. Christ means "anointed." The Messiah was God's Anointed One, born into the lineage of King David. He came to fulfill all the divine promises made to the Chosen People. Many Jews thought the Messiah would be a political ruler, but the Father anointed Jesus with the Spirit to inaugurate God's Kingdom, a reign of peace, love, and service. Jesus accomplished his mission of suffering service through the threefold office of prophet, priest, and king. Each of these is also an appropriate title for Jesus:

- *Prophet.* Jesus is the Word of God who spoke for his Father and taught through his words and deeds the full message of Salvation.

- *High Priest.* Jesus is the perfect mediator between God and humanity. He offered his life for all on the altar of the Cross. Today, Jesus the Christ continues his priestly role at each celebration of the Eucharist.

- *King.* Jesus, as the rightful ruler of the universe, does not lord it over others. He did not come to be served, but to serve through suffering and dying for us and thus accomplish our Salvation. Jesus rules with gentleness, compassion, and love. Along with the gift of the Holy Spirit, Christ's example inspires us to love and serve others in imitation of him.

Son of God

The Old Testament sometimes referred to angels, the Chosen People, and the children and kings of Israel as "sons of God." It did so to show that God had special love for these creatures whom he adopted into a special relationship.

Jesus Christ is the unique Son of God. Only he shares the same divine nature as God the Father. Recall John's Gospel: "In the beginning was the Word, and the Word was with God, and the Word was God" (Jn 1:1).

Simon Peter proclaimed Jesus' divinity when he professed that Jesus was the Son of God. St. Paul professed the same thing to his fellow Jews in the synagogue. This is the very identity that the Father revealed at Jesus' baptism and Transfiguration when the heavenly voice was heard saying that Jesus is "my beloved son" (see Matthew 3:17; 17:5).

Jesus' miracles and his words reveal his divine nature. He alone knows the Father. Although he teaches his followers to call God "Our Father," Je-

sus also reveals a distinction between "my Father and your Father" (Jn 20:17).

After his Resurrection, it became clear to the Apostles what Jesus meant when he said, "The Father and I are one" (Jn 10:30). Our Catholic creed proclaims that Jesus Christ is God's only Son.

Lord

In Biblical times, the title *Lord* could refer to a ruler or another powerful person. It could also mean to address someone like we do when we say "sir." Some people may have used it this way when they were talking with Jesus, especially when they were asking him for a favor.

However, the Church's understanding of "Lord" is something entirely different. *Lord* translates the Greek word *Kurios,* which, in turn, renders the Hebrew word *Adonai. Adonai* was the word the

THE FACE OF JESUS

Jesus Christ is the most famous person who ever lived, yet we have no picture or painting of his real likeness. The Jewish faith of Jesus' day forbade personal portraits for fear of idolatry, the worshiping of false images. Nor do the Gospels give us a physical description of Jesus. We simply do not know if he was short or tall, plain-looking or handsome, dark or fair-skinned.

After several generations, Christians did begin to portray Jesus. The catacombs of Rome contain the earliest images of him. There he appears as a curly-haired young man similar to young King David. At other times he appears as a bearded man with long hair, the style worn by pious Jewish men of Jesus' own day. Other early wall paintings show Jesus as the Good Shepherd, holding a lamb across his shoulders. Jesus appeared as a teacher and a miracle-worker, his two main vocations described in the Gospels. After the emperor Constantine recognized Christianity in 313, Jesus was increasingly shown as a heavenly king crowned in glory.

The early Church Father St. Jerome concluded that some of God's majesty must have shown through Jesus' human body. He wrote:

> Had he not had something heavenly in his face and his eyes, the Apostles never would have followed him at once, nor would those who came to arrest him have fallen to the ground.

Christian artists of later centuries largely adopted St. Jerome's view. Although a true representation of Jesus can never be captured, artists decided that paintings and statues of Jesus should be compatible with the beauty of the mystery of God becoming flesh. Jesus is God-made-man.

Only after about the year AD 1000 did paintings of Jesus as a suffering, crucified Savior become widespread. Depiction of a crucified Jesus appeared first in Byzantine art and then spread to the West. By the time of the Renaissance, artists increasingly portrayed a human Jesus. Rembrandt, for example, chose Jewish men from his city of Amsterdam as his models for Jesus. His paintings are excellent classic representations. They portray a truly human Jesus.

In the nineteenth century, cheap, "syrupy" paintings of Jesus began to appear. Perhaps you have seen some of these in which Jesus is portrayed with delicate, soft features. Missing is the virile manliness that can be associated with driving money changers from the Temple. Certainly, Jesus was not an unassertive, waxen, or plastic man.

However we imagine Jesus, we must consider three facts:

- Jesus was a Jew who spent many hours on the road outdoors in the sun. He was surely tan, rugged, strong, and chiseled by the elements. Traveling up and down the roads of Palestine took fierce drive and commitment.
- Jesus was a carpenter. He was a working man with calloused hands. It takes strength and skill to hoist up cross beams, to cut timber, and to work wood into useful implements.
- Jesus attracted all kinds of people. Strong, rough fishermen dropped their nets to follow him. The rich invited him to dinner. The poor, the sick, and children longed for his touch. Women followed him around and cared for his needs. All types of people wanted to be his friend. There had to be something incredibly attractive about Jesus of Nazareth, both inside and out.

Chosen People used whenever the most holy name for God—*YHWH*—would appear in the Hebrew Scriptures.

Therefore, to call Jesus Lord is to proclaim that he is God. Jesus has the same sovereignty as God, and his Death and Resurrection have won for us eternal life, a gift that only God can bestow. Jesus is the Lord of life, the One who deserves our total devotion and obedience. The power, honor, and glory that are owed God the Father are also due Jesus. When we put together these four words—our Lord Jesus Christ—we are saying something very profound. Jesus, our Savior, is the promised Messiah. He is God himself! He belongs to us and we belong to him. This is great news indeed.

Son of Man

"Son of Man" is the title that Jesus most frequently used about himself. This title occurs over eighty times in the Gospels and only four times outside the Gospels. Its Old Testament background reveals that in one sense the term meant a human being as distinct from God. Perhaps Jesus used it this way when he was emphasizing his ordinary human nature, his identification with us. He may also have used it as a way to refer to himself without using the personal pronoun "I," again stressing his humility.

However, another Old Testament meaning of the word comes from Daniel 7:13–14 and the Jewish books of Enoch and Esdras. These books use the term Son of Man to describe a supernatural figure, God's agent who will help usher in the fullness of God's Kingdom. The Son of Man, in this case, would also serve as the judge of all humanity. Undoubtedly, Jesus used the title in the sense of a Messianic King when he proclaimed what would happen at the end of time:

> And then they will see "the Son of Man coming in the clouds" with great power and glory. (Mk 13:26)

Perhaps Jesus described himself as "Son of Man" more than any other way because he could shape it to his own meaning. People often misunderstood the suffering aspect of his Messiahship. Therefore, he may have used Son of Man to emphasize his claim to be human like us, but also his divine identity as God's Son.

For Review

1. How is Jesus the unique Son of God?
2. What is the Christian understanding of "Lord"?
3. Which title did Jesus prefer for himself?
4. What is the threefold office related to the title of Christ?
5. Define *idolatry*.

For Reflection

Check the following Gospel verses to see what the titles reveal about Jesus: Matthew 1:23, Matthew 2:23, Matthew 9:15, Mark 14:61, and Luke 1:32.

The Early Church Preaches the Good News

The Acts of the Apostles reports on the early days of the Church and the spread of the Gospel of Jesus Christ around the Roman Empire. The history of the Church really begins with the account of how the Holy Spirit descended on the Apostles on Pentecost, the birthday of the Church (see Acts 2). On that glorious day, the Spirit showered gifts on the Apostles, including the courage to proclaim the Gospel with faith and conviction. Another prominent gift was the **gift of tongues**. The Apostles spoke in various languages and were understood by the many

gift of tongues

A supernatural gift that was designed to build up the early Church; on Pentecost the disciples were heard speaking in languages that everyone could understand.

Council of Jerusalem

A crucial meeting of the Church that resolved a conflict of unity on whether or not Jewish Law should be applied to Gentile converts. The decision ultimately was that Christianity was no longer tied to Judaism.

pilgrims who had come from all over the Empire for the religious festival. This miracle of tongues reversed the confusion of languages that overtook the people who built the Tower of Babel. It showed that the birth of the Church created a new human community that was under the power of the Holy Spirit.

Kerygma in the Early Church

Acts records eighteen different sermons that capture what the early Church preached about Jesus. The great saints Peter, Paul, and Stephen delivered these sermons. A typical example is one preached by Peter on Pentecost Sunday (Acts 2:14–40; 3:11–26). First, there is an introduction, when Peter assured his audience that the Apostles were not drunk, as some of his listeners assumed. Peter reminded them of the prophecy from Joel that the Lord promised to pour out his Spirit on the people. That day of the Lord has now arrived, Peter said to them. Then Peter proclaimed the *kerygma*, that is, the essential message or proclamation about Je-

sus Christ. The main elements of this preaching include:

1. The Old Testament prophecies have been fulfilled in Jesus of Nazareth. The new age has dawned. Jesus of Nazareth is the Messiah.

2. Jesus was born of David's family. He worked mighty deeds, proving how God's reign worked through him. He was put to death on a cross, but as was prophesied, God raised Jesus from the dead. His disciples have witnessed these events. He ascended to Heaven, is exalted at the right hand of the Father, and reigns as the Lord of the living and the dead. The crucif Jesus is both Lord and M

3. As he promised, Christ has sent the Holy Spirit, whose power the audience can see and hear for themselves. The Spirit is the sign and assurance of the Lord's presence in the Church until the Lord comes again at the end of time as Judge and Savior of the world.

4. Because all of the above is true, people must respond to the

Famous Sermons in Acts

Read the following kerygmatic sermons from Acts. In your journal, identify the various elements that are included using the four-point outline summarized on pages 248-249.

- Peter and Cornelius: Acts 10:34-48
- Paul at the Synagogue in Perga: Acts 13:16-41

Good News. "Repent and be baptized, every one of you, in the name of Jesus Christ for the forgiveness of your sins; and you will receive the gift of the Holy Spirit" (Acts 2:38).

Peter's Pentecost sermon had an electrifying effect on his hearers. Three thousand people accepted his message and were baptized on that day alone. The Church was well underway.

Apostle to the Gentiles: St. Paul

A good portion of the Acts of the Apostles is devoted to telling the story of the great missionary and theologian St. Paul. Born around AD 10 in Tarsus (in modern-day Turkey), Saul was a Roman citizen who received an excellent Greek education and learned the occupation of a tentmaker. His Jewish name was that of the first king of Israel. Both he and King Saul were from the Jewish tribe of Benjamin. As a Roman citizen, Saul also had a Roman name—Paul (Paulus), a well-known family name. His upbringing in Tarsus exposed him to Gentile religions, philosophies, and customs. This background would help him preach the Gospel of Christ to Gentiles.

Acts of the Apostles recounts that, as a young man, Saul studied under the famous rabbi Gamaliel to be a rabbi himself in Jerusalem. He became a strict Pharisee. Trained in the Law, he was hostile to Christians and violently opposed the preaching that a condemned criminal was the Messiah. For him, this claim was blasphemy, worthy of death. Saul was present at the death of St. Stephen (Acts 7:54–8:1), the first Christian martyr, and consented to his execution.

However, a great a turning point in history took place when Saul was converted to Christ. Paul's conversion at Damascus is mentioned three times in Acts (9:3–19; 22:3–21; 26:9–18). The Lord appeared to him in a blinding light that caused Saul to fall to the ground. "Saul, Saul, why are you persecuting me?" a voice asked (Acts 9:4). When Saul questioned the

Conversion of Saint Paul (though there is no mention of a horse in Scripture).

voice, the Lord replied, "I am Jesus, whom you are persecuting" (Acts 9:5). By persecuting the Church, Saul learned that he was persecuting the Lord.

Blinded for three days by this life-changing event, Paul was baptized in Damascus. He spent time in the Arabian desert praying and reflecting. He then returned to Damascus, where he preached for a time and then made his way to Jerusalem, where he met Peter and James. After another few years spent in his native province, probably in Tarsus, Barnabas invited Paul to help minister in Antioch, the third-largest city in the Roman Empire. Using this as a base of operation, between AD 46–58, Paul engaged on three extensive missionary journeys with various assistants that took him all over the eastern Mediterranean. He preached the gospel first in synagogues and then, after meeting rejection, to the surrounding Gentile communities.

At the end of his first missionary journey, Paul made a historic trip in AD 49 to the **Council of Jerusalem**. There he successfully argued for Gentiles to be allowed into the Church without their first converting to Judaism. On subsequent journeys,

Paul spent eighteen months in Corinth and then more than two years in Ephesus. His hope was one day to make it to Rome, a hope realized in AD 61 when he was taken there as a prisoner after confinement for two years in Caesarea. One tradition holds that the emperor Nero beheaded Paul in AD 64, at about the same time Peter was martyred. Another tradition claims he was released from prison, traveled to Spain, where he preached the Gospel, and then returned to Rome, where he was killed by Nero in AD 67.

Known as the Apostle to the Gentiles, St. Paul allowed Jesus Christ to use him as an instrument to spread the Gospel. Paul movingly wrote, "I live, no longer I, but Christ lives in me; insofar as I now live in the flesh, I live by faith in the Son of God who has loved me and given himself up for me" (Gal 2:20). This love of Christ moved Paul to found countless local churches, preach the Good News to Gentiles, write faith-filled letters to his communities, and inspire loyal followers to continue his work of instruction.

The Letters of St. Paul

The New Testament attributes thirteen letters to St. Paul. Later study by theologians acknowledges that that seven of the letters (Romans, 1 and 2 Corinthians, Galatians, Philippians, 1 Thessalonians, and Philemon) were surely written by Paul. Whether Paul was the sole author of the other six (Ephesians, Colossians, 2 Thessalonians, 1 and 2 Timothy, and Titus) has been debated by theologians and scholars and studied by the Church Magisterium. The conclusion is that if they were not composed by Paul himself, these letters were written by close disciples of his.

In these letters, Paul reveals his bedrock faith in Jesus Christ. He explains clearly the Death and Resurrection of Jesus Christ as the center of God's plan of Salvation. He shows how Christ's message is not just for the Jews, but for all people. He understands the role of the Church as the Body of Christ. He explains how Jesus redeems us. He teaches how the gifts of Baptism and faith in the Lord are gifts that justify and reconcile us before God. Finally, he emphasizes the role of the Holy Spirit in the life of the Church, the one who builds up the Body of Christ and enables us to call God Abba, Father.

What Paul Taught about Jesus

Paul explains who Jesus is and what he has done for us. Here are a few of the main points of St. Paul's proclamations about the Risen Lord and Savior. These points, and many others in St. Paul's letters, help us understand who Jesus truly is:

1. *The crucified Jesus truly rose from the dead!* The Paschal Mystery of the Passion, Death, and Resurrection of Jesus Christ is decisive in Salvation History. Christ's Resurrection is essential to our Salvation. St. Paul writes, "If Christ has not been raised, then empty [too] is our preaching; empty, too, your faith. Then we are also false witnesses to God. . . . If Christ has not been raised, your faith is vain; you are still in your sins" (1 Cor 15:14–15; 17). Faith is dependent on the Resurrection of Jesus Christ. It is the foundation of our belief.

2. *The crucified Christ has been exalted by the Father.* He sits in glory at the right hand of the Father in Heaven. Jesus, the perfect example of humility, will come again to restore all things (1 Thes 1:10). The Letter to the Philippians teaches that Jesus:

   Who, though he was in the form of God,
       did not regard equality with God something to be grasped.
   Rather, he emptied himself,
       taking the form of a slave,
       coming in human likeness;
       and found human in appearance,
       he humbled himself,
       becoming obedient to death,
       even death on a cross.
   Because of this, God greatly exalted him
       and bestowed on him the name

that is above every name,
that at the name of Jesus
every knee should bend,
of those in Heaven and on
earth and under the earth,
and every tongue confess
that Jesus Christ is Lord,
to the glory of God
the Father.
(Phil 2:6–11)

3. *Jesus is the Son of God.* The hymn from Philippians taught that Jesus is Lord. He is God! Paul proclaims that Jesus is the Son of God. In the Letter to the Galatians, he writes, "I live by faith in the Son of God who has loved me and given himself up for me" (Gal 2:20). "He is the image of the invisible God. . . . [A]ll things were created through him and for him. He is before all things, and in him all things hold together" (Col 1:15–17). Jesus is the glory of the Father in whom God brings all things together.

4. *Jesus is the Christ.* The title Christ (Messiah) appears 379 times in the thirteen letters ascribed to St. Paul. After his conversion, it is very clear to St. Paul that Jesus is the Messiah promised to the Chosen People. Jesus Christ must now be preached to Jew and Gentile alike. Believers must accept the new life in Christ. They must believe the Good News that has been proclaimed, turn from their sins, be baptized into Christ's Church, and allow the Holy Spirit to help them to live Christlike lives. They must also worthily celebrate the Eucharist to derive life from the Risen Lord (1 Cor 11:17–34).

5. *Jesus is the New Adam.* The first Adam disobeyed and brought death to the world, but "through the obedience of one [Jesus Christ] the many will be made righteous" (Rm 5:19).

6. *Jesus is the Savior and Redeemer of the World.* The Son of God became man and died to atone for the sins of humanity: "the Lord Jesus Christ, who gave himself for our sins that he might rescue us from the present evil age" (Gal 1:3–4). Paul compared the blood Jesus shed on our behalf to the Jewish ritual of **atonement** (Rm 3:24–25). Jesus is the true Passover lamb: "For our paschal lamb, Christ, has been sacrificed" (1 Cor 5:7). Jesus took on the sins of others to make us righteous before the Father. Using words like justification, Salvation, reconciliation, expiation, redemption, freedom, sanctification, and similar theological concepts, Paul describes how the sinless one won eternal life for believers. He is our **Redeemer**.

7. *Jesus sends the Holy Spirit to give life to his followers.* Jesus works through the power of the Holy Spirit. The Spirit's life unites Catholics to the Risen Christ and enables them to proclaim that Jesus is Lord. The

atonement
A word that means amends or reparation for a sin or a fault. In Christianity, the reconciliation between God and humans is brought about by the redemptive life and Death of Jesus Christ.

Redeemer
Redemption is the process that frees us from the slavery of sin. Jesus Christ is our Redeemer because he paid the price of his own sacrificial Death on the Cross to save us from sin.

SAMPLING PAUL

Along with St. Augustine and St. Thomas Aquinas, St. Paul is one of the Church's greatest theologians. His teachings are fundamental to understanding the meaning of Salvation History, the role of Jesus, the Church, and life in the Spirit. Paul's instructions on prayer, Christian living, and Church administration remain as valid today as when he wrote them.

Below are some summary statements that capture the heart of St. Paul's rich teaching. Study these statements carefully. Then read the passages given, some of the most important ones in all of Paul's Epistles. For each reading, jot down in your journal several significant points Paul makes for that particular passage and any other information on the passages that you can glean from a Biblical commentary.

1. *Salvation takes place through Jesus Christ, the Lord of the universe* (see Colossians 1:15-20).

2. *The heart of the Good News is the Death and Resurrection of Jesus Christ* (see 1 Corinthians 15:1-19).

3. *Christians will participate in the Resurrection of Jesus Christ* (see 1 Corinthians 15:20-28).

4. *Salvation is a free gift of God that demands faith. We cannot earn it* (see Romans 5:1-11).

5. *Christians are bound together in one body, the Church, of which Jesus is the Head* (see 1 Corinthians 12:12-30).

6. *The Holy Spirit is the life of the Church who enables us to call God Abba* (see Galatians 4:1-7).

7. *The brothers and sisters of Jesus should treat each other with dignity. We must love* (see Ephesians 4:17-32).

8. *Following Jesus means that we must gladly suffer for him* (see Philippians 2:1-18).

Holy Spirit showers his gifts on the members of the Lord's Body, the Church. Jesus is the head of the Church; believers are the members. These gifts are not meant for personal or selfish reasons. Rather, the Spirit's gifts are meant for the benefit of all: to build up the Body of Christ, the Church, and to attract nonbelievers to the worship of Jesus Christ. The greatest gift of all is the gift of love. A Christ-centered life is Spirit-filled, resulting in positive virtues or fruits that everyone recognize (see Galatians 5:22–23).

These points merely scratch the surface of St. Paul's beliefs about Jesus Christ, but they offer an idea of the exciting truths this great Apostle of Christ was preaching to people in the early decades of Christian history.

Lessons about Jesus in Other New Testament Epistles

There are nine other **Epistles** in the New Testament that reveal key beliefs about Jesus and offer guidance for Christian living.

The Letter to the Hebrews is associated with Paul because of a reference to Timothy in Hebrews 13:23, though Paul did not write it. Hebrews was written for a local church that had suffered in the past for its faith but then became lifeless. Seven New Testament Epistles—James; 1 and 2 Peter; 1, 2, and 3 John; and Jude—are called "Catholic Epistles" because, in part, they were intended as messages for the entire Church. The final book of the Bible, the Revelation to John, is highly symbolic and imaginative. Written in an apocalyptic style, it, too, reveals much about Christ. More information about each of these Epistles and what they teach us about Jesus Christ follows.

Jesus in the Letter to the Hebrews

The Letter to the Hebrews (composed in the 60s or 80s) is a written homily that develops the theme of Jesus Christ as our supreme High Priest, the model of our faith. A role for priests is to offer sacrifices. Jesus willingly offered his life as a sacrifice "for us" and "for our sins." He is the High Priest who not only offered the sacrifice on our behalf, but he is himself the sacrifice offered. Christ's sacrifice instituted the New Covenant foretold by Jeremiah.

The Letter to the Hebrews often refers to Jesus as the Son. It is the only New Testament writing that calls Jesus an Apostle, that is, a messenger or representative of God (see Hebrews 3:1). The letter stresses that Jesus is far superior to the angels and greater than any Old Testament prophet. Compared to Moses, Jesus "is worthy of more 'glory' than Moses, as the founder of a house had more 'honor' than the house itself" (see Hebrews 3:3).

The Letter to the Hebrews was written for a local church that had suffered for its belief in Christ; however, the members were now living at a time when their faith had become weak. The letter tries to encourage these listless Christians to persevere in their faith. It offers the example of Jesus Christ, who himself was tempted and suffered, yet he remained faithful:

> Therefore, since we have a great high priest who has passed through the heavens, Jesus, the Son of God, let us hold fast to our confession. For we do not have a high priest who is unable to sympathize with our weaknesses, but one who has similarly been tested in every way, yet without sin. So let us confidently approach the throne of grace to receive mercy and to find grace for timely help. (Heb 4:14–16)

The advice given in Hebrews holds true for us today. Distracted by a world that often ignores Christ and his message, we should take to heart the words of Hebrews: "Let us rid ourselves of every burden and sin that clings to us and persevere in running the race that lies before us while keeping our eyes fixed on Jesus, the leader and perfecter of faith" (Heb 12:1–2).

Epistle
A word that means "letter." In the New Testament they are letters intended for public reading. Most Epistles have these elements: an opening address; a thanksgiving; the body of the letter with a main doctrinal teaching; a final salutation.

Suffering Servant

The image from Isaiah 53:7—8 of a Servant who dies for the Salvation of all that was embodied in the Life and Death of Jesus Christ.

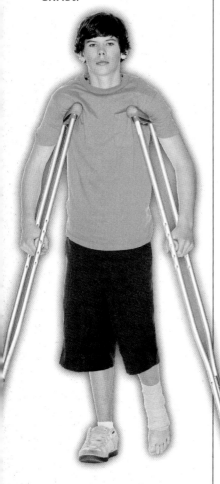

Arianism

A fourth-century movement named for an Alexandrian priest, Arius, whose followers denied the true divinity of Christ. At the Council of Nicaea in AD 325, the Church affirmed that the Son was begotten, not made, and of the same substance as the Father.

Jesus in the Catholic Epistles

The seven New Testament writings—James; 1 and 2 Peter; 1, 2, and 3 John; and Jude—that are termed "Catholic Epistles" are called that because they contain general advice that is helpful to all the churches. Also, both the Western and Eastern churches universally accepted these letters. Finally, they help us to understand how the Catholic, that is, worldwide or universal, Christian Church developed.

The Letter of James contains much practical advice on how to live a Christian life (for example, how to handle temptation, control the tongue, love one's neighbor, and so forth). The letter stresses the need for Christ's followers to put their faith into action. Good works go hand-in-hand with faith in Jesus.

The First Letter of Peter develops the theme of Jesus as the **Suffering Servant**. Christ's followers should imitate Jesus' patient suffering. When Christians are enduring trials for Christ they are entering into his sufferings and attracting others to him. Jesus is the model for this way of living:

> When he was insulted, he returned no insult; when he suffered, he did not threaten; instead, he handed himself over to the one who judges justly. He himself bore our sins in his body upon the cross, so that, free from sin, we might live for righteousness. By his wounds you have been healed. (1 Pt 2:23–24)

The Letter of Jude and the Second Letter of Peter both dealt with people who entered the Church only to engage in immoral behavior or teach heretical beliefs. The letters condemn both the immoral practices and the false teachings, especially teachings that denied that Christ will come again. The Second Letter of Peter emphatically states that there will be a Parousia (Second Coming of Christ) because the Lord said he would return and the Lord keeps his word. The Letter admits that we do not know the time when this will occur, but we should always be ready because "the day of the Lord will come like a thief, and then the heavens will pass away with a mighty roar and the elements will be dissolved by fire, and the earth and everything done on it will be found out" (see 2 Peter 3:10).

All three Letters of John, written around AD 100, deal with heresies that had crept into the Church. The First Letter of John combats heretics known as Gnostics. These heretics claimed that they received special knowledge from mystical experiences with Christ. They believed that Christ came to teach only a few disciples the secrets of eternal life.

The Gnostic brand of heresy in question in the First Letter of John was Docetism, the same heresy challenged by the Prologue of John's Gospel, which insists that the Word of God took on human flesh. Docetism, like most Gnostic heresies, saw the physical world as evil; therefore, the heretics could not believe that God would become man in Jesus Christ.

EXPLAINING THE FAITH

Why do some people try to change what the Church teaches about Jesus Christ?

This has been a problem in the Church from the earliest years. For example, we have seen how Gnosticism tried to restrict Jesus' message to a very few. It claimed that Jesus taught secret knowledge that only select people could understand. The Church condemned this arrogant approach because it excluded most people from the Lord's Good News. Jesus came for all people, and his message is open to all people. The Church invites all people to approach Christ. The Gospel must be preached to everyone, and it can be understood by simple folk as well as learned scholars.

Distortions often set in because people did not like what Jesus taught or found his teachings hard to follow. Others result from downplaying Jesus' suffering and Death. That is precisely what the Docetists did because they had a hard time seeing how God would so lower himself to become a man who could suffer like other humans. Again, the Church condemned false teachings like these because they simply did not correspond with Apostolic teaching. The author of the First Letter of John, for example, made it very clear that he was reporting "what we have heard, what we have seen with our eyes, what we looked up on and touched with our hands concerns the Word of life" (1 Jn 1:1).

Between the second and fourth centuries some authors, curious about the life of Jesus, would make up their own Gospels that would fill in details that did not appear in the canonical Gospels. An example is the Gospel of Judas, a relatively recent discovery. It is a Gnostic text that makes Judas Iscariot, the one who betrayed Jesus, a hero. Obviously, it clashes with the true portrait of Judas given in the four Gospels and thus it was excluded from the canon and condemned by Church authorities.

In those early centuries, heresies also sometimes arose about Jesus because people were trying to explain who Jesus was and who Jesus is. A classic example was _____, started by the priest Arius in the fourth century. Arius accepted that Jesus was the Son of God, but he claimed that the Son was *created* by God and thus was not equal to God. In short, he denied the divinity of Jesus. This teaching clearly contradicted what the Apostles and St. Paul taught (for example, when they proclaimed Jesus as the Word of God who always existed and is God). The first ecumenical council of the Church, the Council of Nicaea (AD 325), condemned Arianism.

Today, people are still trying to figure out who Jesus is. Most theologians and biblical scholars are responsible in their scholarship. They respect Sacred Tradition and look to the Magisterium to guide them in their studies. Others, though, buy into a contemporary mindset that denies that God can intervene in the natural world. For example, one group of mostly Protestant scholars meets as a group in what is called the "Jesus Seminar" in an attempt to explain away the miracles of Jesus by using natural, scientific arguments. Unfortunately, their work often denies God's unique intervention and revelation in human history in the Incarnation and calls into question the true divinity of Jesus Christ. For each generation, the Church must call all followers of Christ to true belief, belief that rests ultimately on Sacred Scripture and Sacred Tradition. Simply put, the Incarnation itself is the great miracle. If God can become man in Jesus of Nazareth, then Jesus could certainly perform miracles. The Church reminds us of this simple truth.

For them, Jesus was only a spiritual being, a "light-bearer," whose mission was to teach only a few. This dangerous heresy denied the Incarnation of Jesus Christ and thus denied the possibility that any of us could ever be saved by his Death and Resurrection. If Jesus only seemed to be a man, then he only seemed to die and rise from the dead, and we only seem to be saved.

The First Letter of John attacks the heretical views of Docetism by teaching that Christians must have true belief in Jesus Christ. Jesus is the Son of God. He is the Messiah whose blood cleanses us from sin. Jesus is Light, Love, and our Savior. He is also true God and true man who came to us in the flesh:

> This is how you can know the Spirit of God: every spirit that acknowledges Jesus Christ come in the flesh belongs to God, and every spirit that does not acknowledge Jesus does not belong to God. This is the spirit of the antichrist that, as you heard, is to come, but in fact is already in the world. (1 Jn 4:2–3)

True belief is one mark of a Christian, but this letter also teaches that belief must show itself in concrete acts of love. In some of the most beautiful words of Sacred Scripture, The First Letter of John instructs:

> Beloved, let us love one another, because love is of God; everyone who loves is begotten by God and knows God. Whoever is without love does not know God, for God is love. In this way the love of God was revealed to us: God sent his only Son into the world so that we might have life through him. In this is love: not that we have loved God, but that he loved us and sent his Son as expiation for our sins. Beloved, if God so loved us, we also must love one another. No one has ever seen God. Yet, if we love one another, God remains in us, and his love is brought to perfection in us. (1 Jn 4:7–12)

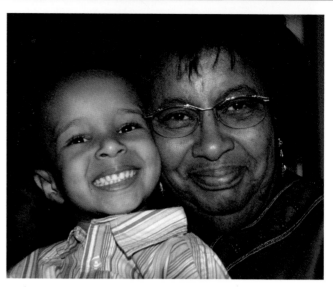

Jesus in the Book of Revelation

The Revelation to John, also known as the Apocalypse, is the last book in the Bible, and it is one of the most difficult to understand. Filled with elaborate symbolism, it is written in the apocalyptic style. Jewish apocalypses were popular between 200 BC and AD 200. Written in times of crises, apocalypses focus on the end of the world, when God will usher in a final age of peace and justice.

The book of Revelation borrows many symbols from the Old Testament, especially the books of Ezekiel, Zechariah, and Daniel. It was written at a time when Christians were being persecuted, probably around the year AD 90 under the reign of the emperor Domitian (AD 81–96). This emperor was requiring his subjects to worship him as a god. The crime for disobedience was death. Much of the use of symbolic language had to do with the Christians fearing persecution from the Roman leaders if they were caught practicing their faith.

A main focus of Revelation is on Jesus. The prophet John (a person who most likely knew the author of John's Gospel) writes that Jesus sent him visions about what is going to be unveiled in the future. Behind all the symbolism and strange visions of this complicated book, the basic message of Revelation is simple. Final Salvation and victory will take place at the end of the present age when Jesus

Christ will return in glory at his Second Coming. Therefore, although there is suffering and hardship in the present world, a Christian should endure these in order to achieve God's reward. The Lamb of God has triumphed! Victory is ours! Jesus assures us, "Yes, I am coming soon" (Rv 22:20).

The purpose of this section is not to analyze verbatim the Revelation to John with its many symbolic descriptions, that is, taking the text word for word at face value. Rather, some of the titles of Jesus that appear in Revelation are noted below. They reveal the depth of faith that a community of persecuted Christians had in the Lord who will surely triumph at the end of time. These titles are:

- *Lamb.* Jesus is called Lamb twenty-eight times in Revelation. The title refers to Jesus' great sacrifice that won us Salvation. "They cried out in a loud voice: 'Salvation comes from our God, who is seated on the throne, and from the Lamb'" (Rv 7:10).

- *Alpha and Omega.* These are the first and last letters of the Greek alphabet. They reveal the eternal nature of Jesus Christ, who is Lord God. He is the beginning and the end. "'I am the Alpha and the Omega,' says the Lord God, 'the one who is and who was and who is to come, the almighty'" (Rv 1:8).

- *The Amen.* Jesus is the "Yes" to God the Father. He is the God of Truth. As Revelation beautifully puts it, "The Amen, the faithful and true witness, the source of God's creation" (Rv 3:14).

- *Lion of the Tribe of Judah.* The lion is the king of the animals. This title emphasizes Jesus as the Messiah, the promised King in the royal line of David. "The lion of the tribe of Judah, the root of David, has triumphed" (Rv 5:5).

- *King of kings and Lord of lords.* Jesus is supreme and will conquer the evil one and his minions. "They will fight with the Lamb, but the Lamb will conquer them, for he is Lord of lords and king of kings, and those with him are called, chosen, and faithful" (Rv 17:14).

- *Morning Star.* Near the end of Revelation, Jesus says, "I, Jesus, sent my angel to give you this testimony for the churches. I am the root and offspring of David, the bright morning star" (Rv 22:16).

Revelation also uses many of the familiar titles of other New Testament writings, for example, Son of God, Lord, Word of God, and Christ. This book is testimony to the great faith in our majestic Lord and Savior, the one who conquers sin, death, and the evil one. The book ends, as does the Bible itself, with these marvelous words: "Amen! Come, Lord Jesus! The grace of the Lord Jesus be with all" (Rv 22:20–21).

For Review

1. What were the main elements in the kerygmatic sermon delivered by St. Peter on Pentecost Sunday?

2. What did Saul of Tarsus learn when the Lord appeared to him on the road to Damascus?

3. Why is St. Paul known as the Apostle to the Gentiles?

4. Discuss five points in the message St. Paul proclaimed about Jesus.

5. What is the predominant image of Jesus in the Letter to the Hebrews?

6. What are the "Catholic" Epistles? How did they get their name?

7. What is Gnosticism? How did 1 John combat it?

8. Discuss three reasons some people change what the Church teaches and believes about Jesus.

9. What is the purpose of the book of Revelation?

10. Discuss three titles of Jesus that appear in Revelation.

🌐 For Reflection

- List three ways the Lord has shown his love for you. Reflect on your life. Write a short paragraph telling the Lord how you show your love for him by sharing it with others.

- When was a time you had to defend your faith in Jesus Christ? What was the result?

Making a Commitment to Really Know Jesus

The grace you have received at Baptism and the gifts of faith, hope, and love on which discipleship are based offer you a firm and lasting foundation for knowing and following Jesus. As you reach the conclusion of this text and course on the Revelation of Jesus Christ in Scripture, now would be a good time to reflect even more deeply on who is Jesus Christ *for you?* How has God revealed Jesus in your life? How has the Holy Spirit led you to love and serve him?

Truly, all disciples of Jesus are just at the beginning of their study of him. It is important to know about the Savior of the world; it is more important to know him *personally*. Do you know Jesus? Is he your friend? Do you want to grow closer to him? Will you say "Amen" to the questions he puts to you?

- Do you accept me as God's only Son, your Savior, a friend who loves you beyond what you can imagine?

- Will you spend time talking to me in prayer, listening to my word in Scripture, enjoying the love I have for you?

- Are you willing to express your sorrow to me in the Sacrament of Reconciliation, where you can ask for my forgiveness and be assured of my love and the help of the Holy Spirit to help you live as a worthy child of my Father?

- Will you receive me in the Eucharist every week?

- Will you make an effort to recognize me in other people?

- Will you form your conscience in light of the teachings of the bishops and the Holy Father, who are my representatives on earth?

- Will you try to imitate me, especially by serving others? Will you reach out in a special way to help those who are especially close to me— the poor, the handicapped, the sick, victims of injustice, and so forth?

In short, Jesus asks, "What do you think of me, my sister, my brother? I love you! My Father loves you. And our Holy Spirit is our gift to you so that you may love, too."

As the book of Revelation ends, so too does this text. God bless you and keep you. "Amen! Come, Lord Jesus! The grace of the Lord Jesus be with all" (Rv 22:20–21).

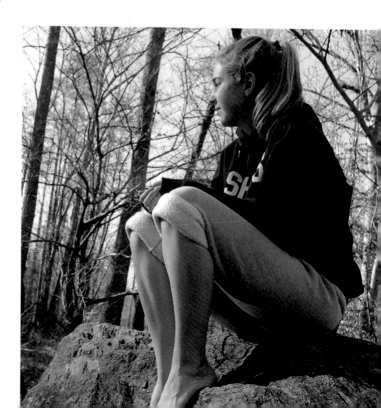

Main Ideas

- Besides knowing about Jesus, each person must answer the question "Who is Jesus for me?" (p. 240).

- The Gospels reveal many appealing human qualities of Jesus (pp. 241–244).

- Jesus was a faithful friend (pp. 241–242).

- Jesus exhibited strength in his ministry with a sense of compassion (p. 242).

- Jesus modeled all of his teaching; among these were the lessons of humility and honesty (p. 242).

- Jesus was revolutionary for his time in the way he related to women; he demonstrated by his relationships with women that they were to have equal status with men (pp. 243–244).

- Several important titles for Jesus that are introduced in the Gospels teach more about his identity; they include: Christ, Son of God, Lord, and Son of Man (pp. 244–247).

- The Acts of the Apostles details how the early Church spread the essential message (*kerygma*) that Jesus Christ is Risen (pp. 247–249).

- Much of the missionary success of the early Church is attributed to St. Paul, whose efforts are told in the Acts of the Apostles (pp. 249–252).

- Nine other Epistles in the New Testament tell about Jesus and offer guidance for Christian living (pp. 252–257).

- The Letter to the Hebrews models Jesus as the High Priest (p. 253).

- The seven "Catholic Epistles" relate universal messages the Church taught about Jesus and how his teachings were to be applied (pp. 254–257).

Terms, People, Places

Complete each sentence by choosing the correct answer from the list of terms below. You will not use all the terms.

theologians

kerygma

atonement

Epistle

Arianism

gift of tongues

Council of Jerusalem

Redeemer

Suffering Servant

1. The issue of how Gentiles would belong and participate in the Church was settled by the _____.

2. _____ summarizes the essential message of our faith.

3. Jesus Christ, the _____, is called such because he paid the price of his own Death on the Cross to save us from sin.

4. Jesus is called the _____ based on a passage from the Book of Isaiah.

5. _____ is a word that means making amends or reparation for a sin or a fault.

6. _____ refers to people who study the nature of God and religious truth.

Primary Source Quotations

Embracing Humanity

This communitarian character is perfected and fulfilled in the work of Jesus Christ, for the Word made flesh willed to take his place in human society. He was present at the wedding feast at Cana, he visited the house of Zacchaeus, he sat down with publicans and sinners. In revealing the Father's love and humanity's sublime calling, he made use of the most ordinary things of social life and illustrated his words with expressions and

Chapter 10 Quick View

imagery from everyday life. He sanctified those human ties, above all family ties, which are the basis of social structures. He willingly observed the laws of his country and chose to lead the life of an ordinary craftsman of his time and place.

—*Gaudium et Spes*, 32

The Unique Christ

St. Paul is profoundly aware that Christ is absolutely original and absolutely unique. If He were only a wise man like Socrates, if he were a "prophet" like Muhammad, if He were "enlightened" like Buddha, without any doubt He would not be what He is. He is the one mediator between God and humanity.

—Pope John Paul II,
Crossing the Threshold of Hope

Living for the Lord

I am no longer my own. Whether I live or whether I die, I belong to my Savior. I have nothing of my own. God is my all, and my whole being is His. I will have nothing to do with a love that would be for God or in God. I cannot bear the word for or the word in, because they denote something that may be in between God and me.

—St. Catherine of Genoa

With the Lord by our side, there is nothing we cannot do. Separated from Him, we will collapse almost immediately. With so good a friend and Captain ever present, Himself the first to suffer, everything can be borne. He helps. He strengthens. He never fails. He is the true friend.

—St. Teresa of Avila

Write a letter addressed to Jesus that tells him some things you promise to do to enhance your friendship with him.

Ongoing Assignments

As you cover the material in this chapter, choose and complete at least three of these assignments.

1. Write an essay focusing on these two points:

    - How *you* are most like Jesus?

    - Why would Jesus want to be your friend?

2. If you have talent with words, write a descriptive paragraph of how you picture the face of Jesus. If you have artistic talent, sketch the face of Christ as you imagine him.

3. Prepare a PowerPoint presentation on the face of Christ using images from the Internet. Check out these sources:

    - http://news.bbc.co.uk/2/hi/uk_news/1244037.stm

    - www.sindone.org/en/welcome.htm

    - http://catholic-resources.org/Art/index.html

4. Report on the title "Son of Man" from the *Catholic Encyclopedia* online: www.newadvent.org/cathen/14144a.htm.

5. Interview five Catholic adults and three Catholic teens on what they believe about Jesus. Present your interview in the form of an audio or video documentary.

6. Research ten titles of Jesus not discussed in this chapter or elsewhere in the book. Give a biblical reference for each title and a brief explanation of its meaning. Some websites to get you started include:

    - http://catholic-resources.org/Bible/Christological_Titles.htm

    - www.joyfulministry.com/titlesf.htm

    - www.studylight.org/con/ttt/view.cgi?number=T568

7. Prepare an illustrated lecture on icons of Jesus.

8. Imagine that you are an early Christian missionary. Write a short letter to your converts to encourage them to remain strong in their faith in Jesus Christ. Discuss some reasons why Jesus should be the center of their lives.

9. Check the LifeTeen website to see a discussion of C.S. Lewis's challenge of deciding whether Jesus was a liar, a lunatic, or Lord. Summarize the arguments presented there: www.lifeteen.com/default.aspx ?PageID=JCHOME

10. After examining the following websites, create a PowerPoint presentation of an illustrated travelogue of one of Paul's journeys.

    • The Journeys of St. Paul: www .luthersem.edu/ckoester/Paul/Main.htm

    • Footsteps of Paul: www.abrock.com/ Greece-Turkey/FootstepsIntro.html

    • Paul's Missionary Journeys: http:// unbound.biola.edu/acts/index.cfm.

11. Scholars recognize Philippians 2:5–11 as an early Christian hymn. Research several Christian musicians. After listening to their works, pick out a favorite song, duplicate its lyrics, and write a short reflection on the Christian themes or virtues the song highlights.

12. Construct a set of twenty-five questions and answers on beliefs about Jesus that can be used as a quiz with fourth graders. Present it as a booklet with images and symbols downloaded from the Internet.

13. Create a collage of symbols of Jesus. Incorporate several from the Book of Revelation.

Prayer

Pray with the following prayer attributed to St. Patrick as a way to summarize your faith and hope in Jesus.

> Christ to protect me today
> against poison, against burning,
> against drowning, against wounding,
> so that there may come abundance
>   of reward.
> Christ with me, Christ before me,
>   Christ behind me,
> Christ in me, Christ beneath me,
>   Christ above me,
> Christ on my right, Christ on my left,
> Christ where I lie, Christ where I sit,
>   Christ where I arise,
> Christ in the heart of every man who
>   thinks of me,
> Christ in the mouth of every man who
>   speaks to me,
> Christ in every eye that sees me,
> Christ in every ear that hears me.

• *Reflection*: Where in your life do you need Jesus Christ? Where does Jesus Christ need you?

• *Resolution*: Resolve to pray to our Lord as to a friend for ten minutes every day for the next three weeks.

CATHOLIC HANDBOOK FOR FAITH

A. Beliefs

From the beginning, the Church expressed and handed on its faith in brief formulas accessible to all. These professions of faith are called "creeds" because their first word in Latin, credo, *means "I believe." The following creeds have special importance in the Church. The Apostles' Creed is a summary of the Apostles' faith. The Nicene Creed developed from the Councils of Nicaea and Constantinople and remains in common between the Churches of both the East and West.*

Apostles' Creed

I believe in God, the Father almighty,
Creator of Heaven and earth.

I believe in Jesus Christ, his only son, our Lord.
He was conceived by the power of the Holy Spirit,
and born of the Virgin Mary.
He suffered under Pontius Pilate,
was crucified, died, and was buried.
He descended into hell.
On the third day he rose again.
He ascended into Heaven,
and is seated at the right hand of the Father.
He will come again to judge the living and the dead.

I believe in the Holy Spirit,
the holy catholic Church,
the communion of saints,
the forgiveness of sins,
the resurrection of the body,
and the life everlasting. Amen.

Nicene Creed

We believe in one God,
 the Father, the Almighty,
 maker of Heaven and earth,
 of all that is seen and unseen.
We believe in one Lord, Jesus Christ,
 the only Son of God,
 eternally begotten of the Father,
 God from God, Light from Light,
 true God from true God,
 begotten, not made, one in Being with the Father.
 Through him all things were made.
 For us men and for our Salvation
 he came down from Heaven:
by the power of the Holy Spirit
 he was born of the Virgin Mary, and became man.
For our sake he was crucified under Pontius Pilate;
 he suffered, died, and was buried.
 On the third day he rose again in fulfillment of
 the Scriptures;
 he ascended into Heaven and is seated at the
 right hand of the Father.
He will come again in glory to judge the living and
 the dead,
 and his kingdom will have no end.

We believe in the Holy Spirit, the Lord, the giver
of life,
who proceeds from the Father and the Son.
With the Father and the Son he is worshiped
and glorified.
He has spoken through the Prophets.
We believe in one holy catholic and apostolic Church.
We acknowledge one baptism for the forgiveness
of sins.
We look for the resurrection of the dead,
and the life of the world to come. Amen.

Gifts of the Holy Spirit

1. Wisdom
2. Understanding
3. Counsel
4. Fortitude
5. Knowledge
6. Piety
7. Fear of the Lord

Fruits of the Holy Spirit

1. Charity
2. Joy
3. Peace
4. Patience
5. Kindness
6. Goodness
7. Generosity
8. Gentleness
9. Faithfulness
10. Modesty
11. Self-control
12. Chastity

The Symbol of Chalcedon

Following therefore the holy Fathers, we unani-
mously teach to confess one and the same Son, our
Lord Jesus Christ, the same perfect in divinity and
perfect in humanity, the same truly God and truly
man composed of rational soul and body, the same
one in being (*homoousios*) with the Father as to the
divinity and one in being with us as to the humanity,
like unto us in all things but sin (cf. Heb 4:15). The
same was begotten from the Father before the ages
as to the divinity and in the later days for us and our
Salvation was born as to his humanity from Mary
the Virgin Mother of God.

We confess that one and the same Lord Jesus
Christ, the only-begotten Son, must be acknowledged in two natures, without confusion or change,
without division or separation. The distinction between the natures was never abolished by their
union but rather the character proper to each of the
two natures was preserved as they came together in
one person (*prosôpon*) and one hypostasis. He is not
split or divided into two persons, but he is one and
the same only-begotten, God the Word, the Lord
Jesus Christ, as formerly the prophets and later Jesus Christ himself have taught us about him and as
has been handed down to us by the Symbol of the
Fathers.

—From the General Council of Chalcedon
(AD 451)

B. Faith in God: Father, Son, and Holy Spirit

*Our profession of faith begins with God, for God
is the First and the Last, the beginning and end of
everything.*

Attributes of God

St. Thomas Aquinas named nine attributes that seem
to tell us some things about God's nature. They are:

1. *God is eternal.* He has no beginning and no
   end. Or, to put it another way, God always
   was, always is, and always will be.
2. *God is unique.* There is no God like YHWH
   (see Isaiah 45:18). God is the designer of a

one-and-only world. Even the people he creates are one of a kind.

3. *God is infinite and omniscient.* This reminds us of a lesson we learned early in life: God sees everything. There are no limits to God.

4. *God is omnipresent.* God is not limited to space. He is everywhere. You can never be away from God.

5. *God contains all things.* All of creation is under God's care and jurisdiction.

6. *God is immutable.* God does not evolve. God does not change. God is the same God now as he always was and always will be.

7. *God is pure spirit.* Though God has been described with human attributes, God is not a material creation. God's image cannot be made. God is a pure spirit who cannot be divided into parts. God is simple, but complex.

8. *God is alive.* We believe in a living God, a God who acts in the lives of people. Most concretely, God assumed a human nature in the divine Person of Jesus Christ, without losing his divine nature.

9. *God is holy.* God is pure goodness. God is pure love.

The Holy Trinity

The Holy Trinity is the central mystery of the Christian faith and of Christian life. Only God can make it known to us by revealing himself as Father, Son, and Holy Spirit. Viewed in the light of faith, some of the Church dogmas, or beliefs, can help our understanding of this mystery:

- *The Trinity is One.* There are not three Gods, but one God in three Persons. Each one of them—Father, Son, and Holy Spirit—is God whole and entire.

- *The three Persons are distinct from one another.* The three Persons of the Trinity are distinct in how they relate to one another. "It is the Father who generates, the Son who is begotten, and the Holy Spirit who proceeds" (Lateran Council IV, quoted in *CCC*, 254). The Father is not the Son, nor is the Son the Holy Spirit.

- *The Three Divine Persons of the Blessed Trinity relate to one another.* While the three Persons are truly distinct in light of their relations, we believe in one God. The three Persons do not divide the divine unity. The Council of Florence taught, "Because of that unity the Father is wholly in the Son and wholly in the Holy Spirit; the Son is wholly in the Father and wholly in the Holy Spirit; the Holy Spirit is wholly in the Father and wholly in the Son" (quoted in *CCC*, 255).

St. John Damascus used two analogies to describe the doctrine of the Blessed Trinity.

Think of the Father as a root,
of the Son as a branch,
and of the Spirit as a fruit,
for the substance of these is one.

The Father is a sun
with the Son as rays
and the Holy Spirit as heat.

Read the *Catechism of the Catholic Church* (232–260) on the Holy Trinity.

Faith in One God

There are several implications for those who love God and believe in him with their entire heart and soul (see *CCC* 222–227):

- It means knowing God's greatness and majesty.
- It means living in thanksgiving.
- It means knowing the unity and dignity of all people.
- It means making good use of created things.
- It means trusting God in every circumstance.

C. Deposit of Faith

"Deposit of Faith" refers to both Sacred Scripture and Sacred Tradition handed on from the time of the Apostles, from which the Church draws all that she proposes is revealed by God.

Canon of the Bible

There are seventy-three books in the canon of the Bible, that is, the official list of books the Church accepts as divinely inspired writings: forty-six Old Testament books and twenty-seven New Testament books. Protestant Bibles do not include seven Old Testament books in their list (1 and 2 Maccabees, Judith, Tobit, Baruch, Sirach, and the Wisdom of Solomon). Why the difference? Catholics rely on the version of the Bible that the earliest Christians used, the *Septuagint*. This was the first Greek translation of the Hebrew Scriptures, begun in the third century BC. Protestants, on the other hand, rely on an official list of Hebrew Scriptures compiled in the Holy Land by Jewish scholars at the end of the first century AD. Today, some Protestant Bibles print the disputed books in a separate section at the back of the Bible, called the *Apocrypha*.

The twenty-seven books of the New Testament are detailed in Chapter 2. The New Testament is central to our knowledge of Jesus Christ.

There are forty-six books in the Old Testament canon. The Old Testament is the foundation for God's self-Revelation in Christ. Christians honor the Old Testament as God's Word. It contains the writings of prophets and other inspired authors who recorded God's teaching to the Chosen People and his interaction in their history. For example, the Old Testament recounts how God delivered the Jews from Egypt (the Exodus), led them to the Promised Land, formed them into a nation under his care, and taught them in knowledge and worship.

The stories, prayers, sacred histories, and other writings of the Old Testament reveal what God is like and tell much about human nature, too. In brief, the Chosen People sinned repeatedly by turning their backs on their loving God; they were weak and easily tempted away from God. YHWH, on the other hand, *always* remained faithful. He promised to send a messiah to humanity.

Listed on the following page are the categories and books of the Old Testament.

The Old Testament

The Pentateuch

Genesis	Gn
Exodus	Ex
Leviticus	Lv
Numbers	Nm
Deuteronomy	Dt

The Historical Books

Joshua	Jos
Judges	Jgs
Ruth	Ru
1 Samuel	1 Sm
2 Samuel	2 Sm
1 Kings	1 Kgs
2 Kings	2 Kgs
1 Chronicles	1 Chr
2 Chronicles	2 Chr
Ezra	Ezr
Nehemiah	Neh
Tobit	Tb
Judith	Jdt
Esther	Est
1 Maccabees	1 Mc
2 Maccabees	2 Mc

The Wisdom Books

Job	Jb
Psalms	Ps(s)
Proverbs	Prv
Ecclesiastes	Eccl
Song of Songs	Sg
Wisdom	Wis
Sirach	Sir

The Prophetic Books

Isaiah	Is
Jeremiah	Jer
Lamentations	Lam
Baruch	Bar
Ezekiel	Ez
Daniel	Dn
Hosea	Hos
Joel	Jl
Amos	Am
Obadiah	Ob
Jonah	Jon
Micah	Mi
Nahum	Na
Habakkuk	Hb
Zephaniah	Zep
Haggai	Hg
Zechariah	Zec
Malachi	Mal

The New Testament

The Gospels

Matthew	Mt
Mark	Mk
Luke	Lk
John	Jn
Acts of the Apostles	Acts

The New Testament Letters

Romans	Rom
1 Corinthians	1 Cor
2 Corinthians	2 Cor
Galatians	Gal
Ephesians	Eph
Philippians	Phil
Colossians	Col
1 Thessalonians	1 Thes
2 Thessalonians	2 Thes
1 Timothy	1 Tm
2 Timothy	2 Tm
Titus	Ti
Philemon	Phlm
Hebrews	Heb

The Catholic Letters

James	Jas
1 Peter	1 Pt
2 Peter	2 Pt
1 John	1 Jn
2 John	2 Jn
3 John	3 Jn
Jude	Jude
Revelation	Rv

How to Locate a Scripture Passage

Example: 2 Tm 3:16–17

1. Determine the name of the book.

   The abbreviation "2 Tm" stands for the book of Second Timothy.

2. Determine whether the book is in the Old Testament or New Testament.

   The book of Second Timothy is one of the Catholic letters in the New Testament.

3. Locate the chapter where the passage occurs.

   The first number before the colon—"3"—indicates the chapter. Chapters in the Bible are set off by the larger numbers that divide a book.

4. Locate the verses of the passage.

   The numbers after the colon indicate the verses referred to. In this case, verses 16 and 17 of chapter 3.

5. Read the passage.

   For example: "All Scripture is inspired by God and is useful for teaching, for refutation, for correction, and for training in righteousness, so that one who belongs to God may be competent, equipped for every good work."

Relationship Between Scripture and Tradition

The Church does not derive the revealed truths of God from the holy Scriptures alone. The Sacred Tradition hands on God's Word, first given to the Apostles by the Lord and the Holy Spirit, to the successors of the Apostles (the bishops and the pope). Enlightened by the Holy Spirit, these successors faithfully preserve, explain, and spread it to the ends of the earth. The Second Vatican Council fathers explained the relationship between Sacred Scripture and Sacred Tradition this way:

It is clear therefore that, in the supremely wise arrangement of God, Sacred Tradition, Sacred Scripture, and the Magisterium of the Church are so connected and associated that one of them cannot stand without the others. Working together, each in its own way, under the action of the one Holy Spirit, they all contribute effectively to the Salvation of souls. (*Dei Verbum*, 10)

Relevant Church Teaching on Reading and Studying Scripture

If one carefully reads the Scriptures, he will find there the word on the subject of Christ and the prefiguration of the new calling. He is indeed the hidden treasure in the field—the field in fact is the world—but in truth, the hidden treasure in the Scriptures is Christ. Because he is designed by types and words that humanly are not possible to understand before the accomplishment of all things, that is, Christ's second coming.

—St. Irenaeus (second century AD)

[Christ's words] are not only those which he spoke when he became a man and tabernacled in the flesh; for before that time, Christ, the Word of God, was in Moses and the prophets . . . [their words] were filled with the Spirit of Christ.

—Origen (third century AD)

You recall that one and the same Word of God extends throughout Scripture, that it is one and the same Utterance that resounds in the mouths of all the sacred writers, since he who was in the beginning God with God has no need of separate syllables; for he is not subject to time.

The Scriptures are in fact, in any passage you care to choose, singing of Christ, provided we have ears that are capable of picking out the tune. The Lord opened the minds of the Apostles so that they understood the Scriptures. That he will open our minds too is our prayer.

—St. Augustine of Hippo
(fifth century AD)

My dear young friends, I urge you to become familiar with the Bible, and to have it at hand so that it can be your compass pointing out the road to follow. By reading it, you will learn to know Christ. Note what St. Jerome said in this regard: "Ignorance of the Scriptures is ignorance of Christ" (PL 24,17; cf. *Dei Verbum*, 25). A time-honoured way to study and savor the Word of God is *lectio divina* which constitutes a real and veritable spiritual journey marked out in stages. After the *lectio*, which consists of reading and re-reading a passage from Sacred Scripture and taking in the main elements, we proceed to *meditatio*. This is a moment of interior reflection in which the soul turns to God and tries to understand what his Word is saying to us today. Then comes *oratio* in which we linger to talk with God directly. Finally we come to *contemplatio*. This helps us to keep our hearts attentive to the presence of Christ whose Word is "a lamp shining in a dark place, until the day dawns and the morning star rises in your hearts" (2 Pet 1:19). Reading, study and meditation of the Word should then flow into a life of consistent fidelity to Christ and his teachings.

St. James tells us: "Be doers of the word, and not merely hearers who deceive themselves. For if any are hearers of the word and not doers, they are like those who look at themselves in a mirror; for they look at themselves and, on going away, immediately forget what they were like. But those who look into the perfect law, the law of liberty, and persevere, being not hearers who forget but doers who act—they will be blessed in their doing" (1:22–25). Those who listen to the Word of God and refer to it always, are

constructing their existence on solid foundations. "Everyone then who hears these words of mine and acts on them," Jesus said, "will be like a wise man who built his house on rock" (Mt 7:24). It will not collapse when bad weather comes.

To build your life on Christ, to accept the Word with joy and put its teachings into practice: this, young people of the third millennium, should be your programme! There is an urgent need for the emergence of a new generation of Apostles anchored firmly in the Word of Christ, capable of responding to the challenges of our times and prepared to spread the Gospel far and wide. It is this that the Lord asks of you, it is to this that the Church invites you, and it is this that the world—even though it may not be aware of it—expects of you! If Jesus calls you, do not be afraid to respond to him with generosity, especially when he asks you to follow him in the consecrated life or in the priesthood. Do not be afraid; trust in him and you will not be disappointed.

—Pope Benedict XVI
(twenty-first century AD)

D. Church

The Church is the Body of Christ, that is, the community of God's people who profess faith in the Risen Lord Jesus and love and serve others under the guidance of the Holy Spirit. The Church is guided by the pope and his bishops.

Marks of the Church

1. *The Church is one.* The Church remains one because of its source: the unity in the Trinity of the Father, Son, and Spirit in one God. The Church's unity can never be broken and lost because this foundation is itself unbreakable.

2. *The Church is holy.* The Church is holy because Jesus, the founder of the Church, is holy, and he joined the Church to himself as his body and gave the Church the gift of the Holy Spirit. Together, Christ and the Church make up the "whole Christ" (*Christus totus* in Latin).

3. *The Church is catholic.* The Church is catholic ("universal" or "for everyone") in two ways. First, she is catholic because Christ is present in the Church in the fullness of his body, with the fullness of the means of Salvation, the fullness of faith, sacraments, and the ordained ministry that comes from the Apostles. The Church is also catholic because she takes its message of Salvation to all people.

4. *The Church is apostolic.* The Church's apostolic mission comes from Jesus: "Go, therefore, and make disciples of all nations" (Mt 28:19). The Church remains apostolic because she still teaches the same things the Apostles taught. Also, the Church is led by leaders who are successors to the Apostles and who help to guide us until Jesus returns.

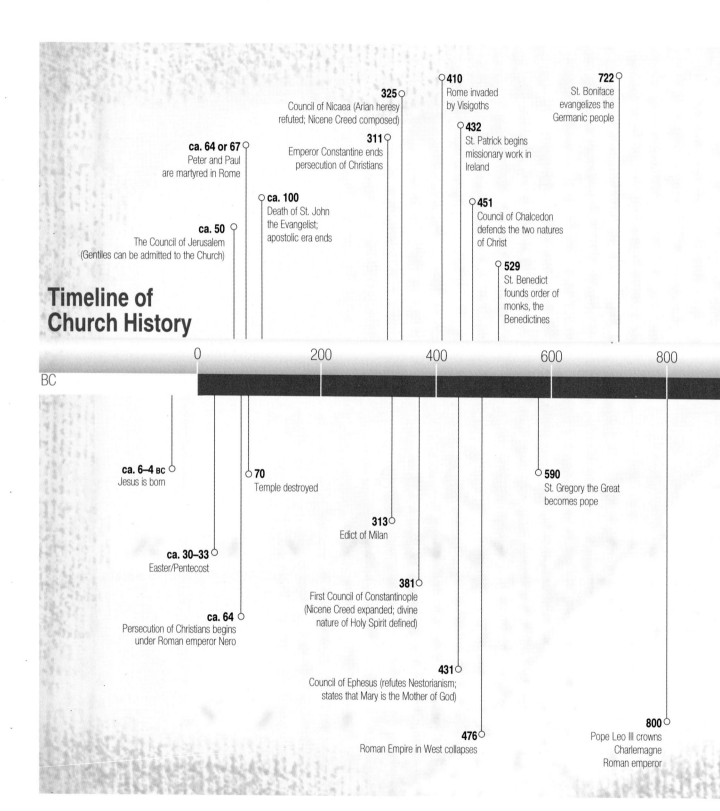

Timeline of Church History

410
Rome invaded
by Visigoths

722
St. Boniface
evangelizes the
Germanic people

325
Council of Nicaea (Arian heresy
refuted; Nicene Creed composed)

ca. 64 or 67
Peter and Paul
are martyred in Rome

311
Emperor Constantine ends
persecution of Christians

432
St. Patrick begins
missionary work in
Ireland

ca. 100
Death of St. John
the Evangelist;
apostolic era ends

451
Council of Chalcedon
defends the two natures
of Christ

ca. 50
The Council of Jerusalem
(Gentiles can be admitted to the Church)

529
St. Benedict
founds order of
monks, the
Benedictines

0   200   400   600   800

BC

ca. 6–4 BC
Jesus is born

70
Temple destroyed

590
St. Gregory the Great
becomes pope

ca. 30–33
Easter/Pentecost

313
Edict of Milan

381
First Council of Constantinople
(Nicene Creed expanded; divine
nature of Holy Spirit defined)

ca. 64
Persecution of Christians begins
under Roman emperor Nero

431
Council of Ephesus (refutes Nestorianism;
states that Mary is the Mother of God)

476
Roman Empire in West collapses

800
Pope Leo III crowns
Charlemagne
Roman emperor

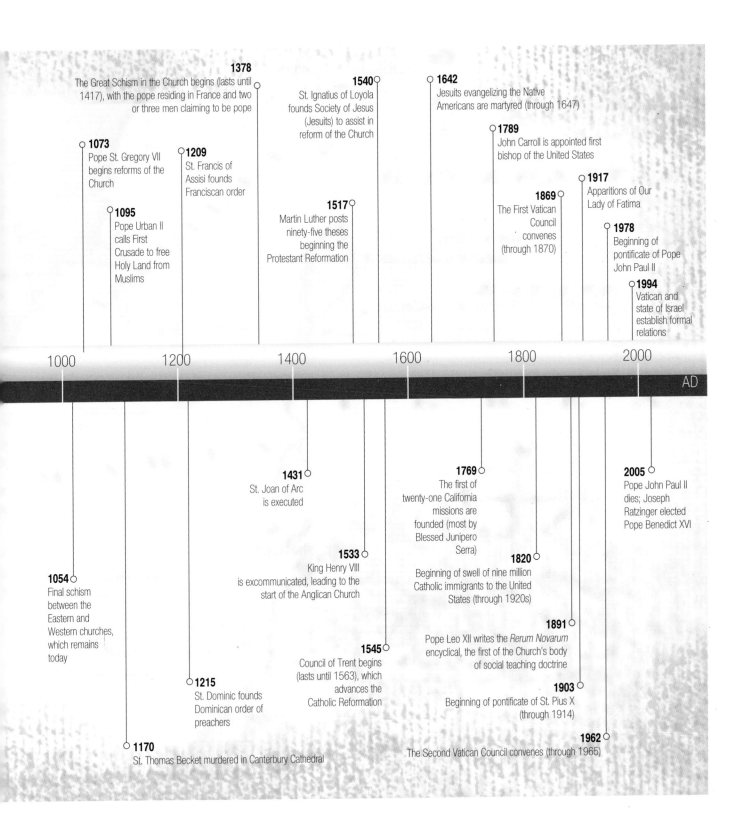

1378
The Great Schism in the Church begins (lasts until 1417), with the pope residing in France and two or three men claiming to be pope

1073
Pope St. Gregory VII begins reforms of the Church

1095
Pope Urban II calls First Crusade to free Holy Land from Muslims

1209
St. Francis of Assisi founds Franciscan order

1540
St. Ignatius of Loyola founds Society of Jesus (Jesuits) to assist in reform of the Church

1517
Martin Luther posts ninety-five theses beginning the Protestant Reformation

1642
Jesuits evangelizing the Native Americans are martyred (through 1647)

1789
John Carroll is appointed first bishop of the United States

1869
The First Vatican Council convenes (through 1870)

1917
Apparitions of Our Lady of Fatima

1978
Beginning of pontificate of Pope John Paul II

1994
Vatican and state of Israel establish formal relations

1000   1200   1400   1600   1800   2000

AD

1054
Final schism between the Eastern and Western churches, which remains today

1170
St. Thomas Becket murdered in Canterbury Cathedral

1215
St. Dominic founds Dominican order of preachers

1431
St. Joan of Arc is executed

1533
King Henry VIII is excommunicated, leading to the start of the Anglican Church

1545
Council of Trent begins (lasts until 1563), which advances the Catholic Reformation

1769
The first of twenty-one California missions are founded (most by Blessed Junipero Serra)

1820
Beginning of swell of nine million Catholic immigrants to the United States (through 1920s)

1891
Pope Leo XII writes the *Rerum Novarum* encyclical, the first of the Church's body of social teaching doctrine

1903
Beginning of pontificate of St. Pius X (through 1914)

1962
The Second Vatican Council convenes (through 1965)

2005
Pope John Paul II dies; Joseph Ratzinger elected Pope Benedict XVI

The Apostles and Their Emblems

St. Andrew

Tradition holds that Andrew was crucified on an X-shaped cross, called a *saltire*.

St. Bartholomew

Bartholomew was flayed alive before being crucified. He was then beheaded.

St. James the Greater

James the Greater, the brother of John, was beheaded by Herod Agrippa. It is the only death of an Apostle mentioned in Scripture (Acts 12:2). The shell indicates James's missionary work by sea in Spain. The sword is of martyrdom.

St. James the Less

James the Less is traditionally known as the first bishop of Jerusalem. The saw for his emblem is connected with the tradition of his body being sawed into pieces after he was pushed from the pinnacle of the Temple.

St. John the Evangelist

John was the first bishop of Ephesus. He is the only Apostle believed to have died a natural death, in spite of many attempts to murder him by his enemies. One attempt included his miraculous survival after drinking a poisoned drink.

St. Jude

Some traditions have Sts. Jude and Peter martyred together. It is thought that he traveled throughout the Roman Empire with Peter.

St. Matthew

Matthew's shield depicts three purses, reflecting his original occupation as tax collector.

St. Matthias

Matthias was the Apostle chosen by lot to replace Judas. Tradition holds that Matthias was stoned to death and then beheaded with an ax.

St. Peter

Simon Peter was the brother of Andrew. The first bishop of Rome, Peter was crucified under Nero, asking to be hung upside down because he felt unworthy to die as Jesus did. The keys represent Jesus' giving Peter the keys to the Kingdom of Heaven.

St. Philip

Philip may have been bound to a cross and stoned to death. The two loaves of bread at the side of the cross refer to Philip's comment to Jesus about the possibility of feeding the multitudes of people (Jn 6:7).

St. Simon

The book with fish depicts Simon as a "fisher of men" who preached the Gospel. He was also known as Simon the Zealot.

St. Thomas

Thomas is thought to have been a missionary in India, where he is thought to have built a church. Hence, the carpenter's square. He may have died by arrows and stones. It is then thought that he had a lance run through his body.

The Pope

The bishop of Rome has carried the title "pope" since the ninth century. Pope means "papa" or "father." St. Peter was the first bishop of Rome and, hence, the first pope. He was commissioned directly by Jesus:

> And so I say to you, you are Peter, and upon this rock I will build my church, and the gates of the netherworld shall not prevail against it. I will give you the keys to the kingdom of Heaven. Whatever you bind on earth shall be bound in Heaven; and whatever you loose on earth shall be loosed in Heaven. (Mt 16:18–19)

Because Peter was the first bishop of Rome, the succeeding bishops of Rome have had primacy in the Church. The entire succession of popes since St. Peter can be traced directly to the Apostle.

The pope is in communion with the bishops of the world as part of the Magisterium, which is the Church's teaching authority. The pope can also define doctrine in faith or morals for the Church. When he does so, he is infallible and cannot be in error.

The pope is elected by the College of Cardinals by a two-thirds plus one majority vote in secret balloting. Cardinals under the age of eighty are eligible to vote. If the necessary majority is not achieved, the ballots are burned in a small stove inside the council chambers along with straw that makes dark smoke. The sign of dark smoke announces to the crowds waiting outside St. Peter's Basilica that a new pope has not been chosen. When a new pope has been voted in with the necessary majority, the ballots are burned without the straw, producing white smoke and signifying the election of a pope.

Recent Popes

Since 1900 and up to the pontificate of Pope Benedict XVI, there have been ten popes. Pope John Paul II was the first non-Italian pope since Dutch Pope Adrian VI (1522–1523). The popes of the twentieth century through Benedict XVI with their original names, place of origin, and years as pope:

- Pope Leo XIII (Giocchino Pecci): Carpineto, Italy, February 20, 1878–July 20, 1903.
- Pope St. Pius X (Giuseppe Sarto): Riese, Italy, August 4, 1903–August 20, 1914.
- Pope Benedict XV (Giacomo della Chiesa): Genoa, Italy, September 3, 1914–January 22, 1922.
- Pope Pius XI (Achille Ratti): Desio, Italy, February 6, 1922–February 10, 1939.
- Pope Pius XII (Eugenio Pacelli): Rome, Italy, March 2, 1939–October 9, 1958.
- Pope John XXIII (Angelo Giuseppe Roncalli), Sotto il Monte, Italy, October 28, 1958–June 3, 1963.
- Pope Paul VI (Giovanni Battista Montini): Concessio, Italy, June 21, 1963–August 6, 1978.
- Pope John Paul I (Albino Luciani): Forno di Canale, Italy, August 26, 1978–September 28, 1978.
- Pope John Paul II (Karol Wojtyla): Wadowice, Poland, October 16, 1978–April 2, 2005.
- Pope Benedict XVI (Joseph Ratzinger): Marktl am Inn, Germany, April 19, 2005–present

Fathers of the Church

Church Fathers, or Fathers of the Church, is a traditional title that was given to theologians of the first eight centuries whose teachings made a lasting mark on the Church. The Church Fathers developed a significant amount of doctrine that has great authority in the Church. The Church Fathers are named as either Latin Fathers (West) or Greek Fathers (East). Among the greatest Fathers of the Church are:

Latin Fathers	Greek Fathers
St. Ambrose	St. John Chrysostom
St. Augustine	St. Basil the Great
St. Jerome	St. Gregory of Nazianzus
St. Gregory the Great	St. Athanasius

Doctors of the Church

The Doctors of the Church are men and women honored by the Church for their writings, preaching, and holiness. Originally the Doctors of the Church were considered to be Church Fathers Augustine, Ambrose, Jerome, and Gregory the Great, but others were added over the centuries. St. Teresa of Avila was the first woman Doctor (1970). St. Catherine of Siena was named a Doctor of the Church the same year. The list of Doctors of the Church:

Name	Life Span	Designation
St. Athanasius	296–373	1568 by Pius V
St. Ephraim the Syrian	306–373	1920 by Benedict XV
St. Hilary of Poitiers	315–367	1851 by Pius IX
St. Cyril of Jerusalem	315–386	1882 by Leo XIII
St. Gregory of Nazianzus	325–389	1568 by Pius V
St. Basil the Great	329–379	1568 by Pius V
St. Ambrose	339–397	1295 by Boniface VIII
St. John Chrysostom	347–407	1568 by Pius V
St. Jerome	347–419	1295 by Boniface XIII
St. Augustine	354–430	1295 by Boniface XIII
St. Cyril of Alexandria	376–444	1882 by Leo XIII
St. Peter Chrysologous	400–450	1729 by Benedict XIII
St. Leo the Great	400–461	1754 by Benedict XIV
St. Gregory the Great	540–604	1295 by Boniface XIII
St. Isidore of Seville	560–636	1722 by Innocent XIII
St. John of Damascus	645–749	1890 by Leo XIII
St. Bede the Venerable	672–735	1899 by Leo XIII
St. Peter Damian	1007–1072	1828 by Leo XII
St. Anselm	1033–1109	1720 by Clement XI
St. Bernard of Clairvaux	1090–1153	1830 by Pius VIII
St. Anthony of Padua	1195–1231	1946 by Pius XII
St. Albert the Great	1206–1280	1931 by Pius XI
St. Bonaventure	1221–1274	1588 by Sixtus V
St. Thomas Aquinas	1226–1274	1567 by Pius V
St. Catherine of Siena	1347–1380	1970 by Paul VI
St. Teresa of Avila	1515–1582	1970 by Paul VI
St. Peter Canisius	1521–1597	1925 by Pius XI
St. John of the Cross	1542–1591	1926 by Pius XI
St. Robert Bellarmine	1542–1621	1931 by Pius XI
St. Lawrence of Brindisi	1559–1619	1959 by John XXIII
St. Francis de Sales	1567–1622	1871 by Pius IX
St. Alphonsus Liguori	1696–1787	1871 by Pius IX
St. Thérèse of Lisieux	1873–1897	1997 by John Paul II

Ecumenical Councils

An ecumenical council is a worldwide assembly of bishops under the direction of the pope. There have been twenty-one ecumenical councils, the most recent being the Second Vatican Council (1962–1965). A complete list of the Church's ecumenical councils with the years each met:

Nicaea I	325
Constantinople I	381
Ephesus	431
Chalcedon	451
Constantinople II	553
Constantinople III	680
Nicaea II	787
Constantinople IV	869–870
Lateran I	1123
Lateran II	1139
Lateran III	1179
Lateran IV	1215
Lyons I	1245
Lyons II	1274
Vienne	1311–1312
Constance	1414–1418
Florence	1431–1445
Lateran V	1512–1517
Trent	1545–1563
Vatican Council I	1869–1870
Vatican Council II	1962–1965

E. Morality

Morality refers to the goodness or evil of human actions. Listed below are several helps the Church offers for making good and moral decisions.

The Ten Commandments

The Ten Commandments are a main source for Christian morality. The Ten Commandments were revealed by God to Moses. Jesus himself acknowledged them. He told the rich young man, "If you wish to enter into life, keep the commandments" (Mt 19:17). Since the time of St. Augustine (fourth century), the Ten Commandments have been used as a source for teaching baptismal candidates.

I. I, the Lord, am your God: you shall not have other gods besides me.

II. You shall not take the name of the Lord, your God, in vain.

III. Remember to keep holy the sabbath day.

IV. Honor your father and your mother.

V. You shall not kill.

VI. You shall not commit adultery.

VII. You shall not steal.

VIII. You shall not bear false witness against your neighbor.

IX. You shall not covet your neighbor's wife.

X. You shall not covet your neighbor's goods.

The Beatitudes

The word *beatitude* means "happiness." Jesus preached the Beatitudes in his Sermon on the Mount. They are:

Blessed are the poor in spirit, for theirs is the kingdom of God.

Blessed are they who mourn, for they will be comforted.

Blessed are the meek, for they will inherit the land.

Blessed are they who hunger and thirst for righteousness, for they will be satisfied.

Blessed are the merciful, for they will be shown mercy.

Blessed are the clean of heart, for they will see God.

Blessed are the peacemakers, for they will be called children of God.

Blessed are they who are persecuted for the sake of righteousness, for theirs is the kingdom of Heaven.

Cardinal Virtues

Virtues—habits that help in leading a moral life—that are acquired by human effort are known as moral or human virtues. Four of these are the cardinal virtues, as they form the hinge that connects all the others. They are:

- Prudence
- Justice
- Fortitude
- Temperance

Theological Virtues

The theological virtues are the foundation for moral life. They are gifts infused into our souls by God.

- Faith
- Hope
- Love

Corporal (Bodily) Works of Mercy

1. Feed the hungry.
2. Give drink to the thirsty.
3. Clothe the naked.
4. Visit the imprisoned.
5. Shelter the homeless.
6. Visit the sick.
7. Bury the dead.

Spiritual Works of Mercy

1. Counsel the doubtful.
2. Instruct the ignorant.
3. Admonish sinners.
4. Comfort the afflicted.
5. Forgive offenses.
6. Bear wrongs patiently.
7. Pray for the living and the dead.

Precepts of the Church

1. You shall attend Mass on Sundays and on holy days of obligation and rest from servile labor.
2. You shall confess your sins at least once a year.
3. You shall receive the Sacrament of Eucharist at least during the Easter season.
4. You shall observe the days of fasting and abstinence established by the Church.
5. You shall help to provide for the needs of the Church.

Catholic Social Teaching: Major Themes

The 1998 document Sharing Catholic Social Teaching: Challenges and Directions—Reflections of the U.S. Catholic Bishops *highlighted seven principles of the Church's social teaching. They are:*

1. Life and dignity of the human person
2. Call to family, community, and participation
3. Rights and responsibilities
4. Preferential option for the poor and vulnerable
5. The dignity of work and the rights of workers
6. Solidarity
7. God's care for creation

Sin

Sin is an offense against God.

Mortal sin is the most serious kind of sin. Mortal sin destroys or kills a person's relationship with God. To be a mortal sin, three conditions must exist:

- The moral object must be of grave or serious matter. Grave matter is specified in the Ten Commandments (e.g., do not kill, do not commit adultery, do not steal, etc.).

- The person must have full knowledge of the gravity of the sinful action.

- The person must completely consent to the action. It must be a personal choice.

Venial sin is less serious sin. Examples of venial sins are petty jealousy, disobedience, "borrowing" a small amount of money from a parent without the intention of repaying it. Venial sins, when not repented, can lead a person to commit mortal sins.

Vices are bad habits linked to sins. Vices come from particular sins, especially the seven capital sins: pride, avarice, envy, wrath, lust, gluttony, and sloth.

F. Liturgy and Sacraments

The sacraments and the Divine Office constitute the Church's liturgy. The Mass is the most important liturgical celebration.

Church Year

The cycle of seasons and feasts that Catholics celebrate is called the Church Year or Liturgical Year. The Church Year is divided into five main parts: Advent, Christmas, Lent, Easter, and Ordinary Time.

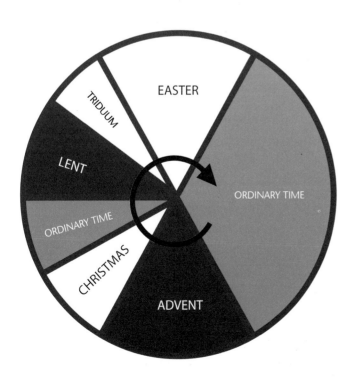

Holy Days of Obligation in the United States

1. Immaculate Conception of Mary
    December 8
2. Christmas
    December 25
3. Solemnity of Mary, Mother of God
    January 1
4. Ascension of the Lord
    Forty days after Easter
5. Assumption of Mary
    August 15
6. All Saints Day
    November 1

The Seven Sacraments

1. Baptism
2. Confirmation
3. Eucharist
4. Penance and Reconciliation
5. Anointing of the Sick
6. Matrimony
7. Holy Orders

How to Go to Confession

1. Spend some time examining your conscience. Consider your actions and attitudes in each area of your life (e.g., faith, family, school/work, social life, relationships). Ask yourself, Is this area of my life pleasing to God? What needs to be reconciled with God? with others? with myself?
2. Sincerely tell God that you are sorry for your sins. Ask God for forgiveness and for the grace you will need to change what needs changing in your life. Promise God that you will try to live according to his will for you.
3. Approach the area for confession. Wait at an appropriate distance until it is your turn.

4. Make the Sign of the Cross with the priest. He may say: "May God, who has enlightened every heart, help you to know your sins and trust his mercy." You reply: "Amen."

5. Confess your sins to the priest. Simply and directly talk to him about the areas of sinfulness in your life that need God's healing touch.

6. The priest will ask you to pray an Act of Contrition. Pray an Act of Contrition you have committed to memory. Or, say something in your own words, like: "Dear God, I am sorry for my sins. I ask for your forgiveness, and I promise to do better in the future."

7. The priest will talk to you about your life, encourage you to be more faithful to God in the future, and help you decide what to do to make up for your sins—your penance.

8. The priest will then extend his hands over your head and pray the Church's official prayer of absolution:

> God, the Father of mercies, through the Death and Resurrection of his Son, has reconciled the world to himself and sent the Holy Spirit among us for the forgiveness of sins; through the ministry of the Church may God give you pardon and peace, and I absolve you from your sins in the name of the Father, and of the Son, and of the Holy Spirit.

> You respond: "Amen."

9. The priest will wish you peace. Thank him and leave.

10. Go to a quiet place in church and pray your prayer of penance. Then spend some time quietly thanking God for the gift of forgiveness.

Order of Mass

There are two main parts of the Mass, the Liturgy of the Word and the Liturgy of the Eucharist. The complete order of Mass is as follows:

The Introductory Rites

> The Entrance
> Greeting of the Altar and of the People Gathered
> The Act of Penitence
> The *Kyrie Eleison*
> The *Gloria*
> The Collect (Opening Prayer)

The Liturgy of the Word

> Silence
> The Biblical Readings (the reading of the Gospel is the high point of the Liturgy of the Word)
> The Responsorial Psalm
> The Homily
> The Profession of Faith (Creed)
> The Prayer of the Faithful

The Liturgy of the Eucharist

> The Preparation of the Gifts
>> The Prayer over the Offerings
>> The Eucharistic Prayer
>>> Thanksgiving
>>> Acclamation
>>> Epiclesis
>>> Institution Narrative and Consecration
>>> Anamnesis
>>> Offering
>>> Intercessions
>>> Final Doxology
> The Communion Rite
>> The Lord's Prayer
>> The Rite of Peace
>> The Fraction (Breaking of the Bread)
>> Communion
>> Prayer after Communion

The Concluding Rites

Communion Regulations

To receive Holy Communion properly, a person must be in the state of grace (free from mortal sin), have the right intention (only for the purpose of pleasing God), and observe the Communion fast.

The fast means that a person may not eat anything or drink any liquid (other than water) one hour before the reception of Communion. There are exceptions made to this fast only for the sick and aged.

Three Degrees of the Sacrament of Holy Orders

There are three degrees of the Sacrament of Holy Orders: the ministries of bishop, priest, and deacon.

The bishop receives the fullness of the Sacrament of Orders. He is the successor to the Apostles. When he celebrates the sacraments, the bishop is given the grace to act in the person of Christ, who is the head of the Body of the Church.

Priests are ordained as coworkers of the bishop. They, too, are configured to Christ so that they may act in his person during the Sacraments of Eucharist, Baptism, and the Anointing of the Sick. They may bless marriages in the name of Christ and, under the authority of the bishop, share in Christ's ministry of forgiveness in the Sacrament of Penance and Reconciliation.

Deacons are ordained for service and are configured to Christ the servant. Deacons are ordained to help and serve the priests and bishops in their work. While bishops and priests are configured to Christ to act as the head of Christ's body, deacons are configured to Christ in order to serve as he served. Deacons may baptize, preach the Gospel and homily, and bless marriages.

G. Mary and the Saints

The doctrine of the communion of saints flows from our belief that we Christians are closely united as one family in the Spirit of Jesus Christ. Mary is the Queen of the Saints. Her role in the Church flows from an inseparable union with her Son.

Mother of God

Mary, the Mother of Jesus, is the closest human to cooperate with her Son's work of redemption. For this reason, the Church holds her in a special place. Of her many titles, the most significant is that she is the Mother of God.

The Church teaches several truths about Mary.

First, she was conceived immaculately. This means from the very first moment of her existence she was without sin and "full of grace." This belief is called the Immaculate Conception. The feast of the Immaculate Conception is celebrated on December 8.

Second, Mary was always a virgin. She was a virgin before, in, and after the birth of Jesus. As his Mother, she cared for him in infancy and raised him to adulthood with the help of her husband, Joseph. She witnessed Jesus' preaching and ministry, was at the foot of his cross at his crucifixion, and present with the Apostles as they awaited the coming of the Holy Spirit at Pentecost. With her whole being, she is as she stated: "I am the handmaid of the Lord" (Lk 1:38).

Third, at the time of her death, Mary was assumed body and soul into Heaven. This dogma was proclaimed as a matter of faith by Pope Pius XII in 1950. The feast of the Assumption is celebrated on August 15.

The Church has always been devoted to the Blessed Virgin. This devotion is different from that given to God—Father, Son, and Holy Spirit. Rather, the Church is devoted to Mary as the first disciple, the Queen of all Saints, and the Church's own

Mother. Quoting the fathers of the Second Vatican Council:

> In the meantime the Mother of Jesus, in the glory which she possesses in body and soul in Heaven, is the image and the beginning of the Church as it is to be perfected in the world to come. Likewise she shines forth on earth, until the day of the Lord shall come, a sign of certain hope and comfort to the pilgrim People of God. (*Lumen Gentium*, 68)

Marian Feasts Throughout the Year

January 1	Solemnity of Mary, Mother of God
March 25	Annunciation of the Lord
May 31	Visitation
August 15	Assumption
August 22	Queenship of Mary
September 8	Birth of Mary
September 15	Our Lady of Sorrows
October 7	Our Lady of the Rosary
November 21	Presentation of Mary
December 8	Immaculate Conception
December 12	Our Lady of Guadalupe

Canonization of Saints

Saints are those who are in glory with God in Heaven. *Canonization* refers to a solemn declaration by the pope that a person who either died a martyr or who lived an exemplary Christian life is in Heaven and may be honored and imitated by all Christians. The canonization process first involves a process of beatification that includes a thorough investigation of the person's life and certification of miracles that can be attributed to the candidate's intercession.

The first official canonization of the universal Church on record is St. Ulrich of Augsburg by Pope John XV in 993.

Some non-Catholics criticize Catholics for "praying to saints." Catholics *honor* saints for their holy lives but we do not pray to them as if they were God. We ask the saints to pray with us and for us as part of the Church in glory. We can ask them to do this because we know that their lives have been spent in close communion with God. We also ask the saints for their friendship so that we can follow the example they have left for us.

Patron Saints

A patron is a saint who is designated for places (nations, regions, dioceses) or organizations. Many saints have also become patrons of jobs, professional groups, and intercessors for special needs. Listed below are patron saints for several nations and some special patrons:

Patrons of Places

Americas	Our Lady of Guadalupe, St. Rose of Lima
Argentina	Our Lady of Lujan
Australia	Our Lady Help of Christians
Canada	St. Joseph, St. Anne
China	St. Joseph
England	St. George
Finland	St. Henry
France	Our Lady of the Assumption, St. Joan of Arc, St. Thérèse of Lisieux
Germany	St. Boniface
India	Our Lady of the Assumption
Ireland	St. Patrick, St. Brigid, St. Columba
Italy	St. Francis of Assisi, St. Catherine of Siena
Japan	St. Peter
Mexico	Our Lady of Guadalupe
Poland	St. Casmir, St. Stanislaus, Our Lady of Czestochowa
Russia	St. Andrew, St. Nicholas of Myra, St. Thérèse of Lisieux

Scotland	St. Andrew, St. Columba
Spain	St. James, St. Teresa of Ávila
United States	Immaculate Conception

Special Patrons

Accountants	St. Matthew
Actors	St. Genesius
Animals	St. Francis of Assisi
Athletes	St. Sebastian
Beggars	St. Martin of Tours
Boy Scouts	St. George
Dentists	St. Apollonia
Farmers	St. Isidore
Grocers	St. Michael
Journalists	St. Francis de Sales
Maids	St. Zita
Motorcyclists	Our Lady of Grace
Painters	St. Luke
Pawnbrokers	St. Nicholas
Police Officers	St. Michael
Priests	St. John Vianney
Scientists	St. Albert
Tailors	St. Homobonus
Teachers	St. Gregory the Great, St. John Baptist de la Salle
Wine Merchants	St. Amand

H. Devotions

Catholics have also expressed their piety around the Church's sacramental life through practices like the veneration of relics, visits to churches, pilgrimages, processions, the Stations of the Cross, religious dances, the rosary, medals, and many more. This section lists some popular Catholic devotions.

The Mysteries of the Rosary

Joyful Mysteries

1. The Annunciation
2. The Visitation
3. The Nativity
4. The Presentation in the Temple
5. The Finding of Jesus in the Temple

Mysteries of Light

1. Jesus' Baptism in the Jordan River
2. Jesus Self-manifestation at the Wedding of Cana
3. The Proclamation of the Kingdom of God and Jesus' Call to Conversion
4. The Transfiguration
5. The Institution of the Eucharist at the Last Supper

Sorrowful Mysteries

1. The Agony in the Garden
2. The Scourging at the Pillar
3. The Crowning with Thorns
4. The Carrying of the Cross
5. The Crucifixion

Glorious Mysteries

1. The Resurrection
2. The Ascension
3. The Descent of the Holy Spirit
4. The Assumption of Mary
5. The Crowning of Mary as the Queen of Heaven and Earth

How to Pray the Rosary

Opening

1. Begin on the crucifix and pray the Apostles' Creed.
2. On the first bead, pray the Our Father.
3. On the next three beads, pray the Hail Mary. (Some people meditate on the virtues of faith, hope, and charity on these beads.)
4. On the fifth bead, pray the Glory Be.

The Body

Each decade (set of ten beads) is organized as follows:

1. On the larger bead that comes before each set of ten, announce the mystery to be prayed (see above) and pray one Our Father.
2. On each of the ten smaller beads, pray one Hail Mary while meditating on the mystery.
3. Pray one Glory Be at the end of the decade. (There is no bead for the Glory Be.)

Conclusion

Pray the following prayer at the end of the Rosary:

Hail, Holy Queen

Hail, holy Queen, Mother of Mercy,
our life, our sweetness, and our hope.
To thee do we cry,
poor banished children of Eve.
To thee do we send up our sighs,
mourning and weeping in the valley of tears.
Turn then, most gracious advocate,
thine eyes of mercy toward us;
and after this our exile,
show unto us the blessed fruit of thy womb,
Jesus.
O clement, O loving, O sweet Virgin Mary.

Pray for us, O holy Mother of God,
that we may be made worthy of the
promises of Christ.
Amen.

Stations of the Cross

The Stations of the Cross is a devotion and also a sacramental. (A sacramental is a sacred object, blessing, or devotion.) The Stations of the Cross are individual pictures or symbols hung on the interior walls of most Catholic churches depicting fourteen steps along Jesus' way of the cross. Praying the stations means meditating on each of the following scenes:

1. Jesus is condemned to death.
2. Jesus takes up his cross.
3. Jesus falls the first time.
4. Jesus meets his Mother.
5. Simon of Cyrene helps Jesus carry his cross.
6. Veronica wipes the face of Jesus.
7. Jesus falls the second time.
8. Jesus consoles the women of Jerusalem.
9. Jesus falls the third time.
10. Jesus is stripped of his garments.
11. Jesus is nailed to the cross.
12. Jesus dies on the cross.
13. Jesus is taken down from the cross.
14. Jesus is laid in the tomb.

Some churches also include a fifteenth station, the Resurrection of the Lord.

Novenas

The novena consists of the recitation of certain prayers over a period of nine days. The symbolism of nine days refers to the time Mary and the Apostles spent in prayer between Jesus' Ascension into Heaven and Pentecost.

Many novenas are dedicated to Mary or to a saint with the faith and hope that she or he will intercede for the one making the novena. Novenas to St. Jude, St. Anthony, Our Lady of Perpetual Help, and Our Lady of Lourdes remain popular in the Church today.

Liturgy of the Hours

The Liturgy of the Hours is part of the official, public prayer of the Church. Along with the celebration of the sacraments, the recitation of the Liturgy of the Hours, or Divine Office (office means "duty" or "obligation"), allows for constant praise and thanksgiving to God throughout the day and night.

The Liturgy of Hours consists of five major divisions:

1. An hour of readings
2. Morning praises
3. Midday prayers

4. Vespers (evening prayers)
5. Compline (a short night prayer)

Scriptural prayer, especially the Psalms, is at the heart of the Liturgy of the Hours. Each day follows a separate pattern of prayer with themes closely tied in with the liturgical year and feasts of the saints.

The Divine Praises

These praises are traditionally recited after the benediction of the Blessed Sacrament.

> Blessed be God.
> Blessed be his holy name.
> Blessed be Jesus Christ, true God and true man.
> Blessed be the name of Jesus.
> Blessed be his most Sacred Heart.
> Blessed be his most Precious Blood.
> Blessed be Jesus in the most holy sacrament of the altar.
> Blessed be the Holy Spirit, the Paraclete.
> Blessed be the great Mother of God, Mary most holy.
> Blessed be her holy and Immaculate Conception.
> Blessed be her glorious Assumption.
> Blessed be the name of Mary, Virgin and Mother.
> Blessed be St. Joseph, her most chaste spouse.
> Blessed be God in his angels and his saints.

I. Prayers

Some common Catholic prayers are listed below. The Latin translation for three of the prayers is included. Latin is the official language of the Church. There are several occasions when you may pray in Latin; for example, at a World Youth Day when you are with young people who speak many different languages.

Sign of the Cross

> In the name of the Father,
> and of the Son,
> and of the Holy Spirit. Amen.

In nómine Patris,
et Filii,
et Spíritus Sancti.
Amen.

Our Father

> Our Father
> who art in Heaven,
> hallowed be thy name.
> Thy kingdom come;
> thy will be done on earth as it is in Heaven.
> Give us this day our daily bread
> and forgive us our trespasses
> as we forgive those who trespass against us.
> And lead us not into temptation,
> but deliver us from evil.
> Amen.

Pater Noster qui es in celis:
sanctificétur Nomen Tuum;
advéniat Regnum Tuum;
fiat volúntas Tua,
sicut in caelo, et in terra.
Panem nostrum
cuotidiánum da nobis hódie;
et dimítte nobis débita nostra,
sicut et nos
dimíttimus debitóribus nostris;
Et ne nos inducas in tentatiónem,
sed libera nos a Malo.
Amen.

Glory Be

Glory be to the Father
and to the Son
and to the Holy Spirit,
as it was in the beginning,
is now,
and ever shall be,
world without end. Amen.

Glória Patri
et Filio
et Spiritui Sancto.
Sicut erat in princípio,
et nunc et semper,
et in sae'cula saeculórum.
Amen.

Hail Mary

Hail Mary, full of grace,
the Lord is with thee.
Blessed art thou among women
and blessed is the fruit of thy womb, Jesus.
Holy Mary, Mother of God,
pray for us sinners now
and at the hour of our death. Amen.

Ave, María, grátia plena,
Dóminus tecum.
Benedicta tu in muliéribus,
et benedíctus fructus ventris
tui, Iesus.
Sancta María, Mater Dei,
ora pro nobis peccatoribus
nunc et in hora mortis nostrae.
Amen.

Memorare

Remember, O most gracious Virgin Mary,
that never was it known
that anyone who fled to your protection,
implored your help,
or sought your intercession was left unaided.

Inspired by this confidence,
I fly unto you,
O virgin of virgins, my Mother,
To you I come, before you I stand,
sinful and sorrowful.
O Mother of the word incarnate,
despise not my petitions,
but in your mercy hear and answer me. Amen.

Hail, Holy Queen

Hail, holy Queen, Mother of Mercy,
our life, our sweetness and our hope!
To you do we cry,
poor banished children of Eve;
to you do we send up our sighs,
mourning and weeping in this valley of tears.
Turn then, O most gracious advocate,
your eyes of mercy toward us,
and after this exile,
show us the blessed fruit of your womb, Jesus.
O clement, O loving, O sweet Virgin Mary.
V. Pray for us, O holy Mother of God.
R. that we may be made worthy of the promises
of Christ. Amen.

The Angelus

V. The angel spoke God's message to Mary.
R. And she conceived by the Holy Spirit.
Hail Mary . . .
V. Behold the handmaid of the Lord.
R. May it be done unto me according to your
word.
Hail Mary . . .
V. And the Word was made flesh.
R. And dwelled among us.
Hail Mary . . .
V. Pray for us, O holy Mother of God.
R. That we may be made worthy of the promises
of Christ.
Let us pray: We beseech you, O Lord, to
pour out your grace into our hearts. By the
message of an angel we have learned of the

Incarnation of Christ, your son; lead us by his Passion and cross, to the glory of the Resurrection. Through the same Christ our Lord. Amen.

Regina Caeli

Queen of Heaven, rejoice, alleluia.
The Son you merited to bear, alleluia,
has risen as he said, alleluia.
Pray to God for us, alleluia.

V. Rejoice and be glad, O Virgin Mary, alleluia.
R. For the Lord has truly risen, alleluia.
Let us pray.
God of life, you have given joy to the world by the Resurrection of your son, our Lord Jesus Christ. Through the prayers of his Mother, the Virgin Mary, bring us to the happiness of eternal life. We ask this through Christ our Lord. Amen.

Grace at Meals

Before Meals

Bless us, O Lord,
and these your gifts,
which we are about to receive from your
   bounty,
through Christ our Lord. Amen.

After Meals

We give you thanks, almighty God,
for these and all the gifts
which we have received
from your goodness
through Christ our Lord. Amen.

Guardian Angel Prayer

Angel of God, my guardian dear, to whom God's love entrust me here, ever this day be at my side, to light and guard, to rule and guide. Amen.

Prayer for the Faithful Departed

V: Eternal rest grant unto them, O Lord.
R: And let perpetual light shine upon them.
   May their souls and the souls of all faithful departed, through the mercy of God, rest in peace.
R: Amen.

Morning Offering

O Jesus, through the Immaculate Heart of Mary, I offer you my prayers, works, joys, and sufferings of this day in union with the holy sacrifice of the Mass throughout the world. I offer them for all the intentions of your Sacred Heart: the Salvation of souls, reparation for sin, the reunion of all Christians. I offer them for the intentions of our bishops and all members of the apostleship of prayer and in particular for those recommended by your Holy Father this month. Amen.

Act of Faith

O God,
I firmly believe all the truths that you have
   revealed
and that you teach us through your Church,
for you are truth itself
and can neither deceive nor be deceived.
Amen.

Act of Hope

O God,
I hope with complete trust that you will give me,
through the merits of Jesus Christ, all necessary
   grace in this world
and everlasting life in the world to come,
for this is what you have promised
and you always keep your promises.
Amen.

Act of Love

O my God, I love you above all things, with my whole heart and soul, because you are all good and worthy of all my love. I love my neighbor as myself for the love of you. I forgive all who have injured me, and I ask pardon of all whom I have injured. Amen.

Prayer for Peace (St. Francis of Assisi)

Lord, make me an instrument of your peace.
Where there is hatred, let me sow love;
where there is injury, pardon;
where there is doubt, faith;
where there is despair, hope;
where there is darkness, light;
where there is sadness, joy.
O Divine Master,
grant that I may not seek so much to be con-
    soled as to console;
to be understood, as to understand,
to be loved, as to love.
For it is in giving that we receive,
it is in pardoning that we are pardoned,
and it is in dying that we are born to eternal life.

GLOSSARY

agnosticism
The belief that God's existence cannot be known.

anthropomorphic
A literary device in which human emotional qualities (e.g., sadness, anger) and physical traits (e.g., eyes) are attributed to God.

anti-Semitism
Unfounded prejudice against the Jewish people.

apocalypse
A Greek word for "revelation." It also refers to a type of highly symbolic literature that contains apparitions about the future and the Final Judgment. This form of literature was used to give hope to a persecuted people that God's goodness will triumph over evil.

apocryphal books
Apocryphal is a Greek word that means "hidden." For Catholics, it refers to pious literature related to the Bible but not included in the canon of the Bible. Two examples from Old Testament times are 1 Esdras and the Book of Jubilees. However, Protestants and Jews also use this term to refer to several Old Testament books that Catholics consider inspired—Sirach, Wisdom, Baruch, 1 and 2 Maccabees, Tobit, and Judith. These books were not part of the Jewish canon of the Hebrew Scriptures at the end of the first century, although they were found in the early Christian Greek translations of the Old Testament. Catholics refer to this same list of books as "deuterocanonical."

apostasy
The denial of God and the repudiation of faith.

Arianism
A fourth-century movement named for an Alexandrian priest, Arius, whose followers denied the true divinity of Christ. At the Council of Nicaea in AD 325, the Church affirmed that the Son was begotten, not made, and of the same substance as the Father.

atheist
A person who denies the existence of God.

atonement
A word that means amends or reparation for a sin or a fault. In Christianity, the reconciliation between God and humans is brought about by the redemptive Life and Death of Jesus Christ.

beatified
From the word for "blessed," a person who is beatified has been declared by the Church to have the ability to intercede for those who pray in his or her name. It is a step toward canonized sainthood.

"beloved disciple"
Since the term is not found in any of the other Gospels, it is understood to refer to John the Evangelist, the author of the Gospel.

blasphemy

Any thought, word, or act that expresses hatred or contempt for God, Christ, the Church, saints, or holy things.

canon

The official list of inspired books of the Bible. Catholics list forty-six Old Testament books and twenty-seven New Testament books in their canon.

catechesis

Process of systematic education in the faith for young people and adults with the view of making them disciples of Jesus Christ.

Christology

The study of Jesus Christ; that is, trying to understand who he is.

Church Father

A traditional title given to theologians of the first eight centuries whose teachings made a lasting mark on the Church.

circumcision

The surgical removal of the male foreskin; it was the physical sign of the covenant between God and Abraham.

concupiscence

An inclination to commit sin that arises from our human desires or appetites. It is one of the temporal consequences of Original Sin, even after receiving the Sacrament of Baptism.

conscience

A practical judgment of reason that helps a person decide the goodness or sinfulness of an action or attitude. It is the subjective norm of morality we must form properly and then follow.

Council of Jerusalem

A crucial meeting of the Church that resolved a conflict of unity on whether or not Jewish Law should be applied to Gentile converts. The decision ultimately was that Christianity was no longer tied to Judaism.

covenant

A binding and solemn agreement between human beings or between God and people, holding each to a particular course of action.

Dead Sea Scrolls

Discovered in 1947 in caves near the Dead Sea, these manuscripts belonged to the Jewish Essene sect, which lived in a monastery at Qumran. The scrolls contain Essene religious documents, commentaries on certain Hebrew Scriptures, and ancient Old Testament manuscripts. They have proved very valuable to scholars in studying the Old Testament and for learning about some Jewish practices at the time of Jesus.

Deposit of Faith

"The heritage of faith contained in Sacred Scripture and Tradition, handed down in the Church from the time of the Apostles, from which the Magisterium draws all that it proposes for belief as being divinely revealed" (*Catechism of the Catholic Church*, Glossary).

deuterocanonical

The Greek term for "second canon." It refers to those books in the Old Testament that were not found in the Hebrew scriptures. These books are Sirach, Wisdom, Baruch, 1 and 2 Maccabees, Tobit, Judith, and certain additions to Esther and Daniel.

devil

The name for a fallen angel who refused to accept God or his Kingdom. Another word for the devil is *Satan*, or the "Evil One." The devil and other demons were at first good angels, but became evil due to their own choices and actions.

didache

A Greek word that means "teaching." In Christian times this term refers to the earliest known writing in Christianity aside from the New Testament.

disciple

A follower of Jesus. The word means "learner."

Divine Revelation

The way God communicates knowledge of himself to humankind, a self-communication realized by his actions and words over time, most fully by his sending us his divine Son, Jesus Christ.

Docetism

An early heresy that was associated with the Gnostics that taught that Jesus had no human body and only appeared to die on the Cross.

dogma

A central truth of Revelation that Catholics are obliged to believe.

Elohim

A common Semitic word for God used in the Bible. Elohim appears in Hebrew names like Mich-a-EL, Dan-i-EL, and Ari-EL.

Emmanuel

A name for Jesus that means "God is with us." This is the name given to Jesus as foretold in the Old Testament (see, for example, Isaiah 7:14 and 8:8) and recounted to Joseph, the foster father of Jesus, in a dream.

Enuma Elish

The Babylonian creation myth.

ephod

Typically in the Old Testament an ephod was a vestment worn by Hebrew priests; however in the example connected with Gideon, an ephod was likely an idol fashioned to worship as a false god.

Epiphany

The feast that celebrates the mystery of Christ's manifestation as the Savior of the world.

Epistle

A word that means "letter." In the New Testament they are letters intended for public reading. Most Epistles have these elements: an opening address; a thanksgiving; the body of the letter with a main doctrinal teaching; a final salutation.

Evangelist

One who proclaims in word and deed the Good News of Jesus Christ. "The Four Evangelists" refers to the authors of the four Gospels: Matthew, Mark, Luke, and John.

exegesis

The process used by scholars to discover the meaning of the biblical text.

exorcism

The public and authoritative act of the Church to liberate a person from the power of the devil in the name of Christ.

faith

A gift from God; one of the three theological virtues. Faith refers to personal knowledge of God; assent of the mind to truths God has revealed, made with the help of his grace and on the authority and trustworthiness of his revealing them; the truths themselves (the content of faith); and the lived witness of a Christian life (living faith).

false prophets

Jesus said of false prophets, "By their fruits you will know them" (Mt 7:16). Jesus said to be aware of people who claimed to speak in the name of God without being inspired by him.

Feast of Dedication

Commonly known as Hanukkah ("Festival of Lights"), it marks the time when the Temple was rededicated in the days of the Maccabees.

Feast of Tabernacles

Also called Sukkot, or the Feast of Booths, it commemorates the forty years the Jews spent in the desert when they had to protect themselves by constructing huts or booths. It begins five days after Yom Kippur and lasts for eight days.

Gentile

A term for non-Jews.

gift of tongues

A supernatural gift that was designed to build up the early Church; on Pentecost the disciples were heard speaking in languages that everyone could understand.

Glory of God

The visible Revelation of the power of the invisible God.

Golden Rule

The Golden Rule is described by Jesus and recorded in Matthew 7:12: "Do to others whatever you would have them do to you."

grace

God's gift of friendship and life that enables us to share his life and love. Grace introduces us to the intimacy of life with the Blessed Trinity.

Hanukkah

The Jewish Feast of Dedication, which celebrates the recovery and purification of the Temple from the Syrians in 164 BC. It is an eight-day feast that takes place during December. Also known as the Feast of Lights, Hanukkah is normally celebrated with gift giving.

Hasmonean Dynasty

Descendants of the Maccabees who ruled in Judea after the ousting of the last of the Syrians in 141 BC until the establishment of Roman authority in 63 BC. John Hyrcanus was the first ruler of this dynasty and ruled until 128 BC.

Hell

Eternal separation from God that results in a person's dying after freely and deliberately acting against God's will (that is, not repenting of mortal sin).

Hellenism

The diffusion of Greek culture throughout the Mediterranean world after the conquests of Alexander the Great.

hospitality

The act of welcoming, receiving, or hosting.

idolatry

Giving worship to something or someone other than the true God.

Incarnation

The dogma that God's eternal Son assumed a human nature and became man in order to save us from our sins. (The term literally means "taking on human flesh.") Jesus Christ, the Son of God, the Second Person of the Trinity, is both true God and true man.

INRI

INRI is an abbreviation of Jesus' crime in the Latin language: I=Jesus, N=Nazareth, R=King, I=Jews.

intercessory prayer

To intercede means to "come between" or "mediate" between two parties. Jesus is our model intercessor, one who mediates between us and God the Father.

irreligion

A vice contrary to the virtue of religion that directs us away from what we owe to God in justice.

John Rylands Greek papyrus

Generally accepted as the earliest record of a New Testament text, it is a fragment that measures 2.5 x 3.5 inches that includes lines from John 18:31–33.

It is kept at the John Rylands Library in Manchester, United Kingdom.

judges

In ancient Israel, judges were those who acted as temporary military leaders, as well as arbiters of disputes within and between tribes. Judges were also expected to remind the people of their responsibility to God.

kerygma

The core or essential message of the Gospel that Jesus Christ is Lord. One example is found in Acts 2:14–36.

Kingdom (or reign) of God

The Kingdom of God (also called the reign of God) was proclaimed by Jesus and began in his Life, Death, and Resurrection. It refers to the process of the Father's reconciling and renewing all things through his Son, to the fact of his will being done on earth as it is in Heaven. The process has begun with Jesus and will be perfectly completed at the end of time.

kingdom of Israel

The name of the northern kingdom that split with Judah after the death of Solomon. This revolt involved people and territory from ten of the twelve tribes.

kingdom of Judah

The name of the southern kingdom after the splitting of the monarchy. It included the territory originally belonging to just two of the twelve tribes, Judah and Benjamin.

literal sense (of the biblical text)

"The *literal sense* is the meaning conveyed by the words of Scripture and discovered by exegesis, following the rules of sound interpretation" (*CCC*, 116).

literary genre

A type of writing that has a particular form, style, or content.

liturgy

The liturgy is the official public worship of the Church. The liturgy is first Christ's work of Redemption, and his continuing work of Redemption as he pours out his blessings through the sacraments. The Holy Spirit enlightens our faith and encourages us to respond. In this way, the liturgy is the participation of the People of God in the work of the Trinity. The sacraments and the Divine Office constitute the Church's liturgy. Mass is the most important liturgical celebration.

Liturgy of the Hours

The prayer of the Church; it is also known as the Divine Office. The Liturgy of the Hours utilizes the Scriptures, particularly the Psalms, for specific times of the day from early morning to later evening.

Logos

The Greek term for "Word." In the Old Testament, Logos referred to creation, the Law, God's Revelation through the prophets and his presence among the people. John's Gospel reveals that Jesus is the Word of God who has existed forever.

Lost Tribes of Israel

The term "Lost Tribes of Israel" refers to the ten tribes from the northern kingdom who disappeared from history after being enslaved and exiled by the Assyrians.

lust

The "disordered desire for or inordinate enjoyment of sexual pleasure" (*CCC*, 2351).

Magisterium

The official teaching authority of the Church. The Lord bestowed the right and power to teach in his name on Peter and the Apostles and their successors.

The Magisterium is the bishops in communion with the successor of Peter, the Bishop of Rome (pope).

major prophets
Four of the latter prophets, Isaiah, Jeremiah, Ezekiel, and Daniel, whose books in the Old Testament are quite lengthy.

Maranatha
An Aramaic phrase that means "Come, O Lord."

minor prophets
The twelve prophets of the Old Testament whose recorded sayings are much briefer than those of the major prophets: Hosea, Joel, Amos, Obadiah, Jonah, Micah, Nahum, Habakkuk, Zephaniah, Haggai, Zechariah, and Malachi.

miracles
Powerful signs of God's Kingdom worked by Jesus.

missionaries
People who are "sent" to share the Good News of Jesus Christ with others. St. Paul was the Church's greatest missionary.

monotheistic
Religions that believe there is only one God. Christianity, Judaism, and Islam are three great monotheistic world religions.

Mount Gerizim
One of the two mountains in the immediate vicinity of the West Bank city of Nablus. The mountain is sacred to the Samaritans, who believe it to be the location chosen by YHWH for the holy temple. The mountain continues to be the center of the Samaritan religion to this day.

mystical
Inspiring a sense of mystery, the word also refers to having direct communication with God.

Nativity
The Nativity of Jesus is the story of our Savior's birth in Bethlehem. Two different accounts of the Nativity are given in the New Testament, one in the Gospel of Matthew, the other in the Gospel of Luke.

oaths
Oaths are solemn, formal declarations of promise. They are false when an oath is contrary to a person's dignity or communion with the Church.

omnipotent
An attribute of God that he is everywhere, unlimited, and all-powerful.

Original Sin
The sin of disobedience committed by Adam and Eve that resulted in their loss of original holiness and justice and their becoming subject to sin and death. Original Sin also describes the fallen state of human nature into which all generations of people are born. Christ Jesus came to save us from Original Sin (and all sin).

Paraclete
A name for the Holy Spirit. In John 14:26, Jesus promised to send an Advocate, a Helper, who would continue to guide, lead, and strengthen the disciples.

Parousia
The Second Coming of Christ when the Lord will judge the living and the dead.

Paschal Mystery
Christ's work of redemption, accomplished principally by his Passion, Death, Resurrection, and glorious Ascension. This mystery is commemorated and made present through the sacraments, especially the Eucharist.

patriarchs

The "fathers of the faith," male rulers, elders, or leaders. The patriarchs of the faith of Israel are Abraham, Isaac, and Jacob.

polytheistic

Religions that believe in the existence of many gods and goddesses.

pontiff

A term with roots from the Latin *Pontifex,* which translates "bridge-builder." Originally the term was associated with the highest leaders of any religion; now the term is reserved almost exclusively for the pope.

Pool of Siloam

A rock-cut pool located outside the walls of the old city of Jerusalem. The pool is mentioned other times in the Bible (e.g., Isaiah 8:6; 22:9).

prehistory

A period of time that refers to events or objects that date before the written record existed.

prophet

The word *prophet* is from the Greek, meaning "one who speaks before others." God entrusted the Hebrew prophets with delivering the divine message to rulers and the people. Most of them were unpopular in their own day. Their style was poetic and memorable. Most of their prophecies were written only at a later time.

proselytes

From a Greek word for "stranger," the term refers to a convert to Judaism.

rabbi

Hebrew word for a Jewish master or teacher of the Torah.

Redeemer

Redemption is the process that frees us from the slavery of sin. Jesus Christ is our Redeemer because he paid the price of his own sacrificial Death on the cross to save us from sin.

reincarnation

A false teaching that holds that people return to earth after they die. Instead, death is the end of our earthly pilgrimage and the beginning of eternal life.

religion

The relationship between God and humans that results in a body of beliefs and a set of practices: creed, cult, and code. Religion expresses itself in worship and service to God and by extension to all people and all creation.

remnant

The exiles and former exiles who remained faithful to YHWH during the time of captivity and who were expected to restore Jerusalem.

Sacred Scripture

The written record of Divine Revelation found in the books of the Old Testament and the New Testament.

Sacred Tradition

The living transmission of the Church's gospel message found in the Church's teaching, life, and worship. It is faithfully preserved, handed down, and interpreted by the Church's Magisterium.

Salvation History

The story of God's saving action in human history.

Samaritans

Descendants of a mixed population of Israelites who survived the Assyrian deportations and various pagan settlers imported after the northern kingdom fell. They worshiped YHWH on Mt. Gerizim but only considered the Pentateuch inspired. Ordinary Jews of our Lord's day despised the Samaritans.

Sanhedrin

The seventy-one member supreme legislative and judicial body of the Jewish people. Many of its members were Sadducees.

scribes

People trained to write using the earliest forms of writing before literacy was widespread.

secularism

An indifference to religion and a belief that religion should be excluded from civil affairs and public education.

Septuagint

An important ancient Greek translation of the Old Testament. The word "Septuagint" comes from the Latin word for "seventy," referring to the legendary seventy (or seventy-two) scholars who translated the work in seventy-two days.

Sermon on the Mount

A section in Matthew's Gospel (Mt 5:1–7:29) in which Jesus delivers the first of five discourses recorded in the Gospel. The Sermon on the Mount begins with the sharing of the Beatitudes. The Beatitudes are also found in the Sermon on the Plain in Luke 6:20–26.

Servant Songs

The name for four distinct poems accredited to Second Isaiah that deal with a specific individual, "the servant," whom God will use to usher in a glorious future.

Suffering Servant

The image from Isaiah 53:7–8 of a Servant who dies for the Salvation of all that was embodied in the life and Death of Jesus Christ.

synagogues

Meeting places for study and prayer introduced by the Pharisees to foster study of the Law and adherence to the covenant code.

tabernacle

The portable sanctuary in which the Jews carried the Ark of the Covenant throughout their travels in the desert.

theologians

People who study the nature of God and religious truth.

theological virtues

Three foundational virtues that are infused by God into the souls of the faithful: faith (belief in and personal knowledge of God), hope (trust in God's Salvation and his bestowal of the graces needed to attain it), and charity (love of God and love of neighbor as one loves oneself).

theophany

An appearance or manifestation of God, as when he "appeared" to Moses in a burning bush.

transcendence

A trait of God that refers to his total otherness and being infinitely beyond and independent of creation.

Transfiguration

The mystery from Christ's life in which God's glory shone through and transformed Jesus' physical appearance while he was in the company of the Old Testament prophets Moses and Elijah. Peter, James, and John witnessed this event.

Twelve Tribes of Israel

The name for the descendents of the twelve sons of Jacob (Israel). See Exodus 1:2–5, Numbers 1:20–43, or 1 Chronicles 1:1–2.

virtues

"Firm attitudes, stable dispositions, habitual perfections of intellect and will that govern our actions, order our passions, and guide our conduct according to reason and faith" (*CCC*, 1804).

Vulgate

St. Jerome's fifth-century Latin translation of the Bible into the common language of the people of his day.

Zoroastrianism

The official religion of the Persian Empire, which understood the universe to be caught in a constant struggle between light and darkness.

Photography Credits

Associated Press
page 130

Corbis
page 6, 26, 35, 39, 48, 72, 74, 147, 156, 160, 162, 182, 196, 212, 215, 219, 238

SuperStock
cover, page 11, 13, 18, 33, 37, 40, 51, 57, 67, 75, 78, 80, 83, 85, 88, 89, 98, 103, 105, 108, 113, 115, 128, 132, 134, 142, 154, 159, 164, 167, 176, 186, 192, 224, 232, 241, 245, 248, 249, 251, 252, 254

Veer
page 46, 205

Bill Wittman
page 24